Introduction
to the PDP-11
and its
Assembly Language

PRENTICE-HALL SOFTWARE SERIES
Brian W. Kernighan, advisor

Introduction
to the PDP-11
and its
Assembly Language

THOMAS S. FRANK

Le Moyne College
Syracuse, New York

Prentice-Hall, Inc., Englewood Cliffs, New Jersey 07632

Library of Congress Cataloging in Publication Data

Frank, Thomas S. (date)
   Introduction to the PDP-11 and its assembly
language.

   (Prentice-Hall software series)
   Includes index.
   1. PDP-11 (Computer)—Programming.   2. Assembler
language (Computer program language)   I. Title.
II. Series.
QA76.8.P2F73   1983   001.64′2   82-16590
ISBN 0-13-491704-9

Editorial/Production Supervision: LYNN S. FRANKEL
Cover Design: DIANE SAXE
Manufacturing Buyer: GORDON OSBOURNE

Printed in the United States of America

10   9   8   7   6   5   4   3   2

ISBN 0-13-491704-9

Prentice-Hall International, Inc., *London*
Prentice-Hall of Australia Pty. Limited, *Sydney*
Editora Prentice-Hall do Brazil, Ltda., *Rio de Janeiro*
Prentice-Hall Canada, Inc., *Toronto*
Prentice-Hall of India Private Limited, *New Delhi*
Prentice-Hall of Japan, Inc., *Tokyo*
Prentice-Hall of Southeast Asia Pte. Ltd., *Singapore*
Whitehall Books Limited, *Wellington, New Zealand*

Contents

B. THE INPUT/OUTPUT MACROINSTRUCTIONS   381

C. TABLE OF ASCII CODES   397

D. PDP-11 ASSEMBLER CONVENTIONS   398

INDEX   405

Preface

This text is designed for a one-semester course in basic computer hardware, and computer programming at the hardware and assembly language level. The conscientious student who completes this material will have a fundamental understanding of computer components and their intercommunication, as well as the machine instructions in their various forms. He or she will also be a reasonably proficient assembly language programmer. Perhaps of greatest consequence, the successful student will be in an excellent position to make rapid progress in a number of areas of computer science—data structures, computer architecture, microcomputing, system programming—in brief, those areas that require some depth of understanding of machine and machine-language fundamentals.

The prerequisites are quite modest. Specifically, no prior electronics background is required, since the hardware is discussed more at a *concepts* rather than *electronics* level. Thus, while we may speak of a device controller placing an interrupt vector address on the data bus, the electronics involved in latching that data onto the bus is not discussed. Similarly, just how the hardware deals with destructive memory reading is not investigated, although the *idea* and *consequences* of destructive reading are. Hence, much of the detail of the electronics required to achieve many of the hardware functions is intentionally omitted, for to do otherwise would detract from the main purpose of the text and would require more background than we choose to assume. These details are more appropriately dealt with in courses in computer architecture and digital electronics, once the student knows *what* the problems are, *how* they arise and *why* they need to be solved.

We informally assume that the student has had some prior contact, however fleeting, with computer programming, perhaps (or even preferably) in some high-level language. General programming concepts—problem analysis, logical program development, algorithm design and construction—are discussed only briefly, and even then these ideas are assumed to be already familiar. The student without a minimal background in these areas would be at a disadvantage, having to learn programming in general while coping simultaneously with fairly difficult concepts. Likewise, program structure and style is transmitted more by example than precept. Finally, most students approach their first contact with computers with an understandable impatience to get on with "making the machine do something." An earlier course or experience will have satisfied this urge to some extent, for in using this text the student will not be in a position to do any programming until some necessary background material has been assimilated.

The most serious prerequisite for any student who studies the topics of this text is *perseverance*. Programming at a machine or assembly language level can be a frustrating business at best, even for the experienced practitioner; the program bugs are far more prolific and obscure than in high-level languages. An ability to cope with and learn from persistent errors will pay greater dividends than almost any other quality the student can bring to a course dealing with this material.

To some extent, the text is machine-independent. Discussions of main memory, various registers, peripheral devices, instruction execution, and so forth, apply to a wide variety of computers. But to develop skills in these areas, the student must "do computing"—write, debug, and execute programs on a physical machine—to illustrate and understand the hardware capabilities of a modern computer. In this regard the illustrative machine could well be almost any computer, from one of the large mainframes to most any of the microsystems. We have chosen the ubiquitous PDP-11 because of the wide variety of its models and because we consider its architecture to be reasonably typical of the currently available hardware. To be sure, much of the text deals explicitly with the PDP-11 structure and its instruction set, but the topics are treated with an emphasis on the *concepts* themselves—what *any* machine must do to cope with an external interrupt, what *in general* must be done to achieve proper subroutine returns, and so forth. Hence, it is the intention of the text to familiarize the student with the PDP-11 hardware and its assembly language in such a way that this knowledge is transportable to most other machines with a minimum of retooling.

A conscious effort has been made to concentrate on those hardware features which are common to all PDP-11 models. Thus, some topics (for example, the floating-point instruction set, memory management, cache memory) are mentioned only in passing, if at all. A few machine features which are not universally applicable—the extended instruction set, for instance—*are* treated, but care is taken to alert the reader to the fact that a particular feature or instruction may not be implemented on some PDP-11 models, and suggestions are often given for their emulation on the more basic processors. Likewise, we recognize that not all PDP-11 models treat certain instructions identically. Occasional mention is made of these differences, in particular those that relate to the stack pointer (R6) and to addressing schemes, but those that do not affect programming at this level are not discussed in any depth.

If not completely independent of a specific machine, the material *is* operating system-independent. The large number of commercially available operating systems for the PDP-11, along with numerous "home-brewed" interactive and batch systems, precludes the possibility of complete coverage. To orient the text toward a specific operating system would be most helpful to students whose PDP-11 installation implemented that particular software, but it could only place additional burdens on those whose programs will be run on different systems. For this reason we consider the sin of total omission to be less severe than that of partial commission. Nonetheless, some operating system features *are* discussed. For example, Chapter 9 investigates the question of loading, relocation, object-file editing, linking and execution, but here again only the *concepts* are discussed, not how a *particular* operating system might deal with the specifics of these problems. Thus, the student will learn what information must be passed from the source program to the assembler, in turn to the loader and relocator, then to the linker and finally to the run-processor, but will not be told how a *particular* operating system treats these processes.

All of this places a certain unavoidable onus on the instructor, who will have to supply information relative to the local installation, for example the format of commands to the assembler and linker. Similarly, supplementary materials on and instruction in text creation and editing may be necessary, and system error messages will require explanation. We have attempted to relieve the overall burden somewhat by the inclusion of macroinstructions which provide the student with an early ability to perform input and output, one of the most difficult areas to deal with in a course of this nature. These modules (which are listed in Appendix B) also contain the necessary data format conversion routines, and these can provide instructive reading for the student who has developed some background and proficiency in assembly language programming.

The hardware and programming topics are developed in a sequential fashion. Thus, the discussion of main memory leads to the contents of memory locations, which in turn introduces the ideas of number representations, computer number systems, and the stored-program concept. In a similar fashion, the TRAP instruction leads naturally to interrupts and the hardware necessary to manage peripheral devices. Because of this text structure, the instructor will not find a vast horde of topics from which a one-semester course may (or must) be constructed. Most of the material is essential to the development. On the other hand, it is certainly possible to dwell at some length on a particular hardware feature, perhaps interrupts, at the expense of a topic such as conditional assemblies. Conversely, careful glossing over of some hardware concepts is possible to allow time for more extensive programming projects. But, basically, the text is intended as a self-contained, one semester package, with an emphasis on clarity of development.

The text is not simply a reference book—it is an instructional tool. As such, it is explicitly designed to be *read with understanding* by the student. Many sample programs and program segments are included with complete discussions to aid in this process. Topics are frequently introduced by stating some easily understood problem and then developing the hardware features and programming techniques necessary to solve it. All of the details required for a depth of understanding of the concepts are supplied, and in some instances the level of detail may appear somewhat overwhelming. For this we make no apologies. For example, the student with a fuzzy understanding of precisely *when* in the instruction execution cycle register autoincrementing takes place will never feel comfortable with a construction such as CMP (R2)+, (R2). Numerous exercises are included to develop the student's skills and confidence. These range from routine computational problems, questions (which might be called "oral exercises"), to the writing of program segments and complete programs. Large-scale, involved "term project" types of exercises are not given here, although other problems and some of the text material might suggest them. Rather, it is felt that the individual instructor, drawing on his or her own interests, experience and expertise, can better devise such projects consonant with the student's particular environment.

Exercises are found at the ends of the chapters and are numbered $C.S.n$, where C is the chapter number, S is the chapter section number to which the exercise applies, and n is the sequential exercise number within that section.

The author wishes to express his appreciation to the editorial staff of Prentice-Hall for their assistance and guidance in the preparation of this book. Finally, gratitude is given to Paul R. Laba, former director of Le Moyne's computer center, for putting up with the author's frequent and unannounced usurping of equipment during the course of the text's development; for reading and commenting on several chapters; and for innumerable conversations that have contributed significantly to whatever clarity and precision will be found here.

THOMAS S. FRANK

Introduction

to the PDP-11

and its

Assembly Language

1

Basic Computer Systems

1.1 INTRODUCTION

This book will investigate computers and, to a large extent, one in particular, the Digital Equipment Corporation PDP-11. However, we shall not attempt to *define* what is meant by the term *computer* since no satisfactory definition really exists. To be sure, it may be possible to give an abstract definition of a *specific* machine in terms of its architecture and capabilities, but that scarcely bears on the general concept of a computer. At present the number and variety of computers are so great that a general, universally applicable definition seems out of reach. The variety of machines includes special-purpose computers such as those used to control machine tools and robots, or the trip computers found in some automobiles; the increasingly popular and inexpensive micro-computers; the moderately sized and priced general-purpose minicomputers, of which the PDP-11 is an example; and the large and very powerful so-called mainframe machines. (*Large* and *powerful* are vague terms at best when applied to computers. A "large, powerful automobile" is a fairly well understood concept. When applied to computers, *large* generally refers to the machine's ability to store a great deal of data, while *powerful* implies an ability to process a large amount of data in a small amount of time.) Even the pocket calculator has grown so sophisticated that the distinction between this useful little device and what we normally think of as a computer has become somewhat fuzzy. Thus our brief discussion here will be more descriptive than definitive.

A computer is a machine; thus it has precisely those characteristics and capabilities that were designed into it. In fact, compared with many of the machines with which we make daily contact, a computer is really quite simple. The number of *different* things it can do is relatively limited. What makes a computer *appear* complex is that the limited actions it can take can be combined into a very wide variety of *sequences* of such actions. In addition to the wealth of combinations of simple activities, the *speed* with which these actions are performed tends to reinforce the idea of complexity. One-millionth of a second is a good average figure to keep in mind for the completion of a single such action, although computers that act several times as fast are no longer uncommon.

As the name implies, computers are designed to *compute*—to *do arithmetic*. There is nothing new about a machine that does arithmetic, since mechanical calculators have been common for decades, but the distinguishing feature of a computer is that these calculations take place *electronically* rather than mechanically. It is essentially this idea that accounts for the computer's speed—electronic components can react to commands much faster than mechanical components can.

Finally, like other kinds of machines, a computer must be *controllable* to be useful. The actions or sequences of actions it takes must be able to be predetermined. The collection of commands given to the machine to control its actions is called a **controlling program,** or, more simply, a **program.**

1.2 A MINIMAL COMPUTER SYSTEM CONFIGURATION

Despite the fact that we have been unable to produce a satisfactory *definition* of a computer, we can describe what we shall mean by a **minimal computer system.** The description, while specific to the PDP-11, is equally applicable to a wide variety of other machines. For our purposes a computer system will consist of the following:

- A **central processing unit** or **processor**
- **Main memory**, or **main storage**, or, more simply, **memory** or **storage**
- **Peripheral devices**
- **Buses**

The remainder of this chapter will describe these basic components, although only in the most general terms. Much of the remainder of the text is devoted to a study of what these components are, what their functions are and how they perform them, and how they interact with one another. Shown in Fig. 1.2.1 is a block diagram of a minimal system that may be helpful here and throughout the text in visualizing the various components and their relationships with one another.

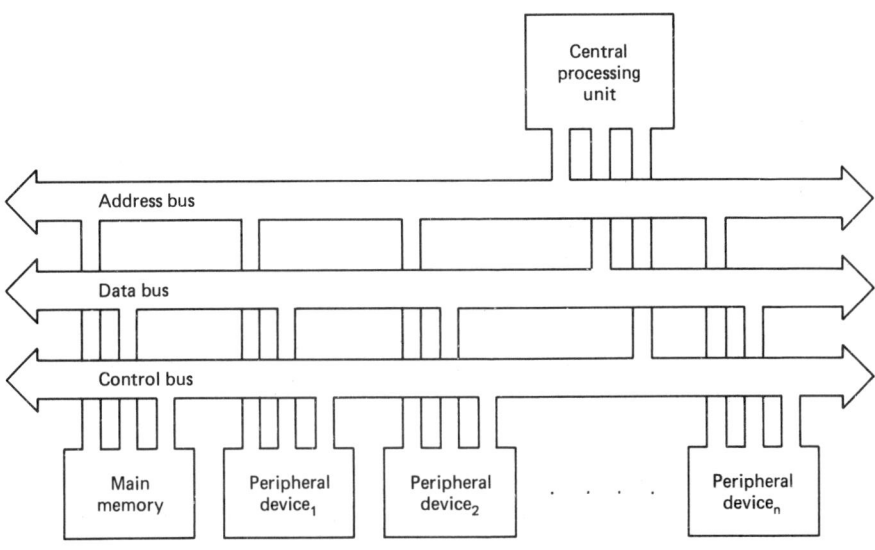

Figure 1.2.1

1.3 THE CENTRAL PROCESSING UNIT

Of the various components that make up a computing system, the central processing unit (CPU) is by far the most complex, both from a physical (electronics) standpoint and from a consideration of its capabilities. The central processing unit or processor consists of a number of interconnected subunits, which we shall briefly describe here.

- **Arithmetic-logic unit** (ALU). As its name implies, the responsibility of this unit is to *do arithmetic*—additions, subtractions, and so forth. In addition, this unit performs other *logical* operations, which are described is some detail in Chapter 3.
- **Control unit.** This unit controls the flow of information within the processor—sending data to the ALU for some arithmetic processing, for example. It is also in this unit that decisions are made about which command the processor is to carry out, using a **decoder,** which *interprets* commands.
- **Registers.** These are electronic units in which information can be *stored,* usually on a temporary basis.

At this point it is not expected that the reader will have a particularly sound grasp of the function of the central processor, and, in fact, it is not likely that the addition of the details given above has done much to illuminate the situation. Suffice it to say that most of the computer system's activities are centered in the processing unit, and much of the text is devoted to a clarification of its capabilities and operations.

1.4 MAIN MEMORY

We indicated in the preceding section that the central processing unit contains registers that could be used to *store* information. While this is true, the typical task performed by the system involves the management of thousands of pieces of data, far more than can be handled by the few registers that are internal to the processor. Thus some sort of *mass* storage device is required to "hold" this large amount of information; we refer to such a device as **main memory.** The next chapter is devoted to a rather close look at this concept.

1.5 PERIPHERAL DEVICES

The computer system, by means of its central processing unit, processes data with the assistance of main memory, which it might use for obtaining information or storing intermediate or final results of arithmetic operations. And while it is fine to construct a machine that can, for example, add two numbers, its utility is certainly limited if *we* cannot specify which numbers are to be operated on, and if the system cannot report back to *us* the results of the requested operation. Some device is required that will provide a channel of communication between the computing system and the real world. Devices that perform this task are called **communication devices** and they make up one category of computer **peripheral devices.**

A peripheral device is one that is directly connected to the processor but is *not* an integral part of the processor itself and is *not* main memory. At present perhaps the most common peripheral device is the **computer terminal,** the typewriterlike device that allows the user (more-or-less) direct communication with the processor. Other peripherals include printers, card readers, plotters, and so forth. These devices provide communication between the processor (and main memory) and the outside world. A second category of peripherals is **bulk storage devices.** They provide extensions of main memory on which information can be stored, usually in a form that is not directly usable by the outside world. Examples are magnetic disks and drums, as well as magnetic tapes.

1.6 BUSES

Implicit in the discussion above is the concept of *moving about* of information within the computer system—data are moved into and out of main memory and between the central processor and various peripherals. Information is transmitted by electric currents on sets of wires called **buses.** In Fig. 1.2.1 we have indicated three such buses (collections of wires), which have been labeled the **address bus, data bus,** and **control bus.** While it will be some time before we examine in any detail just *how* some of these buses are used, the reader is cautioned against trying to assign any deep meaning to them. They are as described —collections of wires over which information may be transmitted between components within the computer system.

2

Main Memory and
Computer Arithmetic

2.1 INFORMATION

The formal concept of **information**—what it is, how it is transmitted, how it is affected by "noise pollution," and so forth—is so complex that an entire mathematical, physical, and engineering discipline is devoted to it. And while information is absolutely central to a study of computers—computers, after all, *process information*—the type with which we shall have to deal here is so simple (we are tempted to use the word *crude*) that we shall be able to take a highly unsophisticated approach to it with very satisfactory results.

We are constantly being bombarded with vast amounts of information, mostly visual or auditory, and all of this information is *processed* in some way or another. Much of it is simply ignored (usually at a subconscious level). For example, when we look at some object across the room, we are receiving much more visual information than that coming from the object in question, but this other information is considered to be "noise"—unwanted information—and we fairly effectively manage to suppress it. In addition to the amount of information we receive, the *complexity* of that information can vary greatly. There is, for example, a tremendous amount of information contained in a recording of Beethoven's Third Symphony, or in a half-hour television program. At the other extreme consider the honking of an automobile horn. If we ignore such qualities as pitch (frequency) and duration of the sound, we find that the information transmitted is very simple indeed. In fact only *one* piece of information has been made available—the *presence* of a sound, as opposed to its *absence*. The way we *process* this particular piece of information may be quite

6

complex and may depend upon the circumstances. (Our reactions to this simple information would likely differ if we were standing on the sidewalk or in the street.)

As another familiar example of this simple type of information, consider walking into a room and observing whether the light is on or off. The information being transmitted here is again of this simple sort—the presence or absence of something. Some of the information we process on a daily basis is of this simple yes-no or on-off nature, although the majority of it is far more complex. One of the features that make computers so conceptually simple is the fact that the information with which they must deal is precisely of this yes-no or on-off variety.

2.2 THE STORAGE OF INFORMATION

The concept of **stored information** is a very familiar one. Books consist of stored information, as do tape recordings and photographic film. These are all **storage devices.** The storage device we wish to pursue here briefly is the human brain—in particular, that portion of the brain that deals with **memory.** Just how humans remember things is not very well understood, but we can make some general observations about the process.

Human memory has the property that information can be stored in it for later retrieval, and this storing process seems to fall into three broad categories. Information that appears to be of little significance to us is stored in **short-term memory**—the information is available for a short period of time and then later seems to disappear. For example, we can probably remember what we had for breakfast this morning, or even yesterday morning, but it is unlikely that we can remember what breakfast we ate 7 years ago today. Other information seems to be placed in **long-term memory** without any conscious effort on our part. We can easily recall on demand certain particularly pleasant events. Unfortunately we can also easily remember especially unpleasant events, but unlike a tape recorder, we seem to have no means of erasing these memories. Finally, some information can be stored in long-term memory by the conscious effort of **memorization**. The reader may not recall the agonies he went through in memorizing the multiplication table, but he surely remembers the table itself. It is this last type of information storage that will be of significance to us.

Memorized information is useful for three principal reasons. First, the information is **specific** rather than random, as is frequently found in short-term memory; that is, we consciously *select* precisely what information we want to remember. Second, that information can be **stored** in memory by some conscious effort. And finally, the information may be **retrieved** whenever it is needed. (For example, a carpenter may consciously store the information that a 2-by-4 board actually has dimensions of $1\frac{1}{2}$ by $3\frac{1}{2}$ inches; this information is then available whenever it is needed.) It is these three characteristics—the ability to *select*, *store*, and *retrieve* information—that we shall demand of *computer* memory.

Our brief discussion of human memory has been presented because some useful analogies with computer memories can be illustrated. It was not our intention here to endow computers and their memories with any human characteristics—mercifully the "giant brain" concept so often associated with the early computers has all but faded from the scene. On the other hand, computers are designed by humans to emulate certain human brain functions; thus it is quite natural that the analogies exist and that certain of the terminology is somewhat anatomic.

2.3 COMPUTER STORAGE DEVICES

In the preceding section it was suggested that for us to use a computer storage device effectively, we should have the capability of storing some selected information in it in such a way that we can later retrieve that information. In Chapter 1 it was stated that computers are *electronic* devices and are therefore controlled by electric currents. Thus in seeking devices that can act as storage devices for a computer, we shall be looking for components that react in a predictable way to the presence or absence of an electric current.

As a first step in this direction, consider the device known as a **capacitor,** which has the property that it becomes charged when a voltage is applied across it; that is, one side of the capacitor will be at 1 volt, for instance, while the other side will be at 0 volts. (See Fig. 2.3.1, where we arbitrarily assume a voltage source of 1 volt.) Once charged, the capacitor can maintain the difference in the voltage level of the two sides even if the voltage source is *removed*. Thus capacitors are frequently thought of as devices that "store" electricity.

A capacitor may be in a *charged* state, as described above, or it may be in the opposite, or *discharged*, state. It is easy to detect in which state a capacitor is at any time; we need only place a *meter* across the two sides of the capacitor, as shown in Fig. 2.3.2. If the capacitor is charged, a current will flow through

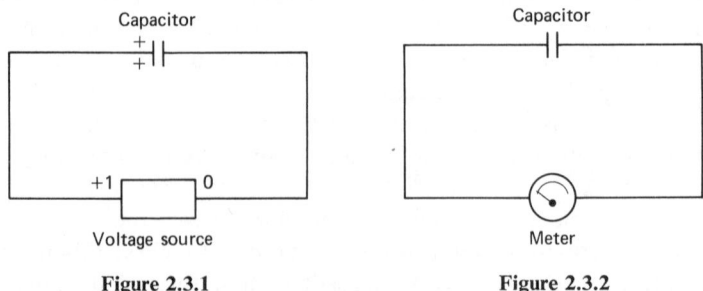

Capacitor

Voltage source

Figure 2.3.1

Capacitor

Meter

Figure 2.3.2

the meter, which will cause a deflection of the indicator needle. If the capacitor is not charged, no such deflection will be detected.

The capacitor seems to be the sort of device we are seeking to store information because it can evidently exist in one of two distinct states—charged or discharged. Such devices, which can be in one of two specific and distinguishable states, are called **bistable devices**. Furthermore, the state of a capacitor can be *set* by a conscious action—by charging or discharging it. (Discharging a capacitor amounts simply to connecting a wire across the two sides of the capacitor—*shorting* it—so that both sides are at the same voltage level.) Finally, the state can be *determined*, by the use of a meter, for example. Thus a capacitor may be used to store retrievable information, but notice how crude the information is—only one of two possible pieces of information can be stored. A capacitor's information is of the yes-no or on-off variety, which gives us no more information than the observation that a room light is on or off. Nonetheless this is a start at what we are trying to accomplish.

As a storage device a capacitor has a couple of nasty properties. Conceptually they are of no real concern to us, since they can be coped with by appropriate engineering, but they are worthy of mention anyway. The reader may have inferred that once a capacitor is charged, it will remain in its charged state indefinitely. In fact, over a period of time capacitors tend to lose, or "leak," this charge. Thus it may be necessary to "refresh" the state of the capacitor from time to time to ensure that it is not later incorrectly interpreted as being in a discharged state when in fact it was supposed to be charged. The second problem is a bit more severe, but it can also be dealt with. When we choose to determine the state of a given capacitor, we place a meter across it to see if a current flows through the meter. Unfortunately, the act of determining the capacitor's state, in the event that it was charged, will *discharge* it, thus placing it in the *opposite* state. Of course, if we detect that the capacitor *was* charged, we can *recharge* it to bring it back to its original state since we are aware that we have discharged it in the course of determining its state.

When a capacitor is set to one of its two states, we say that information has been **written** into the capacitor. When the state of the capacitor is determined (for instance, by a meter), we say that the information has been **read**. The act of reading information from a capacitor in such a way that that information is destroyed, and thus must be restored, is called **destructive reading**.

While we now have a device that can store information, it should be noted that the information stored is so limited that evidently some further development will be required before we can assert that we have uncovered a scheme that is at all practical. This will be done in the next section and throughout the remainder of the chapter, but before expanding on these ideas we look briefly at another bistable device that has been in common use as a computer storage device for some time—the **magnetic core**.

A magnetic core is a "doughnut" of material that can be magnetized. If a wire is placed through the "hole" in the doughnut and a current is then passed through the wire in a particular direction, the core will become magnetized in one of two possible directions—clockwise or counterclockwise—depending upon the direction of the current. In Fig. 2.3.3, the result of passing a current through the wire in the direction shown is the magnetizing of the core in a clockwise direction, as viewed from above. If the current is applied in the opposite direction, the core will be magnetized in the other direction. Thus information—the direction of magnetization—may be *written* into the core by passing a current through the **write-wire** in one direction or the other. Once the core has been magnetized in one direction or the other, it is no longer necessary to maintain the current in the write-wire. The core will remain magnetized indefinitely in the given direction without the presence of this current. The feature that no refreshing of its state is required is one of the aspects of a core that has made it so desirable for computer memory.

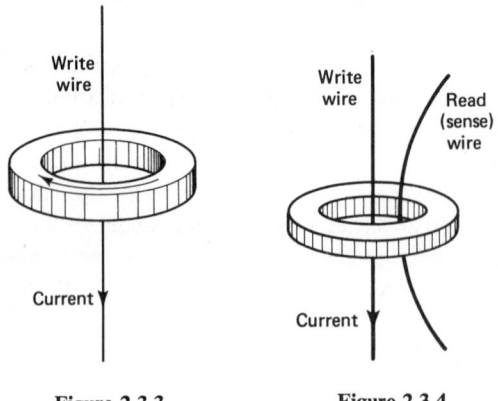

Figure 2.3.3   **Figure 2.3.4**

The state of a core—the *direction* in which it is magnetized—is relatively easy to determine. We insert another wire, called a **read-wire**, or **sense-wire**, through the hole in the core. Suppose we now pass a current through the write-wire *in a fixed direction*, as shown in Fig. 2.3.4. One of two things will take place. If the core is magnetized in a clockwise direction (when viewed from above), then nothing will happen, since the current in the write-wire tends to magnetize the core in its current direction. However, if the core is magnetized in a counterclockwise direction, then the current in the write-wire will force the magnetization of the core into its opposite (clockwise) direction. When the direction of magnetization reverses, there is a change in the magnetic field within the core. That changing field is detected as a current in the read-wire. Thus to read a core we need only pass a current through the write-wire in a known direction and see if a current is induced in the read-wire. But notice again that this type of reading is destructive, so it may be necessary to rewrite it to its original state in order to preserve the state of the core after reading it.

Despite the desirable properties of cores they need no refreshing and in fact once set, they do not even require that power be applied to them to maintain their states—they are relatively expensive and slow to react to currents. For these reasons core-type memories, while of great significance in the historical development of computers, have now generally been replaced by a variety of faster, less-expensive *transistorized* devices.

2.4 MEMORY UNITS

Capacitors and cores are two examples of bistable devices that can exist in one of two states, which may be set (written) by means of an electric current and may later be determined (read) by some electrical means. These are the properties of memory devices that are essential characteristics of such storage devices. The information held in one of these devices is as fundamental as it can be— of an on-off nature. In fact, any less information would be no information at all. In the remainder of the text we shall not concern ourselves with *what* device is being used for storage. Rather we shall assume that some bistable device is being used to hold information. We shall refer to the device itself as a **memory cell** and we shall call its two states simply a and b, rather than specifically *charged* and *discharged, clockwise* and *counterclockwise,* and so forth.

The *amount* of information that can be held in a *single* memory cell is so small that it is all but useless except in very unusual circumstances. However, consider a **memory unit** made up of *two* such cells, each of which can be written and read independently of the other. Then the "values" that such a unit can take on are shown in Fig. 2.4.1, where C_1 and C_2 are the two individual cells making up the unit.

$U_2 = C_1$	C_2
a	a
a	b
b	a
b	b

Figure 2.4.1

This unit, then, can store *four* distinct pieces of information, and this is certainly the direction of progress. Notice, however, that the individual cells C_1 and C_2 must be *ordered* for this much information to be stored. One of the cells, which we have here labeled C_1, must be *first* or *leftmost,* for otherwise there would be no way to distinguish between the configurations *ab* and *ba.*

We take this idea one further step, this time combining *three* cells into a memory unit. As we see from Fig. 2.4.2 there are now *eight* distinguishable sets of states in which these three cells can exist. Again, we assume the independence of the cells—the setting of one cell in no way influences the setting of any other cell in the unit.

$U_3 = C_1$	C_2	C_3
a	a	a
a	a	b
a	b	a
a	b	b
b	a	a
b	a	b
b	b	a
b	b	b

Figure 2.4.2

It is not difficult to verify that if n such bistable cells are independently combined into a memory unit, then that unit U_n can exist in any one of 2^n states. Each such state is then represented by a string of a's and b's—for example, *abbbaabaaabb*.

Thus we can store as much information in a computer storage device as we might want, simply by considering a memory unit with sufficiently many cells. But what kind of information are we storing? That is, how is a string of a's and b's to be *interpreted*? We shall return to this question after a brief digression for some fundamental facts about *number systems*.

2.5 NUMBER REPRESENTATIONS

When we refer to "the number 142," we are guilty of an imprecision, or at least a sloppiness with which we have learned to live. What we intend in such a phrase is "the number whose *representation* is 142," and it would not be out of order to refer equivalently to "the number whose representation is CXLII." While we do not want to go out of our way to be pedantic about this matter, nonetheless there *is* a difference between a number and one of its many representations, and that difference will be of some consequence to us in this and subsequent sections.

Number is an abstract concept, and a rather difficult one at that. When we refer to the "thirteen stripes on the flag" we are attributing to this set of stripes the abstract quality of "thirteenness." Likewise, a quartet is an example of "fourness," as is the collection of states in which two independent memory cells can exist. The 13 in the phrase "13 stripes" is a symbolic representation of an abstraction, the number named *thirteen*. It is this symbolic representation that we wish to pursue briefly.

If the symbols 142 are a representation of the abstract number that we call "one hundred forty-two," then what role is played by the individual symbols 1, 4, and 2, and why are these particular symbols used? The representation is a composite of the symbols 1, 4, and 2, a composite that stems from the fact that

$$142 = 1 \cdot 100 + 4 \cdot 10 + 2$$
$$= 1 \cdot 10^2 + 4 \cdot 10^1 + 2 \cdot 10^0$$

an expression that could as well be written as

$$142 = 1 \cdot x^2 + 4 \cdot x^1 + 2 \cdot x^0$$

provided we know that $x = 10$. That is, the symbolic representation of a number is a **polynomial in x**, where $x = 10$. By agreement, we do not write the polynomial itself as the number representation, but simply write down the polynomial's *coefficients* (in this case, 1, 4, and 2). As the reader is aware, this convention requires some care. Coefficients are written from left to right, with the higher powers of 10 coming first, and coefficients with the value 0 *must* be included— it would not be correct to represent $1 \cdot 10^4 + 4 \cdot 10^2 + 2 \cdot 10^1$ as 142.

The symbols used in the representation, namely, 0, 1, . . ., 9, are of no particular consequence except that they must be *distinguishable* and we must know the *meaning* of each. Theoretically, symbols such as @, #, . . ., $ would do just as well, although the usual numeric symbols are so universal that a change in symbolism would be pointless. The significance of the choice of x as 10 doubtless stems from the fact that we have 10 fingers, which has led us to a particular *counting* scheme. We count as follows (although beginning the count at zero is perhaps a bit unusual):

> no-fingers, one-finger, two-fingers, . . ., nine-fingers
> one-complete-set-of-fingers-plus-no-fingers, one-complete-
> set-of-fingers-plus-one-finger, . . .

which corresponds to the written representation

$$0, 1, 2, \ldots, 9, 10, 11, \ldots$$

(The verbalization becomes a bit awkward beyond the representation 99— "nine-complete-sets-of-fingers-plus-nine-fingers.") If we each had only three fingers on each hand, we would unquestionably count "no-fingers, one-finger, . . ., five-fingers, one-complete-set-of-fingers-plus-no-fingers, . . .," or, symbolically, 0, 1, . . . , 5, 10, 11, and so on. The value of x—the "number of fingers"— in the number representation is called the **base** of the number representation system. Thus in the first case above, the base is 10, whereas in the second example, the base is 6.

In light of this, what interpretation are we going to give to the polynomial

$$142 = 1 \cdot x^2 + 4 \cdot x^1 + 2 \cdot x^0$$

The answer depends on what value we use for x, for if we take x to be 10, then 142 means $1 \cdot 100 + 4 \cdot 10 + 2$. On the other hand, if $x = 6$, then 142 means $1 \cdot 6^2 + 4 \cdot 6^1 + 2 \cdot 6^0 = 1 \cdot 36 + 4 \cdot 6 + 2$, the number that we think of (base 10) as being represented by the symbol 62. Equations such as $142 = 62$ are non-sense, of course, but the reader will recognize the problem—the two sides of the equality refer to *different* number representation bases. Confusion can be eliminated by stating, for example, 142 (with $x = 6$) = 62 (with $x = 10$), or, more compactly, $142_6 = 62_{10}$. The reader should verify that $142_{10} = 354_6$.

In representing numbers in base 6, it was necessary to devise six distinguishable symbols to be used as **numerals** in the representation, and we used 0, 1, 2, 3, 4, and 5, since these were readily available symbols with well-determined meanings. Suppose now, however, that we decide to represent numbers in base sixteen. We need sixteen distinguishable symbols, and among the usual numerals there are only ten. Thus we shall have to invent some new symbols, and we choose for these A, B, C, D, E, and F, where A stands for what we think of in base 10 as ten, B for eleven, . . . , and F for fifteen. Thus the base sixteen counting scheme—referred to as the **hexadecimal** representation system—is

$$0, 1, 2, \ldots, 8, 9, A, B, C, D, E, F, 10, 11, \ldots,$$
$$19, 1A, 1B, 1C, 1D, 1E, 1F, 20, \ldots, 98, 99, 9A, \ldots,$$
$$9F, A0, A1, \ldots$$

(Once again the reader should verify that $142_{10} = 8E_{16}$.)

In grade school we learn to do base ten arithmetic, including a variety of algorithms or procedures to do addition, subtraction, and so forth, with their attendant handling of "carries" and "borrowing." It is easy to establish that these algorithms, while aimed specifically at base ten arithmetic, are actually independent of the base—they work as well for base sixteen or base six. Thus performing arithmetic computations in bases other than ten requires that we learn nothing new, only that we overcome the lack of familiarity with these other bases. To illustrate this fact we provide below a few examples of these procedures. The reader should verify the correctness of each of these, perhaps by converting the numbers to the more comfortable base 10 and then performing the computations. It would also be wise to take advantage of the practice provided in the exercises.

$$
\begin{array}{ccc}
1273_8 & DA5_{16} & 142_6 \\
+5646_8 & -2F9_{16} & \times\ 54_6 \\
\hline
7141_8 & AAC_{16} & 1052_6 \\
& & 1234_6 \\
& & \hline \\
& & 13432_6
\end{array}
$$

It is clear that there are infinitely many different bases we can use for number representations. While bases much larger than sixteen or twenty become highly unwieldy because of the number of numerals required and the fact that we must remember what each of these stands for, theoretically there is no upper limit on the size of the base. But there *is* a lower limit, namely, 2. This representation is referred to as the **binary representation system**. In its favor, base 2 has the desirable feature that only two numerals, 0 and 1, are required for the representation of any number. Thus, for example,

$$142_{10} = 10001110_2$$
$$= 1 \cdot 2^7 + 0 \cdot 2^6 + 0 \cdot 2^5 + 0 \cdot 2^4$$
$$+ 1 \cdot 2^3 + 1 \cdot 2^2 + 1 \cdot 2^1 + 0 \cdot 2^0$$

The clear disadvantage of a base 2 representation is that, even for rather modest size numbers, a great many base 2 digits (numerals) will be required for the representation.

In summary, we have seen that a number—as an abstract concept— may be represented in a wide variety of ways, depending upon the base chosen. The arithmetic of numbers in any base is no more complicated, although perhaps less familiar, than it is in base 10. Large bases for number representations result in compact expressions requiring few digits, although the opposite is true if the base is small. From the standpoint of experience, base 10 is probably the most convenient for us to use, while base 2 seems to be one of the least desirable, considering compactness. Despite this inefficiency of representation, the binary system is the one that will be of most significance to us.

2.6 A CHANGE IN NOTATION

In Sec. 2.3 we investigated devices that could exist in one of two states, a and b. Then we combined such devices into groups, or memory units, of length n, each capable of taking on as a "value" a string of length n of such states, such as *abbbaabaaabb*. Just what information such a string might convey is anyone's guess, but an almost trivial change in the notation will be most illuminating.

Suppose that instead of the notation a and b we substitute the symbols 0 and 1, respectively. Then the value of the memory unit mentioned above, namely *abbbaabaaabb*, becomes 011100100011. And if we *interpret* this string of 0's and 1's as the *binary* (base 2) *representation* of a *number* (which happens to be 1827_{10}), then this memory unit contains information that has substantial meaning. We are tempted to say that this memory unit "contains the number $011100100011 = 1827_{10}$," but this would be patent nonsense. The memory unit *consists* of *individual memory cells*, each of which can be in one of two *states*. It is the *notation*—0 and 1—along with our *interpretation* that leads us to this imprecision. Memory units, if they hold anything, hold sequences of cell states. Nonetheless the numeric interpretation is so appealing that we shall be unable to resist the temptation to say, for example, that a memory unit "contains the binary number 110101, or, equivalently, the decimal number 53." Thus here and throughout the remainder of the text, we shall refer to a memory unit containing a number, or a number being in a memory unit. Thinking of the contents of memory units as numbers is the most natural view of these devices, and at least in this case the imprecision will do us no harm. Indeed, to insist upon the formality described above would only hamper the development.

While we can write specific numbers in their binary format into memory units in such a way that they can later be read, computers are supposed to *process* data; so unless we devise some methods for the manipulation of these stored numbers, the scheme will be minimally useful at best.

2.7 COMPUTER WORDS AND NUMBER SYSTEMS

The memory units discussed so far, consisting of individual memory cells, can hold binary number representations. The size of the numbers that can be so represented depends upon the *number* of memory cells that make up a unit. In constructing a computer's main memory of these memory-cell units, we must keep in mind that it is not just *one* such unit that is involved—main memories consist typically of thousands, hundreds of thousands, or even millions of such units. The decision about the number of cells that are to make up a memory unit is constrained by the fact that, from an engineering standpoint, *each* memory unit should (and to be practical, *must*) consist of the *same* number of memory cells. (There are a few machines that are exceptions to this constraint, although they are not in the PDP-11 family.) Thus whatever decision is made at this point will have far-reaching consequences—if we decide that each unit will consist of 3 cells, then binary number representations between 0 and 7 will be possible (in binary, 000 to 111). If 15 cells are grouped into a unit, then a much wider range is possible, from 0 to 32,767. And while we might be inclined to build memory units consisting of many cells so that they would be capable of storing very large numbers, we must also be aware of certain *economic* constraints. It is simply not economically feasible to build main memories that consist of arbitrarily large numbers of memory units, each comprising an arbitrarily large number of individual cells. Thus the decisions made in this regard involve a trade-off—the cost of memory against the number of memory units and the number of cells that make up each unit. Regardless of what decision is made, of course, a limit is imposed on the largest number that can be represented in any unit since any unit is made up of a *finite* number of such cells.

It is time to change some of our terminology so that it conforms to what is currently in common use. The memory units that make up the computer's memory are called computer **words** and each word consists of a fixed number of memory cells called **bits** (a contraction of **binary digits**). Thus, for example, when we speak of a 24-*bit-word computer*, we mean a computer whose main memory is organized into words (units), *each* of which consists of 24 bits (cells).

As indicated previously, the word size (in bits) selected for a computer's memory will determine the size of the largest number any of the memory units can hold. Some currently popular sizes are 8 bits per word (used, for the most part, in the memories of microcomputers), 12 and 16 bits per word (frequently used in minicomputers), and 24, 32, 36, and 48 bits per word. For the moment we shall investigate in some detail the behavior of a 4-bit word computer. It is clear that this word size, which provides only for the storage of numbers between (decimal) 0 and 15, is too small to be of any practical significance. However, the concepts we shall uncover here can be transferred to machines of any word size without alteration, and the 4-bit word is somewhat more manageable than larger sizes.

We shall think of each 4-bit word as being made up of four cells, which we name the 3 bit, 2 bit, 1 bit and 0 bit as shown in Fig. 2.7.1. Each of the x's will have a value 0 or 1. Notice that the names of the bit positions correspond to the power of 2 represented by that bit. Thus, for instance, bit 2 corresponds to $2^2 = 4$. Bit 3 is called the **most-significant bit** of the word, and bit 0 the **least-significant bit**. (This bit-numbering, or bit-naming, scheme, while quite natural, is nonetheless somewhat arbitrary. Some computer systems adopt the opposite terminology—the most-significant bit is named bit 0, the least-significant, bit 3.)

3	2	1	0	Bit position
x	x	x	x	

Figure 2.7.1

At this point we need to make some assumptions about the capabilities of the central processing unit (CPU). Specifically, we assume that the CPU can **increment**—add 1 to— a 4-bit word, so the word 1001, for example, can be incremented to a value of 1010. In addition, we assume that the CPU can **complement** a 4-bit word; that is, the CPU contains appropriate circuitry to reverse the state of each bit of a 4-bit word, so 1001 will be complemented to 0110. (We shall see in the next chapter that the design of circuits to accomplish these arithmetic tasks is not difficult.) With these assumptions in place, consider the 4-bit word all of whose bits are 0 and thus represents the number 0000 = 0. If this word is incremented, its contents becomes 0001 = 1. We continue to increment this word, with the results being shown in Fig. 2.7.2. If we now attempt a further increment of this word, whose current contents is 1111, we encounter a phenomenon that will be of major significance.

$$\begin{array}{r} 1111 \\ + \quad 1 \\ \hline 10000 \end{array}$$

The result of the addition, which is decimal 16, requires *five* bits for its representation, and our word contains only *four* bits. This 1, which resulted from a *carry* out of bit 3 into the nonexistent bit 4, is *lost*, and thus the arithmetic shown above should have been displayed as

$$\begin{array}{r} 1111 \\ + \quad 1 \\ \hline 0000 \end{array}$$

or 1111 + 0001 = 0000 (in decimal: 15 + 1 = 0), which is clearly incorrect. Let us see if we can track down the problem.

	Word contents
Binary	Decimal equivalent
0000	0
0001	1
0010	2
0011	3
0100	4
0101	5
0110	6
0111	7
1000	8
1001	9
1010	10
1011	11
1100	12
1101	13
1110	14
1111	15

Figure 2.7.2

First, the fault does *not* lie with the processor's incrementing circuitry; it has performed exactly as it was designed to perform. Indeed, any other 4-bit result would have been just as "incorrect." The difficulty lies with the fact that the word contains only 4 bits and thus cannot hold the correct 5-bit result. But if we had selected a larger word size, we would simply have been postponing the problem; no matter what the word size, eventually, we would have encountered this carry out of the most significant bit. Part of the blame lies also with our *interpretation* of these 4 bits—strings of 0's and 1's—as the representation of a binary number. That interpretation served us well up to this point, but the interpretation failed when the word contained the particular bit configuration 1111. Thus we should probably not even say that the result is incorrect—what happened here was completely predictable.

The phenomenon results from our interpretation of memory-word contents as binary number representations, along with the fact that any such word can hold only finitely many bits. Thus a computer's number system is *finite* and, when viewed from the standpoint of successive incrementing of a word, is *circular;* that is, it wraps back around on itself (Fig. 2.7.3).

Let us return to the "equation" that prompted this latest investigation: $1111 + 0001 = 0000$. While this result is not correct, we determined that it is a consequence of the finiteness of the number system, coupled with our interpretation of memory contents. But suppose that we *reinterpret* the number representation 1111 as *negative one* rather than as *positive fifteen*. The equation then becomes correct: $-1 + 1 = 0$. But then what should 1110 mean? Since

1110 is one less than 1111, 1110 should be interpreted as -2. If we continue in this fashion, we must ultimately conclude that $0001 = -15$ and the next step, $0001 - 1 = 0$, leads us to the statement $-15 - 1 = 0$, which is no more satisfying than $15 + 1 = 0$. There is really nothing new here. Our reinterpretation has merely imposed a *different* number scheme on these 4-bit words, and from a standpoint of the finiteness of the system, its circularity, and the "incorrectness" of certain arithmetic operations, it is no more satisfactory than the earlier positive-number scheme. Nonetheless it will be useful to expand upon Fig. 2.7.2 to include this second interpretation (Fig. 2.7.4).

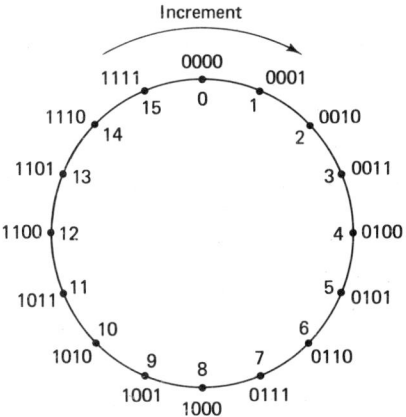

Figure 2.7.3

We now have two *different* interpretations of our 4-bit words as number representations, and we are going to introduce still another. In practice we shall want to store and manipulate *both* positive *and* negative numbers in these words; thus *neither* of the schemes shown in Fig. 2.7.4 will be adequate. Some kind of compromise will have to be made, and we maintain that the following is as

		Interpreted as	
Binary		*Positive*	*Negative*
0000		0	0
0001		1	-15
0010		2	-14
0011		3	-13
0100		4	-12
0101		5	-11
0110		6	-10
0111		7	-9
1000		8	-8
1001		9	-7
1010		10	-6
1011		11	-5
1100		12	-4
1101		13	-3
1110		14	-2
1111		15	-1

Figure 2.7.4

reasonable as any: For those 4-bit configurations in which bit 3 is 0, we use the *positive-number* interpretation. For those in which bit 3 is 1, we use the *negative-number* interpretation. The result is a **signed-number system** that contains both positive and negative numbers. This scheme appears to be potentially useful, since half of the 4-bit configurations are now interpreted as negative numbers, the other half as positive or zero. This compromise is shown in Fig. 2.7.5.

Binary	Interpreted as a signed number
0000	0
0001	1
0010	2
0011	3
0100	4
0101	5
0110	6
0111	7
1000	−8
1001	−7
1010	−6
1011	−5
1100	−4
1101	−3
1110	−2
1111	−1

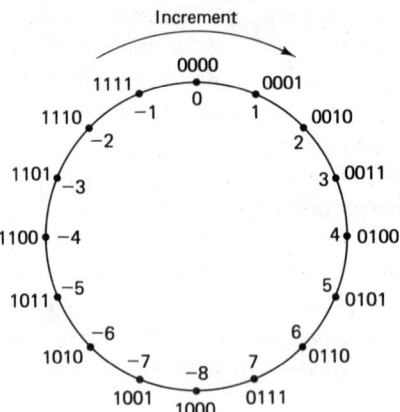

Figure 2.7.5   **Figure 2.7.6**

This number system is still finite, of course, and it is still circular (Fig. 2.7.6), although in this case the discontinuity in the system occurs between 7 and −8, rather than between 15 and 0, as before.

Evidently this interpretation of a 4-bit word as a *signed* number places special importance on the most-significant bit, bit 3. If this bit is 0, the number is interpreted as positive or zero. If it is 1, the number is negative. For this reason the most-significant bit is referred to as the **sign bit**.

2.8 1's-COMPLEMENTS AND 2's-COMPLEMENTS

When the sign bit of a 4-bit signed number is 0, the *value* of the number is easily calculated—we simply ignore the sign bit and evaluate the remaining three bits. Thus, for example, the value of 0101 is just the value of 101, namely 5. However, if the sign bit is 1, the situation is somewhat more complicated. We cannot simply sweep off the sign bit, evaluate the remaining three bits, and then negate the result. For if this were the case, then the value of 1101, for example, would be the negative of the value of 101, namely -5. But in fact 1101 is interpreted as -3, not -5.

To evaluate a negative number, it would suffice to be able to *negate* it. Thus, for example, if we could determine that the *negative* of 1101 was 0011, then we could declare that the value of 1101 was *negative* 3. This prompts a more general question, the calculation of the negative of *any* number and not just one whose sign bit is 1.

The following is an interesting scheme that is easily implemented and introduces a pair of important concepts. Consider a 4-bit (signed) number k. Given the bit configuration for k, we wish to find the configuration for the number $-k$. Consider the (valid) equations $-k = 0 - k = (1 - 1) - k = -1 - k + 1 = (-1 - k) + 1$. Thus to calculate the value of $-k$ we need only subtract k from -1 (1111) and then add 1 (0001). The significance of the subtraction from -1 is that the subtraction is always possible and never requires *borrowing*. In fact, it is easy to verify that the subtraction of a 4-bit number from 1111 (-1) amounts to *reversing* the bits in the 4-bit number; that is, the 0's are changed to 1's and the 1's are changed to 0's. This bit reversal in the number k is called the **1's-complement** of k. We can now complete the process of finding the negative of k by adding 1 to the 1's-complement of k, which results in the negative of k, called the **2's-complement** of k. We show below the process of finding $-k$, where $k = 1101$.

$$
\begin{array}{rl}
1111 & (-1) \\
-1101 & (\text{less } k) \\
\hline
0010 & (\text{the 1's-complement of } k) \\
+0001 & (\text{plus } 1) \\
\hline
0011 & (\text{the 2's-complement of } k; \text{ that is, } -k)
\end{array}
$$

Since we have assumed appropriate circuitry in the processor to form complements—1's-complements—and to increment a 4-bit word, the processor can now *negate* numbers.

In our discussion of 4-bit words interpreted as *unsigned* numbers— numbers in the range 0 to 15—we determined that an arithmetic problem occurred when 1 was added to 1111 that was the result of a carry *out of* bit 3. In the case of *signed* numbers, that same carry causes no problem, for adding 1 to 1111 yields 0000, which is *correct*: $(-1) + 1 = 0$. However, a new problem arises here, namely the incrementing of (adding 1 to) the number 7 (0111). The arithmetic is

$$
\begin{array}{r}
0111 \\
+0001 \\
\hline
1000
\end{array}
$$

Interpreted as unsigned numbers, this addition states that $7 + 1 = 8$. But as *signed* numbers, the corresponding equation becomes $7 + 1 = -8$, and something has gone awry. Notice, however, that the problem here is *not* the result of a carry out of the sign bit. Rather the equation is incorrect because of a carry *into* the sign bit—a carry from bit 2 into bit 3. The effect of the incrementing was to *turn the sign bit on*—make it a 1 where it was 0 before the incrementing.

2.9 THE CARRY AND OVERFLOW INDICATORS

In the preceding sections we investigated 4-bit words and, as a result of various interpretations, we imposed two different number systems on them, unsigned and signed binary. We saw that under certain circumstances, as a result of carries into and out of the most-significant bit, things have not gone so well as we might have wished, from an arithmetic standpoint: The computations were correct in some cases and incorrect in others. And while it is far from satisfactory for a machine to produce a result of questionable arithmetic correctness, we did uncover the source of the difficulties—the finiteness of the computer's word size, along with our interpretation of word contents as representing binary numbers. In any event, the carries that led to these problems have not gone unnoticed by the processor.

The processor contains two indicators, the **carry indicator** and the **overflow indicator**, which we may think of as 1-bit "miniwords." Each of these may be *set* (given the value 1) or *cleared* (given the value 0) by the processor. The carry indicator is *normally* associated with a carry *out of* the most-significant bit, while the overflow indicator is *usually* set by carries *into* the most-significant bit. Thus upon completion of an operation in which a carry out of bit 2 and into bit 3 occurred, the processor might be expected to set the overflow indicator. If such a carry did not take place, the overflow indicator would typically be cleared. The carry indicator would be treated in an analogous fashion. The significance of these indicators is that, upon completion of an operation by the processor, we can examine them. If their states indicate that an arithmetically incorrect result possibly occurred, some appropriate corrective action can be taken. It will be some time before we see just how these indicators are examined; in the meantime we have the assurance that while some arithmetic results may be "incorrect," at least we have some control over what up until now has appeared to be a chaotic situation.

The way in which the processor manages these indicators is by no means as straightforward as suggested in the preceding paragraph. The reader may have the impression that if, at the completion of an operation, a carry out of bit 3 occurred, then the carry indicator will *always* be set, otherwise it will be cleared; likewise, a carry into bit 3 will set the overflow indicator, which will be cleared otherwise. In fact the way in which the processor handles these indicators depends on *what operation is being performed*, not merely on which carries did or did not take place. In some cases, they will be treated as described above. In others, one or the other of them might be set or cleared *regardless* of whether a carry into or out of bit 3 actually occurred. In still other cases, the indicators might simply be unaffected. For example, when the PDP-11 increments a word, it sets the overflow indicator if a carry into the sign bit (bit 3) occurred; if not, the indicator is cleared. But the carry indicator is left unaffected, regardless of whether or not a carry out of bit 3 took place. Thus in this case carries out of the most-significant bit are *undetected*.

It is not possible to give general rules for the conditions under which these indicators are set, cleared, or left unaffected; the CPU's actions depend upon the operation it is performing. Suffice it to say that the hardware has been designed in such a way that these indicators will provide us with useful information in a variety of circumstances.

2.10 SOME FURTHER 4-BIT ARITHMETIC

In this section we look at two further examples of word manipulation, addition and subtraction. Here again we assume that the processor has the necessary circuitry to perform these operations. Consider first the simple addition problem

$$
\begin{array}{r}
0011 \\
+0010 \\
\hline
0101
\end{array}
$$

Considered as unsigned addition, this represents $3 + 2 = 5$. In the signed case, the addition becomes $(+3) + (+2) = +5$. In either case, the result is correct, and we note that neither a carry out of bit 3 nor a carry from bit 2 into bit 3 occurred.

Consider next

$$
\begin{array}{r}
0101 \\
+0011 \\
\hline
1000
\end{array}
$$

In both the unsigned and signed cases, this is $5 + 3$. In the unsigned case, the result is 8, which is correct. In the signed case, the result is -8, which is arithmetically incorrect. But we may be able to detect this incorrectness since a carry into bit 3 occurred.

The addition

$$
\begin{array}{r}
1101 \\
+0101 \\
\hline
0010
\end{array}
$$

is incorrect in the unsigned case: $13 + 5 = 2$. But in the signed case, it is correct: $-3 + 5 = 2$. Notice here that *both* carries occurred—into and out of the most-significant bit.

Finally, consider

$$\begin{array}{r} 1010 \\ +1001 \\ \hline 0011 \end{array}$$

Here both the unsigned and signed interpretations yield an incorrect result—$10 + 9 = 3$ and $-6 + (-7) = 3$, respectively. Note that a carry out of bit 3 occurred, but there was no carry *into* bit 3.

We now make some generalizations that the reader is asked to verify in the exercises. If the words that enter into a 4-bit word addition are interpreted as representing *unsigned* numbers, then the result of the addition will be arithmetically correct provided no carry out of the most-significant bit took place. If the words are interpreted as *signed* numbers, then the result will be arithmetically correct provided (a) *neither* a carry into or out of the most-significant bit occurred or (b) *both* of these carries occurred.

Now that we have seen the conditions under which additions result in correct and incorrect answers, we may ask how the processor manages its carry and overflow indicators in this case. If a carry out of bit 3 occurs, the carry indicator is set; if not, the carry indicator is cleared. Thus the state of the carry indicator—cleared or set—upon completion of an addition operation indicates the correctness or incorrectness, repectively, of *unsigned* addition. The overflow indicator will be set if the two numbers being added were of the same sign but the result of the addition is of the opposite sign; it is cleared otherwise. (Another way of putting this is to say that the overflow indicator is set *if and only if* precisely *one* of the carries into or out of the sign bit occurred.) Thus the state of the overflow indicator—cleared or set—can be used to determine the correctness or incorrectness, respectively, of *signed* addition. The preceding is an example of the processor's setting of these indicators in a way that, while perhaps not completely straightforward, offers maximum information. (We should note that the processor's behavior relative to these indicators applies specifically to the PDP-11, although its actions are not unique—other processors deal with addition in the same way.)

We shall treat subtraction in a somewhat more cursory fashion. Consider the following subtraction problem.

$$\begin{array}{r} 1001 \\ -0011 \\ \hline 0110 \end{array}$$

The computations here are perfectly straightforward, although note that a borrow was required, from bit 3 to bit 2, and finally to bit 1. In the unsigned case, the result is $9 - 3 = 6$, which is correct. However, in the signed case, it is $(-7) - 3 = 6$ which is, of course, incorrect.

Next consider

$$
\begin{array}{r}
0011 \\
-1001 \\
\hline
?010
\end{array}
$$

There is a difficulty here, since the subtraction in bit 3 cannot be accomplished without borrowing, and yet there seems to be nothing from which to borrow. There are two ways we can manage this subtraction. First, consider the minuend to be 10011, rather than 0011. (This bit of trickery assumes that the minuend is actually 5 bits long, but it is not so outrageous as it may appear.) The subtraction now becomes

$$
\begin{array}{r}
10011 \\
-\ \ 1001 \\
\hline
1010
\end{array}
$$

with a borrow from the nonexistent bit 4. The result, 1010, is actually correct, as is easily verified by the addition $1001 + 1010 = 0011$.

The other way to treat subtraction, which avoids the problem encountered above and is in fact the way the PDP-11 deals with this operation, is to rewrite a subtraction such as $A - B$ as the addition $A + (-B)$. Thus we need only negate the subtrahend and add it to the minuend. Since the negative of 1001 is 0111, the present example becomes

$$
\begin{array}{r}
0011 \\
-1001 \\
\hline
\end{array}
\quad \text{is equivalent to} \quad
\begin{array}{r}
0011 \\
+0111 \\
\hline
1010
\end{array}
$$

Observe that in the unsigned case, the subtraction is $3 - 9 = 10$; in the signed case it is $3 - (-7) = -6$. Thus in both cases, the result is arithmetically incorrect.

As a final example, consider

$$
\begin{array}{r}
1101 \\
-1010 \\
\hline
\end{array}
\quad \text{is equivalent to} \quad
\begin{array}{r}
1101 \\
+0110 \\
\hline
0011
\end{array}
$$

In both the unsigned and the signed cases—$13 - 10 = 3$ and $(-3) - (-6) = 3$, respectively—the answer is arithmetically correct.

The reader will not be surprised to find that the correctness or incorrectness of the results of subtractions, as with additions, is dependent upon whether or not various carries into or out of the most-significant bit occurred, and he is asked in Exercises 2.10.6 and 2.10.7 to determine what these conditions are. To see how the processor sets the carry and overflow indicators, we must keep in mind that it handles subtraction as an *addition*: $A - B =$

$A + (-B)$. If this addition results in a carry out of the most-significant bit, then the carry indicator is *cleared;* otherwise it is *set.* Observe that this is precisely the reverse of the carry indicator behavior for addition. The carry indicator, when set, implies that a borrow from the nonexistent bit 4 was required to perform the subtraction. The overflow indicator will be set if the numbers to be subtracted were of opposite sign (had opposite 3 bits) and the result of the subtraction has the same sign (3 bit) as the subtrahend; otherwise the overflow indicator is cleared.

A little experimentation will reveal the following facts: As in the case of addition, the state of the carry indicator—cleared or set—indicates the correctness or incorrectness, respectively, of *unsigned* subtraction. Similarly, a cleared or set overflow indicator signals the correctness or incorrectness, respectively, of *signed* subtraction. Finally, recalling again that the processor handles subtraction as an addition, the carry indicator is set if and only if there was *no* carry out of the most-significant bit (bit 3), and the overflow indicator is set if and only if there was precisely *one* carry into or out of the sign bit.

2.11 EXERCISES

2.4.1. Show that a memory unit made up of n independent memory cells can assume 2^n distinct configurations. How can this result be interpreted if $n = 0$?

2.5.1. Describe the number 100 in terms of fingers and sets of fingers.

2.5.2. Convert each of the following number representations (in the indicated base) to a representation in the specified base.
  (a) $142_5 = $ _____$_{10}$
  (b) $142_{10} = $ _____$_5$
  (c) $142_8 = $ _____$_{10}$
  (d) $142_{10} = $ _____$_8$
  (e) $100110010_2 = $ _____$_4$
  (f) $100110010_2 = $ _____$_8$
  (g) $316_8 = $ _____$_4$
  (h) $1212_4 = $ _____$_8$
  (i) $316_8 = $ _____$_2$
  (j) $1212_4 = $ _____$_2$

2.5.3. Convert each of the following decimal number representations to a binary (base 2) representation.
  (a) 20   (d) 32   (g) 1024
  (b) 5   (e) 65   (h) 2047
  (c) 15   (f) 127   (i) 129

2.5.4. Convert each of the following binary (base 2) number representations to a decimal representation.
  (a) 101   (d) 100001   (g) 101010
  (b) 1001   (e) 111111   (h) 100000
  (c) 1101   (f) 100100   (i) 111011

2.5.5. Convert each of the decimal numbers in Exercise 2.5.3 to its octal (base 8) representation.

2.5.6. Convert each of the binary numbers in Exercise 2.5.4 to its octal (base 8) representation.

2.5.7. Convert each of the following octal (base 8) number representations to hexadecimal (base 16).

    (a) 102235   **(c)** 47   **(e)** 70452

    (b) 16   **(d)** 77777   **(f)** 177776

2.5.8. Convert each of the following hexadecimal (base 16) number representations to octal (base 8).

    (a) $1F$ **(c)** $F1$ **(e)** $FFFF$

    (b) $E7$ **(d)** $ABCD$ **(f)** $1FFE$

2.5.9. Perform the indicated arithmetic operations in the bases specified. (Check the results by converting all numbers to a base 10 representation.)

    (a) 126_7 **(d)** 77204_8 **(g)** 1044_6

        $+\ 662_7$ $-\ \ 1655_8$ $\times\ \ 305_6$

    (b) 126_8 **(e)** 101110_2 **(h)** 1011_2

        $+\ 662_8$ $-\ \ 11101_2$ $\times\ 1101_2$

    (c) 101101_2 **(f)** 6346_8 **(i)** $572_8 \div 24_8$

        $+\ \ 11011_2$ $\times\ \ 447_8$

2.5.10. The addition of the two base 4 numbers 132 and 33 would be performed as shown below (using the standard addition algorithm), where the numbers at the top indicate carries.

$$
\begin{array}{r}
11 \\
132 \\
+\ \ \ 33 \\
\hline
231
\end{array}
$$

Show in this particular case that the addition algorithm is simply the result of the addition of the two polynomials $1 \cdot x^2 + 3 \cdot x^1 + 2 \cdot x^0$ and $3 \cdot x^1 + 3 \cdot x^0$ (where $x = 4$), with the appropriate grouping and reduction of coefficients.

2.5.11. Show that the number of digits required to represent a number in base n may be as many as k times the number of digits required in base n^k. (Thus, for instance, the binary representation of a number can require as many as three times the digits needed in octal.)

2.7.1. Determine the largest (decimal) integer which can be held in 8-bit, 12-bit, 16-bit, 24-bit, 32-bit, and 36-bit words.

2.7.2. Show that if a memory word consists of n bits, then the largest number that can be held in that word is $2^n - 1$.

2.8.1. Show that if a memory word consisted of only *one* bit, then incrementing that word would amount to complementing it—reversing its state.

2.8.2. Show that if a memory word consisted of just *two* bits, then incrementing that word would amount to complementing bit 0 and, if the result in bit 0 was 0, also complementing bit 1. (See Exercise 2.8.1.)

2.8.3. Show that the results of Exercises 2.8.1 and 2.8.2 can be generalized to 4-bit words (in fact, to n-bit words). To increment such a word, begin at bit 0 and complement each bit until the result of the last complementing is 1.

2.8.4. Find the 1's-complement and 2's-complement of each of the following 4-bit word configurations.

(a) 1010   (b) 1111   (c) 0000   (d) 1000   (e) 0111

2.8.5. Ordinarily, the only number that equals its own negative is the number 0. If 4-bit words are interpreted as representations of *signed* binary numbers, show that $-0 = 0$, but also that $-(-8) = -8$.

2.8.6. In constructing a *signed* number system for 4-bit words, we chose the scheme $0, 1, \ldots, 7, -8, -7, \ldots, -1$, in which the most significant bit—bit 3—was used to determine whether a number was negative or nonnegative. It was claimed in the text that this system, inasmuch as it split the negative and non-negative numbers into equal groups, was as reasonable as any such scheme. Show in fact that it is the *only* reasonable system, in the sense that in any other scheme, a carry into the most-significant bit could not be used to determine the correctness of arithmetic results.

2.10.1. Perform the following operations on the 4-bit words shown. In each case state whether a carry out of or into bit 3 occurred, how the carry and overflow indicators are set, and whether, considered as signed or unsigned words, the arithmetic is "correct."

(a)   0101   (c)   1101   (e)   1110
     $+\ 0011$ $-\ 0011$ $-\ 1000$

(b)   1010   (d)   1010   (f)   0011
     $+\ 1010$ $+\ 0011$ $-\ 1010$

2.10.2. If 4-bit words are interpreted as *unsigned* numbers, show that the result of the addition of two such words will be arithmetically correct *if and only if* no carry out of bit 3 occurred.

2.10.3. If 4-bit words are interpreted as *signed* numbers, show that the result of the addition of two *positive* numbers will be arithmetically correct *if and only if* no carry into bit 3 occurred.

2.10.4. If 4-bit words are interpreted as *signed* numbers, show that the result of the addition of two *negative* numbers will be arithmetically correct *if and only if* a carry into bit 3 occurred. Notice that a carry out of bit 3 will always occur in this case.

2.10.5. If 4-bit words are interpreted as *signed* numbers, show that the result of the addition of a *negative* number and a *positive* number will *always* be correct, and a carry into the sign bit will occur *if and only if* a carry out of the sign bit also occurs.

2.10.6. If 4-bit words are interpreted as *unsigned* numbers, find the carry conditions (out of and into bit 3) under which the result of a subtraction will be arithmetically correct.

2.10.7. If 4-bit words are interpreted as *signed* numbers, find the carry conditions (out of and into the sign bit) under which the result of a subtraction will be arithmetically correct.

3

Logic

3.1 STATEMENTS AND CONNECTIVES

We consider the main task of a computer to be the processing of information, which usually involves operating on data. When we think of the operations performed by a computer, the basic arithmetic operations—addition, multiplication, and so forth—come to mind. In the last chapter we explicitly assumed that our 4-bit word machine had certain of these capabilities. But these traditional arithmetic operations are fairly high on a scale of complexity when compared with some other operations performed by the computer's electronic circuitry. This chapter will investigate the fundamental building blocks that are used to form these more complex computer functions. The reader may find the historical background of these fundamental objects somewhat interesting and surprising.

When we speak or write in English we rarely do so in simple sentences with a subject-verb-object construction. Rather, such simple sentences are frequently *compounded*—joined together by special-purpose words called **connectives**. Examples of these are *AND*, *OR*, *UNLESS*, *IF . . . THEN*, and *BUT*. Our investigation will center on the properties of just a few of these; we shall not attempt a formal approach to what is known as **propositional logic** since at this level the formalism would do little to add to our understanding of computers and computing. The more informal development given here will move us along fairly quickly to the ultimate goal: the construction of circuitry to perform simple but important **logical operations**.

By a **sentence** we shall mean a grammatical (syntactically acceptable) English sentence. A **statement** is a *declarative* sentence whose *truth* or *falsity* can be determined in a *unique* way. Thus a sentence such as "Today is Tuesday" is a statement since it is a declarative sentence and its truth or falsity can be determined. The **truth value**—**true** or **false**—that we assign to this sentence is not of any real consequence; our concern here is simply that it be *possible* to make such an assignment. The assignment of a truth value to a sentence may be confusing, so it will be worthwhile to look at two examples of sentences that are *not* statements according to the description above.

First, consider the sentence "Watch your weight." This is certainly an English sentence, but it is no more true than it is false. Truth and falsity are simply characteristics that our experience shows cannot be assigned to such a sentence. There is also some question whether this sentence is even declarative. As a second example, consider the classic sentence "This sentence is false." This is surely an English sentence, and it is declarative—it makes an assertion. However, if we try to assign it a truth value the situation begins to come apart. For if we say that "This sentence is false" is **true**, then this *true* sentence asserts its own *falsity*. And conversely, assigning this sentence the value **false** implies that it is false that "This sentence is false"—that is, the sentence itself is *true*. Thus we have been unable to assert the sentence's truth or falsity in a *unique* fashion. We shall exclude sentences such as these from the collection of *statements*. Henceforth we shall not concern ourselves with just what *information* a statement might convey. Rather our interest centers on the fact that a sentence may take on, in a unique but otherwise undetermined way, exactly *one* of the values true or false.

Recall that our immediate interest lies in **compound sentences**—sentences made up of simple sentences and connectives that join them. Now there is no reason why a compound sentence cannot itself be a *statement*, and it is this idea that we wish to pursue. Suppose a compound sentence is made up of two statements, to each of which we can assign a truth value. If this compound sentence is to be a statement, then we must be able to assign a truth value to it, and the obvious question is how we should assign a truth value to a compound sentence made up of two statements and a connective. In a sense we can make this assignment any way we want, but English-language usage dictates that the truth value of a compound statement is dependent upon the values of its component statements.

To gain some insight into this question, we consider the common connective *AND* and, as an illustrative example, the compound sentence "Today is Friday *AND* it is raining." This sentence is clearly made up of the individual sentences "Today is Friday" and "It is raining," each of which is a statement. Our experience with the language leads us to conclude that this compound sentence is **true** if in fact it is Friday and also raining; that is, the compound sentence is **true** *provided* each of its components is **true**. On the other hand, if today is *not* Friday, then the compound sentence is **false**, regardless of the state of the weather. Conversely, on a sunny day the sentence will be **false** on *any* day of the week.

The preceding example suggests a formal way of assigning a truth value to a **conjunction**—a compound sentence made up of simple statements connected by *AND*—in such a way that the assignment depends upon the assignment of values to the individual statements: The conjunction is **true** if *both* individual statements are **true**; otherwise the conjunction is **false**. We summarize these results in Fig. 3.1.1, where we use P to represent the first statement (Today is Friday) and Q to represent the second statement (It is raining). The letters **T** and **F** stand for the truth values **true** and **false**, respectively.

P	Q	P AND Q
T	T	T
T	F	F
F	T	F
F	F	F

Figure 3.1.1

Note that we included in the table all possible combinations of truth values for P and Q. The connective *AND* is normally replaced by the symbol $\wedge$ where the *structure* of sentences rather than their *meaning* is the primary concern; thus the table above could be rewritten as shown in Fig. 3.1.2.

P	Q	$P \wedge Q$
T	T	T
T	F	F
F	T	F
F	F	F

Figure 3.1.2

Another connective in common use is *OR*. A sentence that results from the joining of two statements by *OR* is called the **disjunction** of the two statements. In Fig. 3.1.3 we present the definition of the connective *OR*, whose logical symbol is $\vee$.

P	Q	$P \vee Q$
T	T	T
T	F	T
F	T	T
F	F	F

Figure 3.1.3

If we take as an example the two simple statements used above (P: Today is Friday, Q: It is raining), the reader will probably agree that our definition of *OR* is consistent with everyday usage. But in English we sometimes use the word *OR* in a slightly different way. We have no special word for this type of disjunction; we rely on the *context* to signal the modified usage. Consider, for example, the disjunction "For our vacation, we are going to the mountains *OR* we are going to the shore." Implicit here is the rarely appended phrase "but not both." This is a strictly *different* use of the connective *OR*, one that *excludes* the possibility that *both* simple statements are **true**. This is the *EXCLUSIVE OR*, whose symbol is $\underline{\vee}$, and whose definition requires a modification of the first line of the table making up the definition of *OR* (Fig. 3.1.4).

P	Q	$P \underline{\vee} Q$
T	T	F
T	F	T
F	T	T
F	F	F

Figure 3.1.4

P	$\sim P$
T	F
F	T

Figure 3.1.5

The foregoing are all the connective definitions we shall need for our purposes, and in fact we have gone even a bit further than necessary. We do need one more idea that, while quite simple, is *not* a connective but a **modifier** that operates on single statements rather than joining two statements. The modifier is called *NOT*, its symbol is $\sim$, and when applied to a statement, it gives that statement the *opposite* truth value (Fig. 3.1.5).

Statements may be more complex than the simple $P \wedge Q$ or $P \vee Q$ we have seen here, but they are fairly easily managed. Consider, for example, the statement $\sim(P \vee Q)$. To determine the truth value of this statement for given values of the individual statements P and Q, we first need handle only the $P \vee Q$ part of the construction and then negate (*NOT*) the result (Fig. 3.1.6).

P	Q	$P \vee Q$	$\sim(P \vee Q)$
T	T	T	F
T	F	T	F
F	T	T	F
F	F	F	T

Figure 3.1.6

As another example, consider the statement $\sim P \wedge \sim Q$. Again, we can determine the values of this statement from the values of P and Q by evaluating the expression one part at a time (Fig. 3.1.7).

These last two examples have an interesting property that has some consequences for us. Notice that for each particular assignment of truth values for the simple statements P and Q, *both* compound statements have the *same*

P	Q	~P	~Q	~P ∧ ~Q
T	T	F	F	F
T	F	F	T	F
F	T	T	F	F
F	F	T	T	T

Figure 3.1.7

value. If two statements S_1 and S_2 are made up (by means of connectives and modifiers) of the simple statements $P, Q, R, \ldots$ and if for each assignment of values to the statements $P, Q, R, \ldots$ the two statements S_1 and S_2 take on the same value, then S_1 and S_2 are said to be **equivalent**, written $S_1 \equiv S_2$. If we apply this definition to the examples above, we have $\sim(P \vee Q) \equiv \sim P \wedge \sim Q$. A number of other examples will be found in the exercises.

3.2 SWITCHING CIRCUITS

A **switch** is a device that can exist in one of two states—**closed** or **open**. When the switch is closed, it allows current to flow in a circuit; when open, it prevents the flow of current. We shall diagram switches as shown in Fig. 3.2.1. Since a *closed* switch is difficult to differentiate from a straight-through wire, we shall henceforth show switches in their open position and rely on the text to determine the state of the switch.

Closed   Open

Figure 3.2.1

The simplest circuit containing a switch is shown in Fig. 3.2.2. We assume some voltage source, which we take to be 1 volt, although the actual voltage is of no consequence. The output of the circuit can be measured with a meter (voltmeter), and we see that if the switch is *open*, then no current flows and the output will be 0 volts. If the switch is *closed*, however, a current flows through the meter, indicating an output of 1 volt. We summarize these results in Fig. 3.2.3.

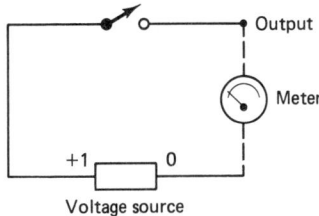

Output

Meter

+1   0

Voltage source

Figure 3.2.2

Switch	Output
closed	1
open	0

Figure 3.2.3

Since the output of the circuit is directly related to the switch position, we adopt the following notation: A closed switch is said to have the *value* 1, and an open switch has the *value* 0. The table above can now be rewritten as shown in Fig. 3.2.4.

Switch	Output
1	1
0	0

Figure 3.2.4

Since this situation is too simple to be of any real interest, consider a slightly more involved circuit, containing two switches in **series** (Fig. 3.2.5). Since there are now two switches, A and B, which we assume can be set independently of one another, the output table requires four lines to indicate the various switch settings. Again, we use 1 for a closed switch, 0 for an open switch (Fig. 3.2.6).

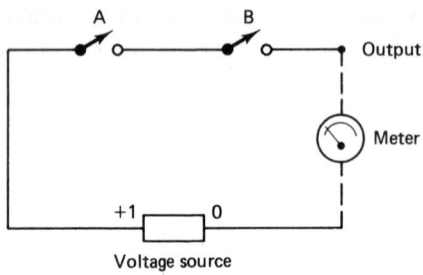

Figure 3.2.5

Switch		Output
A	B	
1	1	1
1	0	0
0	1	0
0	0	0

Figure 3.2.6

Another switching circuit involving two switches is given in Fig. 3.2.7, in which the switches are shown in **parallel**. We do not show the meter here, nor shall we in the future, because we assume that the output can be measured in some way or another. The reader should have no difficulty verifying that the output table is as shown in Fig. 3.2.8.

These two examples, circuits in which switches are in series or in parallel, are the only circuits containing two switches. Circuits can, of course, contain more than two switches. We show an example in Fig. 3.2.9. The reader should verify that this circuit can be described by the table of Fig. 3.2.10.

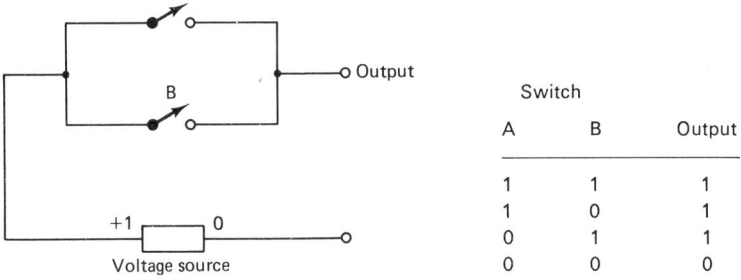

Figure 3.2.7

| Switch | | |
A	B	Output
1	1	1
1	0	1
0	1	1
0	0	0

Figure 3.2.8

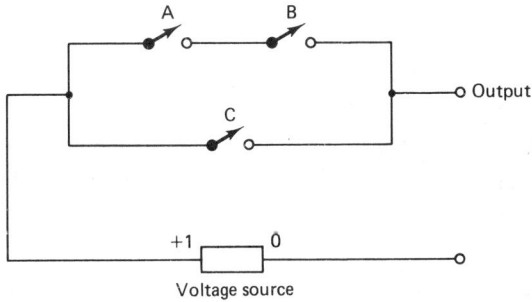

Figure 3.2.9

| Switches | | | |
A	B	C	Output
1	1	1	1
1	1	0	1
1	0	1	1
1	0	0	0
0	1	1	1
0	1	0	0
0	0	1	1
0	0	0	0

Figure 3.2.10

3.3 STATEMENTS REVISITED—A CHANGE IN NOTATION

Fig. 3.3.1 reproduces the definitions from Sec. 3.1 of the connectives *AND*, *OR*, and *EXCLUSIVE OR*, as well as the modifier *NOT*, with the following change in notation: The **T**'s and **F**'s (trues and falses) have been changed to 1's and 0's respectively.

	P	Q	P ∧ Q
(a)	1	1	1
	1	0	0
	0	1	0
	0	0	0

	P	Q	P ∨ Q
(b)	1	1	1
	1	0	1
	0	1	1
	0	0	0

	P	Q	P $\veebar$ Q
(c)	1	1	0
	1	0	1
	0	1	1
	0	0	0

	P	~P
(d)	1	0
	0	1

Figure 3.3.1

A comparison of the tables of Fig. 3.3.1 (a) and Fig. 3.2.6 shows that aside from the *names* of the elements, they are *identical*. Thus a series-switching circuit may be interpreted as a *physical representation* of the connective *AND*, provided only that we interpret a closed switch as representing a true statement, an open switch as a false statement, and an output of 1 as a true conjunction, 0 a false conjunction. The opposite view is equally valid: A series-switching circuit can be represented by the logical statement connective *AND*. In a similar fashion, we see from the tables of Fig. 3.3.1(b) and Fig. 3.2.8 that parallel switching circuits and the disjunction *OR* are simply different representations of the same abstract concept. (The switching-circuit representation of the *EXCLUSIVE OR* and of the modifier *NOT* are not quite so easily managed; we shall postpone further discussion of these until the next section.) We note also that the circuit of Fig. 3.2.9 has, as its logical equivalent, the statement $(A \wedge B) \vee C$.

We shall develop some of the consequences of this dual representation of these concepts in the next section; we shall expand upon others, which bear less directly on the computer applications of these ideas, in the exercises. In any event, the reader should be aware that, with the proper interpretations, we now have a method of evaluating logical statements *physically*—constructing electric circuits that represent certain logical statements.

3.4 RELAYS AND GATES

We are now well on our way to the principal objective of this chapter: the construction of components that can "do logic"—which behave in the same way as the logical connectives and the modifier *NOT*. For as we shall see, these components will form the basic building blocks of the computer's hardware. However, we shall have to deal with a problem here. In our development of computer hardware (for example, the devices that make up memory cells), we insisted that components be able to react to electric currents, and from that point of view the switches we discussed in this chapter are not satisfactory. We represented them as being of the hand-operated type, such as an ordinary light switch, and thus we shall have to take some steps to modify them. Fortunately, this will not be difficult.

Consider an iron rod with a wire wound around it. When a current flows through the wire, the rod becomes a magnet (Fig. 3.4.1(a)). When no current is flowing, the rod is not magnetized. Suppose that we modify this so-called **electromagnet** by placing a piece of spring steel with a contact on its end close to the iron rod (Fig. 3.4.1(b)). When a current flows through the wire, the spring steel is attracted by the magnetized rod, and contact is made between the steel and a fixed contact. When no current flows, no contact is made. These contacts act as a switch, which is controlled by the current in the winding wire. Such an arrangement is called a **relay**. Thus the switching that we used to advantage in the preceding two sections can be performed by the presence or absence of a current, and we can now rebuild the switching circuits that represent *AND* and *OR* using these relays.

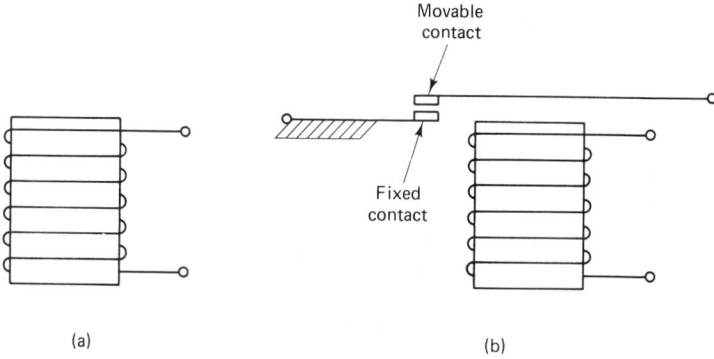

Figure 3.4.1

In Fig. 3.4.2 the lines labeled A and B are called *inputs* to the switching circuit. If A is at 0 volts, then no current is flowing through the leftmost relay, it is not magnetized, and hence the contacts—the switch labeled S_A—are open. If A is at 1 volt, then a current flows through this relay and S_A becomes a closed switch. Switch S_B is similarly controlled by the absence or presence of a voltage at input B. It is not difficult to determine that the output of this circuit will be 1 *if and only if* A and B are both 1—that is, this circuit represents the *AND*ing of A and B. Wires that are shown as crossing by $+$ are *not connected* at their point of intersection. Connected wires will be shown as $+$ or $+$ We shall shortly explain the dashed line that surrounds most of this figure.

In a similar fashion the reader may verify that Fig. 3.4.3 is a circuit that represents the *OR*ing of the inputs A and B. Thus we see that it is possible to design circuits with two inputs, A and B, each of which can be 0 or 1, and a

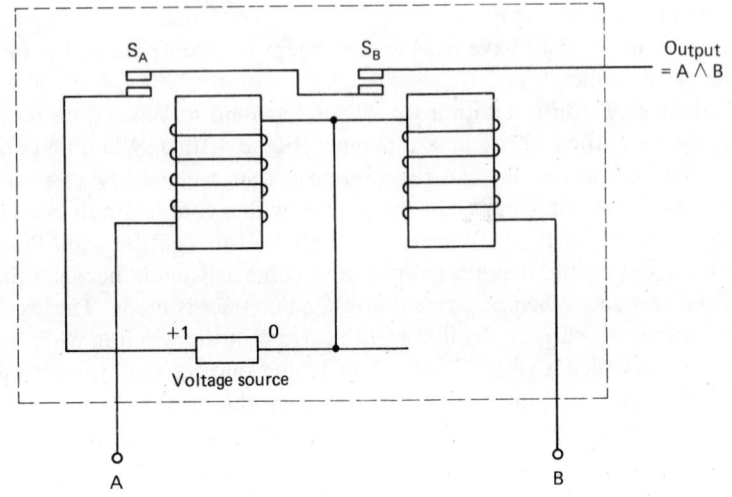

Figure 3.4.2

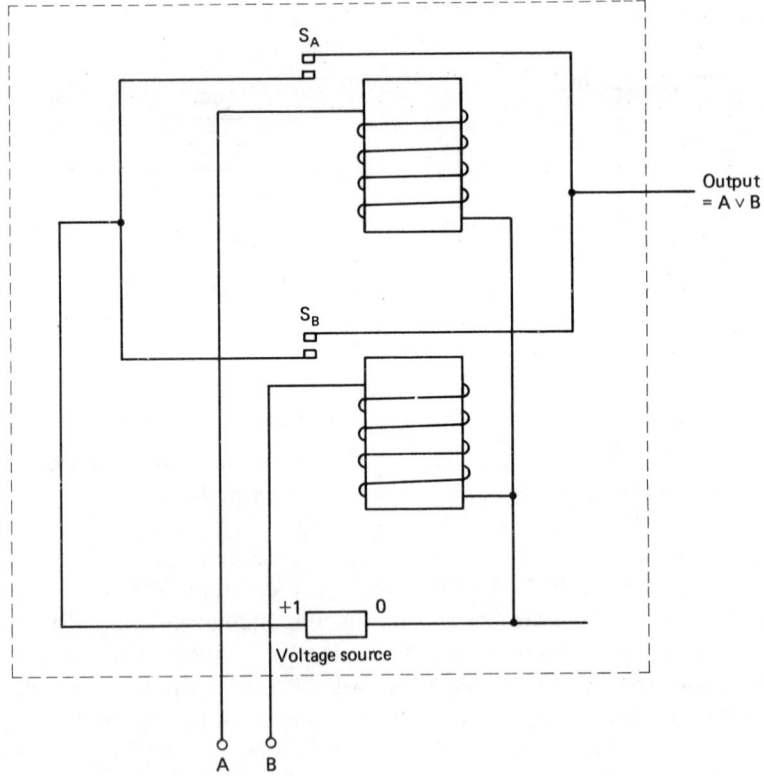

Figure 3.4.3

single output whose value of 0 or 1 will depend upon the inputs. In the first case, the output is A $\wedge$ B, in the second it is A $\vee$ B.

At this point our interest focuses only on the *existence* of such circuits, and we shall no longer be concerned with precisely *how* they are constructed. In our examples we built these circuits from relays, but relays have not been used for these purposes in computers for many years. Such circuits are more typically built from transistors, which have the same capability to act as switches, but which can switch their states much more rapidly than the rather slow relays. No matter—what is of importance is that there *are* such circuits.

Thus the circuitry contained within the dashed lines in Fig. 3.4.2 and 3.4.3 can be reduced to "black boxes," allowing us to concentrate on the inputs and outputs (Fig. 3.4.4). Of course as we have seen, these black boxes also require some voltage source, which we have not shown. Such circuits are usually called **gates** and have standard symbols associated with them, which are shown in Fig. 3.4.5.

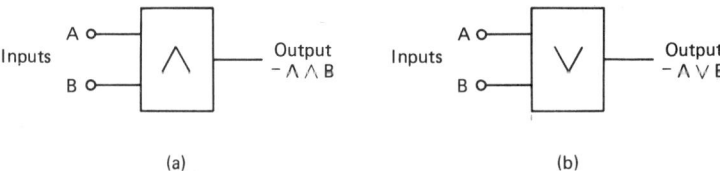

(a)   (b)

Figure 3.4.4

Inputs A ——[⊃ AND-gate ⊃]—— Output = A $\wedge$ B   Inputs A ——[⊃ OR-gate ⊃]—— Output = A $\vee$ B

AND-gate   OR-gate

Figure 3.4.5

We can also use a relay to construct a physical representation of the logical modifier *NOT*. We need only rearrange the relay contacts so that the relay is *normally closed*. That is, the contacts are closed in the *absence* of a current and open in the *presence* of a current. Figure 3.4.6 shows such a circuit, as can easily be verified. Again we reduce this circuit to a black box called an **inverter**, (sometimes referred to as a *NOT* gate), whose symbol is shown in Fig. 3.4.7. Notice that this gate has a *single* input.

We can now finally deal with the heretofore neglected connective *EXCLU-SIVE OR*. The symbol for an *EXCLUSIVE-OR* gate or, for short, an *XOR* gate, is shown in Fig. 3.4.8. It is now relatively easy to construct this gate using *AND* gates, *OR* gates, and inverters. Figure 3.4.9 shows two circuits, each of which represents *XOR*, as the reader should verify.

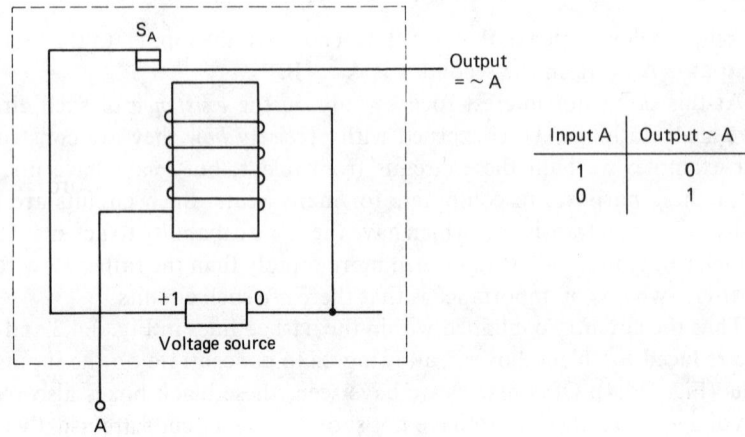

Input A	Output ~ A
1	0
0	1

Figure 3.4.6

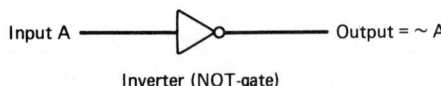

Inverter (NOT-gate)

Figure 3.4.7

EXCLUSIVE-OR-gate

Figure 3.4.8

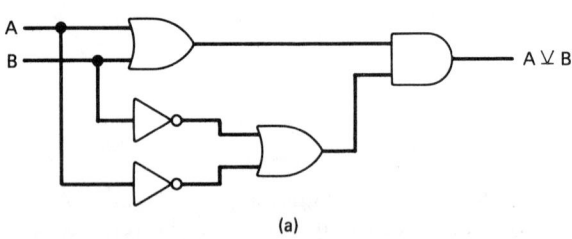

(a)

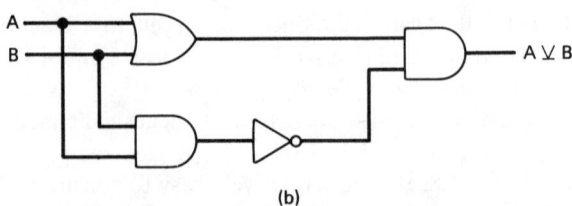

(b)

Figure 3.4.9

3.5 TWO ARITHMETIC CIRCUITS

In this chapter we briefly discussed the logic of statements, which led us to switching circuits, relay circuits, and gates—devices that are physical representations of the logical connectives. But the reader may wonder what this development has to do with computers, and in particular with the 4-bit word machine discussed in some detail in the preceding chapter.

We asserted that these physical representations form the basic building blocks of the computer's processing hardware, and the time has come to verify this. Recall that in Sec. 2.7 we asserted the possibility of designing computer circuitry that would *increment* (by 1) a 4-bit word. The circuit of Fig. 3.5.1 actually increments such a word. Here we take $x_3 x_2 x_1 x_0$ as the 4-bit word to be incremented and $y_3 y_2 y_1 y_0$ as the resulting 4-bit word ($x_3 x_2 x_1 x_0 + 1$). Since we interpret each of the x_k's as a 0 or 1, we can use each as an input to the *XOR* and *AND* gates. The output of each *XOR* gate is again a 0 or 1, which we interpret as the value of the y_k's. Notice that the circuit also has a *fixed* input of 1.

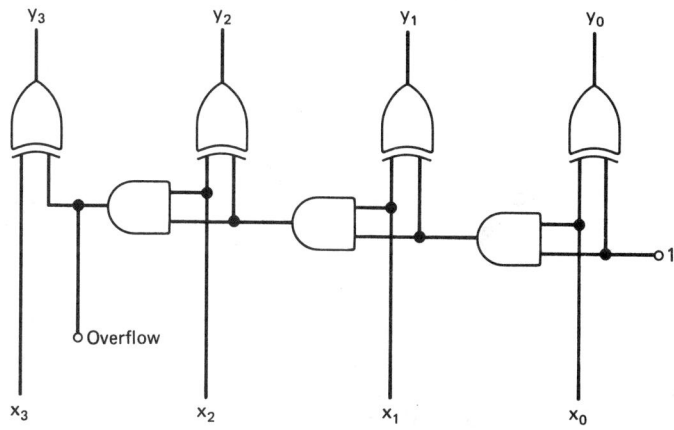

Figure 3.5.1

The reader should analyze this simple circuit to verify that it does the incrementing. In the course of the analysis, it will be seen that the *XOR* gates do the actual incrementing, while the *AND* gates keep track of any carries from one bit into the next higher order bit. In this circuit we also made provision for "capturing" any carry into bit 3 and thus appropriately setting the overflow indicator, as is normally done on an increment.

In Sec. 2.10 we assumed that circuitry existed for the *addition* of 4-bit words. We require a somewhat more complex circuit than the incrementing one shown above, since now there are *two* inputs to the circuit, corresponding to the two words to be added. In Fig. 3.5.2 we show a *partial* circuit to perform 4-bit addition (or *n*-bit addition, for that matter). We show the circuitry required

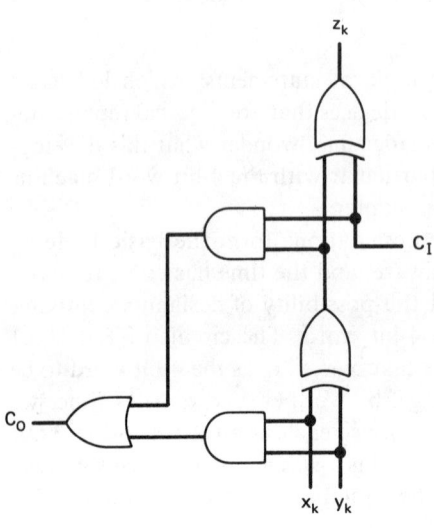

Figure 3.5.2

to add the kth bit of one word $(x_3x_2x_1x_0)$ to the kth bit of a second word $(y_3y_2y_1y_0)$ to obtain the kth bit of the result $(z_3z_2z_1z_0)$. The line labeled C_I stands for the *carry in* from the preceding (lower-order) bit. Thus C_I is either 0 or 1, according as a carry did or did not occur from the addition of the $(k-1)$st bits. Similarly, C_O represents the *carry out* into the next higher order bit as a result of the addition of these kth bits. Thus to form a complete 4-bit word addition circuit, we need only tie four of these circuits together. At the bit-0 level, it would suffice to set C_I to 0, although there are slightly simpler ways to handle this special case. The reader should verify that this circuit will perform as claimed as well as determine how the carry and overflow indicators should be wired in the full 4-bit addition circuit.

The only claim we make for the circuits described in this section is that they do perform the desired tasks. There may be equivalent circuits that are more efficient, in the sense of consisting of fewer components. And while any computer should be able to increment and add, a particular machine may well use circuits different from those shown to accomplish these functions, depending on its overall architecture. Such circuits would be a part of the arithmetic-logic unit (ALU) of the CPU. This unit would also contain the circuitry, or—as it is frequently called—the **logic**, for the other fundamental arithmetic operations. In our development we have purposely ignored certain problems, primarily engineering in nature, involved in the actual implementation of the manipulation of the bits and 4-bit words, and we could investigate much in these directions. However to push these matters further would divert us from our main objective— an overview of what computers are, what they do, and, in rather general terms, how they do it.

3.6 EXERCISES

3.1.1. Define, by means of a table of truth values, each of the following connectives.
    (a) *IF . . . THEN*   **(b)** *BUT*   **(c)** *UNLESS*

3.1.2. Let P, Q, and R be statements. Define what would be meant by $P \wedge Q \wedge R$ and by $P \vee Q \vee R$. (*Suggestion:* Show that $(P \wedge Q) \wedge R \equiv P \wedge (Q \wedge R)$.)

3.1.3. **(a)** Show that $P \wedge (Q \vee R) \equiv (P \wedge Q) \vee (P \wedge R)$.

    (b) Show that $P \lor (Q \land R) \equiv (P \lor Q) \land (P \lor R)$.

    (c) Show that $\sim P \lor \sim Q \equiv \sim(P \land Q)$.

3.1.4. Show that $P \veebar Q \equiv (P \lor Q) \land (\sim P \lor \sim Q)$ and that $P \veebar Q \equiv (P \lor Q)$ $\land \sim(P \land Q)$.

3.1.5. Show that $P \land Q \equiv \sim\sim(P \land Q) \equiv \sim(\sim P \lor \sim Q)$.

3.1.6. Define the connective *IMPLIES*, whose symbol is $\Rightarrow$, as follows.

P	Q	$P \Rightarrow Q$
T	T	T
T	F	F
F	T	T
F	F	T

Figure 3.6.1

    (a) Show that $P \Rightarrow Q \equiv \sim(P \land \sim Q) \equiv \sim P \lor Q$.

    (b) Show that the value of the statement $(P \land (P \Rightarrow Q)) \Rightarrow Q$ is *always* **true**, regardless of the values of P and Q. Such a statement is called a **tautology**.

    (c) Each of the connectives defined in the text has the property that $P \triangle Q \equiv Q \triangle P$, where $\triangle$ is any of the symbols $\land$, $\lor$ or $\veebar$. Show that *IMPLIES* $(\Rightarrow)$ does *not* have this property.

3.3.1. Show that the switching circuit of Fig. 3.2.9 is a physical realization of the logical statement $(A \land B) \lor C$.

3.4.1. Show that if one of the inputs to an *OR* gate is 0, then the output of the *OR* gate is equal to the other input. That is, in this case the *OR* gate is acting as a straight-through wire relative to the other input.

3.4.2. Show that if one of the inputs to an *AND* gate is 1, the output of the *AND* gate is equal to the other input.

3.4.3. Show that the two defining circuits for an *XOR* gate (shown in Fig. 3.4.9) are *equivalent* in the sense that for given inputs A and B, the outputs of the two circuits will be the same. Show this in the following ways.

    (a) By determining the output of each circuit for all possible combinations of inputs.

    (b) By using the results of Exercise 3.1.4. Specifically, show that the circuit of Fig. 3.4.9 (a) is a physical realization of the logical statement $(A \lor B)$ $\land (\sim A \lor \sim B)$, while (b) realizes $(A \lor B) \land \sim(A \land B)$.

3.4.4. Show that the output of the circuit

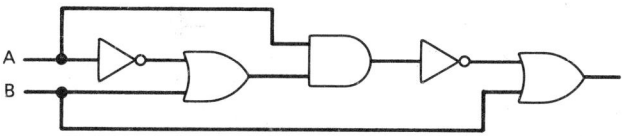

Figure 3.6.2

will always be 1, regardless of the states of the inputs A and B (a) by finding the output for all possible combinations of inputs and (b) by comparing this circuit with the results of Exercise 3.1.6 (a) and (b).

3.4.5. By writing a logical statement equivalent to the following circuit and then manipulating that logical statement, show that the circuit

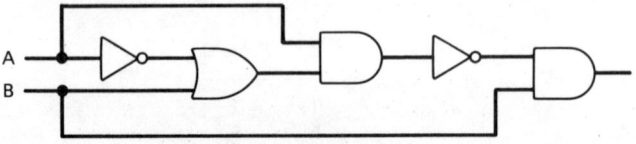

Figure 3.6.3

can be reduced to the equivalent circuit.

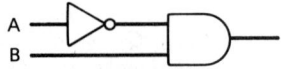

Figure 3.6.4

3.4.6 Show that if one of the inputs to an *XOR* gate is held at 1, then the *XOR* gate acts as an *inverter* for the other input.

3.4.7. Consider a new type of gate, which we shall call simply an *X* gate, whose corresponding logical symbol is $\times$ and whose definition and graphic symbol are shown below.

Inputs

A	B	Output = A $\times$ B
1	1	0
1	0	0
0	1	0
0	0	1

Inputs   A ▷ B   Output = A $\times$ B

X-gate

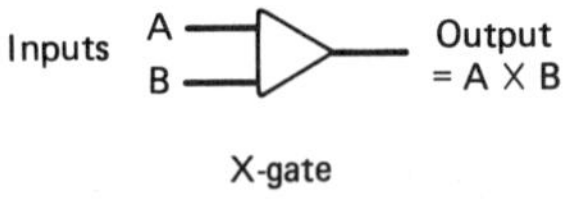

Figure 3.6.5

(a) Show that if B is held fixed at 0, then the *X* gate acts as an *inverter* for the input A. That is,

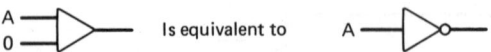

Figure 3.6.6

(b) Show that *X* gates can be used to construct the equivalent of an *OR* gate, namely,

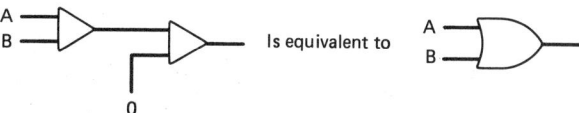

Figure 3.6.7

(c) Show that X gates can be used to construct the equivalent of an AND gate. (Use the fact that X gates can be used to construct *inverters* and OR gates, along with Exercise 3.1.5.)

(d) Show that *all* of the gates of Sec. 3.4 could have been constructed of X gates, thus concluding that this *one* primitive component can be used to fabricate any of these circuits or the circuits of Sec. 3.5. (In fact, an X gate is nothing more than an OR gate followed by an *inverter*; that is, an X gate is equivalent to the circuit of Fig. 3.6.8.

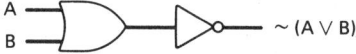

Figure 3.6.8

The usual symbol for this gate is shown in Fig. 3.6.9; it is customarily referred to as a *NOR* gate.)

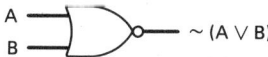

Figure 3.6.9

3.5.1. Verify that the circuit of Fig. 3.5.1 increments a 4-bit word.

3.5.2. Design a circuit to *decrement* a 4-bit word by 1. (*Suggestion:* At each bit, the input to an *EXCLUSIVE OR* gate is the output from the preceding lower-order gate and one of the inputs to that gate.)

3.5.3. What is the effect of the circuit shown below on a 4-bit word? That is, what is the relationship between the output $y_3 y_2 y_1 y_0$ and the input $x_3 x_2 x_1 x_0$? (*Suggestion:* Consider the 4-bit words as *signed* numbers.)

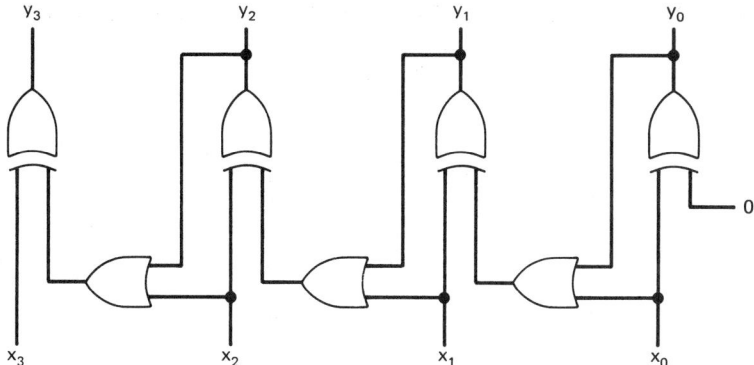

Figure 3.6.10

45

3.5.4. Use the partial circuit of Fig. 3.5.2 to construct a full 4-bit-word addition circuit, paying particular attention to the carry and overflow indicators and to the handling of the addition of the 0-bits. The carry and overflow indicators should be set as described in Sec. 2.10.

3.5.5. Consider the circuit shown below.

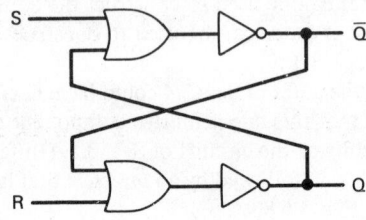

Figure 3.6.11

(a) Show that if $S = 0$ and $R = 1$, then $Q = 0$ and $\bar{Q} = 1$.

(b) With the state as described in part a (that is, $S = 0$ and $R = 1$), show that setting R to 0 does *not* change the outputs Q and $\bar{Q}$.

(c) With the state as described in part b, show that setting $S = 1$ reverses the states of the outputs Q and $\bar{Q}$.

(d) Finally, show that returning S to 0 does not affect the outputs Q and $\bar{Q}$.

This circuit is called a **latch**. Since its principal output Q may be set to 0 or 1 by appropriately setting R and S, and since this output is *unaffected* by returning the inputs R and S to 0, a latch is a potential *memory cell*. In fact, latches are used as memory devices when the high-speed setting of the state of the memory cell is desired or required.

4

16-bit Words and Memory Addressing

4.1 16-BIT-WORD MACHINES

We mentioned in Chapter 2 that the 4-bit words investigated there were so small that the range of numbers they could hold—0 to 15 (unsigned) or −8 to +7 (signed)— was too limited to be of any practical value. And yet that 4-bit-word machine has served us well in introducing a variety of concepts: computer number systems, sign bit, various carries, arithmetic, and so forth. We now move on to a more practical word size, one that will store more realistically usable numbers. We choose a 16-bit word for a number of reasons. First, it is large enough for a fairly wide range of numbers without being unwieldy. Second, 16-bit-word machines have become one of the standards of the industry —a wide variety of minicomputers use this word size. And the PDP-11—the machine of particular interest to us—is a 16-bit-word machine.

There is nothing new to learn about the words themselves, their number systems, or their arithmetic behavior. Aside from the fact that they are 12 bits longer than the familiar 4-bit word, their behavior is identical. We summarize these similarities in the table of Fig. 4.1.1.

Feature	4-bit word	16-bit word
Bit names	3-bit, . . . , 0-bit	15-bit, . . . , 0-bit
Sign bit	3-bit	15-bit
Number system	0 to 15 (unsigned)	0 to 65,535 (unsigned)
	−8 to +7 (signed)	−32,768 to +32,767 (signed)
Carries	Carry from 2-bit	Carry from 14-bit
	into 3-bit	into 15-bit
	Carry out of 3-bit	Carry out of 15-bit

Figure 4.1.1

The carry and overflow indicators are set and cleared, as a result of the arithmetic operations, in a fashion analogous to that of the 4-bit-word case.

4.2 NUMBER REPRESENTATIONS

Despite the fact that the various concepts involved with 4-bit words carry over without substantial change to the 16-bit case, we encounter a problem when dealing with these larger word sizes that was not evident—in fact, did not really exist—in our discussions of 4-bit words. The problem is one of *representation*. Yes, we can say that a 4-bit word contains the binary number 1011, for example, and with either the signed or unsigned interpretation, we can fairly easily grasp the number being represented. But consider now the 16-bit number 1001110001001101. It is very difficult to obtain any feel for what such a number might be, although we can say that in the signed case, it is negative. It is also a rather long string of binary digits to write to express the contents of a memory word. And in its verbalized form, it is all but hopeless:

one-oh-oh-one-one-one-oh-oh-oh-one-oh-oh-one-one-oh-one

We need some means for compressing the notation into fewer digits. We can do this as follows: By breaking up the binary representation of the number into groups of *two* digits each and treating each such pair of digits as the binary representation of a base *four* number, we can write the 16-bit number as a base 4 number containing only half as many digits. For example,

$$\begin{array}{cccccccc} 10 & 01 & 11 & 00 & 01 & 00 & 11 & 01 \\ \wedge & \wedge & \wedge & \wedge & \wedge & \wedge & \wedge \\ 2 & 1 & 3 & 0 & 1 & 0 & 3 & 1 \end{array}$$

Thus $1001110001001101_2 = 21301031_4$. We see that the formation of the base 4 number is quite easy (grouping the base 2 number in sets of two digits and then evaluating), and it is equally easy to reproduce the base 2 number, given the base 4 representation.

We can easily show that this manipulation is valid. In this example,

$$\begin{aligned} 1001110001001101 = \quad & 1{\cdot}2^{15} + 0{\cdot}2^{14} + 0{\cdot}2^{13} + 1{\cdot}2^{12} \\ & +1{\cdot}2^{11} + 1{\cdot}2^{10} + 0{\cdot}2^9 + 0{\cdot}2^8 \\ & +0{\cdot}2^7 + 1{\cdot}2^6 + 0{\cdot}2^5 + 0{\cdot}2^4 \\ & +1{\cdot}2^3 + 1{\cdot}2^2 + 0{\cdot}2^1 + 1{\cdot}2^0 \\ = \quad & (1{\cdot}2 + 0){\cdot}2^{14} + (0{\cdot}2 + 1){\cdot}2^{12} \\ & +(1{\cdot}2 + 1){\cdot}2^{10} + (0{\cdot}2 + 0){\cdot}2^8 \\ & +(0{\cdot}2 + 1){\cdot}2^6 + (0{\cdot}2 + 0){\cdot}2^4 \\ & +(1{\cdot}2 + 1){\cdot}2^2 + (0{\cdot}2 + 1){\cdot}2^0 \\ = \quad & 2{\cdot}4^7 + 1{\cdot}4^6 + 3{\cdot}4^5 + 0{\cdot}4^4 \\ & +1{\cdot}4^3 + 0{\cdot}4^2 + 3{\cdot}4^1 + 1{\cdot}4^0 \end{aligned}$$

This is certainly progress, for we have halved the number of digits required for the representation. However, since eight digits are still quite unmanageable, we make a further attempt at compression, this time taking the binary digits *three* at a time, and obtain the **octal** (base 8) representation of the number.

$$1\ \ 001\ \ 110\ \ 001\ \ 001\ \ 101$$
$$\wedge\quad\wedge\quad\wedge\quad\wedge\quad\wedge$$
$$1\quad 1\quad 6\quad 1\quad 1\quad 5$$

That is, $1001110001001101_2 = 116115_8$. Notice that there is a slight annoyance here, which fortunately is no more than that. When we group the binary digits into sets of three, the most significant bit (bit 15) ends up with no companions in its group since 16 is not divisible by 3. There is no real difficulty here; it simply means that the octal representation of a 16-bit word will always begin with a 0 or 1, according as bit 15 is 0 or 1, respectively. Once again the reader should observe the ease with which either representation (binary or octal) can be converted into the other.

Having managed to reduce the binary representation to one containing only six digits, we make one further attempt at improvement, this time by taking the binary digits *four* at a time. Since four binary digits can represent numbers in the range 0 to 15, the representation will be base 16, or **hexadecimal**, a number base discussed briefly in Sec. 2.5.

$$1001\ \ 1100\ \ 0100\ \ 1101$$
$$\wedge\quad\quad\wedge\quad\quad\wedge$$
$$9\quad\ \ C\quad\ \ 4\quad\ \ D$$

Thus $1001110001001101_2 = 9C4D_{16}$. Any further attempt at compressing the representation of the 16-bit binary number would not seem to hold much promise. Breaking the representation into groups of five digits each would still require four digits in the (base 32) representation, and this number base itself is simply too large to be managed comfortably. Base 16 yields a 4-digit representation of the 16-bit numbers, which is about as compact a notation as we could hope for. Base 16 does have the disadvantage of using "numerals"—*A*, *B*, *C*, *D*, *E*, *F*—with which we are not familiar and to which we would have to become accustomed. In base 8, the representation is slightly longer (six digits) but has the advantage of employing only the familiar numerals $0, 1, \ldots, 7$. At this point it would appear that the use of either octal (base 8) or hexadecimal (base 16) representations is a tossup.

4.3 HALF-WORDS (BYTES)

In Sec. 4.1 we chose to deal with 16-bit words for a number of reasons, one of which was that such a word was sufficiently large to hold meaningful numbers. However, in a number of applications this word size is overly generous. We shall see in Chapter 10, for example, that much of the actual processing done by computers on a day-to-day basis deals with numbers in the range 0 to 127 (decimal). Thus since main memory is limited, even though in some machines it might be quite large, we seek a means of conserving this resource when the numbers to be processed are reasonably small—much smaller than the number that will fit in the full 16 bits. We thus partition each word into two **half-words**, called **bytes**, and we shall see that in some cases it will be possible to manipulate these individual bytes rather than the full words to which they belong.

$$15 \qquad\qquad 8 \quad 7 \qquad\qquad 0 \quad \text{(bit position)}$$

$$\underbrace{x \ldots \ldots x}_{\substack{\text{high-order} \\ \text{byte}}} \quad \underbrace{x \ldots \ldots x}_{\substack{\text{low-order} \\ \text{byte}}}$$

The high-order byte is sometimes referred to as the **left byte**, the **front byte**, or the **more-significant byte**. Similarly, the low-order byte is called the **right byte**, **back byte**, or the **less-significant byte**.

Just as a full word may be represented in its octal or hexadecimal form, so may each individual byte be broken down into groups of 3 or 4 bits to compress its numerical representation. Thus the two bytes 10011100 and 01001101 of the 16-bit word 1001110001001101 may be represented in hexadecimal as

$$\underset{9\qquad C}{1011\ 1100} \quad \text{and} \quad \underset{4\qquad D}{0100\ 1101}$$

and in octal as

$$\underset{2\quad 3\quad 4}{10\ 011\ 100} \quad \text{and} \quad \underset{1\quad 1\quad 5}{01\ 001\ 101}$$

Notice that in the hexadecimal case, the representation of the full word is $9C4D$, its high-order byte is $9C$, and its low-order byte is $4D$. Thus the high-order byte representation consists of the first two digits of the full-word representation; the low-order byte representation, the last two digits. But in the octal representation the situation is far less pleasing. The octal representation of the full word is 116115, its high-order byte is 234, and its low-order byte is 115. Thus in forming the octal representation of the high-order byte we *cannot* simply pick off the first three digits of the full-word representation. And while in this example the representation of the low-order byte does happen to consist of the last three digits of the full-word representation, a little experimentation will show that this is not generally the case. Consider the word whose octal representation is 162524, for example.

Until now we have had no particular reason to favor either the hexadecimal or octal representation of a 16-bit word. The aforementioned unpleasantness in the octal case should tip the balance in favor of the hexadecimal representation, especially if we are going to be dealing to any extent with individual bytes.

For many machines the hexadecimal notation is the most natural. However, there is a feature of the PDP-11 *architecture*, to be discussed in Chapter 7, which so overwhelmingly dictates an octal representation that we shall use it throughout the remainder of the text, even at the expense of some extra calculations when forming bytes from words or words from bytes. Henceforth all number representations, except those that are *obviously* decimal or binary, will be assumed to be octal, unless explicitly noted otherwise.

Before leaving this section we should observe that in dividing words into bytes, or half-words, we have created still another memory structure and with it the corresponding numerical and arithmetic concepts. References to individual bytes, as opposed to full words, carry with them all of the ideas we have discussed for 4-bit and 16-bit words. Specifically, an 8-bit byte may be interpreted as representing an *unsigned* number (in the range 0 to 255) or a *signed* number (between −128 and +127). In the signed case, the most-significant bit is the sign bit. This will be bit 15 or bit 7, depending upon whether the byte is the high-order or low-order byte of the full word. Likewise, the concepts of carries into and out of the most-significant bit apply, along with their possible effects on the carry and overflow indicators.

4.4 MEMORY ADDRESSING

In discussing memory words (4-bit and 16-bit) and bytes in this and previous chapters, we also noted that the main memory of a typical computer consists of thousands or hundreds of thousands of such memory units. It has probably occurred to the reader that if we are going to consider the incrementing of the contents of a word or the addition of the contents of two words, then we shall somehow have to be able to identify just *which* word or words are to be manipulated. And if, as we have claimed, even individual bytes may be operated on, then we shall have to be able uniquely to identify the bytes themselves. We can easily achieve such an identification scheme by associating a unique number, called the **address** of the byte, with each byte of main memory. A portion of main memory with its byte addressing is shown in Fig. 4.4.1.

Notice that we used an octal representation for these addresses and

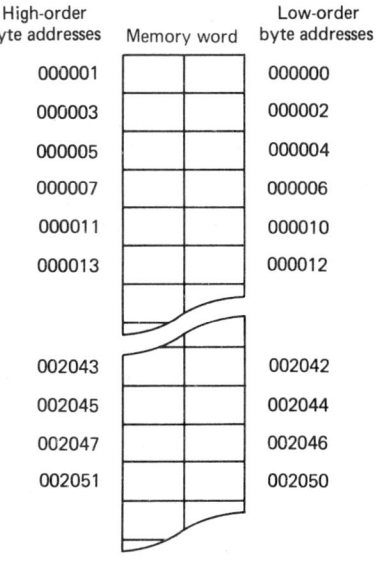

High-order byte addresses	Memory word	Low-order byte addresses
000001		000000
000003		000002
000005		000004
000007		000006
000011		000010
000013		000012
002043		002042
002045		002044
002047		002046
002051		002050

Figure 4.4.1

that we simply used consecutive integers, starting at 0, for these byte addresses. The addresses act very much like house numbers—they are used to *locate* or *identify* a specific byte in main memory. And like house numbers, they are *unsigned;* it would make no sense to speak of the *negative* of the address 002045, for example. Bytes whose addresses differ by 1, such as the bytes with addresses 000202 and 000203, or 104553 and 104554, are called **adjacent bytes**. (By *adjacent* we are referring to the addressing scheme. These two bytes, as 8-celled memory units, are not necessarily physically next to one another in main memory.)

If the contents of a memory byte is to be incremented, then that incrementing will occur in the CPU—more specifically, the arithmetic unit of the CPU. In order to increment the contents of a byte, the CPU will have to obtain the contents from main memory; it does so by specifying the *address* of the byte. Just where that particular byte is located in main memory—that is, just what its address is—is of no consequence to the CPU, since it can access the contents of one byte as easily as that of any other byte. Because of this feature, main memory is frequently referred to as **random access memory** (RAM).

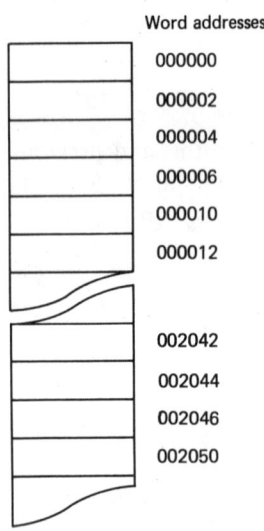

Word addresses

000000
000002
000004
000006
000010
000012

002042
002044
002046
002050

Figure 4.4.2

Having devised an identification (addressing) scheme for the individual bytes, we now turn our attention to full words. Since words can also be operated on by the processor (additions, increments, and so forth), they too must be uniquely identifiable. The word-addressing scheme is very simple: The numeric **address of a word** is equal to the address of the *low-order byte* of that word. (Compare Fig. 4.4.2 with Fig. 4.4.1.)

We can make two obvious but important observations about the consequences of word addressing. First, word addresses are always *even*. Second, the byte- or word-addressing scheme is *not unique*, in the following sense: Let us use the term **memory location** to stand for *either* a byte *or* a word, and consider the operation "increment the contents of the memory location whose address is 002045." There is no question about what this means, for since the address is *odd*, the reference must be to the *byte* whose address is 002045—namely, the high-order byte of the *word* whose address is 002044. But now consider "increment the contents of the memory location whose address is 002050." This statement is ambiguous, for it is not clear whether the contents of the *byte* whose address is 002050 is to be incremented, or the *word* whose address is 002050 is to be incremented. In fact this ambiguity *does* exist, and we see from the previous example that it is unacceptable. However, it is *not* the *addressing* *scheme* which solves the problem—in this sense, the addressing scheme *is* ambiguous—but rather the operation itself. For in fact there *is* no such operation as "increment the contents of the *memory location* whose address is. . . ." Rather, there are *two distinct* such operations: "Increment the contents of the *byte* whose address is . . ." and "Increment the contents of the *word* whose address is. . . ." Throughout the remainder of the text we shall make occasional use of the term *memory location* when referring to a physical word or byte. In all such cases either the context will indicate whether we are referring to a byte or a word, or we shall be explicit in this regard.

We make one final comment about this example. Lest the reader think that incrementing the contents of a particular word is equivalent to incrementing the contents of the low-order byte of that word—in which case the ambiguity previously mentioned would be of no consequence—consider the following word:

$$10011001 \quad 11111111$$

If the *word* is incremented, the result is 10011010 00000000. If the word's *low-order byte* is incremented, the result is 10011001 00000000, since when the contents of the low-order byte is incremented, the byte is considered as a complete memory unit—the carry out of bit 7 does *not* carry *into* bit 8. This is the *only* case in which the two results will be arithmetically different. However, there is one other case in which incrementing a word and incrementing the word's low-order byte can have different consequences. (See Exercise 4.4.3.)

4.5 EXERCISES

4.1.1. Verify that the 16-bit-word number system ranges from (decimal) 0 to 65,535 (unsigned), or $-32,768$ to $+32,767$ (signed).

4.2.1. Convert each of the following base 2 numbers to its equivalent base 4 representation.
   (a) 0100001011111011   **(c)** 1010010001000011
   (b) 1011011101111011   **(d)** 1111111111111111

4.2.2. Convert each of the following base 4 numbers to its equivalent base 2 representation.
   (a) 30303010   **(c)** 12321232
   (b) 01020302   **(d)** 13333331

4.2.3. Show *in general* that a 16-digit base 2 number can be represented as a base 4 number according to the procedure of Sec. 4.2 by proving that

$$\sum_{i=0}^{15} a_i \cdot 2^i = \sum_{j=0}^{7} \left(\sum_{k=0}^{1} a_{2 \cdot j + k} \cdot 2^k \right) \cdot 4^j$$

where $a_i = 0$ or 1.

4.2.4. Show *in general* that a 16-digit base 2 number can be represented as a base 8 number according to the procedure of Sec. 4.2 by proving that

$$\sum_{i=0}^{15} a_i \cdot 2^i = a_{15} \cdot 2^{15} + \sum_{i=0}^{14} a_i \cdot 2^i$$

$$= a_{15} \cdot 8^5 + \sum_{j=0}^{4} \left(\sum_{k=0}^{2} a_{3 \cdot j + k} \cdot 2^k \right) \cdot 8^j$$

where $a_i = 0$ or 1.

4.2.5. State and prove a result that corresponds to Exercises 4.2.3 and 4.2.4 above for the conversion of a base 2 number to its hexadecimal representation.

4.2.6. Convert each of the base 2 numbers of Exercise 4.2.1 to its (a) octal representation, and its (b) hexadecimal representation.

4.2.7. Convert each of the following octal numbers to its equivalent 16-digit binary representation.

    (a) 102343   **(c)** 177276   **(e)** 111111
    (b) 003004   **(d)** 043022   **(f)** 171203

4.2.8. Convert each of the following hexadecimal numbers to its equivalent 16-digit binary representation.

    (a) 84*E*3   **(c)** *FEBE*   **(e)** 9249
    (b) 0604   **(d)** 4612   **(f)** *F*283

4.2.9. Find the 1's-complement and 2's-complement (negative) of each of the 16-bit words represented in octal in Exercise 4.2.7 and in hexadecimal in Exercise 4.2.8. Give the results in octal and hexadecimal, respectively. (*Suggestion:* Use the scheme of Sec. 2.7 to find the 1's-complement, in octal or hexadecimal, then add 1 to find the 2's complement.)

4.2.10. Perform the stated arithmetic of the 16-bit words whose octal representation are given below, indicating carries into and out of the most-significant bit, and specifying the status of the carry and overflow indicators. In each case state whether the result is arithmetically correct in the unsigned and signed interpretation.

    (a)   102306   **(c)**   162662   **(e)**   016302
          + 004035   + 145606   − 060033

    (b)   062404   **(d)**   102306   **(f)**   162662
          + 016333   − 004035   − 145606

4.2.11. Repeat Exercise 4.2.10, with the numbers being represented in hexadecimal.

    (a)   0 10*E*   **(c)**   72*A* 3   **(e)**   *E*4*E* 5
          + 0*B*5*C*   + 0*F*2*A*   − 8020

    (b)   8 283   **(d)**   03*A*4   **(f)**   8020
          + *F*877   − 02*B*9   − *E*4*E*5

4.3.1. Find the contents (in octal) of the high-order and low-order bytes of the 16-bit words whose octal representations are given below.

    (a) 102703   **(c)** 001001   **(e)** 177777
    (b) 000101   **(d)** 101401   **(f)** 077672

4.3.2. Write the octal representation of the 16-bit word whose high-order and low-order bytes (in octal) are given below.

    (a) high $= 000$, low $= 206$ **(d)** high $= 303$, low $= 303$

(b) high = 306, low = 000   (e) high = 200, low = 002
(c) high = 277, low = 277   (f) high = 177, low = 076

4.3.3. What are the 1's-complement and 2's-complement of each of the following *bytes* (expressed in octal notation)?

(a) 177   (b) 377   (c) 000   (d) 276

4.4.1. State the addresses of the bytes that are adjacent to each of the bytes whose address is given below. In each case determine which adjacent byte belongs to the same *word* as the specified byte and state the address of that *word*.

(a) 072303   (c) 000000
(b) 001002   (d) 077777

4.4.2. A byte address can be any (unsigned) number that can be represented in a 16-bit word.

(a) What is the largest (in decimal) byte address?
(b) How many (in decimal) such byte addresses are there?
(c) What is the largest (in decimal) word address?
(d) How many (in decimal) such word addresses are there?

4.4.3. Consider the 16-bit word 0010010101111111 contained in the memory location whose address is 026442, and consider the commands "increment the contents of the word whose address is 026442" and "increment the contents of the byte whose address is 026442." In each case, the resulting *word* is 0010010110000000, and yet the two increments have behaved slightly differently. Why? (*Suggestion:* Consider the state of the overflow indicator.)

5

Stored-Instruction Computers, the Central Processing Unit, and Machine Instructions

5.1 THE STORED-INSTRUCTION CONCEPT

In the preceding chapters we spoke of operating on words and bytes, and in Chapter 1 we indicated that such operations take place in the central processing unit. But the CPU does not simply operate (increment, add, and so on) *at random* on *random* words and bytes—like any other machine, to be useful it must be able to be *controlled*, to perform those and only those operations that we command it to perform. This stipulation leads us to a number of questions that we shall answer in this and subsequent chapters:

1. What *is* a computer operation?
2. How is an operation *performed*?
3. What operations are computers *capable* of performing?
4. How is the CPU *instructed* (*commanded*) to perform one of its operations, and of what does such an instruction *consist*?
5. What is the *source* of these instructions? That is, how does the CPU obtain those instructions that are to be performed?

We must be a bit vague about the answer to question 1, at this time. For the time being it will suffice to think of a computer operation as some kind of (usually arithmetic) manipulation of a word or byte.

Question 2 has already been answered, at least in part. In Chapter 3 we saw two examples of computer circuits, one to do incrementing of (4-bit) words, the other a partial circuit to perform additions. Thus we answer this question by saying that the operations are performed *electronically* by the CPU's *logic* (circuitry). There are, of course, many operations that we did *not* discuss, but the examples of Chapter 3 should have convinced the reader of the *possibility* of designing the circuitry necessary for performing *all* of the tasks of which we want the processor to be capable. That is as far as we wish to develop this idea.

The answer to question 3—possible computer operations—depends upon the particular machine. The operations that can be performed by the PDP-11, the machine of principal interest to us, are described in Appendix A. However, it would be quite premature to launch into a study of all of them at this time. Much preparatory groundwork is required before the majority of those operations will be meaningful. In the meantime if the reader chooses to think of operations such as addition, subtraction, decrementing, and so forth, he will not be misled, but there are other quite standard operations that might be less evident. For example, most processors can perform a bit-by-bit *AND*ing or *OR*ing of two computer words, actions that are reminiscent of the *logical* operations of Chapter 3. And operations such as the shifting of each bit of a word or byte one position to the left or right are also important operations.

We shall temporarily delay the answer to the first part of question 4—how the CPU is instructed to perform an operation—while we examine what such an instruction comprises. Normally it will not be sufficient to tell the CPU just what operation we want performed—it will require further information. Thus while increment may be a valid computer *operation*, it is scarcely an *instruction* (command) since the CPU must know which word or byte to increment. Thus for the time being we shall think of a computer instruction as the specification of a CPU operation, *along with* any further information required to make that operation meaningful, usually in the form of the addresses of the words or bytes on which the operation is to be performed.

We shall deal with question 5 shortly, after gaining further insights later in this and the next chapter. At this point we momentarily divert our attention to the ubiquitous electronic pocket calculator.

Most pocket calculators have the following capabilities, although many are far more sophisticated than described here: Numbers can be input to them by means of a 10-key keypad and can be displayed, typically by a lighted display on the front of the calculator. They can perform the four standard arithmetic operations. Most calculators can store numbers and intermediate results in some sort of memory, although the *amount* of memory is usually quite small, being limited to one, two, or perhaps a half-dozen numbers. Nonetheless these stored (written) numbers can be recalled (read) and displayed or used in further operations.

But then what distinguishes a pocket calculator from a computer? To be sure, the arithmetic capabilities of a computer may extend beyond simple addition, subtraction, and so forth, and a computer's memory is thousands of times as large. Likewise, a computer normally has considerably more elaborate input and output capabilities, such as terminals, printers, and tapes. But these differences are more of *degree* than *substance*. We have said nothing so far about computers that does not apply to pocket calculators. However, there is one feature of a modern computer that makes it something more than a "big" pocket calculator, and that feature involves the *source* of its commands.

Let us analyze the simple addition problem 2 + 3, as done on a pocket calculator. On most calculators this would be accomplished by pressing the key labeled 2, then pressing the key labeled +, followed by pressing the key labeled 3. The result, 5, would appear on the calculator's display when the = key was pressed. We thus issued the following *sequence* of *commands*:

1. Enter the number 2 into memory.
2. Add to that number the next number to be entered.
3. Enter the number 3 and perform the addition specified in step 2.
4. Display the result of the addition.

We are *less* concerned with just what the commands are than we are about *how* the calculator gets those commands—the *source* of the commands. Evidently the calculator is being commanded to perform these operations by our pushing keys on the calculator's keypad; thus the source of the commands is our finger, along with some further complex interaction between finger, vision, and the controlling brain. And while the calculator can perform its operations with speeds that are in the same range as computer operations, it must wait interminably for each command to indicate to it *which* operation is to be performed. Even a fast calculator operator probably cannot do much better than one such entry or command per second, and thus the time involved in performing just a few hundred or a thousand such operations can be quite long—time during which the calculator is, for the most part, idle.

In a *computer*, this inefficiency—the wasted time between the performance of a command and the obtaining of the next instruction, during which the processor is pretty much just "sitting on its hands"—is eliminated in a rather remarkable and ingenious way: The commands themselves are *stored in the computer's main memory*. The significance of this idea lies in the fact that when the CPU is ready to process an instruction, it obtains that instruction from its own memory. Since the accessing of an instruction from memory can be done in about one-millionth of a second, this is an obvious improvement over the calculator situation. Thus if this scheme can be "kept going"—access an instruction from main memory, perform the desired operation, access the next instruction (wherever that might be), perform the operation, and so on—many hundreds of thousands of such instructions might be executed within the span of a single second. This **stored-instruction** concept and its attendant speed is what principally distinguishes the computer from the pocket calculator.

These ideas lead to some interesting questions. For example, if an instruction is stored in main memory, then that instruction must evidently consist of one or more 16-bit words. And recalling that what we mean by *instruction* is an operation (add, increment, or whatever) along with further required information (for example, addresses of words operated on), we infer that an operation, as stored in memory, is a *word*—namely a string of 16 0's and 1's because such strings are the *only* objects that can be stored in memory. It is one thing to command a calculator to perform an addition by pressing the key labeled $+$; it is quite another to issue such a command to a computer, since we cannot "store" the plus sign or the English word *add* in the computer's memory. The information that an addition is to take place will somehow have to be **encoded** into a 16-bit word—some bit configuration which uniquely represents the addition operation. And when this operation is to be performed, the CPU must somehow be able to recognize this bit configuration as the one that represents addition among all $65,536_{10}$ such configurations—that is, this 16-bit word must be **decoded** by the processor. (We have implied here that of the word or words making up an instruction, the operation portion of that instruction takes up precisely one word. This is true in the PDP-11, although in some other machines, typically the microcomputers, an operation may take only a single byte, whereas in others more than one word may be required to encode an operation.)

We said that to achieve the efficiency inherent in the stored-program concept, the CPU, in performing instructions, must be kept going—it must know where to locate an instruction in memory, access it, and perform the specified operation, and then it must know where to find the *next* instruction. The manner in which this information is presented to the CPU is reasonably simple and is discussed in detail in Sec. 5.3.

The question of accessing an instruction leads to another question. The reader has probably inferred from the preceding chapters, in particular, Chapters 2 and 4, that main memory is a place for the storage of *data*—numbers to be manipulated by the computer. But we see now that main memory is also a place for the storage of (encoded) *instructions*. What, then, distinguishes a 16-bit word containing data from one that contains an instruction? The answer is, Nothing. Any 16-bit word in memory *might* be a piece of *numeric data* or it *might* represent the operation portion of an *instruction*. For example, suppose the word whose address is 014426 contains the 16-bit configuration whose octal representation is 005267. This number in decimal is 2743, and it might, for instance, represent the price in cents of some item in a department store. On the other hand, as a *bit configuration* it is 0000101010110111 and as such it is the *code* for the *increment* operation. Such being the case, how can the CPU "look at" a 16-bit word and tell whether it is data or instruction? The answer is that it has no way of distinguishing between these two. The resolution of what appears to be a chaotic situation lies in the fact that, if all goes well, the processor will never be told to look at anything that is *not* an instruction. We shall now examine some of these ideas in detail.

5.2 THE CENTRAL PROCESSING UNIT REGISTERS

In Chapter 1 we stated that one of the hardware components of the CPU was a collection of *registers*, which we shall briefly investigate here and develop more completely later in the chapter. A **register** is a 16-bit word (or, to be very precise, a 16-celled memory unit) and as such it does not differ in its behavior from the 16-bit words in main memory. The contents of registers can be incremented, decremented, added, and so forth, and they display the sign-bit and carry features of main memory words. They *differ* from main memory words in the following respects: First, these registers are *not* in main memory—they "reside" in the CPU. Second, they are designed for high speed. Since much of the CPU's activity takes place in these registers, they are made up of components that can change their states very rapidly—more rapidly than main memory words can be accessed and modified. Finally, the registers are of a more special-purpose nature than are the words of main memory.

We know that the CPU can write words into main memory and also read those words from memory. In fact, later in this chapter we shall see some of the details of those operations. But the reader must also have the impression that *we* can write specific 16-bit configurations into main memory as well. For how else, for instance, could a particular sequence of CPU instructions be placed in main memory so that the CPU will perform the operations required to bring about some desired result? It is true that main memory *can* be written *externally* (that is, by the controlling human) as well as *internally* (by the CPU). Just how *we* can physically write the contents of main memory words is by no means clear at this point, but some explanations will be offered later in this chapter.

The central processing unit's registers fall into one of two categories. The first consists of registers (16-bit words) that are *externally accessible* in the sense described above—they are available for manipulation by the CPU, but they *also* may be read and written from some external source (the controlling human). The second category of registers consists of those that can be manipulated *only* by the processor and *not* by any kind of human intervention. These registers are used by the CPU for a variety of purposes, mostly for the temporary storage of data and addresses. We shall refer to these two categories of registers as **public** and **private**, respectively, although *externally accessible* and *not externally accessible* would be equally acceptable terms.

We, of course, have no hope (or need, as it turns out) of accessing the CPU's private registers. But there is a problem concerning the accessible public registers. Since these registers do not reside in main memory, they do *not* have numeric *addresses*, and thus there is some question as to how they can be referenced (addressed). The answer lies in the fact that the 16-bit configuration that specifies a CPU *operation* contains information about which of these external registers is being referenced. We are getting a bit ahead of ourselves in this regard, but by the end of Chapter 7, we shall have completely resolved the matter.

5.3 THE PROGRAM COUNTER (PC) AND INSTRUCTION FETCHING

We can now explain how the CPU can determine where in main memory to obtain the code for an instruction, access that word, perform the specified operation, and then get the *next* instruction—the crux of "keeping the CPU going." First, we introduce some convenient terminology. At any time any register contains a *number*—a 16-bit configuration of 0's and 1's that we interpret as a binary number representation. *If* that number is *interpreted* as the *address* of a *memory location* (word or byte), then we shall say that the register is **pointing at** that memory location. Thus, for example, if the contents of some register is 004232, then we say that the register is pointing at the memory location whose address is 004232, or—less precisely but a bit more succinctly—is pointing at 004232. In addition, since the phrase *the contents of* will occur frequently, we devise a notation for it, namely, c(...). Thus in the foregoing example, if we temporarily name the register in question R, we would say that c(R) = 004232 and thus R points at the location whose address is 004232. Notice that we say nothing here about c(004232), the contents of the memory location whose address is 004232.

One of the CPU's public, or externally accessible, registers is known as the **Program Counter**, abbreviated (PC), and it plays a central role in the execution of CPU operations. When the processor is ready to perform an operation, it obtains the *contents* of the *PC*—the number that is c(PC)—and places this number in a private CPU register. The CPU then *increments the contents of the PC by 2*, an action whose significance we shall see in a moment. The original contents of the PC is used as an *address*. The CPU now obtains the contents of the memory *word* having this address. The CPU then interprets the 16-bit word so obtained as the code for an instruction, decodes the bit configuration, and performs whatever operation is specified there. Consider the following example. Here and in the sequel we shall display various memory addresses and their contents in the octal notation.

	address	contents
PC ⟶	062044	005201
	062046	005405
	062050	------

We suppose that at the present time, c(PC) = 062044, that is, the PC is pointing at location 062044. We used the arrow in the figure above to indicate this. Suppose now that the CPU is ready to process an instruction. It accesses the contents of the PC—062044—and places this number in a private CPU register, which we call the **instruction address register**. Then it increments the contents of the PC *by* 2, so at this point c(PC) = 062046. The CPU now accesses the *contents* of the memory location whose address is in the internal instruction address register. That is, the CPU obtains the contents of the memory location whose address is 062044. It then *interprets* the number thus obtained—005201—as a *processor operation*, and performs that operation. (Just what operation this is is not of consequence to the discussion—it happens to involve the incrementing of one of the CPU's other public registers.) Upon completion of the processing of this instruction, the situation will be as follows:

address	contents
062044	005201
PC ⟶ 062046	005405
062050	——————

Having completed the execution of the operation located at the word whose address is 062044, the CPU is now in a position to process another instruction. It does so by again accessing the PC's contents (now 062046), saving this number in its instruction address register, incrementing the PC's contents by 2 (so now c(PC) = 062050), and then accessing the contents of the memory location whose address is in the instruction address register. Since that register contains 062046, the CPU accesses the contents of the location, getting the number 005405. It again decodes this 16-bit word and performs the specified operation. (In this case, the instruction directs the processor to clear—set to 0—the contents of still another of the CPU's public registers.) Upon completion of this instruction, the situation will appear as follows:

address	contents
062044	005201
062046	005405
PC ⟶ 062050	——————

The CPU now once again looks at and increments the PC, obtains the next instruction, and so forth.

While these processes may appear relatively simple, such important concepts are involved here that we shall spend some time reviewing them. First, we note that since the *contents* of the program counter is used by the CPU as the address of a *word* of main memory (as opposed to a byte), the contents of the PC must be *even*. And the CPU's action of incrementing the contents of the PC by 2 each time it accesses it maintains this evenness of c(PC). Next, observe that the process as outlined above does, in fact, keep the CPU going, which is one of the fundamental properties of a computer. Once the CPU has been started in its execution process, it will continue accessing consecutive words of main memory for the processing of operations—that is, execution will proceed *linearly* through main memory (a concept that raises a number of questions).

We summarize the process by which the CPU obtains an instruction as follows:

1. The CPU obtains the contents of the PC and saves this number in a temporary private register, which we call the instruction address register.
2. The CPU increments the contents of the PC by 2.
3. The CPU accesses the contents of the memory location whose address is in the temporary private instruction address register.

(The CPU now decodes and performs the indicated operation.) Steps 1 to 3 above are referred to as an **instruction fetch**, or, more simply, a **fetch**. Throughout the remainder of the text we shall use the word *fetch only* in this way. And while all of the aspects of this concept are significant, we wish to impress upon the reader the *incrementing* of the PC by 2 and also the *timing* of that incrementing—it is done immediately after the PC has been accessed. Should the reader feel that we are placing undue importance on this idea, he will see shortly that its importance here and throughout the remainder of the text cannot be overemphasized.

The short example given above of a few sequential CPU instructions was somewhat contrived, in the following sense: The two operations involved there—*increment* the contents of some register and *clear* (set to 0) the contents of some other register—required only a *single* word of main memory for their encoding. Consider the following more realistic example:

	address	contents
PC $\longrightarrow$	112030	005237
	112032	045662
	112034	------

As before, we assume that when the CPU is ready to execute an instruction, the PC contains the number (address) 112030. In this case, the *instruction* consists of *two* words—those located at addresses 112030 and 112032. The first word (005237) contains the code for the *increment* operation, while the second word (045662) contains the *address* of the word whose contents is to be incremented. The processor now does a *fetch*, moving the contents of the PC up to 112032 and obtaining the contents of the memory location whose address is 112030, namely, 005237. Ultimately the contents of the word whose address is 045662 will be incremented and the CPU will be ready for the fetching and execution of the *next* instruction.

Because the CPU looks to the PC for the address of the next word to be fetched, it would appear that c(PC) = 112032 and thus the CPU will access the number 0045662—the address of the location to be incremented as a result of the *last* instruction—rather than the contents of 112304—the first word of the *next* instruction. However, as it turns out, all is well. In fact, by the time the CPU is ready for the next operation, the contents of the PC will be 112034, as required. The hidden *additional* incrementing of the PC (by 2) was *not* the result of a further *fetch*. Rather, it was one of the effects of the *increment* operation itself (whose code is 005237). We shall not determine exactly what occurred here until Chapter 7. In the meantime we assure the reader that when the CPU is confronted with multiple-word instructions upon completion of its processing of the words of one instruction, the PC will be pointing at the first word of the *next* instruction.

5.4 THE INSTRUCTION EXECUTION CYCLE

In the preceding section we stated that it was the function of the PC to point at the next processor operation in its encoded form in main memory. The CPU then executed that instruction by fetching the word and performing the indicated operation. Since the processing of instructions lies at the heart of a computing system, it will be worth spending a little time in looking at a few more of the details of this **instruction execution cycle**—the period spent by the CPU between the completion of processing one instruction and the completion of the next.

After the CPU has executed its last instruction, it takes the following actions:

1. Copies the contents of the PC register to an internal private register—the instruction address register.
2. Increments the contents of the PC by 2.
3. Obtains the *contents* of the *memory word* whose *address* is in the instruction address register.

Obtaining the contents of a word or byte from main memory is a bit complicated from an electronic standpoint, but we can give some indication of how this is done. When the CPU needs to obtain the *contents* of a word from main memory, it places the *address* of that word on the **address bus**. (For the remainder of this discussion the reader will find it helpful to refer to Fig. 1.2.1.) It then sends a signal, called a **read signal**, down the **control bus**. The electronics in main memory responds to the read signal by examining the address currently on the address bus. The *contents* of the word having that address is then placed on the **data bus** and the main memory electronics signals the CPU, by sending a signal down the control bus, that the requested information (contents of the specified word) is available on the data bus. The CPU can now read the data bus to get this information. As we have already noted, steps 1, 2, and 3 are referred to as an *instruction fetch*.

4. Passes the word obtained in step 3 over to the *decoder*—circuitry within the CPU's control unit—to determine what operation is to be performed.

This decoding is conceptually fairly simple. The bit configuration just obtained must be examined and somehow matched up with the codes for the various valid operations. Once the operation to be performed has been determined, various data and, perhaps, addresses are directed to the appropriate electronics for processing—perhaps to the ALU. But the electronics involved is quite complex, and a study at this point of the actual processes would do little to enhance our understanding of the overall execution procedure.

5. Executes (performs) the specified operation.

During this step, the CPU might have to obtain additional information from main memory, since an instruction might consist of the word containing the operation itself, along with one or more additional words specifying, for example, the addresses of memory locations on which the operation is performed.

5.5 LOADING MAIN MEMORY

Now that we see how the CPU processes instructions, we have answered the question of how the CPU can tell the difference between data and instructions. When the CPU is ready to execute an instruction, that instruction will be executed if the PC contains the address of a 16-bit word that is the bit configuration of an *instruction*. If somehow the PC contains the address of what we intended to be a piece of *data*, that datum (as a 16-bit word) will be fetched by the CPU, decoded if possible, and executed. The reader would probably consider this situation—the *execution* of words that were intended to be data—disastrous (it is), but he should also recognize that it is easily avoided. For once the CPU has completed execution of an instruction, it fetches *the next consecutive word of main memory* for execution by referencing the PC. Thus we need only ensure that the instructions we wish executed reside in main memory in *sequential locations*, with any data on which these instructions are to operate kept safely out of the mainstream of these sequentially located instructions. Thus when a sequence of instructions is to be executed, main memory will typically have a layout as shown in Fig. 5.5.1.

Consider the following example. Suppose we wish to add two numbers, and having done so we wish to decrement the resulting sum by 1. Because of the action of the PDP-11's add operation, the sum of the contents of two memory locations will be placed back into the second of these locations. (Thus what we are about to do might be written in a high-level language such as BASIC or FORTRAN as $Y = X + Y - 1$.) Consider main memory to be loaded with the following contents:

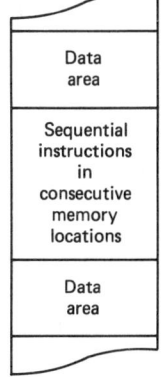

| Data area |
| Sequential instructions in consecutive memory locations |
| Data area |

Figure 5.5.1

	Address	Contents	Comments
PC ⟶	047604	063737	Code for the addition operation—
	047606	100424	adds c(100424) to c(102552) and
	047610	102552	leaves the result in location 102552.
	047612	005337	Code for the decrement operation—
	047614	102552	decrements c(102552).
	047616	000000	Code for "halt the processor."
	047620	------	
	.	.	
	.	.	
	.	.	
	100424	003413	First number to be added.
	.	.	
	.	.	
	.	.	
	102552	022212	Second number to be added.

If we assume that the PC contains the number (address) 047604, the CPU will do a fetch, accessing the contents of the PC and moving the contents of the PC up by 2—so $c(PC) = 047606$—and then obtaining the contents of the location whose address is 047604, namely, 063737. The CPU then decodes this bit configuration and recognizes this to be the add operation. Information in these 16 encoded bits also informs the CPU that it will find the *addresses* of the numbers to be added in the next two consecutive words of main memory, which are at 047606 and 047610. The CPU obtains and adds the contents of the locations with addresses 100424 and 102552 and places the resulting sum back in the location with address 102552. Thus by the time this addition instruction has been completed we have $c(100424) = 003413$, $c(102552) = 025625$ (003413 + 022212), and $c(PC) = 047612$. (Recall that $c(PC)$ had been moved up to 047606 as a result of the CPU's fetch of the contents of location 047604. Why $c(PC)$ has been moved up by an additional 4 to 047612 is *not* the result of any further *fetching* on the part of the CPU. Rather, it involves the add instruction itself. Once again, this will be explained in Chapter 7. In the meantime, we note that the PC is correctly pointing at the next instruction to be executed.) Since $c(PC) = 047612$, the contents of that word is fetched and decoded as the instruction "decrement the contents of the memory word whose address is in the next word." The CPU obtains the contents of the next word (102552) and then decrements the contents of the word having that address. Thus by the time the decrement has been executed, $c(102552) = 025624$ and $c(PC) = 047616$. Again, it is not clear just how the contents of the PC has been incremented by an additional 2, but it has to do with the *form* of the decrement instruction.

Having completed the decrement instruction, the CPU does another fetch—moving $c(PC)$ up by 2 to 047620 and obtaining the contents of the location whose address is 047616, namely 000000—and decodes this word. This is the bit configuration for the operation "halt the processor," so the CPU goes into a stopped state, ceasing the fetch/execute sequence.

Notice that three instructions were executed here: add, decrement, and halt. Observe also that the words fetched by the CPU were obtained from *consecutive* memory locations. Finally, note that we were careful to keep those words that contain the data to be operated on by this sequence of instructions well out of the way of the instructions themselves.

Although we can say that we want certain 16-bit words to be in specific memory locations, how do we ensure that those words are actually so *placed*? That is, how can various words of main memory be *loaded* with *particular* contents? On some machines, including several models of the PDP-11, there is a so-called "front panel" containing switches, which can be used in the following way. We can set 16 of these switches (each to represent a 0 or 1) to a specified address, represented as a binary number. Having *selected* this address, we can now reset the switches to a 16-bit binary number and, by depressing another switch, *deposit* the 16-bit word currently represented by the state of the 16 switches into the previously selected address. In this way we can place (deposit) any particular 16-bit word into any memory location. Having used the switches to set up main memory in whatever way we desired, we may now again use these switches to load a specified number into the *program counter*. And having done so, we may depress a START switch to begin processor execution at whatever address was placed in the PC.

In this way we could have set up the eight words required in the previous example—the six words of instruction between locations 047604 and 047616, inclusive, and the two data words at 100424 and 102552—set the PC to 047604, and then STARTed the CPU. In a few millionths of a second, the CPU would have halted with the PC at 047620, and we could have, if we desired, used the switches to examine the contents of the word whose address is 102552—the "answer." Some of the later models of the PDP-11 do not have these so-called "bit switches" on a front panel. In these, the specifying of memory addresses and the loading of those words with particular contents takes place through the **console terminal**—the terminal in some sense directly connected to the CPU. This terminal can also be used for examining memory words, loading of the PC, and STARTing of processor execution.

It is one thing to load the few words of memory required for the execution of the instructions of the previous example; it would be quite another to do so for a lengthy—several-thousand-word, perhaps—sequence of instructions. In such a case it is simply impractical to load memory by means of these switches; in fact, these switches were never really intended for that purpose. There are far more efficient means of placing words into main memory, and in the sequel we shall see what some of these are. In the meantime the reader is assured of the *possibility* of setting particular memory locations to specified values.

5.6 THE PROCESSOR STATUS WORD (PSW)

In discussing 4-bit-word arithmetic in Chapter 2, we noted that under certain conditions carries into the most-significant bit or out of it, or both, can occur, which in turn can signal possibly incorrect arithmetic results. Of course, the analogous problems can occur in the 16-bit case. We asserted at that time that the CPU would, under certain circumstances, set carry and overflow *indicators* that could then be examined. We could then take appropriate corrective action if some arithmetic computation yielded a result that seemed to have gone awry. Yet we did not explain *what* these indicators were or *how* they might be examined. We shall deal with the *what* part of these indicators in this section and with the *how* immediately afterward.

We have already discussed one of the CPU's public registers, the PC. The CPU has another such externally accessible register, the **processor status word**, abbreviated PSW, or sometimes simply PS. It is aptly named—the contents of this register tells much about the current *status* of the *processor*. A partial layout of this word is shown in Fig. 5.6.1.

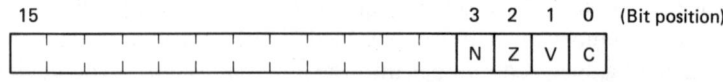

Figure 5.6.1

The four bits of the PSW, which are shown in Fig. 5.6.1, are *named* as follows:

> bit 3 — N — the **negative indicator**, or **negative bit**
>
> bit 2 — Z — the **zero indicator**, or **zero bit**
>
> bit 1 — V — the **overflow indicator**, or **overflow bit**
>
> bit 0 — C — the **carry indicator**, or **carry bit**

(One might expect the overflow bit to be labeled O. We have used V so that no confusion will exist between the use of the *letter O* and the *numeral 0*.) Most of the remaining bits of this word—bits 15 through 4—also have some meaning, although we shall not see what this is until we develop the material of Chapter 12.

Bits 3 through 0 of the PSW are called the CPU's **condition codes**. As we noted in Chapter 2, the setting and clearing of these bits is dependent upon the particular operation being performed, but we can make some general, if not completely accurate, observations about them. When the CPU completes the processing of an arithmetic-type operation, it sets or clears these bits accordingly. In particular, the CPU normally sets the C-bit upon carries out of bit 15, and typically sets the V-bit upon carries from bit 14 into bit 15. Again, we caution the reader that the setting and clearing of these two bits is operation dependent, and the precise details will have to be determined by a careful examination of the description of the operation at hand. (See Appendix A.) The Z- and N-bits, on the other hand, behave more predictably. If the result of an arithmetic operation is *zero*, the CPU will set the Z-bit in the PSW. If not, the CPU will clear the Z-bit. And finally, if the resulting number is *negative*, the CPU will set the N-bit (to 1), otherwise it will clear it (to 0). In this way, at the completion of each instruction, we have some means of determining *what happened* as a result of that instruction, as is shown in the following example.

Consider the addition of the two numbers 064223 and 043002. The result is 127225. As we see, the resulting number is *negative*, it is *nonzero*, a carry from bit 14 into bit 15 occurred, and there was no carry out of bit 15. Thus at the completion of this operation, the condition codes in the PSW will have the following values:

$$N = 1$$
$$Z = 0$$
$$V = 1$$
$$C = 0$$

Thus if we were treating these two numbers as *unsigned* integers, we could conclude on the basis of $C = 0$ that since no carry out of bit 15 occurred, the result is arithmetically correct. If we were treating the numbers as *signed*, then the overflow bit would indicate that a sign change had occurred—a carry into the sign bit—and thus that the arithmetic result is incorrect.

The processor status word is unique among the CPU registers in that it *does* have an address, namely, 777776, and yet it is *not* a main-memory word. Thus we can presumably access the PSW by address, just as we do a word of main memory. And while this is true, we rarely do so. At this point our only interest in accessing the PSW is to determine what its condition codes are, but there are easier ways of testing these bits than actually "looking at" the PSW.

5.7 A CONDITIONAL BRANCH INSTRUCTION

From the discussion of the role played by the program counter in the execution of instructions, we concluded (quite correctly) that instruction execution proceeds *linearly*—one consecutive word after another in main memory is fetched and executed by the CPU, so instruction codes must be loaded in *sequentially* addressed memory words. Yet from his previous programming experience, the reader is doubtless aware that it is common for the logic of a programming procedure to dictate that under certain circumstances, this sequential processing should terminate and control be given over to some other segment of instructions. Indeed, without such transfer-of-control capabilities the stored-instruction concept, which seems so promising, would be severely limited in its utility. The familiar program loops would not be possible, for example. We need some means then of ceasing the processing of instructions in one part of main memory and resuming processing elsewhere in memory—and we have a simple way of doing this.

Let us consider the next example, in which we assume that processing has begun at location 002442 and is allowed to continue down to location 005314 *at which point* we wish to interrupt the linear (consecutive word) processing and pick up execution at 023660. In effect, we wish to jump from 005314 to 023660 as far as the *location* of the operations to be performed is concerned (Fig. 5.7.1). We need only place in the word whose address is 005314 the *code* for the instruction that "puts the number 023660 in the PC." (There is such an instruction.) Let us investigate what takes place when this instruction is encountered.

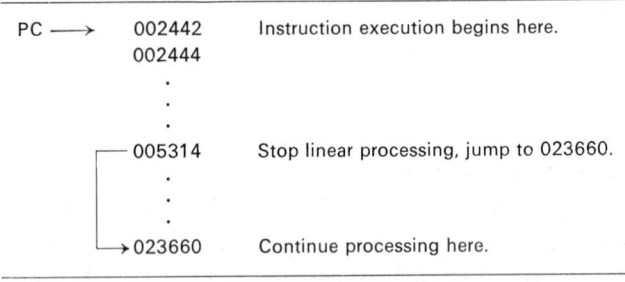

Figure 5.7.1

When execution is ready to commence, the CPU accesses the contents of the PC (namely, 002442), increments c(PC) by 2 to 002444, fetches the contents of location 002442, decodes that 16-bit word, and executes the specified instruction. The CPU then repeats this execution cycle. Eventually the CPU accesses the PC and finds that it contains 005314. The CPU increments c(PC) to 005316 and fetches and decodes the contents of 005314. Recall that we are assuming that the instruction that is located at 005314 is an operation that places the number 023660 in the *PC*. Thus by the time this instruction execution has gone to completion, we have c(PC) = 023660. The CPU is now ready for its next instruction, and, as usual, it accesses the PC to determine the address of the memory location that contains the next instruction. In accessing the PC it now obtains the address 023660, increments the PC to 023662, fetches the contents of 23660, decodes it, and executes it. Thus we see that we have managed to jump the processor's execution from one place (005314) to another (023660) in main memory, simply by adjusting the contents of the program counter. The idea is quite simple; its consequences are far reaching.

The reader who has some experience with programming in a high-level language (BASIC or FORTRAN, for example) will recognize that this jumping from one sequence of instructions to another is not an unusual occurrence in those languages; it is a so-called **unconditional transfer**, frequently represented by the term GOTO. But he is also aware that a more useful type of transfer-of-control statement is the **conditional transfer**, which is often in the form

IF (condition) THEN GOTO (somewhere)

The statement executes as follows: If the specified condition is *true*, then control is transferred to the indicated place to continue processing. But if the condition is *false*, then the statement is simply *ignored* and execution continues linearly, with the next statement. The PDP-11 implements a number of operations, called **conditional branches**, that correspond to these conditional transfers. We examine one such in detail in this section. With the exception of the condition on which the instruction does or does not generate a branch, or jump, all of the conditional branches behave exactly the same way as the one we shall investigate here.

We shall informally call the conditional branch instruction **branch-if-nonzero** and describe its action as follows: If the Z-bit (bit 2) of the PSW is 0 at the time this instruction is decoded, the effect of the instruction will be to produce a branch (to somewhere). If on the other hand the Z-bit is 1 at the time the instruction is decoded, the CPU ignores the instruction and continues processing at the next instruction, that is, at the next word of main memory. Thus in using this branch-if-nonzero instruction we are in effect *examining* one of the PSW's condition codes—the Z-bit—but that examination is less direct than actually "looking at" it (whatever that might mean). Rather we are instructing the *processor* to look at that bit and then to take one action or another, according as it is set or cleared.

Since we saw that a branch, or jump, can be achieved by altering the contents of the PC, the reader might guess that branch-if-nonzero is a *two-word* instruction, the first word being the code for the conditional branch itself, the second word being the *number* (address) to be placed in the PC to produce the branch (if the Z-bit is 0). And while this guess is perfectly reasonable, it turns out that on the PDP-11 the branch-if-nonzero instruction, which we might more accurately call *branch-if-the-Z-bit-is-clear*, is a *one-word* instruction that is formed in a slightly more complicated way. The one idea to keep in mind throughout this discussion, however, is that if a branch, or jump, is to take place, it *must* be achieved by altering the contents of the program counter.

The format of the bit configuration that represents (will be decoded as) branch-if-nonzero is

00 000 010   *xx xxx xxx*

The high-order byte (00 000 010) is the code that is recognized by the decoder as branch-if-nonzero. The low-order byte (*xx xxx xxx*) requires some explanation. The contents of this byte represents an **offset**, a term whose use will be clear shortly.

To effect a branch, the CPU must alter the contents of the PC. The CPU can do this by loading some new number directly into the PC or by *adding* a positive or negative number to the contents of the PC, thereby giving it a new value. Such a number added to c(PC) is called a **program counter displacement**. Thus, for example, if the current contents of the PC is 020042 and the CPU executes an instruction that adds the number 000150 to c(PC), then after execution of that instruction, c(PC) = 020212. We have effected a branch, or jump, from 020042 to 020212. Thus the CPU in some fashion uses the low-order byte of the conditional branch-if-nonzero instruction to displace (adjust) the current contents of the program counter if the PSW's Z-bit is 0 when the instruction is executed.

The reader might assume that the low-order byte of the instruction is the actual number to be added to c(PC), but this is not the case. To see why, consider the numbers, represented here in decimal, that can occupy an 8-bit byte; they range from 0 to 255 if we consider them as unsigned. But if we deal only with unsigned numbers, then any displacing of the PC will always be toward *higher* memory addresses, and there will be no hope of branching *back*, to *lower* memory addresses, which is typically what occurs when a *loop* is constructed in a sequence of instructions. Thus we shall have to consider the 8-bit low-order byte as a *signed* number. The range of such numbers is −128 to +127, with bit 7 acting as the sign bit.

Now observe that the program counter is always pointing at a *word* (containing an instruction) and thus c(PC) is always *even*. Since c(PC) must still be even after displacing, we conclude that if the low-order byte of the branch-if-nonzero instruction is the displacement itself, then it *also* must be even. Thus, in fact, the possible (decimal) numbers that can be used in the low-order byte are −128, −126, . . . , 0, 2, 4, . . . , 124, 126. We conclude that this branch instruction allows us to branch *backward* 128 bytes and *forward* 126 bytes, or, equivalently, backward 64 words and forward 63 words. Note that bit 0 itself is always 0 since, as we have observed, the displacement must be even; thus bit 0 is "wasted" in the low-order byte.

To eliminate the waste associated with bit 0 and at the same time extend (actually double) the range over which the branch can adjust the PC, we take the number in the low-order byte to be the **word offset** rather than the PC byte displacement. Then the processor need only double this word offset to obtain the displacement. In this way, the contents of the PC can be modified by −128 to +127 *words*, or, equivalently, by −256 to +254 *bytes*. A formal description of branch-if-nonzero follows.

> **Branch-if-nonzero:**
> If the Z-bit in the PSW is 1 at the time the instruction is decoded, the instruction is ignored and processing continues at the next word of main memory.
> If the Z-bit in the PSW is 0 at the time the instruction is decoded, the low-order byte of the instruction, taken as a signed number, is *doubled* and the resulting (signed) number is added to the contents of PC.
> $$\text{Symbolically, PC} \leftarrow c(PC) + 2 \times c(\text{low-order byte})$$
> $$= c(PC) + 2 \times (\text{signed word offset})$$

We use the notation ← to mean "is given the value."

The following few simple examples will demonstrate the action of this instruction.

Suppose that when the CPU is ready to execute an instruction, c(PC) = 023042 and c(023042) = 001031.

	address	contents
PC ⟶	023042	001031
	023044	------

The CPU does a fetch, incrementing c(PC) by 2; thus now c(PC) = 023044. The fetched word, 001031, is passed to the decoder, which interprets it as a branch-if-nonzero. If the Z-bit in the PSW is 1, the CPU takes no action and simply begins the next execution cycle, fetching the contents of 023044, and so forth. If the Z-bit is 0, a branch takes place, and we shall calculate the destination of the branch. In binary, the branch-if-nonzero instruction is

$$00 \; 000 \; 010 \qquad 00 \; 011 \; 001$$

The low-order byte—the signed word offset—is (octal) 031, which is doubled to obtain the PC displacement, 062, and then added to c(PC). However, we must be aware that *by now* c(PC) = 023044. Performing the addition we obtain 023044 + 062 = 023126, which becomes the new contents of the program counter. Having completed the processing of this instruction, the CPU, as usual, looks to the PC for the address of the next instruction and finds the number (address) 023126. Thus the branch-if-nonzero instruction has caused a branch to location 023126 from location 023042 (provided, of course, the Z-bit is 0).

As another example, consider the situation

	address	contents
PC ⟶	023042	001315
	023044	------

Again we assume c(PC) = 023042, the CPU does a fetch, moving c(PC) up to 023044, and the instruction is decoded as a branch-if-nonzero. The bit configuration corresponding to the octal number 001315 is

$$00 \; 000 \; 010 \qquad 11 \; 001 \; 101$$

and thus if a branch is to occur—if the Z-bit is 0—the word offset in the low-order byte is (octal) 315. As an 8-bit byte, this number is *negative*—it is the negative of the (8-bit-octal) number 063. Doubling this number yields 146, which is the byte displacement that must be *subtracted* from c(PC). Thus the new value of the PC is 023044 − 146 = 022676, and we have achieved a branch *backward*, into a *lower* address, in main memory.

If the reader is bothered by the fact that we treated positive and negative word offsets in different ways—by adding the byte displacement in the former case and subtracting the negative of the byte displacement in the latter—we offer a uniform scheme that is independent of the sign of the offset and more accurately reflects the actual procedure followed by the processor. Consider a word (private register) whose low-order byte is the same as the low-order byte of the conditional branch-if-nonzero instruction. As we know, this byte is the word offset. We *shift* this byte *left by one bit*, as follows: We shift bit 7 of the byte out of the byte, but save its value, 0 or 1. We shift bit 6 into bit 7, bit 5 into bit 6, . . . , bit 0 into bit 1, and we fill the vacated bit 0 with a 0. We now *fill* the high-order byte of the word with the bit value that was shifted *out of* bit 7. This process is called a **sign extend** into the high-order byte of the word, since the high-order byte has been filled with the original sign bit—bit 7—of the low-order byte. The effect of the procedure is to generate a *word* whose *signed* value is *twice* the signed value of the low-order byte of the conditional branch instruction. (Why?) Thus the low-order byte is doubled, as required, and the sign has been extended into the high-order byte. This word is now simply added to the current contents of the PC to produce the branch, and we note that no decisions had to be made regarding the positiveness or negativeness of the word offset.

Consider again the two examples above. In the first, the low-order byte of the instruction is 00 011 001. When we shift it left one bit, the result is 00 110 010 and, since a 0 was shifted out of bit 7, the high-order byte of the private register is filled with 0's giving the word 0 000 000 000 110 010 = 000062. When we add this word to c(PC) = 023044, the result is 023044 + 000062 = 023126, as before. In the second example, the low-order byte of the branch instruction is 11 001 101. Shifting it left results in 10 011 010 and, since a 1 was shifted out of bit 7, the sign-extended word representing the byte displacement is 1 111 111 110 011 010 = 177632. Adding this to c(PC), we obtain 023044 + 177632 = 022676, as before.

There are numerous other conditional branch instructions which we shall encounter in examples throughout the remainder of the text. They test the other PSW condition codes or, in some cases, *combinations* of these codes. In fact, one of them does no testing at all—it branches *unconditionally*. The conditional branches form one of the most frequently used classes of instructions, as we shall see, and the reader will find that they are indispensable as he develops sequences of instructions to perform various tasks. As we already mentioned, while the high-order bytes of these conditional branches differ—these bits determine what *kind* of test is to be made on the condition codes—in each case the low-order byte is always taken to be a signed word offset. Thus the behavior of the particular branch-if-nonzero instruction is truly typical of all the instructions in this class.

5.8 TWO COMPLETE (IF NOT INTERESTING) PROGRAMS

Up to this point we have carefully avoided using the term *program* insofar as possible, but we can now give an informal definition. By a **program** we shall mean a sequence of CPU instructions, along with the data operated on by those instructions, which, when executed, perform some meaningful function. We might also insist that upon execution of the sequence of instructions, the CPU will ultimately halt. We realize that this definition is quite vague, especially the word *meaningful*, but a formal definition, if one existed at all, would be so abstract as to be useless for our purposes. In the sense of the informal definition, the sequence of instructions of Sec. 5.5 that added two numbers, decremented the result, and then halted is a program. In this section we present two such programs, although their meaningfulness is certainly questionable. Their principal purpose is to introduce the concept of instruction execution *iteration—loops* of instructions that are performed over and over again. The iteration eventually terminates as a result of a branch-if-nonzero instruction testing the PSW Z-bit.

The first program repeatedly increments the contents of a memory word, which we initially assume to contain -3, until the contents of that word is 0. Then the program directs the processor to halt. The addresses at which the instructions are located were chosen arbitrarily.

Address	Contents	Comments
.	.	
.	.	
.	.	
076606	177775	The number to be incremented, -3.
.	.	
.	.	
.	.	
104302	005237	Increment the contents of the location
104304	076606	whose address is 076606.
104306	001375	Branch if nonzero.
104310	000000	Halt the CPU.
104312	------	
.	.	
.	.	
.	.	

We assume that initially $c(PC) = 104302$, so the first instruction to be executed is the two-word instruction to increment the contents of the memory word whose address is 076606. This is done, so that word now contains 177776. As a result of that incrementing, the condition codes are set as follows:

$$N = 1$$
$$Z = 0$$
$$V = 0$$

(The C-bit is not affected by the operation, but we shall not be concerned with it anyway.) The N-bit is set since the resulting number—177776 $(= -2)$—is negative. The Z-bit is cleared since the resulting number is *nonzero*, and this is the bit we are interested in. (The V-bit also is cleared since no carry into bit 15 occurred.) At this point c(PC) = 104306; that is, the PC is pointing at the branch-if-nonzero instruction, which is fetched, and the contents of the PC is moved up to 104310. Since the Z-bit is 0, the branch *will* take place and we must calculate the displacement for the branch. The low-order byte of the instruction (in octal) is 375, a *negative* number, which is the negative of 003. Since this is the word offset, we double this to obtain the byte displacement, −006. We add this number to the PC contents and find the new value of the program counter to be 104310 − 006 = 104302. Thus execution resumes back at the increment instruction.

Again the contents of 076606 is incremented (giving 177777), and since this result is again nonzero, the Z-bit will be cleared and when the branch-if-nonzero instruction is encountered the second time, it will again generate a branch back to the increment instruction. *This* time the number incremented is 177777, and the increment results in 000000. Since this *is* 0, the CPU will *set* the Z-bit (to 1). Once again c(PC) = 104306, so the CPU fetches the contents of 104306 (the branch-if-nonzero instruction), in the course of which c(PC) is advanced to 104310, as before. Since an examination of the Z-bit reveals that it is now set, the CPU ignores the branch instruction and begins another instruction execution cycle. Since c(PC) = 104310, the halt instruction, whose code is 000000, is fetched, and the contents of the PC is incremented to 104312. The instruction is executed, and the CPU halts. Thus, with executing having ceased, we have c(PC) = 104312 and c(076606) = 000000. The contents of the other memory locations are unchanged.

The importance of this example lies in the fact that an instruction—in this case the "increment the contents of the word whose address is 076606" instruction—was executed *repeatedly* and that the repetition was *terminated* upon some *condition*, namely, when the contents of that word went to 0.

Our next example is a bit more meaningful and somewhat more complex, and contains a rather unusual feature: The program actually *modifies* one of its own *instructions* in the course of its execution. The purpose of the program is to add five numbers as follows: One memory location contains the number 5, which will act as a *counter* to control the number of execution iterations of a sequence of instructions. This number will be decremented by 1 each time through this loop, and the loop will exit when this number is 0, the condition being tested by a branch-if-nonzero instruction, as before. The five numbers to be added will be placed in five *consecutive* memory locations, and we shall see the significance of the fact that these locations are consecutive, or *contiguous*. Also, we must be aware that the PDP-11 add instruction calculates the sum of the two numbers and puts the result *back* into the *second* of those numbers. Thus we shall initialize a memory word to 0, and the sum of the numbers will be accumulated in that location. The program is shown in Fig. 5.8.1.

We assume that execution begins at 047032—that is, initially c(PC) = 047032. The word at that location is fetched and decoded, and it is found to be

Address	Contents	Comments
047032	005237	Increment the contents of
047034	047044	the word at 047044.
047036	005237	Increment the contents of
047040	047044	the word at 047044.
047042	063737	Add the contents of the word at ??????
047044	102602	to the contents of the word at 104004
047046	104004	leaving the sum in location 104004.
047050	005337	Decrement the contents of
047052	074010	the word at 074010.
047054	001366	Branch if nonzero to 047032.
047056	000000	Halt the CPU.
.	.	
.	.	
.	.	
074010	000005	Counter (initially = 5).
.	.	
.	.	
.	.	
102604	003013	These
102606	102000	are
102610	000003	the
102612	012340	numbers
102614	100114	to be added.
.	.	
.	.	
.	.	
104004	000000	Sum is accumulated here (initially 0).

Figure 5.8.1

"increment the contents of the word whose address is in the next word (that is, whose address is in 047034)." Thus the word to be incremented is the word whose address is 047044, namely, the word 102602. This word is incremented to 102603 and the next instruction is fetched and decoded. As we see, it is identical to the first instruction processed, and the word at 047044 is incremented again. Thus by now the word at 047044 contains 102604, and $c(PC) = 047042$. The next instruction code—063737—is fetched from location 047042, and this is decoded as "add the contents of the two words whose addresses are in the next two memory locations and place the sum in the second of those words." Here we must proceed with some care. In the listing of the contents of main memory above, the word following the add instruction, that is, the word at 047044, is shown as 102602. But recall that this word has already been incremented (by 1) *twice*. Thus at this point the contents of location 047044 is 102604, which is the *address* of the first of the two words to be added. The address of the second word to be added immediately follows, namely, 104004 (at 047046). Thus $c(102604)$ is added to $c(104004)$, giving $003013 + 000000 = 003013$ as a result, which is then put back into location 104004. Now $c(PC) = 047050$.

The next instruction—decrement the contents of the word whose address is 074010—is fetched and executed, and as a consequence the number in location 074010 is now 4. Since that result is *nonzero,* the Z-bit in the PSW is *cleared* (set to 0). At this point c(PC) = 047054, and the branch-if-nonzero instruction is fetched, with c(PC) being incremented to 047056. Since the Z-bit is cleared, the branch will occur, and we need to calculate the displacement. The low-order byte of the branch instruction (in octal) is 366, which as a signed 8-bit number is −012. Doubling this to generate a byte displacement gives −024, the number to be added to c(PC). Thus by the time this instruction has been executed, we have c(PC) = 047056 − 024 = 047032. Therefore execution resumes here—at 047032—and we find ourselves back at the first of the two increment instructions. The contents of the word at 047044 is again incremented twice, and by the time the add instruction at 047042 is encountered the second time, the CPU is directed to add the contents of the word at 102606 to the contents of the word at 104004 and leave the result in 104004. The addition yields 102000 + 003013 = 105013. The contents of 074010 is then again decremented, this time to 3, and since this result is nonzero (the Z-bit is clear), the branch at 047054 again takes place and control is once more transferred to 047032.

It should now be clear that we have an instruction loop consisting of the two increment instructions, the addition, and the decrement instruction. The result of the decrement is tested by the branch-if-nonzero and the loop is reexecuted. The purpose of the increment instructions is to modify the address portion of the addition instruction, so that each time through the loop the addition will be operating on the *next* word—the *next* of the five numbers. (It should now be evident why we wanted those five numbers to be in *consecutive* memory words.) The loop execution will be repeated until the fifth number has been added into the word at 104000, after which the word at 074010 will be decremented again. *This* time, the result is 0 and the branch-if-nonzero instruction will be ignored. Thus the halt instruction at 047056 will be performed and execution will cease, with the sum of the five numbers in location 104004.

The foregoing example points out how "unknowledgeable" the CPU is concerning which words of main memory are data and which are instruction. The word at location 047044 was treated as *data* by the two increment instructions, and later that word was interpreted as a part of an *instruction*—the address portion of the addition instruction. By now the reader should be convinced that *any* word in main memory, regardless of whether we *think* of it as being *data* or *instruction*, can be manipulated by the CPU in any way of which it is capable. At a high level (when programming in BASIC or Pascal, for example), this is usually not possible—data and instructions are kept carefully separated. But at the *machine* level, as we have seen, this instruction manipulation *is* possible and it can sometimes be a powerful capability. And it is *always* potentially dangerous and sometimes disastrous. We shall see in a few later examples that this instruction code modification can be useful provided it is handled with extreme care.

While the reader probably had little trouble in following the *logic* of this program—why these particular instructions were used and the order in which they were loaded for execution—he might well wonder how we were even aware that such instructions were implemented on the PDP-11 and how we determined what the instruction codes were—what bit configurations would be decoded as increment, add, and so forth. Here we must rely on materials supplied by the computer manufacturer that describe the various operations, how they execute, and what their codes are. Thus if we know that a decrement operation is implemented on the machine and we choose to use it, we can look up in a table the 16-bit word that represents this instruction. For questions about the logic of the program itself, we refer the reader to Chapter 6.

5.9 SOME OTHER CPU REGISTERS

We have spent some time discussing two of the CPU's externally accessible registers—registers that are not private to the processor—namely, the program counter and the processor status word. These are evidently very highly specialized in their behavior and use. But in addition to these, the CPU has public— externally accessible—registers which are not so highly specialized. We shall see in future programming examples (in fact, in the next section) that these registers can be used to hold counters, addresses, and intermediate results, and to accumulate sums and products. In general, they are highly convenient for a wide variety of purposes. These registers, unlike the PSW, do *not* have addresses, and thus for the purposes of our discussions, we shall simply *name* them. Since there are eight such registers, we shall refer to them as R∅ to R7.

$$
\left.
\begin{array}{l}
\text{R}\emptyset \\
\text{R1} \\
\text{R2} \\
\text{R3} \\
\text{R4} \\
\text{R5}
\end{array}
\right\} \quad \text{(general-purpose registers)}
$$

$$
\begin{array}{l}
\text{R6} \\
\text{R7}
\end{array}
$$

The reader will note that the first six of these, R∅ to R5, inclusive, have been labeled **general-purpose registers** to indicate that they may be used for any purpose whatever—as counters, accumulators, and so on. Like any other word in main memory, these are 16-bit words that behave arithmetically and in all other respects just like their main-memory counterparts except, as we said, that they are not numerically addressable. Register 6 is a special case, not because its *behavior* is different from that of R∅ to R5, but because the CPU has a special *use* for this register. For this reason it was not included among the general-purpose registers. The details of how R6 is used by the processor are given in Chapter 8.

We also did not include R7 among the general-purpose registers for a very good reason: It is *the program counter*. And by now we know that R7 (PC) is used by the CPU in a very special way. Again we caution the reader against thinking that just because R7 is the program counter and thus is used by the CPU to point at the next instruction to be executed, that there is something peculiar about R7's behavior, with regard to arithmetic, for instance. Register 7 can be manipulated arithmetically, and, in fact, the conditional branch-if-nonzero does just that, with the expected results. However it is clear that R7 cannot be used as a general-purpose register, for purposes of counting or accumulating, for example. As a general rule, then, we can say that of the eight registers R0 to R7, the general-purpose registers R0 to R5 may be used in any way desired. Registers 6 and 7 play special roles relative to the CPU, and without some depth of understanding of the consequences (which we presently do not have), arbitrary use of them will probably end in disaster.

5.10 PUTTING THE GENERAL-PURPOSE REGISTERS TO USE

In this section we see how the general-purpose registers can be used in various ways by presenting again the addition program of Fig. 5.8.1. This latest version is shown in Fig. 5.10.1.

Address	Contents	Comments
047032	012700	Put the number 5 in register 0 (R0)
047034	000005	to be used as a counter.
047036	012702	Put the number 102604 (address of first
047040	102604	number to be added) in register 2 (R2).
047042	005005	Clear register 5 (that is, set c(R5) to 0).
047044	062205	The add instruction (explained in the text).
047046	005300	Decrement the contents of R0.
047050	001375	Branch-if-nonzero to location 047044.
047052	000000	Halt the processor.
.	.	
.	.	
.	.	
102604	003013	These
102606	102000	are
102610	000003	the
102612	012340	numbers
102614	100114	to be added.

Figure 5.10.1

Again we assume that initially c(PC) = 047032. When the instruction there is fetched, it is decoded as the instruction to "put the number 5 in R∅"—that is, the contents of the 16-bit register ∅ is set to 000005. The next instruction (at 047036) is similar—it puts the number 102604 in register 2, and we noted in the listing of the program that this number is the *address* of the first of the five numbers to be added. We shall see momentarily how this address is used. The next instruction clears register 5—that is, it sets the contents of R5 to 0. This is where the sum of the numbers will be accumulated, and as in the previous version of the program, this word has been initialized to 0. We are now ready to begin adding the numbers into this accumulator R5.

The addition instruction at location 047044, namely 062205, is in a different *form* from its counterpart in the previous version, and its action requires some explanation. The effect of this instruction is to add the contents of the memory location whose *address* is in R2 to the contents of R5, placing the resulting sum back in R5. The contents of R2 is 102604, and this number is taken as the *address* of a memory location whose *contents* is to be added to the current contents of R5. Thus the effect is to add c(102604) to c(R5) and put the result in R5. That is, 003013 + 000000 = 003013 is put in R5. Thus we have added the first number into R5. But the instruction actually does a bit more. When the contents of R2 was accessed by the CPU to obtain the address 102604, the CPU also *incremented* c(R2) by 2, so now we have c(R2) = 102606. The significance of this action is that R2 is now pointing at—contains the address of—the *second* of the five numbers. It is important that the reader understand that the incrementing of c(R2) was *not* the result of some separate instruction to do this. Rather that incrementing took place because of the *form* of the addition instruction 062205. This will be explained in detail in Chapter 7.

Just as in the previous version, the counter (initialized to 5) is now decremented (at location 047046), although in this case the counter is in R∅ rather than in a main-memory word. A test of the PSW's Z-bit is made by the branch-if-nonzero instruction and control is transferred back to location 047044, as the reader should verify. We have returned to the add instruction, and as before, it uses c(R2) as the address of the location whose contents is to be added to c(R5). But note that because of the incrementing (by 2) that occurred the *last* time this addition took place, we now have c(R2) = 102606 and thus the contents of 102606—namely, 102000—is added to the current contents of R5 (003013). Thus R5 now contains the sum of the first *two* numbers, and as before, a further result of this form of the addition operation is that c(R2) has again been incremented by 2; thus we now have c(R2) = 102610, the *address* of the *third* number. Then c(R∅) is decremented, the Z-bit is tested, a branch to 047044 takes place, and so forth, until the last number is added to c(R5). Then c(R∅) is decremented to 0—so no branch occurs—and the processor halts with the sum of the five numbers in R5.

The peculiar add instruction used here requires some further investigation, which will be done in Chapter 7. In the meantime the reader should make note of its very desirable feature, the incrementing of register 2 by two each time it is accessed to obtain the address of one of the summands. As we saw, the effect is that R2, which initially pointed at the first number, was reset to point at the second number, then the third, and so forth. This "stepping through consecutive memory locations" has greatly simplified the *structure* of the program, having eliminated the necessity for our explicitly incrementing (twice) the address portion of the add instruction. In fact, we observe that this latter version does *not* modify any of its own instructions.

Finally, notice that this version is physically *shorter* than that of Fig. 5.8.1. For example, the addition instruction here is a *one-word* instruction as opposed to the three words required earlier. Generally speaking, the use of these general-purpose registers will normally result in shorter, more efficient programs.

5.11 EXERCISES

5.7.1. Suppose each of the following branch-if-nonzero instructions is located at 020332. Find the address of the location to which control is transferred if the branch takes place (that is, if at the time the instruction is decoded, the PSW's Z-bit is clear).

(a) 001023	**(d)** 001176	**(g)** 001376
(b) 001014	**(e)** 001276	**(h)** 001377
(c) 001100	**(f)** 001200	**(i)** 001000

5.7.2. Suppose a branch-if-nonzero instruction is located at 020332. Construct (the 6-digit octal form of) the instruction for each of the "target" addresses below —the address to which control is to be transferred if the PSW's Z-bit is clear.

(a) 020604	**(d)** 012606	**(g)** 020332
(b) 020340	**(e)** 020334	**(h)** 024336
(c) 020302	**(f)** 020000	**(i)** 020330

5.7.3. Suppose that at location 003674 we intend to place the instruction "branch-if-nonzero to location 003274."

(a) Show that the limitation on the size of the word offset in the conditional branch instructions precludes such a branch-if-nonzero instruction.

(b) Show, however, that the following instructions will have the same effect.

address	contents
003674	001402
003676	012707
003700	003274
003702	------

(The instruction whose code is 001402 is a conditional branch meaning branch-if-*equal*-to-zero and the combination

012707

003274

forms the instruction "put the number 003274 in the program counter.")

5.7.4. What would be the consequences, in terms of instruction execution, of the instruction located at 005314 whose effect is to put the number 005314 into the program counter?

5.7.5. In Sec. 5.7 it was asserted that shifting the bits of a byte one place to the left has the effect of doubling its value. Explain why this is the case *provided* bit 7 contains a 0. What happens if bit 7 contains a 1?

5.8.1. Suppose that the second program of Sec. 5.8 (the addition of five numbers) is loaded into main memory as shown in Fig. 5.8.1 on page 77. Suppose next that the program is *executed*; that is, the number 047032 is loaded into the PC and the processor started. Then the five numbers will be added, the sum will be in location 104004, and the processor will halt. Now assume that we reexecute the program simply by reloading the PC with the number 047032 and again starting the processor. Specifically, we do *not* reload these words of main memory. Show that this second execution of this code will *not* again add those five numbers. Determine exactly where the difficulties lie (there are three of them). Finally, explain what *will* take place on this reexecution.

5.10.1. Referring to Exercise 5.8.1, explain why the second version of the addition program, as shown in Fig. 5.10.1, *could* be reexecuted with the expected results. (Exercises 5.8.1 and 5.10.1 demonstrate the sometimes dire consequences of instructions that modify other instructions, and programs that fail to initialize various memory locations prior to their use.)

5.10.2. It was observed that the add instruction of the first version of the addition program was a three-word affair, whereas in the second version only one word was required. Explain where the other two words "went."

6

Assembling (Building) a Program

6.1 PROGRAM CONSTRUCTION

When we set about the task of writing a program, there are a number of (sometimes informal) phases that we go through. First, we ensure that we fully understand what job is to be done and just what information we have at our disposal. Next, we develop a basic approach to the task, deciding, for example, that several methods will do the job, finally selecting the one that appeals to us most, perhaps on the grounds of efficiency, familiarity, or expediency. Then we make a more formal attack on the problem, in which we write out an algorithm, or procedure, to solve the problem. It is at this stage that machine and language considerations are introduced: If we decide to write the program in the Pascal language, for example, the constraints and features of that language will to some extent influence the procedure. Now it is time to transcribe the algorithm into the chosen language, load the resulting code into main memory, and execute it. When writing in a high-level language, such as BASIC, FORTRAN, or Pascal, these last steps are really not too difficult—the real action lies in the algorithm-construction phase; the translation to a particular language is rather anticlimactic.

The programming phases described above apply equally to the programmer who writes in **machine language**—the native or inherent language of the computer itself. (The few little programs we have examined so far are machine-language programs.) And while the last phase—transcribing the algorithm to machine language—may well be an anticlimax, it is here that many difficulties arise. The writing of machine-language programs is a very difficult, time-consuming, and demanding task.

6.2 A SAMPLE PROGRAM

The few machine-language programs we have seen thus far were presented as complete programs, and their various features were then discussed in some detail. In this section we answer the question of where these programs come from; that is, how were the programming instructions constructed in the first place? We illustrate the procedures with a conceptually simple problem.

We shall use the task of finding the largest of a collection of signed numbers as an illustrative example. We shall go through the various phases described in the preceding section and examine the program-writing process in detail. First, provided we are given the numbers whose maximum is to be found, we know what is to be done and that sufficient information is available. We suppose, for the sake of definiteness in the discussion, that we are dealing with five numbers, although it is easy to see that the procedure does not depend on the actual number of numbers. Second, we decide on the following approach to the problem: We look at the *first* of the five numbers and immediately declare it to be the largest. (In fact, this statement is true of all the numbers we have looked at—namely, just one.) Perhaps a better term is *temporary maximum*. We now look at the remaining four $(5 - 1)$ numbers in turn, comparing each with this temporary maximum. If we encounter a number that is *larger* than this temporary maximum, we replace the temporary maximum with it and continue the process. By the time we have examined the remaining four numbers the temporary maximum will, in fact, be *the* maximum of the five numbers.

For a more formal algorithm we write the procedure out in English, assigning symbolic names to some of the program components.

1. Set a COUNTER equal to 4.

   Even though there are five numbers, since the first will be the temporary maximum, there are four numbers remaining to be examined.

2. Set TEMPMAX equal to the first number.

   Make the first number the temporary maximum.

3. Get the next number and call it NUM.

   Go through the numbers, looking at each one in turn.

4. If NUM is less than or equal to TEMPMAX, go to step 6.

   Compare the number with the temporary maximum. If it is not larger, skip step 5.

5. Set TEMPMAX equal to NUM.

   Replace the temporary maximam with the larger number.

6. Reduce COUNTER by 1.   *Decrement the counter to see if there are more numbers to compare.*

7. If COUNTER is not zero, go back to step 3.   *Since there are more numbers to compare, go get the next one.*

8. STOP.   *The procedure is completed, and the largest of the five numbers is in TEMPMAX.*

We must now make some decisions about casting the procedure in machine language. We need a counter, to be initialized to 4, and a register—R0, for example—seems a likely candidate for such a counter. We shall place the five numbers themselves in consecutive memory locations, and our experience with the addition program of Sec. 5.10 indicates that an efficient way to refer to them would be to have the address of the first number in some register and then to let the register step through the addresses of each number in turn. We choose R2 for this purpose and set R2 initially to the address of the first number. While we have decided that the five numbers should be in consecutive memory locations (notice that we could not take advantage of the stepping through of R2 if the numbers were not in *consecutive* locations), we have said nothing yet about just *where* those memory locations will be. While we already know that they can be anywhere in main memory, we shall assume that the five numbers will be placed in main memory immediately following the program instructions. Finally, we shall need someplace to hold the temporary maximum (TEMPMAX in the algorithm), and we select R5 for this purpose. The choices of the various registers to hold these program values are completely arbitrary except, of course, that once a register has been assigned to one purpose it should not be used for any other.

Now that we have given certain registers some initial values, let us go through the procedure informally. First, we transfer the number whose *address* is in R2 (that is, the first of the five numbers) to R5, the temporary maximum. We must now increment R2 by 2 so that it will contain the address of the *second* number. We are now ready to do the comparison. If the number whose address is in R2 (the second of the five numbers) is *greater* than the number in R5 (the temporary maximum), then that number should replace the temporary maximum—that is, the number whose address is in R2 should be transferred to R5. If not, then this last step should be skipped. Next we decrement the counter R0, and if it is not now 0, the program should return control to the point at which R2 was incremented by 2 so that R2 will then contain the address of the next number. On the other hand, if the counter (R0) *is* 0, the program should stop—the maximum will be in R5.

Having determined the procedure—where various counters, numbers, and so forth will be stored, and to some extent even what machine instructions will be used—we are now ready to begin writing down the instructions. The first step is to decide *where* the program is to be loaded in main memory.

We are surely a long way from actually loading the instructions and data into memory, but, as we shall see, some of the instructions require actual memory *addresses*, and we shall have to know what those addresses are. Because of the random-access characteristic of main memory, no particular location is favored over any other, so we may as well start at the first word of memory— the location whose address is 000000. Recall that the first thing we needed to do was to initialize a counter (R∅) to 4. Looking up the machine instruction for "move the absolute number 4 into register ∅" we find it to be a two-word instruction, the first of which is the code for the move operation—012700—and the second is the number 4 itself—000004. Thus we may write (as usual, the first number being the address, used for reference, the second number, the contents of that address)

000000	012700	Move the number
000002	000004	4 into register ∅.

We may feel that we are well launched until we try to write the next instruction. Recall that we made the decision that the *address* of the first of the five numbers would be put in R2. While we can look up the code for "move a number (the address) into R2," unfortunately at this point we do not know just *what* number is to be moved into R2. That number is supposed to be an address, but at present we cannot see far enough ahead to know precisely *where* (at *which* address) the first number will ultimately be loaded. Thus we cannot complete this instruction, although we are aware that it consists of two words, the first of which is the "move an absolute number into R2" operator (whose code is 012702), the second word being the unknown address. The best we can do is to write a *partial* instruction and make a mental note that we shall have to complete it at a later time, when we know the address of the first of the five numbers. Thus we now have

000000	012700	
000002	000004	
000004	012702	Move the (unknown) address of
000006	------	the first number into register 2.

One little setback of this kind is not so bad, so we forge ahead. Assuming now that the address of the first number will be in R2 by the time the program is executing, we want to move the first number into R5 as the temporary maximum. The process we shall be using here—having R2 step through the addresses of the five numbers—is reminiscent of the addition program of Fig. 5.10.1. Recall that in that program R2 contained the addresses of the numbers to be added, and as each number was added, R2 was *automatically incremented by 2*, so it always contained the address of the *next* number to be added. In that case automatic incrementing was a most desirable feature, but here we elect *not* to do this, for reasons that will be clear shortly. Thus we need a variation of the move operator that moves the number whose address is in R2 into R5,

but does so without affecting the value in R2. We look this up and append it
to the program.

```
000000        012700
000002        000004
000004        012702
000006        ------

000010        011205        Move the number whose address is
                            in R2 into R5 (without changing
                            the value of R2).
```

Now that we have given the temporary maximum (R5) its initial value,
we are ready to begin comparing it with the remaining four numbers. But the
address in R2 is that of the *first* number, whereas it should be the address of the
second number. This is an appropriate place to add 2 (two bytes equal one
word) to the contents of R2. Since there is an instruction that increments c(R2)
by 1, we need only include two copies of that instruction here.

```
000000        012700
000002        000004
000004        012702
000006        ------
000010        011205

000012        005202        Increment the contents
000014        005202            of R2 (by 1) twice.
```

We are now ready to compare the number in R5 (the temporary maximum) with the number whose address is in R2. There is a PDP-11 instruction
that does precisely that, and we insert its code at this point in the program.

```
000000        012700
000002        000004
000004        012702
000006        ------
000010        011205
000012        005202
000014        005202

000016        020512        Compare the contents of R5 with
                            the contents of the memory location
                            whose address is in R2.
```

A word of explanation concerning the compare operator is required here.
The operator calculates the *difference* between the first number specified (in this
case, the temporary maximum in R5) and the second number (the number in
the memory location whose address is in R2) and sets the condition codes in

the PSW accordingly. Neither of the numbers themselves is affected by this subtraction—only the condition codes.

How does the flow of the program logic proceed from here? If the result of the "subtraction" that took place in the compare instruction is *positive*, it means that the contents of R5—the temporary maximum—is *larger* than the number being compared with it, so the temporary maximum should not be changed. Even if the result of the comparison is 0, meaning the two numbers are equal, no replacement of the temporary maximum is required. Only if the result of the subtraction in the compare instruction is *negative* should a replacement of the temporary maximum be made. Thus the instruction following the compare should be a conditional branch—skip around (something) if the result of the compare is greater than or equal to 0. The something that should be skipped around is, of course, an instruction or instructions to replace the temporary maximum (in R5) with the number whose address is in R2. Since there *is* a conditional branch instruction of the form branch-if-greater-than-or-equal-to-zero," we should insert it here. Like all the conditional branch instructions, the low-order byte contains the signed word offset. But how many words are we to skip? At this point, it is difficult to anticipate just where we want to branch to, and thus we shall not be able to complete the branch instruction at this time. Again, the best we can do is observe that whatever the instruction, it will occupy one word and note that it will have to be filled in later, when we know the destination of the branch.

000000	012700
000002	000004
000004	012702
000006	------
000010	011205
000012	005202
000014	005202
000016	020512
000020	------

000020 ------   Branch (to where?) if the result of the compare was greater than or equal to 0.

Despite this problem, let us move ahead with the code required to replace the temporary maximum. Recalling that the larger number (the *new* temporary maximum) has the address of its location in R2, we see that we need a form of the move operator that will move the number whose address is in R2 into R5. Its code is 011205. It should now be clear why we wanted to handle the incrementing of R2 ourselves—the double-increment at locations 000012 and 000014—rather than allowing some kind of *autoincrementing*. If R2 had been autoincremented, then it would now contain the address of the *next* of the five numbers, not the number we must move into R5. Our program now looks like the following:

000000	012700
000002	000004
000004	012702
000006	------
000010	011205
000012	005202
000014	005202
000016	020512
000020	------

000022	011205	Move the number whose address is in R2 into R5.

The segment that increments R2, compares it with R5, and replaces it if necessary is now complete. It is time to adjust—decrement—the counter in R∅ and, if not all the numbers have yet been treated, branch back (to somewhere) to reexecute these instructions. We look up and insert in the partial program the instruction to decrement the counter R∅.

000000	012700
000002	000004
000004	012702
000006	------
000010	011205
000012	005202
000014	005202
000016	020512
000020	------
000022	011205

000024	005300	Decrement the contents of R∅.

Now that the counter has been decremented, we must branch back (to somewhere in the program) *provided* the counter is not 0. We need only determine *where* we want to branch to, so that we can calculate the word offset that is to go in the low-order byte of the branch instruction.

Recall that we have just compared the contents of R5 with the number whose address is in R2, and since we did not allow R2 to be automatically incremented, R2 still contains the address of that number. For the next compare, of course, R2 should contain the address of the *next* number. Thus c(R2) should be incremented by 2, and a glance back at the program reveals that the desired adjustment will take place if we simply branch back to location 000012— c(R2) will be incremented by 2, the next compare will take place, and so forth. To determine what form the branch-if-nonzero instruction should have, we must be aware of the following: First, this instruction occupies one word, which will be at memory location 000026. Second, its low-order byte will contain the signed number of words by which the PC is to be adjusted. Third, and probably most crucial, when the program *executes* (and we again remind the reader that we are still far from the execution phase) the CPU will have *fetched* this branch instruction and consequently moved the PC up to 000030, which is the value that must be adjusted to achieve the branch to 000012. Doing a little arithmetic shows us that we must *subtract* 000016 from 000030 to get 000012. Thus the displacement is −16 bytes, or −7 words. (Recall that we require the *word offset*.) Since as a signed 8-bit number −7 = 371, which will go in the low-order byte of the branch instruction, and since the high-order byte of the branch-if-non-zero operator is 002, we can put these bytes together to get

$$00\ 000\ 010\ 11\ 111\ 001 = 001371$$

We are now just about home free. We have just determined the code to be inserted at 000026, and we know that if the branch instruction is *not* to be acted upon, the program is finished and we should simply HALT, the code for which is 000000. Thus we should load 000000 at the word following the conditional branch (namely at 000030). Finally, we can insert the data—the five numbers whose maximum is to be found—starting at location 000032. Our (almost) complete program is shown in Fig. 6.2.1.

000000	012700	
000002	000004	
000004	012702	
000006	------	
000010	011205	
000012	005202	
000014	005202	
000016	020512	
000020	------	
000022	011205	
000024	005300	
000026	001371	Branch back to 000012 if the result of decrementing R∅ was nonzero.
000030	000000	Halt the CPU.
000032	000403 ⎫	The numbers
000034	102304 ⎪	whose
000036	023704 ⎬	maximum
000040	007702 ⎪	is to be
000042	176337 ⎭	found are loaded here.

Figure 6.2.1

The only task remaining is to fill in the ------'s. The first one is quite easy. Recall that we had to leave the word at 000006 blank since it is the address of the first of the five numbers, and at the time we could not anticipate what that address would be. We now see that it is 000032, and we can insert it at

000006. The ------ at location 000020 represents a branch instruction that is to skip around the instruction to replace the temporary maximum. That is, if the result of the comparison at 000016 is greater than or equal to 0, we do *not* want to execute the move instruction at 000022. Rather, we should skip to location 000024—the decrement R$\emptyset$ instruction. To calculate the word offset that goes in the low-order byte of the branch-if-greater-than-or-equal-to-zero instruction, we must be aware that *upon execution*, by the time the instruction has been fetched, the program counter will have been advanced to 000022. Since we want to branch conditionally to 000024, the displacement is clearly 2 bytes, or 1 word. Thus the low-order byte of the instruction shoud be 001, and since the high-order byte of the branch-if-greater-than-or-equal-to-zero instruction is 004, we can put these bytes together to get 002001, the word to be filled in at 000020. The program is now complete, and we show it in its final and annotated form (Fig. 6.2.2).

000000	012700	Move the number
000002	000004	4 into R$\emptyset$ as a counter.
000004	012702	Move the number (address)
000006	000032	000032 into R2.
000010	011205	Move the number whose address
		is in R2 into R5.
000012	005202	Increment the contents
000014	005202	of R2 twice.
000016	020512	Compare the contents of R5 with the
		number whose address is in R2.
000020	002001	Branch to 000024 if the result of
		the compare was greater than or
		equal to zero.
000022	011205	Move the number whose address is
		in R2 into R5.
000024	005300	Decrement the contents of R$\emptyset$.
000026	001371	Branch to 000012 if the result of
		decrementing R$\emptyset$ was nonzero.
000030	000000	Halt the CPU.
000032	000403$\rangle$	The numbers
000034	102304	whose
000036	023704$\rangle$	maximum
000040	007702	is to be
000042	176337$\rangle$	found are loaded here.

Figure 6.2.2

The program construction process is now complete, and we may load the program instructions and data in main memory starting at location 000000; set the PC to 000000, which is where we wish execution to begin; and start the CPU. In so doing, we had best hope that the program will execute properly the first time. For if there is something wrong with it, either in our logical development or in some of our computations, then we may have to make some repairs. Even if the repairs are conceptually minor, they may require inserting or deleting a word or two of instruction here or there. But doing so will change addresses in the program—in particular, in making even *slight* program modifications, we may be altering addresses and displacements that are parts of instructions, which we shall then also have to repair, modify, recalculate, and so forth. Thus even small changes—"small" on the surface—may require extensive rewriting.

In developing the program of this section we went into considerable detail, but a review of what we did will reveal that all of the detail was absolutely necessary. By now the reader must be asking himself if writing a machine-language program is *really* this complicated and painful. The answer is yes; in fact, it is usually much, much *worse*. Our sample program is, after all, fairly simple and very short. Imagine the problems a programmer would face if involved with a program that was hundreds or even thousands of instructions long. We advise the disheartened that help is as near as the next four sections.

At this point, one could legitimately ask: Why are we doing this? Why try to write even simple programs in machine language when convenient and easily learned languages such as BASIC, FORTRAN, and the like are available for use? There are numerous responses, and we offer two. First, recall that our primary interest here is to investigate the workings and capabilities of a modern computer; the machine's instruction set and how it operates are central to the computer's architecture. Thus we shall be using machine language in various ways to illustrate and understand many of the hardware features of computers in general and the PDP-11 in particular. The reader should also be aware that high-level languages (FORTRAN or COBOL, for example), while programmer-convenient are also somewhat inefficient because programs written in them frequently use substantially more main memory than the corresponding program written in machine language (although some recently developed languages are far more efficient in this regard than those mentioned). Thus typical high-level programs not only use more memory, but they also tend to execute more slowly because there are more instructions to process. Hence large programs that are run frequently are sometimes written in the machine's natural language to conserve space and execution time.

6.3 A MNEMONIC LANGUAGE

Having survived the painstaking instruction construction, loading, and executing of the program of the preceding section (it does execute properly, by the way), we pause for a few moments to analyze the process and, in particular, to ask ourselves what in the procedure makes program writing at this level so difficult. The individual phases seem to offer no real problems; we decided initially on an algorithmic approach to the problem of finding the maximum of a set of numbers—a conceptually simple task. Next, we wrote down the specifics of that algorithm, made some decisions about register assignments, and then wrote the actual program. In this last stage we found it necessary to look up the code for a number of machine instructions, to anticipate (rather, to postpone) some addresses, and to calculate a few displacements. None of these by itself is a particularly challenging task. However, when these details encroach on the *logic* of the program, we easily lose track of what we are trying to accomplish—the development of a sequence of machine instructions that will produce a particular effect. We are constantly distracted from the logical flow of the program by having to deal with details. For example, by the time we arrive at the point in the preceding program where the counter is to be decremented, we have probably forgotten not only which register it was, but also what its function was. Thus we must constantly backtrack not only to remind ourselves what registers and memory locations are being used for which purposes, but also to keep reviewing the program logic itself.

    Our having to stop to look up codes, calculate displacements, and so forth, not only lengthens the programming process, but also increases the chance of errors, with their attendant repairs. We might be able to avoid these if we could simply write instructions and not have to deal with these other details. Of course, we ultimately have to tend to the details if we hope ever to execute the program, but it would be desirable if we could separate the two tasks of writing the program itself and looking up codes and addresses, calculating displacements, and so forth. The former task is a creative one; the latter is merely a necessary chore. To achieve this separation of "creating the program" from "building the code"—which is really the *executable* program—most programmers invent their own private "machinelike" language. They use miniwords, or **mnemonics,** (from the Greek *mnēmonikos,* "to remember") to stand for the machine instructions. Thus, for example, if at some point in a program we need to transfer, or move, the contents of register 1 to register 4, we might write

MOV   R1,R4

instead of looking up the code (010104) for this instruction. Of course eventually we shall have to look up the code for this mnemonic instruction, but the point is that we do not have to look it up *at this time.* We can simply write down this mnemonic and move on to the next instruction. And surely, if we need to refer to this instruction later, the mnemonic MOV R1,R4 will be more meaningful to us than the machine code 010104.

    In addition to the mnemonic MOV, of course, we shall be inventing miniwords for other instructions. For instance, there is an instruction that sets a memory location or register to 0, and we might denote this instruction by CLEAR or, more briefly, CLR. We might naturally refer to branch-if-non-zero as BNZ, although in fact the standard PDP-11 mnemonic for this branch instruction is BNE (*B*ranch-if-*N*ot-*E*qual-to-zero). Similarly, BGE could stand for *B*ranch-if-*G*reater-than-or-*E*qual-to-zero. Other possible mnemonics are

INC (increment), CMP (compare), DEC (decrement), and HALT (halt, or stop-the-processor). It is important to recognize that there is nothing God-given about what mnemonics we use—we choose them as an aid to our memory. Some other programmer might prefer XFER (transfer) to MOV, ZERO to CLR, COM to CMP, and so on; so be it—programmer convenience is the key word here.

In developing these mnemonics, we must do more than simply invent miniwords to represent the instructions. We have already seen that a number of the instructions come in a variety of different forms, or *modes*. For example, we can MOV the contents of a register to another register, or we can consider the contents of a register to be an *address* and MOV the contents of that address somewhere—to a register or another memory location, for instance. In each case the basic instruction is MOV, but we are using it in slightly different ways. In fact, we used MOV in still another way in the first instruction of the program of the preceding section when we MOVed the *number* 4 into register 0. In addition to assigning the mnemonic MOV to the instruction that transfers words from one place to another, we shall have to distinguish these various different modes of use by our notation.

Let us agree to the following notation: If we are MOVing the contents of one register to another register, we shall simply write down the **source register** (the register from which the data is coming) and the **destination register** (the register to which the data is going), separated by a comma. Thus

MOV   R5,R2

stands for "move the contents of register 5 to register 2." Its machine code is 010502, and we know that the effect of this instruction is to copy the data in R5 into R2. Such copying or MOVing does not affect the contents of the source register, R5, so after the MOV both registers will have the same contents. But if, for example, we wish to move the contents of some *memory location* into a register, we simply use the numeric address of that location as the source operand. Therefore

MOV   102334,R3

means "transfer (move) a copy of the contents of the memory location whose address is 102334 into register 3 without affecting the contents of location 102334."

Suppose now we wish to move an absolute number, such as 4, into a register. Because of the decision we just made, we cannot write

MOV   4,R∅

since this means "move the *contents of memory location* 000004 into register ∅," and not, as we intended, "move the *number* 4 into register ∅." We need some new notation, and it seems fairly natural to use the number sign ($\#$) to indicate that the source is an absolute *number*. Thus

MOV   #4,R∅

There are two other ways in which we have used the general-purpose registers in some instructions, and we shall need notations for these. First, in the program of the preceding section, the contents of R2 was interpreted as the *address* of a number, rather than the number itself; and second, the compare instruction (at 000016), while it made reference to R5 and R2, was *not* a comparison of the contents of R5 with the contents of R2. Rather, it was a comparison of the contents of R5 with the contents of the memory location whose *address* was in R2. Thus we cannot write

CMP   R5,R2

since this means "compare the contents of R5 with the contents of R2." We must create some notation for this new (and, as we have seen, useful) way of using the registers. Since we have been using the notation c(. . .) to indicate "contents of," let us use (R2) to indicate that we are referring to the contents of the location whose address is in R2, rather than to the contents of R2 itself. Using this convention, we can write the compare instruction of the preceding program mnemonically as

CMP   R5,(R2)

There are still other ways in which we have used the registers. For instance, in the addition program of Fig. 5.10.1, we used R2 as the address of a number to be added, but recall that each time an addition took place, R2 was automatically incremented by 2. Thus we would need some variation on the (R2) notation we just invented to indicate this autoincrementing. The notation (R2)+ is suitable; thus

ADD   (R2)+,R5

indicates that the contents of R2 is incremented by 2 subsequent to being used as the address of the number to be added to c(R5).

6.4 THE SAMPLE PROGRAM AGAIN, WRITTEN IN MNEMONICS

We now have enough mnemonics and register notations to allow us to rewrite the program of Sec. 6.2, this time taking advantage of the instruction abbreviations we have invented. Recall that our chief purpose in creating these mnemonics was to permit us to devote our attention to the logical flow of the program instructions without the constant distraction of worrying about addresses, instruction codes, and displacements. We should find the program-writing task substantially easier and more satisfying this time around. The reader will want to refer to Fig. 6.2.2, where the complete listing of that program is shown. We include here, as any programmer is likely to do, some comments as a further assistance in keeping track of what is going on.

instruction		comments
MOV	#4,R∅	*Move the number 4 to R∅, as a counter.*
MOV	#??????,R2	*Move the* address *of the first number into R2.*

We are not off to a good start. One of the problems encountered before—the inability to anticipate the address of the first number, a so-called **forward reference**—is back to plague us, and it is just this sort of difficulty we had hoped to avoid by using the mnemonic language to write programs. We can circumvent the problem if we simply invent some symbol, such as DATA, to stand for that address. Thus DATA is simply a number, namely, the unknown address of the first of the five numbers whose maximum is to be found. Thus we may insert the instruction

MOV   #DATA,R2

here. We know from Sec. 6.2 that actually DATA = 000032, so this instruction is equivalent to

MOV   #000032,R2

Notice, incidentally, that if we had inadvertently written

MOV   DATA,R2

—the number sign (#) is missing—that this would be equivalent to

MOV   000032,R2

which, according to our notational conventions, would move the *contents* of memory location 000032—namely, the first of the five numbers—into R2. And this is not what we intend here.

Having disposed of this addressing problem, or at least postponed it, we may now continue with the program.

instruction		comment
MOV	#4,R∅	*Move the number 4 to R∅, as a counter.*
MOV	#DATA,R2	*Move the address of the first number into R2.*
MOV	(R2),R5	*Move the first number into R5 (the temporary maximum).*
INC	R2	*Increment c(R2) twice (so it will contain*
INC	R2	*the address of the second number).*
CMP	R5,(R2)	*Compare TEMPMAX with next number.*
BGE	??????	*If the result of the compare is greater than or equal to 0, branch to ??????.*

Here again we encounter the problem of a forward reference: We do not know a future address (in this case, the address of the instruction to which we want to branch). By now we know that we need to branch conditionally around the instruction that replaces the temporary maximum in R5. We can avoid this difficulty in the same way we handled the address of the first number, which we simply *called* DATA. We shall thus call the address to which we must branch by the symbolic name NEXT. This will allow us to continue with the programming and leave the actual construction of the BGE operator to a later time.

	BGE	NEXT	*If the result of the compare is greater than or equal to 0, branch to NEXT.*
	MOV	(R2),R5	*Replace TEMPMAX with current number.*
NEXT:	DEC	RØ	*Decrement the counter.*

Notice what we have done here. We realize that the instruction DEC RØ is in the memory location to which the BGE is to refer in the event that no replacement of the temporary maximum is required. Since we referred to that memory location as NEXT in the mnemonic form of the BGE, NEXT is the address of the location containing the decrement instruction. It is important to understand that NEXT is merely another name for this number. Observe also that the symbol NEXT has been placed to the *left* of the instruction itself. This is perfectly natural, for the following reason: We have not, as before, been writing in the addresses of the memory locations of the various instructions as we went along. Indeed, one of the purposes of the present approach to machine-language programming was to relieve us of this and other burdens. But if we *had* been writing in these addresses, in keeping with what has gone before, we would probably have put them out to the left to keep track of them. Thus the symbol NEXT appears in the leftmost column exactly because it *is* an address, although at the present time we neither know nor care just what its numeric value is. Finally, note that we placed a colon after the symbolic name NEXT. This is not significant; rather, it is to help us distinguish symbolic addresses such as HALT: from the instruction mnemonic HALT.

The next thing to do in the program is to branch back to the first of the two increment instructions in the event the counter is nonzero. We assign the symbolic name LOOP to this increment instruction

LOOP: INC   R2

and then insert the instruction

BNE   LOOP   *Branch back if counter nonzero.*

The only instructions remaining now are the HALT instruction (if the counter *is* 0) and the data. In inserting the data, we must not forget to assign the symbolic name DATA to the address of the first of the five numbers. We now have a finished product, shown in Fig. 6.4.1.

The heading *label* on the leftmost column is consistent with most PDP-11 terminology. These **labels** are, as we know, simply symbolic *names* for the addresses of their respective memory locations. Notice above all, that this listing of program instructions is *readable*. (Compare this with the list of machine

Label	Instruction		Comment
	MOV	#4,RØ	*Move the number 4 to RØ, as a counter.*
	MOV	#DATA,R2	*Move the address of the first*
			number into R2.
	MOV	(R2),R5	*Move the first number into R5*
			(the temporary maximum).
LOOP:	INC	R2	*Increment c(R2) twice (so it will*
	INC	R2	*contain the address of the next number).*
	CMP	R5,(R2)	*Compare TEMPMAX with next number.*
	BGE	NEXT	*If the result of the compare is*
			greater than or equal to 0,
			branch to NEXT.
	MOV	(R2),R5	*Replace TEMPMAX with current number.*
NEXT:	DEC	RØ	*Decrement the counter.*
	BNE	LOOP	*Branch back if counter nonzero.*
	HALT		*Stop if counter is 0.*
DATA:	403		*The five*
	102304		*numbers*
	23704		*whose maximum*
	7702		*is to be*
	176337		*found are loaded here.*

Figure 6.4.1

instructions in Fig. 6.2.2.) It is now fairly easy to look over this program and satisfy ourselves that it is logically correct. Again, the important feature is that we were able to write these instructions, once we were familiar with the mnemonics and other notation, concentrating only on the logic of the program without the constant distraction of having to look up codes, determine addresses, and calculate displacements.

We have now finished the creative aspects of program construction, and the day of reckoning is at hand. What we have produced is not, of course, an executable program. Rather, it is a collection of symbols (mnemonics); but the computer will execute only its own machine code. Thus we have come to the tedious process of transcribing these mnemonics into machine instructions, with all its attendant calculations and drudgery. Once we have done this, we can load main memory with the machine code and data and execute the **machine program.** Before digging into these details, we might ask, Just what has to be done at this point? The answer, as we know, is that we must look up each mnemonic (in a table, for instance) to determine its corresponding machine code and the way the instruction has been used, determine addresses, define symbol values, and calculate a variety of displacements. At this stage no knowledge of the program's logic is required. In fact, no knowledge of programming in general is necessary, only the ability to look up mnemonics and do some careful although trivial calculations. It appears that we could simply hand over the mnemonic form of the program to a clerk who has access to the table of mnemonics and ask that the program be returned some time later with the corresponding machine instructions. And this is precisely what we shall do.

6.5 ASSEMBLING THE MNEMONIC PROGRAM

In this section we shall examine in some detail the tasks confronted by our clerk in **assembling** our mnemonic program. (*Assembling* is the term normally used for the process of converting mnemonic instructions to machine-under-standable code.) Recall that the clerk has a list of the mnemonics given in Fig. 6.4.1, but we might not bother to include the comments, since these would be of no consequence to him. Remember that he has no knowledge of what the program logic is, what the program is intended to do, or even what the mnemonics mean.

As a first step, the clerk will ask where the program should be assembled. That is, at what address will the first word of the program ultimately be loaded? Since we have given him no information in this regard, he will use the value 000000 by *default*. (Recall that knowing this beginning address, and consequently all subsequent addresses, is necessary for the construction of some of the machine instructions.) Next, he might reason as follows: The mnemonic program will probably contain symbolic references, and of course those instructions will not be able to be assembled until the values of the symbols are known. Thus he will make a first pass through the program in order to determine these values. We can see what needs to be done in this regard by looking at the first few instructions of the mnemonic program of Fig. 6.4.1.

The first instruction, MOV   #4,RØ, will be located at 000000, as we noted earlier. But where should the *next* instruction, MOV   #DATA,R2, go? To determine this the clerk must know how many words of main memory will be required for the MOV   #4,RØ instruction. He can look in his table and determine that this type of MOV, that is, MOV an absolute number into a register, requires two words, although at this point he need not concern himself with what those words are. He now knows that the MOV   #DATA,R2 instruction will be located at 000004. Since he is most likely maintaining a counter to keep track of these addresses—called the **location assignmnent counter** —he will move this up to 000004 and examine the next instruction, MOV #DATA,R2. There are two things to note here. First, the instruction is again of the form "move an absolute number into a register," which he knows will take up two words of memory. Thus when he has completed his examination of this instruction, he will have to increment the location assignment counter by 4 (two words equal four bytes). But before moving on to the next instruction, he observes the presence of the symbolic name DATA. At this point he does not know its value, but since it is a program symbol, he makes a note of it in a **symbol table.** Normally he would also include in the table the *value* of the symbol, but since this is unknown, the symbol's entry in the table might look like

$$\text{DATA} \quad \text{******}$$

The asterisks indicate that its value is not known.

Now he looks at the instruction MOV   (R2),R5 and since one word is required, moves the location assignment counter up by 2. By the time the clerk encounters the first increment instruction, his worksheet will look similar to the following:

address	contents	label	mnemonic
000000			MOV #4,RØ
000002			
000004			MOV #DATA,R2
000006			
000010			MOV (R2),R5
000012		LOOP:	INC R2

(The column labeled *contents* has not been filled in. Recall that on this first pass through the mnemonic program, the clerk is concerning himself only with assigning addresses and determining the values of symbols.) Here he encounters another symbol, LOOP. And since it is not in his symbol table, he makes an appropriate entry. But notice that whereas he did not know the value of the symbol DATA, he *does* know the value of LOOP—it is 000012—and the table entry is

$$\text{LOOP} \quad 000012$$

In a similar fashion he scans the remainder of the program, assigning addresses according to his location assignment counter, inserting symbols in the table as he encounters them, and so forth. Notice how he handles the instruction

$$\text{DATA}: \quad 403$$

He recognizes that he has come upon the *definition* of the symbol DATA. Looking at his location assignment counter, he sees that DATA is another name for the address 000032. He also sees that DATA is already in the symbol table, with the (unknown) value ******. Thus he can now erase the asterisks and replace them with 000032. At the end of this first pass his worksheet looks like the following:

address	contents	label	mnemonic
000000			MOV #4,RØ
000002			
000004			MOV #DATA,R2
000006			
000010			MOV (R2),R5
000012		LOOP:	INC R2
000014			INC R2
000016			CMP R5,(R2)

address	contents	label	mnemonic
000020			BGE NEXT
000022			MOV (R2),R5
000024		NEXT:	DEC RØ
000026			BNE LOOP
000030			HALT
000032		DATA:	403
000034			102304
000036			23704
000040			7702
000042			176337

and the symbol table has the following entries, in the order in which they were encountered:

DATA   000032
LOOP   000012
NEXT   000024

He is now ready to do the actual assembly—generate the machine code for each of the instructions—and since each of the symbols is now defined, he should have no difficulty filling in the Contents column. Since we have been through that process in detail previously, we shall not include it here. The clerk will then return the completed worksheet to us, we can load the machine code into main memory, beginning at 000000, and execute the machine program.

Before we leave this section, a few comments are in order. Suppose that we had inadvertently neglected to place the label NEXT on the DEC   RØ instruction. When the clerk first encountered this symbol in the BGE   NEXT instruction, he would have placed it in the symbol table thus, indicating that its value was presently unknown,

NEXT   ******

By the time he finished the first pass, the symbol table would be

DATA   000032
LOOP   000012
NEXT   ******

On the *second* pass, during which the actual machine code is generated, all would be well until he attempted to assemble the instruction BGE   NEXT. Since he must calculate a word offset to go in the low-order byte of the BGE operator, and since he knows the current address—the value of the location assignment counter—he needs to have only the value of NEXT to complete the instruction. Looking in the symbol table, he finds that NEXT has *never* been defined, and thus he will not be able to assemble this instruction. To let us know about this problem, he flags this instruction on his worksheet with an error code, the *U* standing for "reference to an *U*ndefined symbol."

U   000020   *??????*   **BGE NEXT**

As a second example of how things can go wrong, suppose that we had used the identical label, for example, ANSWER:, *more than once* in the mnemonic program. This can happen, especially if the program is fairly long. Assume that we had used this label at 000046 and at 000162. The first time the clerk encounters ANSWER: he looks in the symbol table. Either the symbol ANSWER is not in the table, in which case he makes an entry for it with the value 000046, or it *is* in the table with the value ∗∗∗∗∗∗ (having been referenced earlier), in which case he erases the asterisks and replaces them with 000046. But now at 000162 he *again* encounters ANSWER:. Looking in the symbol table, he finds the entry

ANSWER   000046

and now he does not know which of these values we intended for this symbol. This is a situation with which he cannot cope, and the best he can do is indicate somehow that we have passed him a program containing a multiply-defined symbol.

Next, suppose in our hurry to get the program to the clerk we had forgotten to insert the HALT instruction—more careful review of the finished product would have avoided this. But can we expect the clerk to detect this *logical* error? Certainly not. He knows nothing of programming; his job is to assign addresses, look up instructions, and maintain a symbol table. He cannot be expected to criticize the logical flow of the program. He will return the worksheet to us, having done his job properly with no indication that anything is wrong. Notice, incidentally, that because of the missing HALT instruction in this case, he would have assigned the symbol DATA the value 000030. We would not find out that something was amiss until we loaded the program and executed it. We would have to examine the program logic, notice the missing HALT instruction, insert it in the mnemonic program, and return it to the clerk for another assembly.

Finally, suppose we had made the mistake of writing BNZ LOOP instead of BNE LOOP. When he encountered this line in the program, the clerk would have to announce that he could not find the mnemonic BNZ in his table of mnemonics and that consequently he could not generate any code for it.

We commented earlier that once the clerk's worksheet was returned to us (without any error flags), we could load it into main memory beginning at location 000000. Notice that we could *not* whimsically load it elsewhere, at 001000, for instance, without suffering some consequences. For at location 000006 the clerk has correctly placed the address 000032 of the first word of data. If we try to load the program *as is* at 001000, then the five data words would be in main memory starting at 001032, not at 000032. That is, the MOV #DATA,R2 instruction would put 000032 in R2, and the program upon execution would then be working on five memory locations that are not within our program. Of course, if we were really adamant about loading the program at 001000, we could change the word at 000006 from 000032 to 001032, but in a long program it might be difficult to find the many words that would require such repairing. In brief, we are asking for trouble by trying to move the program away from its intended location, and we are introducing complications—precisely what we have been trying to eliminate in this and the preceding section.

6.6 THE PDP-11 ASSEMBLER

Let us review very briefly the tasks required of our clerk of the preceding section. He needed to initialize a location assignment counter (to 000000) and then maintain it by incrementing it by 2 or 4 as he processed each instruction. He had to be able to look up mnemonics in a table, by doing matches or compares, and recognize some notations, such as # and (. .). He had to recognize the use of symbols, which was a fairly easy task—symbol usage appears in an instruction following an operator mnemonic, and is neither an absolute number nor a register designation. Symbol definition—the use of labels—was also a trivial matter. We assisted him in this regard by putting a colon after labels or symbol definitions. While there are a few additional jobs to which he had to attend, there appears to be nothing in the process that could not be done by the computer itself if it executed an appropriate program. This program would have to scan the lines of the mnemonic program—the so-called **source program**—do table look-ups (undoubtedly with the help of the CMP operator), calculate displacements (using SUB—SUBtract), and so forth. Its output—the **object program**—would, of course, be the machine code for the source (mnemonic) program. Such a translating program is called an **assembler**, and its job would be *precisely* that of our clerk.

Writing an assembler would not be a trivial task. While it is easy to state that the assembling clerk's job is quite straightforward, it is another matter altogether to write a *program* that can scan a line of mnemonics, recognize the various components (such as labels, operators, and register symbols), correctly maintain a location assignment counter, and so forth. But the rewards upon its completion would be great. First, we would be able to dispense with our clerk—clerks, most likely, since a single programmer would be able to keep several clerks busy. And second, we would also get our assemblies in a matter of minutes rather than hours or days because computers work faster than people.

Fig. 6.6.1 shows the output of the PDP-11 assembler for the mnemonic program, or **assembly language program**, as it is usually called, that we have been discussing in this chapter. The conventions used by the PDP-11 assembler are in Appendix D. Note that the assembler has printed each line of mnemonics, or **source code**. This is strictly for our convenience, so that we have a printed copy of each line of instruction and can see how the assembler dealt with it. Next, observe that the assembler has assigned each line of source code a (decimal) line number—the numbers in the leftmost column. Again, this is for programmer convenience. The next column contains the addresses .at which each instruction was assembled, followed by the contents of those memory locations. Note, however, that if an instruction consists of more than one word, the assembler prints only the address of the first of those words. Thus, for instance, in the first instruction of the program—MOV   #4,R∅— we do not see listed the address 000002 in which the number 000004 has been placed. Finally, notice the last line, .END. This is a "statement" we included to indicate to the assembler that it has come to the end of the source program. (We did not do this for our clerk who would assume that when he ran out of mnemonics, the first pass was completed.) The statement. END is *not* a program (machine) instruction, and in fact the assembler did not generate a code for it, nor did it even assign it an address. In contrast to a machine instruction, .END is a statement that directs the assembler to do something—in particular, to stop assembling, since there is no more program. We call this type of statement an **assembler directive**, and we shall see several more of these informational statements in the course of the text. They are easily recognized, since they begin with a dot.

```
 1 000000   012700           MOV    #4,R∅
                000004
 2 000004   012702           MOV    #DATA,R2
                000032
 3 000010   011205           MOV    (R2),R5
 4 000012   005202   LOOP:    INC    R2
 5 000014   005202           INC    R2
 6 000016   020512           CMP    R5,(R2)
 7 000020   002001           BGE    NEXT
 8 000022   011205           MOV    (R2),R5
 9 000024   005300   NEXT:    DEC    R∅
10 000026   001371           BNE    LOOP
11 000030   000000           HALT
12 000032   000403   DATA:    403    403
13 000034   102304           102304
14 000036   023704           23704
15 000040   007702           7702
16 000042   176337           176337
17                           .END
```

Figure 6.6.1

Recall that we commented earlier that the choice of mnemonics is strictly up to the programmer, who can devise any miniwords that make it easiest to remember the hardware instruction to which that mnemonic refers. If the programmer later decides that some other mnemonic might be more suggestive of an instruction than the one originally selected, the change would cause no great problem. But now that a machine-language *program* is doing the assembly, and that program contains a list, in a table, perhaps, of the valid mnemonics, a change in the mnemonics would require a modification of the program (assembler) itself. While this can be done, normally it is not; once we select a set of mnemonics and write an assembler to recognize them, we usually stick with them indefinitely. The PDP-11 assembler mnemonics are listed in Appendix A.

6.7 A MODIFICATION OF THE SAMPLE PROGRAM

The reader may have observed that one of the deficiencies of *all* of the programs so far is that the program simply directed the processor to stop (HALT) after performing the required calculations. Thus while the answer was known and resided in some register or memory location, we made no provision for the program somehow to *announce* the result. We conclude this chapter with a modification of the maximizing program in which the maximum of the five numbers is actually printed, although in so doing we probably raise more questions than we answer. Also, we play a bit more fair with the reader as concerns the listings produced by the assembler—they are more involved than the simple listing shown in Fig. 6.6.1.

Referring to Fig. 6.7.1, we note that **comments** have been included on

```
MAXIMUM

 1                              .TITLE  MAXIMUM
 2                              ;
 3 000000  012700  START:  MOV    #4,R0           ;SET FOR 4 COMPARES
           000004
 4 000004  012702          MOV    #DATA,R2        ;ADDR OF 1ST NO. IN R2
           000074'
 5 000010  011205          MOV    (R2),R5         ;1ST NO. = TEMPMAX
 6 000012  005202  LOOP:   INC    R2              ;INCREMENT THE
 7 000014  005202          INC    R2              ; ADDRESS IN R2 BY 2
 8 000016  020512          CMP    R5,(R2)         ;COMPARE TEMPMAX WITH NO.
 9 000020  002001          BGE    NEXT            ;TEMPMAX BIGGER -- SKIP
10 000022  011205          MOV    (R2),R5         ;REPLACE TEMPMAX
11 000024  005300  NEXT:   DEC    R0              ;DECREMENT COUNTER
12 000026  001371          BNE    LOOP            ;MORE NOS. IF NONZERO
13 000030  010567          MOV    R5,ANSWER       ;GET THE MAXIMUM
           000036
14 000034                  $OUT.OCT #ANSWER,#1   ; AND PRINT IT
15 000070                  $EXIT                  ;RETURN TO OP. SYSTEM
16                              ;
17 000072          ANSWER: .BLKW 1                ;FOR PRINTING MAX
18                              ;
19                              ;THE 5 NUMBERS TO BE MAXIMIZED
20                              ;
21 000074  000403  DATA:   .WORD 403
22 000076  102304          .WORD 102304
23 000100  023704          .WORD 23704
24 000102  007702          .WORD 7702
25 000104  176337          .WORD 176337
26                              ;
27         000000'          .END  START


MAXIMUM
SYMBOL TABLE

ANSWER  000072R      LOOP    000012R      START   000000R
DATA    000074R      NEXT    000024R      $.... = ****** G
```

Figure 6.7.1

many of the lines of source code. The assembler will tolerate these, provided they are preceded by a semicolon. In fact, once the assembler detects the presence of a semicolon, it assumes that it has come to the end of the line of source code. The assembler does nothing with a comment but saves it to be printed later on the program listing. This is another instance of the assembler's doing something strictly for the convenience of the programmer; clearly, the comments are not essential to the generation of machine code. As we see from lines 2 and 19, for example, entire lines may be treated as comments if the semicolon is the first character of the line. Comments, while not essential, are extremely useful in making the mnemonic program more readable and in pointing out the flow of the logic of the program.

Next, observe line 1: .TITLE   MAXIMUM. Here is another example of an assembler *directive:* We are directing the assembler to do something for us other than translate mnemonics, namely, to title or name the source program. Again, this feature is of no real substance; programs need not be titled. However, if the program *is* titled, the title word or words will appear in the *listing header* at the top of each page of the listing. (While we have shown only the title here in the listing header, there is in fact other useful information printed in the header, such as the date and time the listing was printed. Most of these details are self-explanatory.) If no .TITLE directive is given, the assembler supplies .MAIN. as a default title.

The statement at line 14,

$$\text{\$OUT.OCT   \#ANSWER,\#1}$$

requires a great deal of explanation, much of which we are unable to give at this time. Nonetheless we can make some educated guesses about it. According to the comment on this line, evidently we are printing the maximum number here. Thus we might conjecture that $OUT.OCT stands for *OUT*put in *OCT*al format, that the word to be output is in the memory location whose symbolic address is ANSWER, and that one (#1) number is to be printed. All of these conjectures are correct, and if the program is executed we shall see printed

$$023704$$

(Remember that 102304 and 176337 are *negative.*)

Despite the fact that $OUT.OCT   #ANSWER,#1 might look somewhat like the PDP-11 assembler mnemonic for some machine instruction, an examination of the instruction set (Appendix A) reveals that it is not. Nor is it an assembler directive, which normally begins with a dot. Equally curious is the fact that whatever $OUT.OCT really is, it apparently takes up a good bit of memory—000034 to 000066—which is 34_8 bytes, or $16_8 = 14_{10}$ words. The best we can say at this point is that $OUT.OCT is a **macroinstruction** that consists of a number of ordinary PDP-11 machine instructions, which along with their machine code have not been listed, although the assembler has placed that code in these memory locations. The details of how to use this and the other input/output commands for performing data transfers are in Appendix B.

Line 15 contains another macroinstruction, $EXIT, although here we note that this macroinstruction takes up only one word (two bytes) of main memory. Again, the code for the instruction is not listed, but the assembler has filled in that code at location 000070. At this point the best we can say is that $EXIT should be included in any program when we wish *execution* to cease. (Here we are again looking ahead to the time when the program is actually loaded into main memory and executed, even though we are currently in the preliminary assembly phase.) In past examples, when we were through with program execution, we merely instructed the processor to HALT. $EXIT takes the place of the previously used HALT instruction and provides an orderly end to program execution and returns control of the processor to the **operating system**—the environment within which our program will be running.

At line 17, .BLKW (*BLocK* of *Words*) is again an assembler directive, and it requires a little explanation. Recall that as the assembler scans the source program, it maintains a location assignment counter. As the assembler processes each instruction, it moves the counter up by 2 or more, but always by an even number, so that its value will be the address of the memory location of the next instruction. The directive .BLKW   n directs the assembler, at this point, to increment its location assignment counter by 2n, which leaves a 2n-byte (n-word) gap in the object program. The presumption is that the programmer needs some words of storage in the program, that he or she does not care what is in these words, and that *once the program begins execution* these words will be filled in with meaningful data. This is precisely the case here. We are directing the assembler to set aside one word (two bytes) of storage at location 000072 so that upon execution, once the maximum has been found, it can be moved into this location (line 13: MOV   R5,ANSWER) and printed.

Another assembler directive, similar to .BLKW, is .WORD, found in lines 21 to 25. Here, however, instead of directing the assembler to *skip over* a word of main memory, we are requesting that it place a specified value in that word. Thus .WORD   403 at 000074 directs the assembler to insert the word 000403 at memory location 000074, which, as we see, it has done. The reader may be somewhat puzzled by the fact that in the listing of Fig. 6.6.1 (see lines 12 to 16), no .WORD directive was given; rather, the desired numbers were simply inserted into the source code at this point. The reason that the assembler seems to have handled this properly is that when the assembler encounters a line of source code that consists (apart from a possible label) exclusively of a number or numbers, it *defaults* to .WORD. Thus the use of .WORD in these circumstances is optional. In the remainder of the text we shall use .WORD when it appears to be useful to be explicit, otherwise we shall allow the assembler default to take over. If more than one word needs to be generated by the source program, it is permissible to put a string of numbers on the same line of source code, separated by commas. Thus lines 21 to 25 of this program could as well (and more easily) have been written as

DATA :   .WORD   403,102304,23704,7702,176337

or even

DATA :   403,102304,23704,7702,176337

Either of these would establish the specified numbers at locations 000074 to 000104, in the order given.

At the .END statement of line 27, note that the address START has been included. This is where the program is to begin execution. Since the task of the assembler is simply to translate mnemonics and build machine code, but certainly *not* to *execute* the program, the start address has no meaning to it. This start address is frequently referred to as the **transfer address**, that is, the address to which control is to be transferred when execution begins. Nonetheless, the assembler will make a note of this start address for future reference. Just *how*, or *by whom* this start address will be referenced will be made clear somewhat later. Most programs have start or transfer addresses in their .END statements, but there are exceptions.

Another matter needs attention here. The assembler has placed the number 000074 at location 000006, the second word of the MOV #DATA,R2 instruction. This corresponds to the reference in the instruction to the number DATA, and indeed we see that DATA does in fact have the value 000074. However, that value has been flagged with an apostrophe (000074'). The flag has to do with something to which we alluded earlier; that this particular number (the 000074 at 000006) would require repairing if the object program was **relocated**—that is, if the program was loaded at some address other than 000000. (See page 103.) The assembler was able to detect which words would no longer be correct upon program relocation and indicated these on the listing with the apostrophe as a further assistance to the programmer.

Finally, the symbol table is reasonably straightforward. Recall that it was necessary for the assembler to build this table on its first pass in order to know various symbolic addresses and to calculate needed displacements. The table is printed by the assembler for our reference. Notice that the symbols are listed in alphabetic order by columns. Each user-defined symbol is listed, along with the value assigned to it by the assembler. The reader should verify that the symbol values are correct by examining the listing. The R following each symbol value stands for *relocatable*. That is, these symbols have values that are sensitive to program relocation. If the program is moved about in main memory, the values of these symbols will change. Consequently, certain references to them will have to be repaired, as was the reference to the address DATA at location 000006.

There is room for one more obscurity. The "name" $. . . . appears in the symbol table, although in a slightly different format,

$$\$. . . . = ******G$$

This is surely not a user-defined symbol, as a glance at the program listing reveals. In fact, the asterisks seem to indicate, according to our previous discussion of symbols and their values, that the symbol $. . . . was never defined in the program. All of this is true, and yet the assembler seems not to have been perturbed by encountering an undefined symbol. In fact, $. . . . is a symbol used within the macroinstruction $OUT.OCT.

It appears that in giving this rather complete assembler listing of the program we have opened a can of worms, not all of which have been disposed of. While this might be somewhat disturbing to the reader, it is also unavoidable. These mysteries will gradually be unveiled. And while we normally avoid statements such as "don't worry about these details right now," this is probably the best advice we can give at the present time.

6.8 EXERCISES

6.2.1. Write (English-language) algorithms as in the beginning of Sec. 6.2 to do the following tasks. (The reader familiar with a high-level programming language—BASIC or Pascal, for example—may wish to complete the process and transcribe the algorithm into a program.)

(a) Find the sum of the positive integers between 1 and 10 inclusive.

(b) Find the sum of the *odd* positive integers between 1 and 9 inclusive.

(c) Put a collection of 7 integers into increasing order.

(d) Given a collection of 12 positive integers, find the *first* of the numbers that is *odd*; if none such exists, report that all the numbers are even.

6.2.2. Explain how the forward reference problem, encountered when we attempted to move the address of the first of the 5 numbers to be maximized into R2 (see page 87), could have been eliminated if we had decided to load the five numbers *ahead* of (in front of) the program instructions rather than behind them. There was another forward reference encountered in building this program, namely, the branch instruction at 000020 (see page 89). Could that forward reference have been eliminated by changing or rearranging the program steps?

6.2.3. On page 92 it was stated that since the high-order byte of the branch-if-greater-than-or-equal-to-0 instruction is 004 and the displacement (low-order byte) is 001, the instruction code becomes 002001. Why should it not be 004001 instead?

6.2.4. How should the program of Sec. 6.2 be modified if the *minimum* of seven numbers is to be found?

6.2.5. Normally when a program executes, the contents of the general-purpose registers (R0 to R5) are not known until and unless the program itself sets one or more of these registers to some specific values (such as MOV #4,R0, for example). Write a machine-language program to increment register 2 repeatedly until its value is 0. Then the program is to halt. (Note that the initial value of R2 is not known.) Will the program run *indefinitely* if R2 has an initial value that is *positive*? Why or why not? What will the program do if R2's initial value just happens to be 0?

7

Operator Formats and
Addressing Modes

7.1 OPERATORS AND INSTRUCTIONS

In Chapter 5 we informally noted the distinction between an *operator*—one of the actions of which the CPU is capable—and an *instruction*—an operator, along with the registers or memory locations, or both, on which it operates. In this chapter we shall expand upon and be more precise about these notions.

So far, and especially in the preceding chapter, we called upon operators and instructions as needed, and while we explained exactly what they *do*, nonetheless our approach has been somewhat disorganized. For example, in some cases the 16-bit word affected by an operator was a register, and in others it was the memory location whose *address* is in a register. Similarly, sometimes an operator automatically incremented the contents of a register and sometimes not. We saw uses of the single operator MOV, in which the word being moved was an absolute number (MOV #4,RØ), the contents of a register (MOV R1,R4), or the contents of the memory location whose address was in the register (MOV (R2),R5). If the reader has the impression that there are many different ways in which a single operator may be used, he is quite correct. On the other hand, the situation is not nearly so chaotic as we have represented it. Indeed, we shall show that far from being chaotic, the situation is quite well structured and fairly simple.

7.2 INSTRUCTION TYPES AND OPERATOR FORMATS

In the few sample programs thus far, we saw that some instructions require two words of memory; for example,

> 012700   MOV   #4,RØ
> 000004

Others require only one word, such as

> 011205   MOV   (R2),R5

or

> 000000   HALT

The addition instruction in the program of Fig. 5.8.1 requires *three* words, including two addresses, which is as many words as instructions ever use. In each case, the *first* of the (one, two, or three) words specifies the operation itself—that is, what action is to be taken by the CPU—while any additional words in the instruction supply further needed information, such as an absolute number or an address.

The operation portion of an instruction—that is, the first (or only) word of the instruction—may occur in a number of different formats. First, each operator word contains some number of bits that specify to the CPU *what* the operation is. A little review will reveal, for example, that although we used the MOV operation in a number of different ways, *each* of the operators that performs a MOV is of the form

$$01XXXX$$

or, in binary,

$$0\ 001\ xxx\ xxx\ xxx\ xxx$$

It is precisely the leading 4 bits, 0001, that inform the CPU that a MOV is to be performed. In a similar way, the increment operator INC is of the form

$$0052XX$$

or

$$0\ 000\ 101\ 010\ xxx\ xxx$$

In this case, 10 bits, 0000101010, specify the INC operation. Finally, we saw one operator, HALT, in which all 16 bits determine the operation 000000 = 0 000 000 000 000 000. The best we can say about this situation is that the bits of an operator that determine the CPU's action will always number at least 4, may be as many as all 16, but in any event will always be the *leading* (high-order) bits of the operator word. However many, those bits that determine what operation is to be performed by the processor are called the **operation-code bits**, or **op-code bits** for short, or, even more simply, the **op-code** of the operation.

If not all the bits of an operation word are used for op-code bits, what information is transmitted in the remaining bits? We should like to give a straightforward answer to this question, but unfortunately the bits not used for op-code are used in a variety of ways that depend to a large extent on the operation itself. With a few exceptions, in general, the remaining bits are used to specify some register, or some offset, or a combination of these, or they are of no significance to the operation—that is, they are *unused*. All of this seems to belie our claim of the last section that operations are fairly simple and decently structured. If the reader will bear with us for a bit, he will see that the vast majority of operations *are* indeed quite well behaved; the exceptions will then cause us very little trouble.

7.3 THE CONDITIONAL BRANCHES

Aside from the few operations in which all 16 bits are used to specify the operator (HALT, NOP, CLC, and so forth), the structurally simplest operations are the conditional branches and the unconditional branch, BR. We shall say little here about them, except by way of review, since we discussed the operator branch-if-nonzero in detail in Chapter 5, where we noted that *all* of these branch operations are formed in an identical fashion.

Recall that the branch operations are of the form (in binary)

$$0 \ 000 \ 000 \ o \ xx \ xxx \ xxx$$

where the *o*'s represent the op-code (0 000 001 0, in the case of BNE), and the *x*'s represent the signed word offset. Thus if the conditional branch *is* to be executed, then the signed 8-bit offset, *times* 2, is added to the current contents of the PC.

7.4 ONE- AND TWO-OPERAND INSTRUCTIONS

An **operand** associated with an operation is some word or byte location on which the operation operates. That location might be a register or memory location, for example. Some operations operate on a *single* operand—CLR   R2,   DEC   RØ, and NEG   R3 are three examples. Others such as MOV   R1,R4 or ADD   (R2)+,R5, need *two* operands.

Some terminology will be useful here, and we introduce it by examining the familiar MOV instruction. When we write

MOV   R1,R4

we are MOVing a number *from* register 1 *to* register 4. For this reason R1 is called the **source** of the MOV operation and R4 is called the **destination**. If we let *SS* represent the 6 bits making up the source, and *DD* the 6 bits comprising the destination, we may write the MOV operation as

$$0 \ 1 \ S \ S \ D \ D$$

or in binary, expanding the notation somewhat,

$$0 \ 001 \ sss \ sss \ ddd \ ddd$$

In a similar fashion, if an operation has only one operand (such as CLR), we usually refer to it as the destination and write, as the code for CLR, for example,

$$0 \ 0 \ 5 \ 0 \ D \ D$$

or

$$0 \ 000 \ 101 \ 000 \ ddd \ ddd$$

7.5 ADDRESSING MODES

Since the MOV operation is by now so familiar to us, we shall use it as an example to introduce the main topic of this section. We have already noted that in the instruction MOV R1,R4, R1 is the source and R4 is the destination of the operation. In fact, the code for this instruction is 010104 and it is not difficult to pick this code apart as a 16-bit word.

0 001	000 001	000 100
MOV	R1 =	R4 =
op code	source	destination

What is puzzling here, however, is why *six* bits have been allocated for the specification of each of the source and destination registers, when *any* register—R∅ to R7—can be specified in *three* bits—000 to 111. But specifying the register to be used is *not* sufficient to determine the source or the destination or both. To see why, let us review the principal example of Chapter 6—the program to find the largest of five numbers.

Recall that it was necessary to MOV the number whose address was in R2 into R5, first to give R5 an initial value, and then later to replace R5's value with a new value, in the event that a larger number had been encountered. The mnemonic for that instruction is MOV (R2),R5, and its octal code is 011205. But notice that we are *not* MOVing the contents of R2 to R5. Rather, we are using the contents of R2 as the address of the memory location whose contents is to be MOVed to R5. Indeed, from what we said above, we should expect (correctly) that the code for MOV R2,R5 would be

$$0 \ 001 \qquad 000 \ 010 \qquad 000 \ 101$$

However, we have just stated that the code for MOV (R2),R5 is

0 001	001 010	000 101
MOV	(R2) =	R5 =
op code	source	destination

Evidently the 3 bits in the source—001—specify the *way* in which R2 is used as a source—the contents of R2 is not the source, but rather the contents of the memory location whose *address* is in R2 is the source. Thus of the 6 bits specifying a source or destination register, the first 3 bits determine the way in which the register is used—the **addressing mode** of the register. Thus we may view the source or the destination bits of an operation as follows:

m m m	r r r
mode bits	register bits

There are clearly eight possible register modes that can occupy these mode bits (0 to 7—000 to 111), and in fact they are all in use. Likewise there are eight possible registers, R0 to R7, that can be specified in the register bits. The reader will recall that we referred to R0 to R5 as *general-purpose* registers, R7 (PC) enjoys a somewhat distinguished position as the program counter, and we have not mentioned R6. In the remainder of this section, in which we discuss addressing-modes, we shall *include* R6 as one of the permitted registers, with an occasional mention of one of its peculiarities, but we shall *exclude* from consideration the program counter, R7. The reason for setting R7 aside here is *not* that what we are about to say fails to apply to R7. Rather, R7 has one feature that makes it something of a special case—it is *incremented* (by 2) by the CPU whenever a *fetch* is done. The effects of the addressing modes for the PC will be taken up in the next section.

Some additional terminology will be useful in this and subsequent sections. The **effective location** (EL), sometimes referred to in the PDP-11 literature as the EA—effective address—is the 8-bit byte or 16-bit word used as the source or destination of an operation. Thus, for instance, in CLR   R1, R1 is the EL, whereas in DEC   (R3), the EL is the 16-bit word whose *address* is in R3. Similarly, for MOV   (R2),R5, the *source* EL is the word whose address is in R2, while the *destination* EL is R5.

- Mode 0   (000)
  Name: **Register** (or **direct register**) **mode**
  Symbol: Rn

In mode 0 the EL is the specified register itself. This is the simplest of all the addressing modes. Thus, for example, the operation that decrements the contents of register 3, DEC   R3, is coded as

$$\underbrace{0 \ \ 000 \ \ 101 \ \ 011}_{\text{decrement op code}} \quad \underbrace{000 \ \ \underbrace{011}_{\text{reg 3}}}_{\substack{\text{mode 0} \\ \text{destination}}} = 005303$$

Likewise, the operation that transfers (MOV) the contents of R5 to R2, is coded as

$$\underbrace{0 \ \ 001}_{\substack{\text{move} \\ \text{op code}}} \quad \underbrace{000 \ \ \underbrace{101}_{\text{reg 5}}}_{\substack{\text{mode 0} \\ \text{source}}} \quad \underbrace{000 \ \ \underbrace{010}_{\text{reg 2}}}_{\substack{\text{mode 0} \\ \text{destination}}} = 010502$$

- Mode 1   (001)
  Name: **Register deferred mode**
  Symbol: (Rn)

In mode 1 the EL is the 8-bit byte or 16-bit word whose *address* is in the specified register. Thus, for example, if R3 contains the number 014622 and R3 is referenced in mode 1, then the 8-bit byte or 16-bit word that is the source or destination of the operation is the 8-bit byte or 16-bit word whose address is 014622. It is important to note here that the EL is *not* the register itself—the register holds the address of the EL. As an example, we look at an instruction of the principal program of Chapter 6 (Fig. 6.6.1, line 3).

Suppose register 2 contains the number 000032, that is, C(R2) = 000032, and the memory location whose address is 000032 contains 000403 (c(000032) = 000403). Then the instruction MOV (R2),R5 will have as its machine code

$$
\underbrace{0 \;\; 0\,0\,1}_{\substack{\text{move} \\ \text{op code}}} \quad \underbrace{\underbrace{0\,0\,1}_{\text{mode 1}} \; \underbrace{0\,1\,0}_{\text{reg 2}}}_{\text{source}} \quad \underbrace{\underbrace{0\,0\,0}_{\text{mode 0}} \; \underbrace{1\,0\,1}_{\text{reg 5}}}_{\text{destination}} = 011205
$$

After *execution* of this instruction, we shall have c(R2) = 000032, c(000032) = 000403, and c(R5) = 000403.

- Mode 2   (010)
  Name: **Autoincrement mode**
  Symbol: (Rn)+

In mode 2 the effective location is the same as in mode 1—the specified register contains the *address* of the EL. The only difference between mode 1 and mode 2 is that *immediately after* accessing the register to obtain the address of the EL, the CPU *automatically increments* the contents of the specified register. The autoincrementing is by 1 if the operation is a *byte* instruction (such as INCB) and by 2 if the operation is a *word* instruction (such as MOV or CLR). In the case of byte operations, there are two exceptions: R6 and R7 (PC). These two registers are *always* incremented by 2, never by 1, *even though* the instruction that references them is a byte instruction.* In the case of R7 it is fairly obvious why incrementing should always be by 2. Recall that the PC is always pointing at the next *word* to be processed, therefore R7 should always contain an *even* (word) address. We shall say more about this in the next section. Just why R6 should be a special case in this regard will not be evident until we examine the desirability of this peculiar action in the next chapter.

For an example of mode 2, let us return to the last (mode 1) example and recall that c(R2) = 000032, c(000032) = 000403. Consider the instruction MOV (R2)+,R5, whose code is

$$
\underbrace{0 \;\; 0\,0\,1}_{\substack{\text{move} \\ \text{op code}}} \quad \underbrace{\underbrace{0\,1\,0}_{\text{mode 2}} \; \underbrace{0\,1\,0}_{\text{reg 2}}}_{\text{source}} \quad \underbrace{\underbrace{0\,0\,0}_{\text{mode 0}} \; \underbrace{1\,0\,1}_{\text{reg 5}}}_{\text{destination}} = 012205
$$

*Some models of the PDP-11 family of processors do not treat autoincrementing and autodecrementing (mode 4) in the cases of R6 and R7 precisely as described here. A discussion of the architectural differences that result in any such discrepancies is beyond the scope of the present text. However, we shall see that these differences are handled by the processor in such a way that they have no substantive effect on the sample programs, text material, or the programming that the reader might do.

After *execution*, we have c(R2) = 000034, because of the autoincrementing, c(000032) = 000403, and c(R5) = 000403. If the instruction had been a "move *byte*" instead—112205—then the only difference would be that after execution, R2 would contain the number 000033 because of the byte form of the instruction, and R5 would contain 000003. (Why?)

To indicate just *when* in the course of executing an autoincrementing instruction the incrementing takes place, consider the following (admittedly somewhat bizarre) instruction: MOV (R4)+,(R4)+. The machine code for this instruction is 012424. Assume that prior to execution of this instruction, c(R4) = 002642 and that c(002642) = 147306. When the CPU references R4 to obtain the *source* EL—that is, when the CPU obtains the address 002642 of the source—it *then* autoincrements c(R4) by 2. Thus by this time, c(R4) = 002644. The CPU can at this point access the *number* to be MOVed, namely 147306. The *destination* of the MOV operation is the memory location whose address is *currently* in R4—that is, 002644. Then c(R4) is again autoincremented by 2 to 002646. Thus we find that the source address is 002642, its contents is 147306, and the destination address is 002644. At the end of the execution, we have c(R4) = 002646, c(002642) = 147306, and c(002644) = 147306. As strange as this example might seem (and it, or at least instructions with a similar structure, are not so outrageous as may appear), it does point out just *when* in the course of executing the instruction the CPU increments the register contents. This can be of great significance to us in some of our programming.

Although we saw this addressing mode and its usefulness in an earlier example (the addition program of Chapter 5), it will be helpful to discuss again the principal use of autoincrement mode addressing. Suppose we have a collection of numbers in *consecutive* memory locations. By MOVing the address of the first of these numbers into some register, R3 for example, and then referencing R3 in autoincrement mode, we can step through the consecutive numbers. Specifically, a reference to (R3) will, of course, be a reference to the first of the numbers. But a reference to (R3)+ will not only refer to the first number, it will also automatically adjust R3 so that it is then pointing at the second number—more precisely, after the autoincrementing, R3 will contain the address of the second number. Notice that this discussion holds whether the numbers are considered as full words, with reference to R3 made by a word-type instruction, or as single bytes, with reference to R3 made by a byte-type instruction. This happens for us automatically because the incrementing is by 2 or 1, respectively.

We offer a final example (Fig. 7.5.1). Suppose we have seven 16-bit numbers in consecutive memory locations, and we give the first location the symbolic name VECTOR. We wish to find out how many of the numbers are *greater than* their immediate successors in the list. Thus, for example, if the numbers in the given order are

000017   102333   002110   000644   000023   007441   100031 then there are four numbers that are greater than their successors. Specifically, 000017 is greater than 102333 (since 102333 is negative), 002110 is greater than 000644, 000644 is greater than 000023, and 007441 is greater than 100031. Shown below is a complete program to do this little task.

```
 1 000000  005000    START:  CLR    RØ          ;'GREATER THAN' COUNTER
 2 000002  012701            MOV    #6,R1       ;'PAIR' COUNTER
           000006
 3 000006  012703            MOV    #VECTOR,R3  ;ADDR. OF 1ST NUMBER
           000026'
 4 000012  022313    LOOP:   CMP    (R3)+,(R3)  ;COMP. NO. TO NEXT NO.
 5 000014  003401            BLE    CONT        ;LESS THAN OR =
 6 000016  005200            INC    RØ          ;INCREMENT COUNTER
 7 000020  005301    CONT:   DEC    R1          ;MORE PAIRS TO DO?
 8 000022  001373            BNE    LOOP        ;YES -- DO NEXT PAIR
 9 000024  000000            HALT               ;NO -- STOP
10                                              ;
11 000026  000017    VECTOR: 000017             ;THE
12 000030  102333            102333             ; NUMBERS
13 000032  002110            002110             ; TO
14 000034  000644            000644             ; BE
15 000036  000023            000023             ; COMPARED
16 000040  007441            007441             ; IN
17 000042  100031            100031             ; PAIRS
18                                              ;
19         000000'          .END    START
```

Figure 7.5.1

Notice first that at line 1, RØ is cleared to 0 and will act as a counter to keep track of the number of pairs in which the first number is larger than the second. And although there are seven numbers, R1 is set to 6 (line 2) since there are only six consecutive *pairs* of numbers. Then the symbolic address VECTOR, whose value is 000026, is moved into R3. The heart of the program is at line 4: CMP   (R3)+,(R3).

The first time this instruction is executed, the CPU looks at the contents of R3—000026—to get the *address* of the first of the two numbers to be compared. It then autoincrements the contents of R3 to 000030, incrementing by 2, since CMP is a *word* instruction. Thus the first of the numbers to be compared is 000017. Next, the CPU uses R3 again as the address of the second of the numbers to be compared. That address is, as we see, 000030, and the CPU can now access the second number for the compare, 102333. But notice here that for the second operand, R3 is referenced in mode 1, not mode 2. Thus no autoincrementing takes place on this second reference to R3. Hence, c(R3) is still 000030. The comparison now takes place, and the result is found to be positive. Thus the BLE instruction at line 5 is *not* executed, the counter RØ is incremented, R1 is decremented, and we are directed back to the CMP instruction. Recalling that R3 contains 000030, we see that now the second number will be compared with the third, and so forth.

This little example not only points out the great utility of autoincrement mode for the purposes of stepping through memory, it also clearly shows the necessity for a precise understanding of just when the autoincrementing takes place—the CMP instruction at line 4 relies for its proper execution on the fact that this incrementing takes place immediately after the register is accessed to obtain the address of the number, not after the entire instruction has been executed.

- Mode 3   (011)
  Name: **Autoincrement deferred mode**
  Symbol: @(Rn)+

This addressing mode shares with mode 2 the autoincrementing of the specified register, but the differences are quite significant. The first difference lies in the way the EL is calculated. Recall that in both modes 1 and 2, the EL was the memory location whose *address* was in the given register. In mode 3, the EL is determined as follows: The number in the specified register is used as the address of some memory location; the contents of *that memory location* is then taken as the *address* of the EL. An example will clarify these ideas.

Suppose $c(R1) = 024460$ and $c(024460) = 102336$. Then if R1 is referenced in mode 3, the effective location is the byte or word whose address is 102336. The reader will recognize what has happened here—the calculation of the address of the EL has been deferred one additional step beyond what took place in modes 1 and 2.

The second difference between mode 3 and mode 2 is that while the contents of the specified register is incremented immediately after it is used to obtain an address, the incrementing is *always* by 2, *never* by 1, even though the instruction involved might be a byte-type instruction (MOVB, DECB, COMB, and so on) and regardless of which register was specified (R0 to R7). This behavior requires some explanation. Recall that an *address* is a number that might be *odd* (in which case it is the address of the high-order byte of some word), or it might be *even* (and then it is either the address of a full word or the address of the low-order byte of a word). But in any event, an *address* is *always* a 16-bit *word*. Let us introduce some informal symbolism here. Suppose $c(R4) = X$, where X is *even*, and $c(X) = Y$, which may be either even or odd. Consider the instruction CLRB   @(R4)+. The byte to be cleared will be calculated as follows: The contents of R4, namely X, will be used as an address. (The contents of the word whose address is X, namely Y, will be used as the address of the byte to be cleared.) All is well so far, but suppose now, since CLRB is a byte instruction, the CPU was to autoincrement the contents of R4 by 1. Then by the time R4 had been accessed to determine the address of the address of the EL, $c(R4)$ would be $X + 1$, which is *odd*. Could R4 then be again referenced in mode 3? Certainly *not*, for the following reason: Its contents, $X + 1$, being odd, *cannot* be the *address* of a *word* whose contents is the address of the EL. Thus R4, having been incremented by 1, has immediately lost its effectiveness for stepping through a sequence of addresses. For this reason the autoincrementing is *always* by 2 in mode 3.

Because of the double indirectness, or deferment, involved in the calculation of the EL, the reader might legitimately wonder how useful this addressing
mode is. In fact, this mode does not appear frequently in day-to-day programming. Moreover, we decline even to give an example, since at this point in our
development such an example would be quite contrived. We do note, however,
that there are circumstances in which this mode is precisely what is needed,
and without it some awkward programming would be required.

- Mode 4   (100)
  Name: **Autodecrement mode**
  Symbol: $-(Rn)$

The autodecrement mode is analogous to the autoincrement mode (mode
2) in that the specified register contains the *address* of the EL. However, there
are two significant differences. First, as the name implies, the contents of the
register in question is *decremented* rather than incremented. Second, the decrementing of the register takes place *prior* to its being referenced for the address
of the effective location. (Recall that in mode 2, the contents of the register was
incremented *subsequent* to its use as an address.) The decrementing is by 1 for
byte instructions and by 2 for word instructions. Again, R6 and R7 (PC)
are exceptions, the decrementing always being by 2. (But see the footnote,
page 118.)

The *timing* of the decrementing is very important, as it was in the case of
autoincrementing, and as a further reminder to the programmer, the notation
that is used is quite descriptive. Note that in mode 2 we used the symbol $(Rn)+$,
with the plus sign placed *behind* the register, to indicate that incrementing takes
place *after* the register contents have been accessed. In mode 4, we place the
minus sign *in front of* the register symbol to suggest that decrementing takes
place *before* accessing the register for the address of the EL. We offer one simple
example comparing these two modes.

Suppose $c(R\emptyset) = 002306$, and consider the two instructions INC $(R\emptyset)+$
and INC $-(R\emptyset)$. In the first case, the address of the effective location will be
002306, and *after* that address has been determined, $c(R\emptyset)$ will be incremented to
002310. In the second instance, $c(R\emptyset)$ will *first* be decremented to 002304, and
then its contents (002304) will be used as the address of the EL. For these reasons,
mode 2 is sometimes referred to as *post*-autoincrement mode, and mode 4 is
called *pre*-autodecrement mode.

Again, the principal use of mode 4 addressing is to allow the register to
step through memory addresses, but in this case the register steps through them
backwards, from higher addresses to lower addresses. A little care is necessary
here, as shown in the sample program of Fig. 7.5.2. This is a modification of the
program of Fig. 7.5.1, which counts the pairs of numbers in which the first is
larger than the second. Here the numbers are traversed in reverse order, from
back to front.

```
 1 000000  005000  START:  CLR   R0          ;'GREATER THAN' COUNTER
 2 000002  012701          MOV   #6,R1       ;'PAIR' COUNTER
          000006
 3 000006  012703          MOV   #VECTOR,R3  ;ADDR. OF LAST NUMBER
          000042'
 4 000012  021343  LOOP:   CMP   (R3),-(R3)  ;COMPARE THIS NO.
 5                                           ; TO PRECEDING NO.
 6 000014  002001          BGE   CONT        ;GREATER THAN OR =
 7 000016  005200          INC   R0          ;INCREMENT COUNTER
 8 000020  005301  CONT:   DEC   R1          ;MORE PAIRS TO DO?
 9 000022  001373          BNE   LOOP        ;YES -- DO NEXT PAIR
10 000024  000000          HALT              ;NO -- STOP
11                                           ;
12 000026  000017          000017            ;THE
13 000030  102333          102333            ; NUMBERS
14 000032  002110          002110            ; TO
15 000034  000644          000644            ; BE
16 000036  000023          000023            ; COMPARED
17 000040  007441          007441            ; IN
18 000042  100031  VECTOR: 100031            ; PAIRS
19                                           ;
20         000000'          .END  START
```

Figure 7.5.2

Note that we had to make a few modifications. VECTOR is now the symbolic address of the *last* of the numbers, rather than the first. We also altered the CMP instruction at line 4; in fact, the compare takes place in the reverse order. And because of this change, we changed the former BLE CONT instruction to BGE CONT at line 6. (Why?)

· Mode 5 (101)
  Name: **Autodecrement deferred mode**
  Symbol: @ −(Rn)

By now the reader should have little difficulty conjecturing what this mode does. The register is *first* decremented by 2 (*never* by 1, even for byte instructions). Next, the (new) contents of the register is used as the address of a memory word, whose contents is then used as the address of the EL. There are no surprises here, and again the mode is not very useful in ordinary programming situations. We leave it to the reader to supply his own examples of how the EL is calculated, and he is invited to verify his understanding of this mode by trying some of the exercises at the end of the chapter which employ it.

· Mode 6 (110)
  Name: **Index mode**
  Symbol: X(Rn)

This addressing mode is an exceedingly useful one, as we shall see. As the parentheses surrounding the register symbol—(Rn)—seem to indicate, the register contains the *address* of the EL, and this is almost correct. Rather, the contents of the register is obtained by the CPU, and then the *number* X, which is called the **index**, is added to it. It is important to note that the contents of the specified register is *not* altered by this CPU addition. The resulting number is used as the address of the EL. A simple example follows.

Suppose c(R5) = 026301, and consider the instruction COMB   −12(R5). To determine the address of the byte to be COMplemented, we take the contents of R5—026301—and then add the index X, which in this case is −12. We get 026301 + (−12) = 026267. This is the address of the byte that will be replaced by its 1's-complement (after which we shall still have c(R5) = 026301). Thus the address of the effective location in an indexed instruction is the index plus the contents of the register: X + c(Rn).

A more extensive example would also be useful. Recall that in Chapter 6 we spent some time writing a program to find the largest of five numbers, and one of the decisions that we made there was *not* to autoincrement (mode 2) register 2, which contained the address of the number, when using it for the compare with the temporary maximum. Our reasoning there was that although the stepping of this register was certainly desirable and would avoid the awkwardness of having to increment R2 twice, unfortunately if we needed to replace the temporary maximum in R5, the autoincrementing would already have moved R2 *beyond* the address of the number that should replace the temporary maximum. At that time there seemed no efficient way around this difficulty, but we see now that index mode allows us to clean up that program quite a bit. We give a listing of the modified program without further comment (Fig. 7.5.3). The reader will find it worthwhile to examine this in detail and to compare it with the listing shown in Fig. 6.7.1.

```
MAXIMUM

 1                              .TITLE   MAXIMUM
 2                              ;
 3  000000  012700  START:  MOV   #4,R0            ;SET FOR 4 COMPARES
            000004
 4  000004  012702          MOV   #DATA,R2         ;ADDR OF 1ST NO. IN R2
            000072'
 5  000010  012205          MOV   (R2)+,R5         ;1ST NO. = TEMPMAX
 6  000012  020522  LOOP:   CMP   R5,(R2)+         ;COMPARE TEMPMAX WITH NO.
 7  000014  002002          BGE   NEXT             ;TEMPMAX BIGGER -- SKIP
 8  000016  016205          MOV   -2(R2),R5        ;REPLACE TEMPMAX
            177776
 9  000022  005300  NEXT:   DEC   R0               ;DECREMENT COUNTER
10  000024  001372          BNE   LOOP             ;MORE NOS. IF NONZERO
11  000026  010567          MOV   R5,ANSWER        ;GET THE MAXIMUM
            000036
12  000032                  $OUT.OCT #ANSWER,#1  ; AND PRINT IT
13  000066                  $EXIT                  ;RETURN TO OP. SYSTEM
14                              ;
15  000070          ANSWER: .BLKW 1                ;FOR PRINTING MAX
16                              ;
17                              ;THE 5 NUMBERS TO BE MAXIMIZED
18                              ;
19  000072  000403  DATA:   .WORD 403
20  000074  102304          .WORD 102304
21  000076  023704          .WORD 23704
22  000100  007702          .WORD 7702
23  000102  176337          .WORD 176337
24                              ;
25          000000'          .END  START
```

Figure 7.5.3

Before moving on to the last addressing mode, we take a few moments to examine the code generated by the assembler for an indexed instruction and how the CPU deals with such an instruction *upon execution*. As a typical example, consider the instruction CLR   5(R1), which is assembled as follows. The addresses were chosen arbitrarily.

026442	005061	the CLR operation
026444	000005	the index 5

Note that a two-word instruction has been constructed, with the index itself in the second of these words. Let us now examine in detail what actions the CPU takes upon execution of this instruction. We suppose, of course, that just prior to its execution, c(PC) = 026442. The CPU then does a *fetch*—that is, the CPU gets the contents of the memory location whose address is in the program counter, and then *increments the contents of the PC by 2*, the action it *always* takes on a *fetch*. By now, c(PC) = 026444. Now, because of the mode bits (110) in the operator, the CPU recognizes the instruction as being indexed. Thus it knows that the index is in the memory location whose address is currently in the PC, and to obtain the index (which, of course, it needs to calculate the address of the EL), it does another *fetch*, along with the attendant *incrementing of c(PC) by 2*. Notice that the PC is now pointing at the next program instruction. This second *fetch* may not seem to deserve all the emphasis we have placed on it, but we shall see its significance in the next section.

- Mode 7   (111)
  Name: **Index deferred mode**
  Symbol: @X(Rn)

With his experience with the preceding seven addressing modes, the reader can probably guess that the commercial-at in the symbol for mode 7 addressing indicates that the address of the EL is deferred one further step, and this is correct. The address of the EL is calculated by taking the contents of the register, adding the index, and then using the result as the address of a memory location whose *contents* is the *address* of the effective location. A concrete example will be helpful.

Suppose c(R2) = 042662, the index X is 000012, c(042674) = 112002, and c(112002) = 173353. Consider the instruction NEG   @12(R2). Adding the index to c(R2) gives 000012 + 042662 = 042674. The *contents* of the memory location with this address—042674—is the *address* of the EL. Thus the EL has address 112002, and it is the 16-bit word 173353—the contents of the address 112002—that is negated. When the instruction has gone to completion we have c(R2) = 042662, c(042674) = 112002, and c(112002) = 004425 (−173353).

A word of caution about the use of mode 7 is required here. Since the sum of the index and the contents of the specified register is used as the *address* of a *word* whose contents is then used as the address of the EL, evidently X + c(Rn) must be *even*. While this does not necessarily require that *both* X and c(Rn) must be even, it does imply that if *either* is odd, then *both* must be odd. There are potential programming problems lurking here, and mode 7 must be used with some care. This warning does *not* apply to mode 6, although here again some care must be exercised. In mode 6, X + c(Rn) may be odd, provided the instruction that uses this mode is a *byte* instruction.

We make two final comments about index instructions before moving on to the next section. First, in both modes 6 and 7, notice that the contents of the specified register is *unchanged* upon execution of the instruction. Thus it is possible to vary the address of the effective location *without* affecting the contents of the register. (Compare this situation with modes 2, 3, 4, and 5, where the contents of the register *is* altered.) Second, the reader will sometimes see mnemonics containing the register symbol @(Rn). A review of our addressing modes reveals that evidently there *is* no such mode (nor can there be, since we have now examined all possible modes—we have run out of mode bits). For example, a program might contain the mnemonic COM   @(R3). The assembler interprets this construction as if it were written COM   @0(R3); that is, the assembler assumes a mode 7 construction with an index of 0. The effect, of course, is to add the index 0 to the contents of R3—to use c(R3) as the address of the address of the EL. Thus in effect we have created (with the help of the assembler) an addressing mode that is similar to @(Rn)+ or @−(Rn), but *without* the autoincrementing or autodecrementing. And while this can be useful, we note that this is nothing new—it is mode 7 with a 0 index. The assembler has simply been accommodating enough to translate our notation in an appropriate fashion. But it is important to realize that the assembler has generated a *two*-word instruction here, the second of which is the index—000000.

We summarize the eight PDP-11 register addressing modes discussed in this section in the table of Fig. 7.5.4.

7.6 ADDRESSING MODES FOR REGISTER 7 (THE PC)—
A SPECIAL CASE

In the preceding section we explicitly eliminated R7 from consideration because of its behavior at the time of a *fetch*. To see why R7 must be treated as a special case, suppose some instruction *does* reference R7, for example INC   (R7) (or INC   (PC)). Assume further that this instruction is located at memory address 023104.

```
023104        005217        INC   (R7)
023106        ------
```

In order for this increment instruction to be *executed*, the PC must contain the number (address) 023104. If it does, then the CPU will use this number as the address of the memory location containing the next instruction to be executed,

Summary of PDP-11 Addressing Modes

Mode	Symbol	Name	Effective Location (EL)
0	Rn	Register	The register Rn.
1	(Rn)	Register deferred	c(Rn) = address of EL.
2	(Rn)+	Autoincrement	c(Rn) = address of EL. Then c(Rn) is incremented by 1 (byte instruction) or 2 (word instruction). c(R6) and c(R7) are always incremented by 2. (See footnote, page 118.)
3	@(Rn)+	Autoincrement deferred	c(Rn) = address of the address of EL. Then c(Rn) is incremented, always by 2.
4	−(Rn)	Autodecrement	c(Rn) is decremented by 1 (byte instruction) or 2 (word instruction). Then c(Rn) is used as the address of EL. c(R6) and c(R7) are always decremented by 2. (See footnote, page 118.)
5	@−(Rn)	Autodecrement deferred	c(Rn) is decremented, always by 2. Then c(Rn) = address of address of EL.
6	X(Rn)	Index	X + c(Rn) = address of EL.
7	@X(Rn)	Index deferred	X + c(Rn) = address of address of EL.

Figure 7.5.4

will get the contents of this location—005217, the increment instruction—and in the process, before decoding the instruction, *will increment the contents of R7 by 2*—the action always taken by the CPU on an instruction fetch. Thus what complicates using the program counter as we used R∅ to R6 is the fact that by the time the instruction has been fetched, the PC no longer has the value it had *prior* to the fetch. Nonetheless the program counter *can* be used in instructions just as the other registers have been, provided we are cognizant of this special feature and take some care in building PC-type instructions. Thus INC   (PC) is a perfectly legitimate instruction, although as we shall see, mode 1 PC addressing does some strange things upon execution and thus is not very useful.

Since the various addressing modes apply equally to R7, we shall examine each of them, 0 to 7. We shall see that some of these have effects that are most desirable, while others result, upon execution, in consequences which are so bizarre as to make them totally useless except in extremely peculiar circumstances.

(a) Program counter addressing, mode 0 (*000*)

This PC addressing mode can be quite useful, but it can also lead to disaster unless care is taken. To see why, recall that the PC can be used either as the *source* register or the *destination* register of an instruction (or both). In the former case, the contents of the PC will not be changed, whereas in the latter case it will be. And we must be aware that if the contents of the PC is changed, then we have disturbed, perhaps intentionally, the flow of execution of the program. We look at a few simple examples to get some ideas about what can go right and what can go wrong. In each case we assume that the instruction is located at 004602 and that the PC contains this address just prior to execution of the instruction.

```
004602      010702      MOV   PC,R2
004604      ------
```

This instruction is perfectly straightforward—it moves the contents of the PC into R2. But we need to be aware that by the time the instruction has been fetched, the PC has been moved up to 004604. Thus the number moved into R2 is 004604, not 004602. Aside from the fact that c(PC) has been incremented by 2 on the instruction fetch, it is otherwise unaffected by the instruction.

```
004602      060712      ADD   PC,(R2)
004604      ------
```

This also is a perfectly well behaved instruction that again has no effect on c(PC). It adds the contents of the PC (004604) to the number whose address is in R2, and places the sum in the word whose address is in R2.

We present one more example here, which turns out to be a fairly common and useful instruction. The details of what takes place are left to the reader.

```
004602      010746      MOV   PC,-(R6)
004604      ------
```

These three examples have been fairly simple and have left c(PC) unaffected (except for the usual increment-by-2 because of the instruction fetch). But let us look at some examples in which the PC is the *destination* of the instruction.

```
004602      010207      MOV   R2,PC
004604      ------
```

In this case, the instruction is fetched, and c(PC) is incremented by the CPU to 004604. Now the instruction is executed—the contents of R2 is MOVed into the PC. To see the effect of this action, suppose that c(R2) = 045532. Then the MOV will put the number 045532 into the PC, overlaying the value that was there, namely, 004604. Now that this instruction has gone to completion, the CPU is ready to fetch, decode, and execute the *next* instruction. Where does it look for the address of this next instruction? In the PC, of course. What it sees there is 045532, not 004604. Then it fetches the contents of 045532, increments the contents of the PC to 045534, and starts another decoding/execution cycle. Thus this instruction has interrupted the normal sequential flow of execution and transferred control to location 045532—that is, we have jumped to 045532.

This "jumping" will occur any time an instruction modifies the number in the program counter. This can certainly have undesirable effects if it is not expected, and altering the PC in an unexpected fashion will have unpredictable results. On the other hand, we are reminded that affecting the PC by an instruction is not always bad. In fact, the conditional branch instructions do precisely this—they add some number to the contents of the program counter in order to produce the branch, to transfer control of the CPU to some other part of memory.

As desirable as it might be on occasion to adjust the contents of the PC, it must be done carefully. Consider, for example,

004602	060307	ADD	R3,PC
004604	------		

The effect of this instruction is to add the contents of R3 to the contents of the PC and place the resulting sum in the PC. By the time the instruction is executed, the contents of the PC will be 004604. However, suppose $c(R3) = 000423$. Then the value given to the PC will be $000423 + 004604 = 005227$. But now the CPU cannot possibly fetch the next instruction to be executed since the PC does not contain a *word* address—its contents is *odd*.

In looking at these few sample instructions we have by no means exhausted all possible cases, nor shall we be able to in discussing the remaining seven modes of PC addressing. But the reader with a firm understanding of these addressing modes should have no difficulty in understanding the action of the CPU when the register in question is R7.

(b) Program counter addressing, mode 1 (*001*)

To determine the effect of mode 1 PC addressing, it will be useful to calculate the EL of an instruction using it. Suppose $c(PC) = X$. When the instruction at X is fetched, the contents of the PC will be incremented to $X + 2$. Then since the PC is addressed mode 1, the EL will be the word (or possibly byte) whose address is in the PC. That is, the address of the EL will be $X + 2$. This is a peculiar situation, and to illustrate what is going on, let us look at an example.

Suppose again $c(PC) = 004602$ and that the code for INC   (PC) is at 004602. Suppose further that the instruction CLR   R3 is at 004604.

004602	005217	INC	(PC)
004604	005003	CLR	R3
004606	------		

Upon execution, the CPU will fetch the contents of 004602, it will move the contents of the PC up to 004604, and then execute the INC   (PC) instruction.

What will be the EL of this instruction? The answer is, the word whose address is in R7. Since c(R7) = 004604, the word in that memory location, namely, 005003, will be incremented to 005004. Thus at this point, c(004604) = 005004. Now that the CPU has executed this increment instruction, it is ready for the next instruction. It looks in the PC for the address of the next instruction, sees 004604, fetches its contents (005004), moves c(PC) up to 004606, and executes the instruction it has just fetched. But this instruction is CLR   R4, *not* CLR   R3, since its code has been incremented.

Thus it appears that if the PC is used in mode 1 to specify the *destination* of an instruction, some strange and probably not very desirable things will happen. Even if the PC is used in mode 1 as the *source* register of an instruction, the results are not very interesting, although there are some cases in which this might be exactly the mode to use. However, before we abandon mode 1 PC addressing as fruitless, let us consider one more example.

Suppose we wish to move the *number* 224 into register 1, for example. Consider the following machine code:

004602	011701	MOV (PC),R1
004604	000224	(the number 224)
004606	------	

Let us see what happens when c(PC) = 004602 and the CPU is ready to execute an instruction. The CPU uses the contents of the PC as the address of the next instruction, fetches the number, and moves c(PC) up to 004604. The current contents of the PC, namely, 004604, is the address of the the source EL. Thus 000224, the contents of 004604, is the number to be moved. The destination, of course, is R1. Thus the effect of the instruction is to move the number 000224 into R1—precisely what we wanted. But now problems arise. The CPU is now ready for the next instruction and fetches the contents of the memory location whose address is in the PC, moving c(PC) up to 004606. The 16-bit number fetched, and thus to be executed, is 000224. Unfortunately, this cannot be decoded because this bit configuration is not the code for any PDP-11 instruction.

We have *almost* discovered a useful construction—one in which the source is a specified number. The difficulty we encountered would be overcome if the CPU, after obtaining this specified number, would once again *increment* c(PC) *by* 2, so that by the time the present instruction had gone to completion, the PC would be pointing at the *next instruction*, rather than at the specified number. Mode 2 addressing is just what we need for this.

(c) Program counter addressing, mode 2 (*010*)

As we already know, mode 2 addressing behaves identically with mode 1 addressing *except* that, in mode 2, after the register has been accessed to obtain the address of the EL, that register is incremented. Furthermore, in the case of R7 (the PC), the incrementing is always by 2, regardless of the byte or word form of the instruction. Let us reexamine the sample instruction of the mode 1 instruction, this time using mode 2 PC addressing.

```
004602      012701      MOV  (PC)+,R1
004604      000224      (the number 224)
004606      ------
```

We assume that initially c(PC) = 004602, the CPU fetches the contents of this address (012701), and moves c(PC) up to 004604. Again, the source of the MOV is determined to be the number whose address is in the PC, namely the number 000224. But because of the mode 2 addressing, when the address 004604 is obtained from the PC, c(PC) is *autoincremented* to 004606. The MOV is now executed, putting the number 000224 in register 1, and when the CPU is ready for the next instruction, it finds the PC pointing at the next instruction— whatever is in 004606. We have achieved the desired effect. By using mode 2, we have managed to skip the PC around the number to be moved.

In a similar fashion the reader should verify that the following code will successfully add the number 177776 (−2) to the number whose address is in R5:

```
004602      062715      ADD  (PC)+,(R5)
004604      177776      (the number −2)
004606      ------
```

Although this addressing mode is useful when we are using a number as the source of an instruction, it is nonetheless something of a nuisance *for the programmer*, since he or she must remember to use PC addressing mode 2 and then insert the number—to be MOVed, ADDed, SUBtracted, or whatever—in the word following the mode 2 instruction itself. On the other hand, it should not be too difficult to get the *assembler* to generate this code—to use PC mode 2 addressing and then to place a specified number in the word following— provided only that we indicate to the assembler that this is our intent. We do this by replacing the source we have been using—(PC)+—by the *number itself* preceded by the number sign. Thus the preceding two instructions could have been written as MOV #224,R1 and ADD #177776,(R5), respectively. Of course, this notation is not new for we have been using it for some time—in each of our (mnemonic) programs we MOVed some absolute number into some register or other. (It will be worthwhile for the reader to glance back at the preceding programs to see just how this construction was used and what code was generated by the assembler.) Since this addressing mode is so useful (we have even invented a special assembler-recognizable symbolism for it) it is given the distinguished name **immediate mode program counter addressing**.

(d) Program counter addressing, mode 3 (011)

Recall that in the preceding section we dismissed mode 3 register address-ing—autoincrement deferred—as being not especially useful in everyday programming. However, when the specified register is R7, the program counter, we shall find that this addressing mode is highly desirable. Remember that in mode 3 the contents of the specified register is used as the *address* of the *address* of the EL, and that the register is then autoincremented by 2.

Again suppose that c(PC) = X, that c(X) is some instruction referencing the PC in mode 3, and that location $X + 2$ contains the number Y. When the instruction at X is fetched, c(PC) will be moved up to $X + 2$. The EL of the instruction will then be calculated as follows: The current contents of the PC, namely, $X + 2$, contains a number (Y) that is the *address* of the EL. In addition, c(PC) is autoincremented by 2 to $X + 4$. An example using the "test" (TST) instruction will aid our understanding. (See Appendix A for the details of what this instruction does.)

```
004602        005737        TST   @(PC)+
004604        036224        (the number 036224)
004606        ------
```

The number 036224 at 004604 was chosen arbitrarily. We shall see its significance momentarily.

If we assume that c(PC) = 004602, the CPU will fetch the number 005737 and increment the contents of the PC to 004604. Because of the mode 3 PC addressing (the 6 bits 37 in the instruction), the EL is calculated in the following way: The contents of the register—in this case, the PC—is used as the address of a word whose *contents* is the *address* of the EL. Since c(PC) = 004604 and c(004604) = 036224, 036224 is the address of the EL, that is, the word to be TSTed. At this time c(PC) is also incremented to 004606.

The significance of this addressing mode is that this is the first time we have seen a means of referencing a memory location by specifying its numerical address. So far we have done this indirectly, by putting the address in a register and then referencing the register in an appropriate mode. Here we can actually specify the address, either numerically or symbolically. Again, to relieve us of the burden of specifying a PC mode 3 instruction and inserting the address in the word following the instruction, we solicit the help of the assembler. We use the notation @#, followed by the address, in place of the (source or destination) register designation @(PC)+. This addressing mode is called **absolute mode program counter addressing**. Thus we could more easily have written this TST example as TST   @#36224, and we would rely on the assembler to construct the code shown above. In a similar fashion, we may now write instructions such as CLR   @#1124, MOV   @#DATA,R3, ADD   @#104662, @#NUMBER, and so forth. The last example contains *two* absolute mode references, and we display the code generated by the assembler, again assuming that the first word of this instruction is located at 004602. The reader should go through this example in detail and verify that the contents of memory location 104662 has been added to the contents of the memory location whose symbolic address is NUMBER.

004602	063737	ADD @#104662,@#NUMBER
004604	104662	(the number 104662)
004606	NUMBER	(the numeric value of the symbol NUMBER)
004610	------	

(e) Program Counter Addressing, Mode 4 (*100*)

Mode 4 PC addressing exhibits two characteristics that make it sufficiently peculiar to render it all but useless. First, when the PC contains the address of a PC mode 4 instruction, and that instruction is fetched by the CPU, c(PC) is incremented by 2, as usual. But the mode 4 reference to the PC in the instruction itself will again *back up* c(PC) by 2, prior to the register reference, so the PC will once more be pointing at the operation that referenced it. Thus the EL will be the location occupied by the instruction itself, and it is difficult to devise even contrived circumstances in which it would be a useful addressing mode. Second, unless there is some further PC addressing in the instruction that increments c(PC), by the time the instruction execution has been completed, the PC will still contain the address of the *original* instruction. When the CPU is ready to execute the "next" instruction, it will do another PC fetch and end up with identically the same instruction it just processed: The CPU is caught in an infinite loop.

Clearly it is the pre-autodecrementing of c(PC)—an action that in effect undoes the CPU's PC increment-on-fetch—that makes this mode virtually useless and there is little point in devoting more time to it. Again, we emphasize that this mode is *not invalid*; it is simply of little *utility*.

(The reader might be interested in establishing that the instruction

004602	014702	MOV −(PC),R2
004604	------	

does, in fact, catch the CPU in an infinite loop. As a second, more amusing, example he should follow through the first few steps of the instruction

004602	005247	INC −(PC)
004604	------	

to see how quickly the situation falls apart.)

(f) Program Counter Addressing, Mode 5 (*101*)

This is again a pre-autodecrementing mode, although the address of the EL is deferred one additional step. Since the same objections stated for mode 4 apply, and for substantially the same reasons, we shall move on to the next mode.

(g) Program Counter Addressing, Mode 6 (*110*)

This mode—index—is most interesting and useful, so we shall examine it with some care. The operand will be of the form X(PC), where X is the index. The address of the EL is then calculated as $X + c(PC)$; that is, the address of the EL is found by *displacing* the PC by the index. This can be a very important way to determine the EL. Since its significance is not yet evident, we shall look at two examples in detail.

Consider first the following instruction, which once again we assume to be located at 004602:

004602	016703	MOV 1442(PC),R3
004604	001442	The index 1442.
004606	------	

This is an indexed instruction, and the assembler has generated two words, the first being the operation code and the second the index itself. Assuming that c(PC) = 004602 and that the CPU is about to execute the instruction, we see that 016703 is fetched by the CPU and c(PC) is incremented, because of the fetch, to 004604. The CPU recognizes the instruction as being indexed, and consequently it must obtain that index to complete calculation of the address of the EL. It obtains the index (001442) by means of a *fetch*, thereby *incrementing* c(PC) *by* 2, so now c(PC) = 004606. Note that it was the *fetch* that caused the incrementing of c(PC), *not* because there was any autoincrementing associated with the operation itself. The CPU now has all the information required to calculate the address of the EL. It adds the index (001442) to the contents of the PC (004606) to get 006250, which is the address of the EL. The contents of 006250 is MOVed into R3.

Before making further comment on this addressing mode, let us look at a slightly more involved example.

004602	016767	MOV 1442(PC),175454(PC)
004602	001442	(the index 1442)
004606	175454	(the index 175454)
004610	------	

Here both the source *and* destination ELs are determined by indexing the PC, and while the situation is still reasonably straightforward, some care will be required in calculating the addresses of the *source* EL and *destination* EL. The calculation of the address of the source EL does not differ from that of the preceding example—it is 006250. As for the destination, we must be aware that by the time the CPU is even ready to begin its calculation of the destination EL, c(PC) = 004606. Again, the CPU recognizes an index mode destination (referencing the PC) and *fetches* the index, thus moving c(PC) up to 004610. The index fetched is 175454 which, when added to the *current* c(PC) (004610), gives 002264. (Why?) Thus the effect of this three-word instruction is to move the contents of the memory location whose address is 006250 into the memory location whose address is 002264.

We now have three ways of specifying the address of a memory location in an instruction. First, we can put the address of the location in some register, R1 for example, and then refer to (R1) or (R1)+. Second, and most straightforward, we can use PC addressing mode 3, specifying symbolically @#ADDR. Finally, as we have just seen, we can indicate the address as an *index*—a *displacement* to be added to the current contents of the program counter. This last scheme has everything working against it from a practical standpoint. In order to determine the index, in general we must know *where* the instruction itself is in main memory, we must know *where* the address of the EL is, even if this is a forward reference, and then we must correctly calculate the index. This is surely an excessive burden to place on the programmer.

Before dismissing this mode as impractical, however, let us note that the assembler, once it has made its first pass, will know the value of the address of the EL (even if it was given symbolically), will know the address at which the PC index mode instruction is being assembled, and consequently should have no difficulty calculating the proper index (PC displacement). Thus we need only invent some notation that will inform the assembler that we wish the EL address to be determined by PC mode 6 addressing. The assembler will then generate an index instruction, calculate the appropriate index (PC displacement), and insert that index in the word following the operation word. We already invented that notation in the last chapter—to indicate this addressing mode, we use the address of the effective location *without* "punctuation" such as @, or @#, or #.

A simple example will illustrate this type of addressing. In fact, we have already used this sort of instruction, although the reader may not have been aware of it at the time. Refer to the program listing of Fig. 6.7.1, specifically to line 13.

```
000030      010567      MOV   R5,ANSWER
000032      000036
000034      ------
```

We see from the symbol table (and by the end of the first pass the assembler knows) that ANSWER = 000072. Notice that a mode 6 construction—010567—has been generated, and that the index (000036) is precisely correct. By the time the instruction has been fetched from 000030, the PC will contain 000032. The additional fetch required to obtain the index 000036 will have moved c(PC) up to 000034. This PC, when added to the index, will give 000036 + 000034 = 000072, the address ANSWER. This PC addressing mode, by far the most commonly used, is called **relative program counter addressing**, since addresses are determined relative to the current value of the program counter, displaced by the appropriate index.

We seem now to have two different PC addressing modes—3 and 6—that have the same effect. What is the difference between INC BUFFER and INC @#BUFFER? From the programmer's point of view, they seem to be identical in that each of these instructions will increment the word whose (symbolic) address is BUFFER. As we know, the assembler handles these two instructions quite differently. In the former case, the assembler must calculate an appropriate *index* and insert it in the word following the mode 6 increment instruction, to be used as a displacement to BUFFER from the current PC value. In the latter case, the assembler needs only to generate a PC mode 3 instruction and then insert the *number* BUFFER in the word following the operation. Thus as far as the programmer (and even program execution) is concerned, the use of one type of instruction or the other seems to be a tossup. It will not be until we give a thorough discussion of **program relocation** and **position-independent code** that we can explain any advantage of one of these modes over the other. In the meantime the reader should be aware that they have the same effect and should use either of them as his whim might dictate.

(h) Program Counter Addressing, Mode 7 (*111*)

It should come as no surprise to find that the structure of a PC mode 7 instruction is the same as for mode 6, except that the address determined by displacing c(PC) by an appropriate index is *not* the address of the EL, but rather is the address of a memory location whose *contents* is the address of the EL. One simple example should clarify this notion.

004602	005477	NEG	@13422(PC)
004604	013422	(the index 13422)	
004606	------		

The address of the effective location is calculated as follows: When the operation word (005477) is fetched, c(PC) is moved up to 004604. Then another *fetch* is done, thereby incrementing c(PC) to 004606. The index obtained on this second fetch is added to the current PC to get 013422 + 004606 = 020230. The *contents* of the memory location with this address (020230) is the address of the EL. Clearly, the index must be *even* for this mode to make any sense, for when it is added to c(PC)—which is *always* even—the result must be a *word* address.

To indicate to the assembler that we want a PC mode 7 construction, we specify the (numerical or symbolic) address, preceded by the commercial-at symbol, for example, NEG @20230 or TSTB @ADDR. This mode is called **relative deferred program counter addressing**. To illustrate the EL address calculation in this mode, we supply a program *segment*, rather than a complete program. In subsequent programming examples we shall occasionally use this mode, but it is not so commonly used as mode 6 (Fig. 7.6.1).

```
003604   012302       VECTOR:  .WORD    ADDR1
003606   020446                .WORD    ADDR2
003610   026330                .WORD    ADDR3
                                .
                                .
                                .
006332   017703                MOV      @VECTOR+2,R3
006334   175250
006336   ------
                                .
                                .
012302   000072       ADDR1:   .WORD    72
                                .
020446   173005       ADDR2:   .WORD    173005
                                .
026330   002406       ADDR3:   .WORD    2406
                                .
                                .
```

Figure 7.6.1

We are interested, of course, in the MOV instruction at 006332—MOV @VECTOR+2,R3. What number has been MOVed into register 3? First, notice that the assembler has taken certain expected actions. As to the operation itself at 006332, it has correctly formed a mode 7 PC addressing operation—017703. Next, at 006334, it has inserted an index, 175250. Let us verify that this index is correct. By the time the index has been fetched, the contents of the PC is 006336. This number, when added to the index gives $175250 + 006336 = 003606$, which is in fact VECTOR $+ 2$ ($003604 + 2 = 003606$). (Notice, incidentally, that the assembler has been able to cope with the reference to VECTOR $+ 2$, which required of it only a little simple arithmetic.)

Now 003606 is *not* the address of the effective location; that is, the *contents* of 003606 is not MOVed into R3. Rather, the calculation is deferred one additional step—the *contents* of 003606, namely, 020446, is the address of the EL. Thus the contents of memory location 020446 is MOVed into R3. Hence finally we see that it is the number 173005 that is MOVed into R3.

We summarize the program counter addressing modes in a table, as we did for general register addressing, but here we include only those that we have found to be particularly useful (Fig. 7.6.2).

The descriptions of the effective location in this table can be somewhat misleading, and they are included more as a guide than as absolute formulas. For example, in the instruction MOV #3,@A, which will be assembled as

012777
000003
(*displacement to A*)

it *is* true that the immediate mode number 3 is in the word following the operation word. But the index—the displacement to A—is in the *second* word follow-

Summary of (useful) PDP-11 PC Addressing Modes

Mode	Symbol	Name	Effective location (EL)
2	#n	Immediate	Operand n follows the operation word.
3	@#A	Absolute	Address A of the EL follows the operation word.
6	A	Relative	Address A of the EL = operation address + 4 + index (index follows the operation word).
7	@A	Relative deferred	A is the address of the address of the EL, where A = operation address + 4 + index (index follows the operation word).

Figure 7.6.2

ing the operation word. Furthermore, the address A is calculated by taking the operation address and adding 6 plus the index. The reader with a firm grasp of the addressing modes themselves will have no difficulty with these inconsistencies and will probably rely more on his understanding of addressing than on the formulas.

7.7 SOME EXCEPTIONAL CASES

In the last three sections we discussed a large class of instructions—the conditional branches, and those instructions in which the source or destination address, or both, are determined by 3 mode bits and 3 register bits. Also, because of their simplicity, we can consider those instructions that have *no* operands as having been treated as well. There are, however, a few remaining operations that do not fall into any of these categories. We shall discuss some of these—JSR, RTS, TRAP, and so forth—later in the text, when it is most natural to do so. We shall not deal with others at all; we leave it to the reader to investigate their formats, which are in Appendix A. We shall describe a few that are of special interest in this section.

An interesting and highly useful instruction is SOB—*S*ubtract-*O*ne-and-*B*ranch-back. The format of this one-word instruction is

$$0\ 111\ 111\ rrr\ xxx\ xxx$$

or, in octal,

$$077RXX$$

Here, *R* or *rrr* stands for a 3-bit register designation (000 to 110—it will shortly be obvious that R7 would *not* be an appropriate register for this instruction) and *XX* or *xxx xxx* stands for a PC word offset. Its assembler mnemonic is of the form SOB   Rn,ADDR. The following example of this instruction, in fact, could be used further to streamline one of our earlier programs.

The SOB instruction acts as follows: The specified register is *decremented by* 1; if the result is *nonzero*, a branch to ADDR takes place. On the other hand, if the register *is* zero after decrementing, then no branch takes place and control is simply passed to the next instruction. Thus SOB is a *loop-controlling* instruction—we can load a register with a *count* (the number of times we want a loop to be executed), let ADDR be the symbolic address of the first instruction in the loop, and then *end* the loop with the instruction SOB   Rn,ADDR. The loop will be executed, the register decremented, control passed back to ADDR, the loop executed again, and so forth, until finally the register is decremented to 0. Then no branch takes place—that is, we fall out of the loop. Notice, incidentally, that it is *not* the case that the branches take place as long as the register—counter—is *positive*. The branches occur as long as the register is *nonzero*. Observe also that the decrementing of the register takes place *before* the testing for 0 occurs.

As we might expect, the 6 offset bits are used to displace the current PC—that is, to achieve the branch. As was the case with the conditional branch instructions, the offset is taken to be a *word* offset, and for the same reason—a PC displacement must always be *even*. But unlike our treatment of the conditional branches, we do *not* use the high-order bit of these 6 bits as a sign bit. Rather the CPU assumes that the given word offset is to generate a branch *backward*—a *negative* PC displacement. The reason for this construction is twofold. First, an instruction that controls a loop is typically at the *end* of the loop, not at its beginning, and thus we would normally want to branch backward. Second, if the first of the 6 bits was to be used as a sign bit, the remaining 5 bits could hold only numbers as large as 31_{10}, and this would severely limit the length of the loops we could control with this instruction. There is already a 63_{10}-word limitation with which we must cope.

The SOB instruction acts as follows:

$$Rn \longleftarrow c(Rn) - 1$$

$$PC \longleftarrow c(PC) - 2 \times (\text{word offset}) \quad \textit{if } c(Rn) \neq 0$$

(Recall that the symbol $\longleftarrow$ stands for "is given the value. . . .")

As an example of the SOB instruction, consider again the program of Fig. 7.5.3. Recall that R∅ was given the value 4 as a counter, and a loop was controlled by decrementing $c(R\emptyset)$ and then testing to see if it was 0. Specifically, Lines 9 and 10 of that program are

9	000022	005300	NEXT:	DEC	R∅
10	000024	001372		BNE	LOOP

These two instructions could be replaced by the single instruction

9	000022	077005	NEXT:	SOB	R∅,LOOP

As a second interesting and sometimes useful instruction, consider the *EXCLUSIVE OR*, whose assembler mnemonic is XOR. Its operation format is

$$0\ 111\ 100\ rrr\ ddd\ ddd$$

or, in octal,

$$074RDD$$

Here again, R specifies some register, while DD refers to a normal destination consisting of 3 mode bits and 3 register bits. The instruction acts as follows: The destination is replaced by the result of forming the *EXCLUSIVE OR*, bit by bit, of the specified register and the destination. As an example, suppose $c(R4) = 104223, c(R1) = 002644$, and $c(002644) = 036435$. Then the instruction XOR   R4,(R1) will replace the contents of 002644 with 132616, the *EXCLUSIVE OR* of 104223 and 036435.

Note: XOR and SOB are not implemented on some models of the PDP-11. In the case of SOB, this is not of great consequence, since SOB   Rn,ADDR can always be replaced by the two-instruction sequence

DEC   Rn

BNE   ADDR

Our last example deals with MULtiplication and DIVision. We treat multiplication here, leaving it to the reader to examine the details of the instruction DIV, as found in Appendix A. Multiplication, as an arithmetic operation, is peculiar in that in general, the product of two 16-bit numbers will result in a number made up of as many as 32 bits. Since the PDP-11 word size is 16, this creates some problems with which we must deal. The solution is quite interesting; the PDP-11 takes two of its 16-bit registers and "hooks them together" to form a 32-bit superword in which to hold the product. But these cannot be just *any* two registers, as the following notation will show.

The notation $Rn \lor 1$ will mean the register whose register number is the result of logically *OR*ing the numbers n and 1. Thus, for instance, $R2 \lor 1 = R3$, since $2 \lor 1 = 3$, while $R3 \lor 1$ would be R3, since $3 \lor 1 = 3$. With this notation, we can now describe the effect of the MUL operation.

The format of the multiply operator is

$$0\ 111\ 000\ rrr\ sss\ sss = 070RSS$$

Here R is a register and SS represents a (normally formed) source, consisting of 3 mode bits and 3 register bits. The effect of the instruction is to multiply the contents of the specified register by the contents of the source, and to place the resulting 32-bit (signed) product in the 32-bit register combination consisting of R and $R \lor 1$. As a specific example, suppose $c(R2) = 002605$ and $c(R5) = 030024$. Then the instruction MUL   R5,R2, whose code is 070205, will place the product of these two numbers, namely, 00102257144, in R2 and R3 (R3 = R2 $\lor$ 1). Specifically, after execution, $c(R2) = 000411$ and $c(R3) = 057144$.

(Why?) If the product of the two numbers is *negative*, then the high-order bit—that is, bit 15 of the *first* of the two registers—will be set to 1.

What would have happened in the example above if the register we had specified had been R3 instead of R2, that is, if c(R5) = 030024, c(R3) = 002605, and we had performed the operation MUL   R5,R3? The significance of this change would be that R3$\vee$1 = R3. That is, there would apparently be no second register to hold the 32-bit product. Indeed, there would have been no such second register; the 16 low-order (least-significant) bits of the product would be placed in R3, and the 16 high-order (most-significant) bits would be *lost*. We can make two comments in this regard. First, if any bits are lost in this process, that situation can be detected, for in that instance the carry indicator will be set. Thus we could follow such a multiply with an instruction such as BCS   ERROR to transfer control to some instructions to cope with this loss of bits. Second, it may be that we have sufficient information about the numbers being multiplied to know that their product can be held in 16 bits; in this case, we can safely use an odd-numbered register for the product.

Note: Some models of the PDP-11—principally the earlier and smaller machines—do *not* contain the hardware to implement MUL and DIV as hardware instructions. On these machines products and quotients must be calculated by programming—for example, by successive additions and subtractions, respectively.

7.8 THE PDP-11 INSTRUCTION SET

We can now outline the types of PDP-11 operations. In general, they consist of the instructions that take zero, one, and two operands, the branch instructions, and a few exceptional cases. These are categorized below, and in each case we give the mnemonics for the operators that fall into each group, the full descriptions of which will be found in Appendix A. Some of these mnemonics we have already seen; most we have not, although we shall use the majority of them in the remaining chapters. A few special-purpose instructions, which do not apply to all PDP-11 models, are not included here.

The bit notations used below are

$$c = \text{condition code}$$

$$d = \text{destination}$$

$$n = \text{number}$$

$$o = \text{op-code}$$

$$r = \text{register}$$

$$s = \text{source}$$

$$x = \text{word offset}$$

$$- = \text{unused}$$

- Type: No-operand
  Format: *o 000 000 000 000 000*   or   *o 000 000 0--   ---   ---*
  Operators: BPT   EMT HALT IOT NOP RESET RTI RTT
             TRAP WAIT
- Type: One-operand
  Format: *o 000 000 000 ddd ddd*
  Operators: ADC   ADCB   ASL   ASLB   ASR   ASRB   CLR
             CLRB   COM   COMB   DEC   DECB   INC   INCB
             JMP   NEG   NEGB   ROL   ROLB   ROR   RORB
             SBC   SBCB   SWAB   SXT   TST   TSTB
- Type: Two-operand
  Format: *o 000 sss sss ddd ddd*
  Operators: ADD   BIC   BICB   BIS   BISB BIT BITB CMP
             CMPB   MOV   MOVB   SUB
- Type: Branch
  Format: *o 000 000 oxx xxx xxx*
  Operators: BCC   BCS   BEQ BGT BHI BHIS BLE BLO
             BLOS   BLT   BMI BNE BPL BR   BVC BVS
- Type: Register/source   or   Register/destination
  Format: *o 000 000 rrr sss sss*   or   *o 000 000 rrr ddd ddd*
  Operators: ASH ASHC DIV JSR MUL XOR
- Type: Condition code
  Format: *o 000 000 000 ooc ccc*
  Operators: CCC CLc SCC SEc
- Type: Miscellaneous
  Operators: MARK   *o 000 000 000 nnn nnn*
             RTS   *o 000 000 000 000 rrr*
             SOB   *o 000 000 rrr xxx xxx*
             SPL   *o 000 000 000 000 nnn*

7.9 SOME CLOSING REMARKS

We have examined the various addressing modes available on the PDP-11 and in so doing have gone into quite a bit of detail—detail that the reader may have found somewhat ponderous at times. For this we make no apologies, for two reasons. First, a thorough understanding of these modes is essential to good, efficient machine-level programming, and this is certainly one of the goals of the text. Anything less than a solid grounding in these fundamentals can only lead to poorly structured programs, obscure program "bugs," and a fuzzy understanding of the capabilities of the hardware. Second, recall that our intent here is *not* to make an exhaustive study specifically of the PDP-11, but rather to acquire an understanding of the capabilities of *any* modern computer. A sound knowledge of how the PDP-11 accesses memory and registers via its various register modes will allow the reader to write assembly-language programs for other machines with a minimum of "retooling."

If we have given the impression in this chapter that the PDP-11 has a very "rich" instruction set—a number of useful instructions with numerous modes in which they can be referenced—it was intentional. By varying the mode and register bits in the source and destination, we can in fact reference the MOV instruction alone in 4096 different ways, although not all of these are substantially different, nor are all of these especially useful. But this vastness of the repertory of instructions is not peculiar to the PDP-11. Most modern computers are capable of these, and indeed some of the larger machines have substantially more elaborate instruction sets. And the ubiquitous microcomputers, while supporting instruction sets that in some cases are a bit crude by PDP-11 standards, nonetheless have all these capabilities as well, and the reader with a solid understanding of what a machine instruction is and what the CPU does with it should have little problem successfully programming these popular machines.

Finally, recall from the discussion of Chapter 4 that it appeared to be most reasonable to use the *hexadecimal* representation of a 16-bit number; the *octal* representation left much to be desired, especially because the 8-bit byte boundary did *not* coincide with one of the octal digit boundaries. But by now the reader should be convinced that hexadecimal representations would be most difficult to deal with. As an example, consider the 16-bit configuration that represents the instruction BISB   (R4),@−(R2),

$$1\ 1\ 0\ 1\ 0\ 0\ 1\ 1\ 0\ 0\ 1\ 0\ 1\ 0\ 1\ 0$$

In octal, this would be written as 151452, which we can pick apart into its component pieces:

1	5	1	4	5	2
BISB		mode reg		mode reg	
		1 4		5 2	

In hexadecimal, the corresponding representation would be *D32A*, and there is little hope of looking at this base 16 number and deriving much information from it. All of this is due to the way in which the hardware is structured—for the PDP-11, octal representations are most natural; for another machine, hexadecimal representations may be substantially more informative.

7.10 EXERCISES

7.5.1. Suppose $c(R2) = 104505$ and $c(R3) = 026101$. What will be the contents of each of these registers after execution of the instruction MOVB R2,R3? How would the result differ if $c(R2) = 104305$ instead? (The effect of MOVB with a *register* destination—that is, mode 0—is a little tricky. A study of the description of this instruction in Appendix A would be in order.)

7.5.2. Suppose that just prior to the execution of each of the MOV (01$SSDD$) or MOVB (11$SSDD$) instructions, we have

$$c(R2) = 021314$$

$$c(R4) = 002016$$

c(001026) = 103076	c(021312) = 063022
c(002014) = 001026	c(021314) = 104202
c(002016) = 010302	c(021316) = 042104
c(002020) = 030300	c(030300) = 000106
c(010300) = 017772	c(042104) = 101114
c(010302) = 000000	c(063022) = 060662
c(010304) = 100205	c(104202) = 013235

In each case write the mnemonic form of the instruction, determine the source and destination EL, and state which registers or memory locations (or both) are changed by the instruction, along with their new contents.

(a) 010204
(b) 010402
(c) 110204
(d) 110402
(e) 011204
(f) 011402
(g) 111204
(h) 111402
(i) 012204
(j) 112204
(k) 011214
(l) 011224
(m) 013214
(n) 012244

(o) 014204
(p) 014412
(q) 113422
(r) 016204
    000002
(s) 116462
    177777
    000001
(t) 017274
    000002
    177776
(u) 016434
    000002
(v) 015254

7.5.3. On page 124 we illustrated index mode by considering the instruction COMB $-12(R5)$, where $c(R5) = 026301$. How would this differ from the instruction COMB 26301(R5), where $c(R5) = 177766$ (-12)?

7.5.4. Modify the program of Fig. 7.5.1 to find the number of *bytes* that exceed their successors in value.

7.5.5. In the program of Fig. 7.5.1, show that the use of R1 as a counter could have been eliminated if line 7 was changed from DEC R1 to CMP R3,#VECTOR+14.

7.5.6. Figure 7.5.3 is a listing of a modification of the program to find the largest of five numbers. Modify this program further in such a way that R2, instead of being autoincremented, is *autodecremented*.

7.5.7. What would be the effect of the instruction ADD (R1),(R1)? How would this differ from ADD (R1)+,−(R1)? How would it differ from ADD (R1),(R1)+? How would it differ from ASL (R1) or ASL (R1)+?

7.5.8. How could one move the *high-order byte* of R2 into the *high-order byte* of R3, leaving the *low-order byte* of R3 unchanged? (This is by no means completely trivial.)

7.6.1. Assume that the first word of each of the following MOV (01*SSDD*) or MOVB (11*SSDD*) instructions is located at 014626. In each case, state the source and destination EL.

(a) 012715
002313

(b) 016715
003212

(c) 016767
003212
002314

(d) 116767
002313
003212

(e) 010167
172304

(f) 013767
024606
003146

(g) 010377
024030

(h) 013727
024606
003146

7.6.2. Assume that each of the following MOV or MOVB instructions is located at 010224, and that the symbolic addresses ABC and XYZ have the following values: ABC = 002776, XYZ = 017242. Construct the (octal) code for each of the instructions.

(a) MOV   RØ,XYZ

(b) MOV   @#ABC,R2

(c) MOV   @#ABC,XYZ

(d) MOV   #6,ABC

(e) MOV   ABC,XYZ

(f) MOV   XYZ,ABC

(g) MOV   @XYZ,(R3)+

(h) MOVB   @ABC,XYZ+7

(i) MOVB   ABC−7,−(R2)

(j) MOV   #ABC,XYZ

(k) MOV   #XYZ,ABC

7.6.3. In Exercise 6.3.3 we asked what MOV RØ,#206 would mean, if anything. While it is difficult to make sense of such an instruction, the assembler nonetheless will generate the code

010027
000206

for it. Explain what will happen if this operator/operand pair is executed. In a similar way, determine the code generated by the assembler for CLR #4 and INC #622, and explain what will take place for each of these upon execution.

7.6.4. To increment the *high-order* byte of a *word* whose symbolic address is DATA, we need only write INCB DATA+1. But how could we increment the high-order byte of register 4? In particular, show that INCB R4+1 will *not* be properly handled by the assembler.

7.6.5. In the instruction MOV −(PC),R2 of page 133, what number will be MOVed into R2?

7.6.6. What is the difference between the two instructions CMP (R3)+,(R3) and CMP (R3),2(R3)?

7.6.7. The following mnemonic program simply adds the positive integers from 1 to 10, and places the result (55_{10}) in the memory location labeled ANSWER. Assuming that the program is to be assembled beginning at location 000000, generate the assembled machine code. That is, play the part of the assembler or our assembling clerk. Should any words of the machine program be flagged with an apostrophe to indicate that they are sensitive to program relocation? What will the symbol table be?

```
ANSWER:   .BLKW  1
          ;
BEGIN:    CLR    @#ANSWER
          CLR    R4
LOOP:     INC    R4
          ADD    R4,ANSWER
          CMP    R4,#12
          BNE    LOOP
          HALT
          ;
          .END   BEGIN
```

(The resulting code can be verified by submitting the source program to the PDP-11 assembler.)

7.7.1. The SOB RØ,LOOP instruction of page 139 was machine coded as 077005. Why? Specifically, where did the 6 bits 05 come from?

7.7.2. Assume that an SOB instruction is located at 014626, that R2 is the controlling register for the SOB, and that the target address is 014576. Construct the octal form of the SOB instruction.

7.7.3. Consider a program that contains the following SOB instruction. (The numbers represent the addresses at which the instructions are located.)

```
002606     LOOP:  ------
                    .
                    .
                    .
003012            SOB  R5,LOOP
```

What is wrong with this construction? State at least two ways in which it could be repaired.

7.7.4. We stated on page 138 that R7 was *not* an appropriate register for use in an SOB instruction. Why not?

7.7.5. If the *initial* value of Rn is *zero* and Rn is used in an SOB instruction to control the number of times a loop is executed, will the program ever exit the loop? Why or why not?

7.7.6. What is the effect of the following instruction sequence?

```
XOR  R1,R3
XOR  R3,R1
XOR  R1,R3
```

(*Suggestion:* To get some idea of what is going on here, assume that R1 and R3 hold only 4-bit words, for instance, and see what happens when some particular values are chosen for these registers, for example, $c(R1) = 0110$ and $c(R3) = 1101$. At this point it should be fairly easy to conjecture what these instructions do. Now try to establish the conjecture in general, for *any* bit configuration and for *any* word size.)

7.7.7. One of the activities with which computers frequently occupy themselves is that of *sorting* numeric data. Write a program to put a collection of numbers into *increasing* order. There are many techniques for this task; one of the most easily implemented (but scarcely the most efficient) is the so-called **exchange sort**, or **bubble sort**.

The idea is quite simple. For a given collection of numbers, we compare the first two. If they are in the correct order (the first less than or equal to the second), we go on to compare the second and third numbers. If they are *not* in the correct order, we *exchange* them before comparing the next consecutive pair. By the time we have compared (and possibly exchanged) all consectutive pairs, the *largest* of all the numbers will have been moved to the last position. Thus this first pass through the numbers has yielded a partial sort. (Additional passes will be required to complete the sort.) An example will clarify the procedure.

Suppose the numbers (shown here in decimal) are

$$1 \quad -2 \quad 7 \quad 19 \quad 10 \quad -5$$

in that order (read left to right). The first pass is shown below, where the circles show the pair being compared and the double arrows indicate the necessity for an exchange.

1	↔	−2	7	19		10		−5
−2		1	7	19		10		−5
−2		1	7	19		10		−5
−2		1	7	19	↔	10		−5
−2		1	7	10		19	↔	−5
−2		1	7	10		−5		19

Figure 7.10.1

The six numbers are still not sorted, although some improvements have been made. Notice that the largest number, 19, has been moved all the way to the right. (Explain why this will always happen.)

We now repeat the process on the truncated collection

$$-2 \quad 1 \quad 7 \quad 10 \quad -5$$

there being no need now to consider the largest number, 19. After a total of five such passes, each time on a further truncated collection of numbers, the original collection will be ordered.

There are two nested loops here, one to control the individual passes, the other to control the number of passes. Each should be handled by an SOB instruction. Test the program on the (octal) numbers (in the order given)

24, 17726, 0, 177726, 24, 1, 0, 101101, 12345, 120220, 20

7.7.8. How should the program of Exercise 7.7.7 be modified to put the collection of numbers in *decreasing* order?

7.7.9. Shown below is the listing of a program that while it does nothing useful, nonetheless does execute. When the program executes, determine the value that will be in R4 by the time the HALT instruction at line 10 is encountered.

```
 1 001000    010767   START:  MOV    PC,SKIP
             000006
 2 001004    105267           INCB   SKIP+2
             000004
 3 001010    005004           CLR    R4
 4 001012    000402   SKIP:   BR     CONT
 5 001014    005203           INC    R3
 6 001016    000775           BR     SKIP
 7 001020    152767   CONT:   BISB   #14,1031
             000014
             000003
 8 001026    000304           .WORD  000304
 9 001030    000304           .WORD  000304
10 001032    000000           HALT
11                            ;
12           001000           .END   START
```

Figure 7.10.2

7.7.10. We stated in the text that SOB Rn,ADDR could be replaced by

DEC   Rn

BNE   ADDR

and yet these two constructions are *not identical*. What is the difference?

7.7.11. Assuming that XOR is *not* a hardware instruction, write a sequence of instructions that will emulate (for example) XOR R5,R2; that is, c(R2) is replaced by c(R5) $\vee$ c(R2), and c(R5) is unaffected. Is the emulation exact? For instance, are the condition codes set as XOR would set them, as specified in Appendix A?

7.7.12. A 16-bit word places a restriction on the size of the unsigned or signed numbers that it can represent. In order to expand this size, consider two consecutive (adjacent) words of memory as representing a 32-bit, double-precision "superword," with bits 0–15 being interpreted as the bits of the lower-addressed word, and bits 16–31 being the bits of the higher-addressed word. Specifically, let X and Y be the addresses of two such 32-bit "words," whose high- and low-order 16 bits have the symbolic addresses XHIGH and YHIGH, and XLOW and YLOW, respectively. Show how two such 32-bit words may be added and subtracted. Are the carry and overflow indicators set by these double-precision arithmetic operations as expected—as they are for single-precision addition and subtraction? Is it really necessary that the 16-bit words making up a 32-bit superword be *adjacent*?

7.7.13. How can we determine if an unsigned 16-bit word, for example, c(R0), is a power of 2—that is, has precisely *one* bit set to 1? (The result is almost trivial; the problem itself is not.)

7.7.14. If a particular model PDP-11 does not implement multiplication as a *hardware* instruction, then products must be calculated by a *sequence* of program instructions. Write such a sequence to emulate the hardware instruction MUL. Specifically, duplicate the action of MUL R5,R0, and then test the emulation by setting R5 to 000200 and R0 to 012345. After execution of the "multiply" instructions, the contents of the various registers should be

$$c(R5) = 000200$$

$$c(R\emptyset) = 000012$$

$$c(R1) = 071200$$

Does the program segment work properly if either (or both) the multiplier or multiplicand is *negative*? For example, if $c(R5) = 177777$ and $c(R\emptyset) = 012345$, or if $c(R5) = 012345$ and $c(R\emptyset) = 177777$, then after execution,

$$c(R\emptyset) = 177777$$

$$c(R1) = 165433$$

Are the condition codes affected in the same way as in MUL?

7.7.15. In the same fashion as Exercise 7.7.14 above, emulate the hardware instruction DIV. Specifically, suppose that the 32-bit dividend is in the register combination $R\emptyset/R1$ and that the divisor is in R5. Again, analyze various combinations of the signs of the divisor and dividend; also examine the condition codes for compatibility with DIV, as described in Appendix A.

7.9.1. We have assured the reader that with a solid understanding of the concepts of memory addressing, machine instructions, and addressing modes, he should encounter no great difficulty in transferring his knowledge of PDP-11 assembly-language programming to other machines. As evidence of this, we offer below the listing of a source program assembled for the Motorola 6800 microcomputer, a machine that is architecturally quite a bit different from the PDP-11, and ask that he determine what this program will do upon execution.

Some preliminary information will be needed. First, the 6800 is a *byte* machine. That is, the memory groups consist of 8-bit words, and the only 16-bit combinations are used for addresses of these bytes, and for three registers. The listing shows addresses and their contents in hexadecimal representation, that being more useful for the 6800 than octal would be. Rather than having many registers, the 6800 has only *two* general-purpose registers, which are called *accumulators* and are denoted by A and B. In addition, there is a so-called *index register*, denoted by X, which is 16-bit and thus can hold an address. As the name implies, this register is used the same way a PDP-11 register is used in index mode. For example, if $c(X) = 18B6$ and $c(R3) = 014266$ (notice that $18B6_{16} = 014266_8$) then a reference to 6(R3), for example, is the same as the 6800 reference to 6, X. Next, notice that labels are not followed by colons; rather, they are distinguished by beginning in column 1 of the source code. FCB is an assembler directive, *form constant byte*, that is analogous to the PDP-11 .WORD. Similarly, RMB stands for *reserve memory byte* and is similar to .BLKW. Finally, LDA stands for *load accumulator* and LDX stands for *load index register*. We leave it to the reader to guess the meanings of the other mnemonics. Program execution begins at memory location 0006.

Notice the instruction at line 10: INC LOOP+1. The effect is to modify the index (originally set to 0) at line 7. While we have seen examples of programs that modify their own instructions, good programming practice dictates that such instructions should be avoided whenever possible. Because of the limitations of an 8-bit word and a somewhat restricted instruction set, self-modifying

```
0001  0000  11            DATA   FCB    17,24,-6,0,-101
      0001  18
      0002  FA
      0003  00
      0004  9B
0002  0005  0001          ANSWER RMB    1
0003                             ;
0004  0006  C6 05                LDA B  #5
0005  0008  4F                   CLR A
0006  0009  CE 0000              LDX    #DATA
0007  000C  AB 00         LOOP   ADD A  0,X
0008  000E  5A                   DEC B
0009  000F  27 05                BEQ    DONE
0010  0011  7C 000D              INC    LOOP+1
0011  0014  20 F6                BRA    LOOP
0012  0016  97 05         DONE   STA A  ANSWER
0013  0018  7E 0000              XIT
0014                             ;
0015                             END
```

Figure 7.10.3

programs are more common in microcomputer programming. There is no serious objection to using them, provided such instructions are well documented and care is taken in their use.

7.9.2. In Chapter 6 we saw the necessity, brought on by forward references, for the assembler to make two passes through the mnemonic source program, picking up the values of symbolic addresses on the first pass so that they could be used on the second. This two-pass construction of the assembler is nowadays not a problem, for the source program typically resides on some bulk storage device, such as disk or magnetic tape, and the accessing of the source code twice—once for each pass—is a relatively easy and rapid operation. However, in the earlier history of computing, such bulk storage devices did not exist, and most processing was card-oriented. In order to assemble a program, the following steps were required:

1. A deck of cards (which might consist of 1000 or more cards) that contained the code for the assembler itself was first loaded into main memory.
2. The programmer's source statements, on cards, were then loaded.
3. The assembler (now memory-resident) made its first pass on the programmer's card deck.
4. Finally, the programmer's deck was reloaded so that the assembler could make its second pass.

(In fact, the situation was frequently far more complicated and time-consuming than described above.) Thus in order to improve the time required to assemble a program, much thought was given to the concept of a *one-pass assembler*—an assembler that could produce executable code on a single pass, even in spite of forward references. How might it be possible to design such an assembler? (The reader is assured that he now has all the equipment necessary to answer this. He is also advised that the solution is quite complicated.)

8

Stacks and Subroutines

8.1 DATA STRUCTURES

By a **data structure** we shall mean quite informally just any way of organizing data which is convenient from the programmer's point of view. In some of the sample programs in the preceding chapters we imposed a kind of crude structure on the data when we insisted that numbers that were to be added or maximized were in *consecutive* memory locations, so that, for example, we could take advantage of the autoincrementing feature of register addressing. It was not absolutely *essential* for the data to be organized in this fashion, but this structure greatly simplified the program construction—imagine the complications that would have been introduced in these programs had the data simply been randomly placed in main memory.

At a higher level, the reader may already have had some experience with **vectors** (or **linear lists**) and **matrices** (also called **tables** or **arrays**). In implementing these structures, we name a block of main memory, then reference the particular entry in the block by the name and its *position* in the block, the position being specified by one or more **subscripts** or **indices**. For this reason, vectors and matrices are frequently referred to as **subscripted variables**. In using these structures, the programmer is getting some assistance from the particular **translating program** he is using—the BASIC interpreter, the FORTRAN compiler, and the like. For in general, a vector or matrix is stored in main memory as a block of consecutive memory locations, and some arithmetic must be done on the subscripts to find the address of the desired variable entry.

(Some suggestions for the implementation of these structures at the machine level are given in the exercises.)

The data structures mentioned above are examples of **static** data structures, in the following sense: If we specify initially that a vector is to contain 29 integers, then 29 words of main memory will be allocated to this structure and the *size* of the vector—29 words—will remain *fixed* throughout program execution. To be sure, the vector *entries* may and probably will be changed from time to time, but the vector itself will be statically held as a 29-word structure. In contrast to this situation, a **dynamic** structure is one whose *size* may change during the course of program execution. One of these structures is a principal topic of the present chapter.

A **queue** is a familiar example of a dynamic structure. This is a *linear* data structure (in the sense that for any two entries in the queue, one entry can be determined as *preceding* the other), that can grow or shrink dynamically, and such that entries are always *added* at one end of the linear structure, called the **tail** of the queue, and *removed* from the other end, called the **head** of the queue. A diagram of a queue structure is shown in Fig. 8.1.1.

As an everyday example of a queue, consider the checkout line at a supermarket. As customers complete their shopping, they join the end of a line at a checkout counter (are added to the tail of the queue). At the other end, once their order has been processed, they leave the counter (are removed from the queue). The queue might be *empty* (that is, no customers waiting to check out, although personal experience shows this to be a rare occurrence), or on a busy day the queue could theoretically become arbitrarily long. Because the first entry in the queue is also the first entry to be removed—sometimes called *first come–first served*—a queue is referred to as a **first in–first out**, or **FIFO**, structure.

A dynamic linear structure that is less familiar than the queue is the **stack**, or **push-down store**. Unlike a queue, which is double ended in the sense that entries are added at one end and removed at the other, all the action in a stack takes place at *one* end, called the **top** of the stack. Thus entries are added to the stack at the top and also removed from the stack there. This implies that the first entry in the stack available for removal was the last entry to be added to the stack, and for this reason a stack is referred to as a **last in–first out**, or **LIFO**, structure. A diagram of a stack is shown in Fig. 8.1.2.

Everyday examples of stacks are a bit difficult to come by. The discard pile in a game of gin rummy is somewhat stacklike, in that cards are always added (discarded) at the top, and only the top card may be removed. However it is not legal to remove more than one card from the stack, and in this sense the discard pile does not behave like a stack—there is nothing in the construction of a stack as a data structure that precludes removing as many entries as desired from the stack, provided only that the removals always take place one at a time from the top of the stack. As a truly representative example, consider a spring-loaded coin holder into which a supply of nickels can be pushed, one at a time,

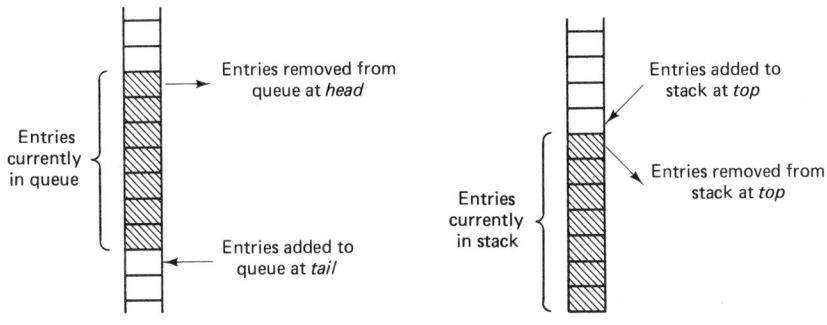

Figure 8.1.1   **Figure 8.1.2**

and then when a nickel is needed, it can be popped out of the top of the coin holder. Since the first nickel to be popped out of the holder was the last one that was pushed into it, this example is an exact analogue of the stack structure. In fact, we shall even borrow some of this terminology and apply it to this data structure. When an entry is added to the top of the stack, we say that it is **pushed onto the stack**; when an entry is removed from the stack, we say that it is **popped off the stack**.

As a final example, consider a stack of plates on a counter (Fig. 8.1.3(a)). When a plate is added to the stack, it is added at the top. In a similar fashion, plates are removed from the top, and thus this stack of plates behaves precisely like the data structure in question. Of course the reader might object that it is possible to add or remove a number of plates at one time, or even to slip a plate out of the middle of the stack, actions that violate the permitted operations for the stack structure. We can counter these objections by using a device employed by many restaurant kitchens. Rather than being stacked on a counter top, plates are stored in a spring-loaded recess in the counter (Fig. 8.1.3(b)). As a plate is added to the stack, all of the plates in the stack drop down one plate level, and as one is removed, the plates rise one level. In this way only the top of the stack is available for pushing or popping.

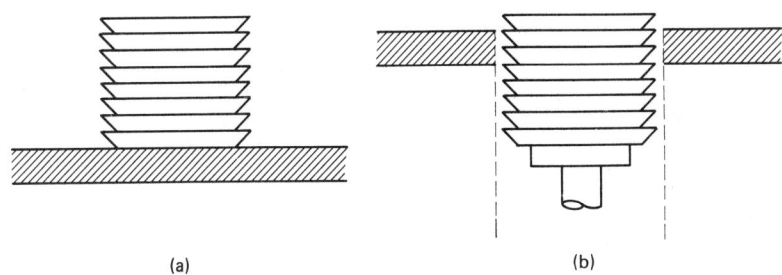

(a)   (b)

Figure 8.1.3

8.2 IMPLEMENTATION OF A STACK IN MAIN MEMORY

We referred to a stack as a data structure and thus, according to our informal definition, a stack consists of a way of organizing data in memory. We shall see in this section that it is quite easy to construct main memory stacks and to maintain them—that is, to push entries onto the stack, pop them off the stack, and keep track of where the top of the stack is.

Consider a register—R3, for example—that contains the number 2404, which we interpret as the *address* 002404. We say that R3 is pointing at the memory location whose address is 002404, and we consider the effect of the following three instructions, executed in the order given:

$$\begin{array}{ll} \text{MOV} & \#17,(\text{R3})+ \\ \text{MOV} & \text{R1},(\text{R3})+ \\ \text{MOV} & \text{ADDR},(\text{R3})+ \end{array}$$

As a result of these instructions the number 17 is put into location 002404 and c(R3) is incremented to 002406. Then the contents of R1 is put into 002406 and c(R3) is incremented to 002410. Finally, the contents of ADDR is put in location 002410 and c(R3) is autoincremented to 002412. A diagram of this situation is shown in Fig. 8.2.1.

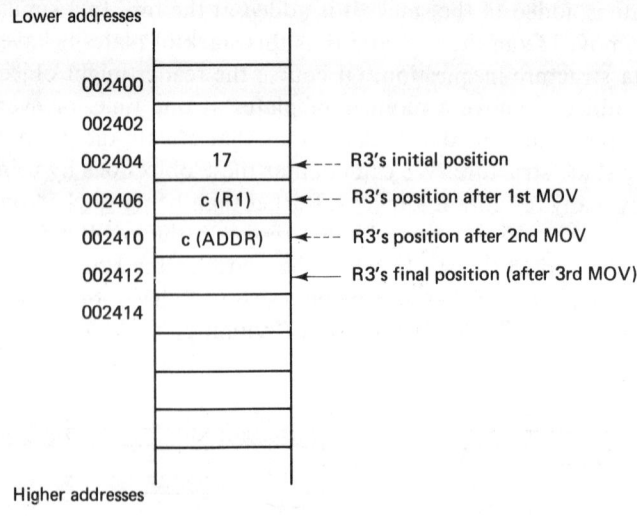

Figure 8.2.1

We may consider the block of main memory beginning at location 002404 and extending into higher addresses (which, according to the figure should be at least as high as 002412) as a *stack*, with R3 acting as a **stack pointer**. That is, R3 contains the address of the top of the stack. (Here we encounter a matter of semantics. If the top of the stack is interpreted as the location containing the

154

last entry put on the stack, then the figure shows that R3 is pointing at the word immediately *beyond* the top of the stack.) And the three MOV instructions above were *pushes* onto the stack.

If a push onto the stack amounts simply to a MOV   ???,(R3)+, then it is fairly easy to see that a pop from the stack is nothing more than execution of the instruction MOV   −(R3),???. For example, given the situation shown in Fig. 8.2.1, if we wish to pop the piece of data, namely, c(ADDR), from the stack into register 4, for instance, we need only to execute MOV   −(R3),R4. The pre-autodecrementing mode will decrement c(R3) by 2 *first* (so c(R3) = 002410) and *then* move the contents of the memory location whose address is in R3 into R4. Thus we see that by using a register as a pointer to the top of the stack, we can easily manage that stack by pushing and popping entries.

There are two slight annoyances here with which we can deal quite simply. We have already mentioned the first, namely, that the stack pointer—in our case, R3—does not quite point to the top entry on the stack. Rather, it points to the first unused memory location above the top of the stack. The second concerns the way we have visualized main memory. We have consistently drawn diagrams in which lower memory addresses are at the top of the diagram and higher addresses are at the bottom. This representation corresponds to assembler *listings*, which show addresses increasing from top to bottom. With this convention, the stack discussed above grows *downward* as items are pushed onto it, whereas it might be more natural to think of a stack as growing upward as new items are piled on top of it. The reader will recognize both of these difficulties as purely conceptual and thus of no consequence as far as stack management is concerned. On the other hand, both "problems" disappear if we simply organize the stack a bit differently.

Suppose we give R3 the initial value (address) 002412 and then execute the following sintructions:

```
MOV    #17,−(R3)
MOV    R1,−(R3)
MOV    ADDR,−(R3)
```

As we see from Fig. 8.2.2, the stack is now growing upward and R3 now *does* point at the top entry in the stack. Evidently the management of this stack is just the reverse of the earlier situation. To *push* an entry onto the stack, we execute an instruction of the form MOV   ???,−(R3), and to *pop* a number from the stack, we use MOV   (R3)+,???.

Returning for a moment to our example of a stack of plates on a counter top, we stated that it is not legitimate to *remove* or *add* plates in the middle of the stack. However, there is nothing to prevent us from observing that the fourth plate from the bottom is blue, that the second plate down is chipped, and so forth. That is, it is permissible to *access* any entry in a stack, provided no removals or additions take place anywhere except at the top. An example will clarify this idea.

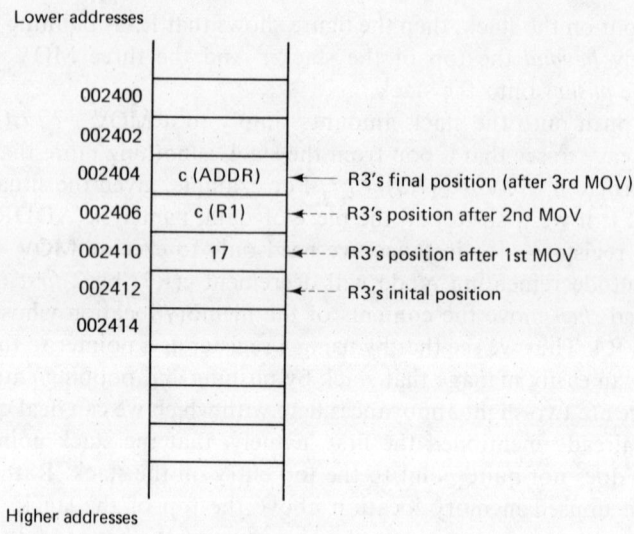

Lower addresses

002400	
002402	
002404	c (ADDR)	← R3's final position (after 3rd MOV)
002406	c (R1)	←--- R3's position after 2nd MOV
002410	17	←--- R3's position after 1st MOV
002412		←--- R3's inital position
002414	

Higher addresses

Figure 8.2.2

Suppose we have a stack established somewhere in main memory that uses R1 as a stack pointer, and assume the stack contains the entries shown in Fig. 8.2.3. The stack is organized so that it grows upward, from higher to lower addresses, as is evident from the diagram. Consider the sequence of instructions

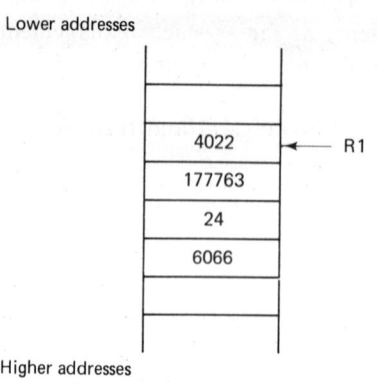

Lower addresses

4022	← R1
177763	
24	
6066	

Higher addresses

Figure 8.2.3

```
ADD    6(R1),R5
ADD    (R1),R5
ADD    2(R1),R5
```

These instructions add to the current contents of register 5 the numbers 6066, 4022, and 177763, in that order. Thus three stack entries have been *accessed*, but the stack itself, as a *structure* containing four entries, has not been changed. We may even use an instruction such as COM 4(R1), which changes the entry 24 to 177753. Again, the structure has been left intact, even though one of its entries has been altered.

We have presented two distinct (in fact opposite) ways of organizing a stack. In the first, the stack grows downward, from lower addresses to higher addresses. In the second, the situation is just the reverse. The latter scheme seems to be a bit more appealing, since *pictorially* the stack seems to be growing upward, and the stack pointer register actually points at the top entry in the stack. We shall normally use this second scheme throughout the remainder of the text and, in fact, for reasons somewhat more compelling than simple aesthetics. But it is important to understand that there is nothing *wrong* with the first scheme. It requires a different type of stack management, but as long as the programmer remains aware of how the stack is organized, no problems should be encountered. Indeed, it is not unusual for a program to contain both types of stacks.

The reader might legitimately question the utility of the stack structure. We have described the structure and have seen that its implementation in main memory is quite simple. It can be used as a place to store entries, but the storage scheme—always taking place at one end—is certainly strange upon first encounter. There seems to be no reason why a stack is any more or less useful than any other block of storage. In this regard, we beg the reader's indulgence for a few sections. We shall see that the stack is one of the most useful devices in the programmer's toolbox.

8.3 SOME POTENTIAL PROBLEMS IN STACK MANAGEMENT

If we choose to implement a stack structure in a program, then we are going to have to set aside some area of main memory in which the stack will reside, and a fundamental question involes *how much* storage should be so allocated. To see how problems of stack management can arise as a result of inappropriately answering this question, consider a program in which a block of eight words is set aside not only as stack space but also as temporary storage of a nonstack nature.

```
001000        BLOCK:  .BLKW  10
001002
001004
001006
001010
001012
001014
001016
001020        START:  MOV     #START,R4
001022                  .
001024                  .
```

The instruction at START, MOV   #START,R4, initializes R4 to the value 001020, so that R4 may be used as a pointer for the user stack. Notice that even though c(R4) = 001020, the *base* of the stack will be at 001016. For the first push onto the stack, MOV   ???,−(R4), will pre-autodecrement c(R4) to 001016 prior to the MOV. Suppose now that the programmer desires temporarily to save the contents of R0, a register that perhaps contains some volatile data but that is for the moment needed for other purposes. A likely place to save this register is on the user stack, so the program executes the instruction MOV   R0,−(R4). The contents of R0 will be moved into 001016, which will then also be the address in the stack pointer, R4. Next, suppose that six numbers need to be read, perhaps with the statement $IN.OCT #BLOCK,#6. These numbers will then reside in locations BLOCK to BLOCK+12 (001000 to 001012) inclusive. So far all is well, but suppose now that two additional pushes onto the stack are made. The first push moves a number into the location whose address is 001014, but the second push is into location 001012, thereby overlaying the sixth number that had previously been read.

The problem is fairly obvious. When the stack pointer was initialized, the stack had the potential to expand to eight entries, but the reading of six pieces of data into BLOCK immediately reduced the stack space to two entries. The third push onto the stack then resulted in a **stack overflow**. (Of course, if by the time the third push had taken place, the data that had been read was no longer of significance, then no damage would have been done.) This double-duty use of a block of storage, resulting as it has in a rather dynamic memory area, is best avoided in a well-written program. It would be far better to allocate storage for the exclusive use of the stack, reserving other blocks for any other needs. But even if we take these precautions, we can still underestimate the necessary size of a stack, and stack overflows can occur.

The opposite problem can also occur. Suppose for example that given a stack that is initially empty, we push three items onto it. Some time later we pop these three items back off the stack. But now, as a result of poor stack management, we attempt an additional pop from the stack. Of course, *something* will be popped from the "stack," but since the program had not pushed it there originally, it will doubtless be data that is meaningless to the program. We have just experienced a **stack underflow**. Stack overflow and underflow result from poor stack management—faulty accounting procedures on the part of the programmer. If a stack is used heavily and frequently, then the only way to avoid problems of this nature is to exercise extreme care.

While we can deal with the situations described above by proper accounting practices, we can less easily manage another problem. Suppose again we have a stack with stack pointer R4, which contains the address 001020, and we assume that the stack is initially empty. Once more we assume that the contents of R0 is pushed onto the stack—MOV R0,−(R4)—so that c(R4) is pre-auto-decremented to 001016. Suppose next that we need to save the *byte* whose symbolic address is ADDR+1, and we elect to push it onto the stack. We can do this with the instruction MOVB ADDR+1,−(R4). Then c(R4) is pre-autodecremented, by *one*, to 001015, and the byte is moved into that location. (Recall that the amount by which a register is autoincremented or autodecremented depends upon whether the instruction is in *word* form or *byte* form.) If the next stack activity is in word form—for example, MOV (R5),−(R4) —we are in trouble. For R4, the stack pointer, presently contains an *odd* address (001015) and the processor cannot execute a *word* MOV if the destination address is *odd*.

There are essentially three ways to cope with this difficulty. The first involves the maintenance of *two* stacks, one for the pushing and popping of *bytes*, the other for *words*. Thus whenever a byte needs to be stacked, it is pushed onto the byte stack. Stacked words go on the word stack. As usual, the programmer must be careful in managing two stacks, but the byte/word problem is completely disposed of, and this solution is by no means unreasonable or unusual.

A second approach to the problem is both unreasonable *and* unusual, but it is worth discussing since it leads naturally to the third solution. Since we know the difficulty lies with the stack pointer's possibly containing an odd address, we need a scheme to ensure that the stack pointer *always* contains an *even* address. We can achieve this whenever a byte push onto the stack occurs by immediately following that push with an instruction that adjusts the stack pointer by an additional 1, so that it will again contain an even address. For example, the instructions

```
MOVB    ADDR+1,-(R4)
DEC     R4
```

will autodecrement c(R4) by 1, move the byte whose address is ADDR+1 into the location whose address is in R4, and then adjust c(R4) back to an even number with the DEC   R4 instruction. Of course, we would have to make a similar adjustment—INC   R4—each time prior to popping a byte from the stack.

Notice that one of the consequences of this scheme is that whenever a byte is pushed onto the stack, the subsequent adjustment of the stack pointer leaves an *unused—wasted*—byte in the stack. Unless many bytes will be stored on the stack at one time in this way, this is not really objectionable since the amount of wasted storage will be insignificant relative to the amount of available main memory. A more serious consequence is that the pushing and popping of entries is now a *nonuniform* process—byte activity requires the aforementioned adjustments, while word activity explicitly requires that such adjustments *not* be made. This technique clearly places additional burdens on the programmer, and the chances for errors will rise accordingly.

Despite these problems, the solution to the byte/word problem outlined above—always ensure that the stack pointer has been adjusted by 2—is intriguing and worth pursuing. We remind the reader that in the preceding chapter we asserted that one of the registers—R6—was *always* adjusted by 2 when used in autoincrement or autodecrement mode (modes 2 and 4), *never* by 1, *regardless* of whether the instruction was in word form or in byte form.* Thus R6 seems

---

*We observed in the footnote of page 118 that some models of the PDP-11 processor treat autoincrementing and autodecrementing of R6 in a slightly different way from what is described here. However, even on such machines the stack is managed properly. For example, in a mix of byte and word pushes, words will be correctly aligned on even (word) addresses. Consequently, any processor may be visualized as behaving as outlined above.

to be a natural register to use as a stack pointer; a word push or pop onto or off of a stack pointed at by R6 will result in the adjustment of c(R6) by 2, and a *byte* push or pop also will yield an adjustment by 2 of c(R6) (with the attendant wasting of 1 byte). Thus if R6 is used as a stack pointer, the byte/word problem simply disappears. It should now be clear that R6's reaction to mode 2 and 4 addressing—which up to now must have struck the reader as peculiar at best— results *precisely* from the fact that R6 is *intended* to be used as a stack pointer. In fact, this register's role in this regard is so strong that R6 is normally referred to as SP (*S*tack *P*ointer), analogous to our use of PC for R7. In giving R6 this special title (SP) we do not want to leave the reader with the impression that R6 is the *only* register that is to be used as a stack pointer. Everything we have described to this point is still true; any register, other than R7, may be utilized as a stack pointer. Register 6 simply has a property relative to some addressing modes that makes it especially useful in this respect.

8.4 THE SPECIAL STACK POINTER SP (R6)
AND THE HARDWARE STACK

Throughout the remainder of the text we shall assume in discussing programs and program segments that whenever needed, a stack has been established in main memory that is pointed at by SP. Thus when we refer to *the* stack pointer we shall always mean SP (R6), and when we refer to *the* stack we shall mean the stack whose pointer is SP. If other stacks are also established in a program, we shall refer to them more explicitly, such as "the stack whose pointer is R3," or "the byte stack," for example.

We shall normally not be explicit about this stack's location nor about how SP was initialized, but will rather assume that this has already been taken care of. The reader who is somewhat uneasy about this lack of definiteness may find his apprehensions allayed in the next chapter. There are numerous ways of establishing this stack. For example, we could agree that our programs are loaded at location 001000, and that the stack pointer is initialized to this same value, thereby leaving the locations between 000000 and 000777 as stack space. This amounts to a potential stack of length 256_{10} words which, under ordinary circumstances, would be more than sufficient (Fig. 8.4.1 (a)). As an alternative scheme we could initialize the stack pointer at an address a few hundred words *beyond* the last address of our program (Fig. 8.4.1(b)). In either case we would have established sufficient

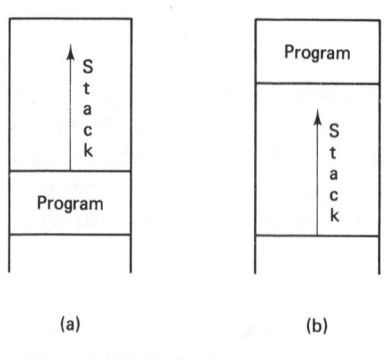

Figure 8.4.1

stack space for most purposes. Notice that while these generous stack sizes all but remove the hazard of stack *overflow* except in unusual cases, they do not remove the potential for stack *underflow*. How the stack is created does not concern us now; we shall simply assume that it exists, with adequate space, and shall feel free to use it whenever it becomes useful to do so.

The stack whose stack pointer is R6 is called the **hardware stack,** a term that requires some elaboration. Indeed, *every* stack is a hardware stack in that it resides in main memory and thus is certainly hardware-dependent. But the stack whose pointer is SP is singled out for this distinction since there are *hardware instructions* that use it. That is, in the course of executing certain instructions, the *CPU itself* uses this stack for the pushing and popping of entries. We have not yet encountered any of these instructions—MOV, INC, CMP, and so forth do *not* use the stack—but they will appear shortly. In the meantime we observe that the existence or nonexistence of this stack is not a matter of arbitrary judgment—this stack *must* exist for the proper execution of some of the hardware instructions.

Before leaving this section we offer an example that shows how the stack can be used to advantage in programming. Figure 8.4.2 shows a revised version of the maximizing program of Fig. 7.5.3 in which the stack is used to hold the temporary maximum, thereby eliminating the need for an additional register (R5). The reader should take special note of line 5, which is a *push;* line 8, which is *not* a push but rather a *replacement* of the top entry on the stack; and

```
MAXIMUM

 1                                .TITLE  MAXIMUM
 2                              ;
 3  000000  012700   START:   MOV   #4,R0          ;SET FOR 4 COMPARES
            000004
 4  000004  012702            MOV   #DATA,R2       ;ADDR OF 1ST NO. IN R2
            000072'
 5  000010  012246            MOV   (R2)+,-(SP)    ;1ST NO. = TEMPMAX
 6  000012  021622   LOOP:    CMP   (SP),(R2)+     ;COMPARE TEMPMAX WITH NO.
 7  000014  002002            BGE   NEXT           ;TEMPMAX BIGGER -- SKIP
 8  000016  016216            MOV   -2(R2),(SP)    ;REPLACE TEMPMAX
            177776
 9  000022  005300   NEXT:    DEC   R0             ;DECREMENT COUNTER
10  000024  001372            BNE   LOOP           ;MORE NOS. IF NONZERO
11  000026  010567            MOV   (SP)+,ANSWER   ;GET THE MAXIMUM
            000036
12  000032           $OUT.OCT #ANSWER,#1 ; AND PRINT IT
13  000066           $EXIT                ;RETURN TO OP. SYSTEM
14                              ;
15  000070           ANSWER:  .BLKW 1               ;FOR PRINTING MAX
16                              ;
17                              ;THE 5 NUMBERS TO BE MAXIMIZED
18                              ;
19  000072  000403   DATA:    .WORD 403
20  000074  102304            .WORD 102304
21  000076  023704            .WORD 23704
22  000100  007702            .WORD 7702
23  000102  176337            .WORD 176337
24                              ;
25          000000'            .END  START
```

Figure 8.4.2

line 11, which is a *pop*, thereby restoring the stack to its original condition—
that is, we are "cleaning up" the stack before EXITing.

8.5 SUBROUTINES

In the course of programming we frequently find ourselves repeating the same
group of instructions in the same program. As an example, consider a matrix
manipulation program in which a block of 25_{10} words, the first of which is
labelled MATRIX, is interpreted *by us* as a 5×5 matrix or array. The first
row of the matrix consists of the words at MATRIX, MATRIX+2, MATRIX
+4, MATRIX+6, and MATRIX+10, the second row extends from MATRIX
+12 to MATRIX+22, and so forth. In the course of manipulating this matrix
we shall probably want to see what values it contains after each significant
change in its entries. Thus we shall want to print this block of storage (in
decimal, say), but simply issuing the command $OUT.DEC   #MATRIX,#31
will result in two rows of nine numbers each, followed by one row of seven
numbers. (See Appendix B, where the output of $OUT.DEC is described.)
Considering the structure we have imposed on this block of numbers, this is
not a particularly convenient form for the output. Thus we choose instead to
do some **formatting** by issuing the *five* commands

$OUT.DEC   #MATRIX,#5
$OUT.DEC   #MATRIX+12,#5
$OUT.DEC   #MATRIX+24,#5
$OUT.DEC   #MATRIX+36,#5
$OUT.DEC   #MATRIX+50,#5

These will do the job very nicely—we shall now see the first five numbers
in the block (what we interpret as the first row of the matrix), followed by the
next five numbers, and so forth. But while the format may be desirable, the
inclusion of these five lines of source code *each* time the matrix is to be printed
is objectionable on two grounds: First, it is a nuisance to write these five lines
each time we want to see the value of the matrix, and second, a fair amount of
main memory is taken up when these five source lines are assembled. (We have
already observed that a reference to one of the input/output commands is made
up of several PDP-11 instructions. In fact, $OUT.DEC takes up 16_8 words
of memory, so printing these five lines requires $5 \times 16 = 106_8 = 70_{10}$ words.)

Evidently we need a scheme by which we can write these five output commands just *once* as a separate routine, called a **subroutine**, to be placed out of
the mainstream of the program execution, then when we want the matrix
printed, we simply pass control over to this routine with a JMP or BR instruction, for example. This technique solves the problem of multiple copies of the
source code, but it introduces another, more serious difficulty. When we need
to print the matrix, we jump to this subroutine, which then executes and prints

the five rows of the matrix, as desired. But *then* what should happen? Apparently we need to return control to the main portion of the programming, but just *where?* Surely we cannot simply execute a JMP to some fixed location, for our intent in writing these five lines as a subroutine was to jump to it from *several* places in the main program, and presumably we would want to pick up main processing where we left off when we jumped to the subroutine. Thus a subroutine must also contain some instructions to achieve a proper return to main processing. To summarize, in order for a subroutine to be useful, we must somehow accomplish the following:

1. Control is passed to the subroutine from the main portion of the program (with JMP or BR).
2. The subroutine executes.
3. Control is returned to the main portion of the program at the instruction following the instruction that gave control to the subroutine.

The situation is diagrammed in Fig. 8.5.1, where the first word of the subroutine is labeled PRINT, and the solid and dashed lines represent the passing of control to PRINT at two *different* places in the main program and then returning to the main program *at the appropriate place.*

It should be clear that whatever difficulties are involved here result from the "return from subroutine" concept, so we shall concentrate our efforts there. What happens when we jump to the subroutine PRINT is what takes place during any kind of jump or branch instruction—the PC is given the value PRINT. Since the value the PC had in the main part of the program is *lost* in the process, there is no hope of getting back to the main program after the subroutine has completed execution *unless,* prior to jumping to the subroutine, we make a note of what the PC was at the time control was passed to PRINT. We shall be able to accomplish this with the instructions that are currently at our disposal.

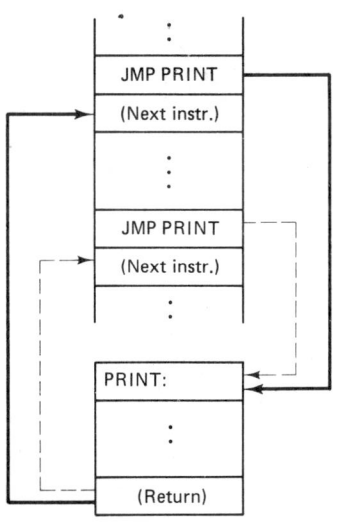

Figure 8.5.1

Since we need to save the PC prior to passing control to the subroutine, we shall save its current value in a register, R5, for instance, with the instruction MOV PC,R5. (The reader might consider the stack to be an equally likely place for saving the PC—MOV PC,–(SP)—and this is quite correct. For the moment, however, we choose to employ a general-purpose register for this task.) Below is a jump-to-subroutine and return-from-subroutine scheme that *almost* works. The addresses shown were chosen arbitrarily.

```
024612                                        ·
024614      010705                      MOV   PC,R5
024616      000167                      JMP   PRINT
024620      021622
024622                                  (next instruction)
024624                                        ·
                                              ·
                                              ·
046444                      PRINT:      (first subroutine instruction)
                                              ·
                                              ·
                                              ·
046552      010507                      MOV   R5,PC
```

When the MOV   PC,R5 instruction is executed, the number (address) 024616 is put in R5, since c(PC) had already been advanced by 2 on the instruction fetch. Control is then passed to the subroutine with the JMP   PRINT instruction. The instruction at 046552—MOV   R5,PC—puts the number 024616 in the PC; thus upon return from the subroutine, program execution picks up at 024616. Unhappily this is not quite where we wanted to return, namely, to 024622. But fortunately we can easily repair the situation in two different ways.

When we are ready to return from the subroutine, R5 contains not the return address, but rather the address of the jump instruction. Since we need to skip around the two words (four bytes) that make up the JMP instruction, all that we need to do is to adjust R5 prior to moving its contents back into the program counter. Thus if we were to change the MOV   R5,PC instruction to

```
046552      062705                      ADD   #4,R5
046554      000004
046556      010507                      MOV   R5,PC
```

then before R5 was moved into the PC, it would contain the value 024622—the correct return address.

The second repair is substantially the same, except in this case we appropriately adjust the contents of R5 *before* passing control to the subroutine. Notice that in this case we cannot simply add 4 to c(R5) as before. Rather, we must add 10 to c(R5), to take into account the four bytes occupied by the ADD instruction itself.

```
024612                                        ·
024614      010705                      MOV   PC,R5
024616      062705                      ADD   #10,R5
024620      000010
024622      000167                      JMP   PRINT
024624      021616
```

024626   (next instruction)
024630   .
                                                  .
                                                  .

046444   PRINT: (first subroutine instruction)
                                                  .
                                                  .
                                                  .

046552   010507   MOV R5,PC

Although this second approach to the proper return address appears to be
a bit more complicated (from the programmer's point of view), we actually
prefer it, for reasons that will be clear shortly. First, we call attention to the
fact that R5, which is being used to save the return address, may well be in use
in the program for other purposes. Thus to avoid the disaster that could occur
by saving c(PC) in it, it would be well as a matter of practice to save c(R5)
prior to its use and then restore it upon return from the subroutine. Since the
stack seems a likely place to save c(R5) temporarily, we modify the jump-to-
subroutine sequence as follows:

                         MOV   R5,−(SP)
                         MOV   PC,R5
                         ADD   #10,R5
                         JMP   PRINT
                         MOV   (SP)+,R5
                         (next instruction)

We now have a technique for passing control to a subroutine and also
properly returning to the main portion of the program that would seem to work
under any circumstances, but actually there are still a few potential problems
here. Suppose, for example, in the course of the main portion of the program
we required printing of the matrix—a jump to the subroutine PRINT—but
we discovered that we were physically close enough to the subroutine to reach
it with a BR instruction rather than a JMP. If we included the jump-to-subroutine code

                         MOV   R5,−(SP)
                         MOV   PC,R5
                         ADD   #10,R5
                         BR   PRINT
                         MOV   (SP)+,R5
                         (next instruction)

we would find that we had misadjusted c(R5) with the ADD   #10,R5 instruction. For BR   PRINT takes only *one* word of memory, whereas JMP   PRINT
takes *two*, and consequently the adjustment should have been ADD   #6,R5

instead. Provided we keep our wits about us when we write the jump-to-subroutine instructions, all will be well, although the procedure is beginning to
become a bit burdensome. But notice that if we had chosen to make the R5
adjustment in the subroutine itself, as proposed on page 164, then there would
be little hope for a proper return. If, as shown, we adjust c(R5) by 4, then a JMP
to PRINT will return correctly, but a BR to PRINT will not. On the other hand,
if the adjustment of c(R5) is by 2, then BR to PRINT will return properly,
whereas a JMP to PRINT will not. For this reason we prefer to adjust R5 in
the main portion of the program where we can determine *how* control will be
passed to the subroutine and can thus properly adjust the return address.

Finally, we note that R5 plays no special role here. Any general-purpose
register would do for saving the return PC, and as we mentioned earlier, even
the stack would be an appropriate place for this. Indeed, as long as the return
address (possibly adjusted) is saved *somewhere* so that control can be returned
to main processing after the subroutine has executed, the jump-to-subroutine
and return-from-subroutine scheme is not only usable but also extremely useful.

8.6 THE JSR AND RTS INSTRUCTIONS

The preceding section should have convinced the reader that the subroutine
concept is quite useful for reducing the amount of code needed in some programs
and consequently, the necessity for the programmer to write that code. But the
instructions needed to set up the return address prior to the subroutine jump,
while not conceptually difficult, nonetheless require some care in their construction which, as always, is thus accompanied by increased chances of error. Also,
the instructions themselves take up a nontrivial amount of main memory.
Fortunately the PDP-11 hardware assists us in this regard.

A brief review of the subroutine jump/return scheme reveals the following
procedure:

1. Save some register on the stack.
2. Put the (correct) return address in that register.
3. Pass control to the subroutine.
4. Reset the PC to the return address and restore the (original) value of the
   register.

The two hardware instructions JSR (*J*ump to *Sub*Routine) and RTS (*ReT*urn
from *S*ubroutine) have *precisely* these effects. The form of the JSR instruction is

$$\text{JSR} \quad \text{Rn, target}$$

Its binary code is

$$0 \ 000 \ 100 \ rrr \ ddd \ ddd$$

or, in octal,

$$004RDD$$

Here R is the register used to save the return PC (R5, in the examples of the preceding section), called the **subroutine transfer register**. DD is, as usual, the subroutine jump destination, and all addressing modes are valid here. The effect of the JSR instruction is as follows:

1. Calculate the destination (subroutine) address.
2. Push the current contents of the transfer register on the hardware stack.
3. Put the current contents of the PC in the transfer register.
4. Put the destination (subroutine) address in the PC; that is, jump to the subroutine.

The details of JSR can be diagramed as follows:

$$\text{TEMP} \leftarrow \text{destination (subroutine) address}$$
$$\downarrow \text{(SP)} \leftarrow \text{c(transfer register)}$$
$$\text{transfer register} \leftarrow \text{c(current PC)}$$
$$\text{PC} \leftarrow \text{c(TEMP)}$$

Here the symbol $\leftarrow$ stands for "is given the value of," $\downarrow$ (SP) represents a push onto the stack, and TEMP is an internal private CPU register.

It is important that the reader understand that *all* of this desirable activity takes place as a result of the JSR instruction. The saving of the current contents of the transfer register, the saving of the current PC, and the jump to the subroutine are now taken over completely by the CPU, leaving the programmer with little to do other than to write the JSR instruction itself. Two observations are necessary here. Note first that this instruction actually *uses the hardware stack* (hence the terminology), the first such instruction we have encountered. This is also by far the most complex instruction we have seen, from a standpoint of the amount of CPU activity involved. Second, the return address is *always* correct, for regardless of the form of the JSR instruction— it may be a one-word or two-word instruction, such as JSR   R5,PRINT, or JSR   RØ,@#SUBR, or JSR   RØ,(R3)—the PC will always have the address of the next instruction following the JSR by the time the current c(PC) is moved into the transfer register.

Now we require a companion instruction to achieve the return from subroutine, and the RTS instruction fills this need. The form of the RTS is

$$\text{RTS} \quad \text{Rn}$$

Its binary code is

$$0\ 000\ 000\ 010\ 000\ rrr$$

or, in octal,

$$00020R$$

where R is the transfer register. Diagrammatically its effect is

$$PC \longleftarrow c(\text{transfer register})$$
$$\text{transfer register} \longleftarrow (SP) \uparrow$$

where $(SP) \uparrow$ represents a pop from the hardware stack.

We include here a final version of the principal subroutine example of the preceding section.

024612		·	
024614	004567		**JSR R5,PRINT**
024616	021624		
024620			(next instruction)
		·	
		·	
		·	
046444		**PRINT:**	(first subroutine instruction)
		·	
		·	
		·	
046552	000205		**RTS R5**

When the PC contains the number (address) 024614, the CPU does a fetch, moving c(PC) up to 024616. Since the instruction is indexed (PC mode 6), the CPU does another fetch, incrementing c(PC) to 024620. Now the JSR is executed: The current contents of R5 is stacked, R5 gets the current c(PC)—024620—and control is passed to PRINT. Upon encountering the RTS   R5 instruction, the CPU puts the current contents of R5, namely, 024620, in the PC and pops the stack into R5. Thus control is returned to location 024620, the instruction following the JSR, as desired.

This is really all that we need to say about the JSR/RTS combination. These instructions handle the transfer of control to subroutines and proper returns quite automatically. And while the programmer does need to be aware of what is taking place when these hardware instructions are executed (as we shall see in a later section), nonetheless the processor and its hardware take a substantial burden off the programmer, in particular in setting up the return address.

Finally, we trust that it is evident that if the transfer register is modified *within the subroutine* to which it refers, the consequences for the RTS instruction can be disastrous since that register holds the return address—the lifeline back to the main portion of the program. In Sec. 8.8 we shall see that modifications of the transfer register done in the subroutine may be desirable and necessary, but they must be made carefully.

8.7 SUBROUTINES THAT REFERENCE OTHER SUBROUTINES

In the preceding section we saw how the JSR/RTS combination—instructions that do precisely everything required for subroutine references—makes use of the hardware stack for the saving of the transfer register. And while we see the desirability of saving the transfer register and might agree that the hardware stack is a convenient place to put this register while it is in use for saving the return PC, the role played by the stack *structure* is not yet clear. In Sec. 8.2 we touted the stack as a highly useful device; it is time to justify our claims.

Let us consider a substantially more complex subroutine situation than those in the preceding sections—one in which we have three subroutines, which we shall refer to as SUBA, SUBB, and SUBC. We also assume some main program that refers to them. For convenience we introduce some terminology. We shall call the main portion of the programming the **mainline program**, and whenever we refer to a subroutine, we shall say that we **call** or **invoke** the subroutine. In the present example we go out of our way to complicate things as much as possible. Rather than simply have the mainline call SUBA, SUBB, and SUBC in turn, which would not differ from the examples we have seen, we assume instead that the mainline calls SUBA, that SUBA in the course of its execution calls SUBB which, in turn, calls SUBC. The reader might conclude that this subroutine call nesting would cause no severe difficulties *provided* that *different* transfer registers were used for each call. But we are going to use the *same* register—R2—for all three subroutine calls. It might appear that disaster will strike when SUBB is called, since c(R2) will be destroyed in the process, thereby causing SUBA to lose its ability to return to the mainline. But as we shall see, it is precisely the *stack* structure that completely eliminates these difficulties.

In Fig. 8.7.1 we again assigned addresses arbitrarily. In the course of following through the subroutine calls we shall pay particular attention to the state of the hardware stack, which is the key to the proper disposition of the subroutine calls and returns. We assume the stack to be empty initially, although there is no reason that it has to be. In the mainline program, we give R2 the value 12 at location 002410, only so that we will know explicitly c(R2).

The effect of the JSR R2,SUBA instruction at location 002414 bears a detailed examination. When the JSR instruction is fetched from location 002414, the CPU increments c(PC) to 002416. Since the instruction is indexed (mode 6), another fetch is required to obtain the index, 004270. This moves c(PC) up again, to 002420. Now the destination address is calculated, by adding the index to the current contents of the PC, to obtain 002420 + 004270 = 006710. Next, the current contents of the transfer register R2, 000012, is pushed onto the stack, the current contents of the PC (002420) is put into R2, and the PC gets the destination address, 006710. The stack at this point is shown in

002406		(mainline program)
002410	012702	MOV #12,R2
002412	000012	
002414	004267	JSR R2,SUBA
002416	004270	
002420		(next mainline instruction)
002422		.
		.
		.
006710	SUBA:	(first SUBA instruction)
		.
		.
		.
006744	004267	JSR R2,SUBB
006746	001360	
006750		(next SUBA instruction)
		.
		.
		.
007204	000202	RTS R2
		.
		.
		.
010330	SUBB:	(first SUBB instruction)
		.
		.
		.
011402	004267	JSR R2,SUBC
011404	005414	
011406		(next SUBB instruction)
		.
		.
		.
011722	000202	RTS R2
		.
		.
		.
017022	SUBC:	(first SUBC instruction)
		.
		.
		.
020034	000202	RTS R2

Figure 8.7.1

Fig. 8.7.2. Execution picks up at SUBA and continues until the JSR   R2,SUBB
instruction is encountered at location 006744. Once again the destination address
is calculated and found to be 010330, during which c(PC) has been moved up
to 006750. Next the *current* contents of the transfer register, R2—002420—is
stacked, R2 is given the value of the PC (006750), and the PC is given the destination address. Figure 8.7.3 shows the current stack. Execution in the subroutine
SUBB   proceeds   until   JSR   R2,SUBC   is   encountered.   The   destination
address (017022) is calculated, the current contents of R2 (006750) is stacked,

R2 gets the current c(PC) (011406), and PC is given the destination address (Fig. 8.7.4). We are now executing in SUBC, where processing continues until the RTS   R2 instruction is encountered at location 020034. The effect of this instruction is to give the PC the value currently in the transfer register, R2—namely, 011406—and then to pop the top of the stack into that transfer register. Thus after execution of this RTS   R2 instruction, the various registers and the stack have the values shown in Fig. 8.7.5. Since c(PC) = 011406, execution continues in SUBB at the instruction immediately following the call to SUBC. When the RTS   R2 instruction at 011722 is executed, the return process is repeated—the PC gets the current contents of R2 (006750), and the

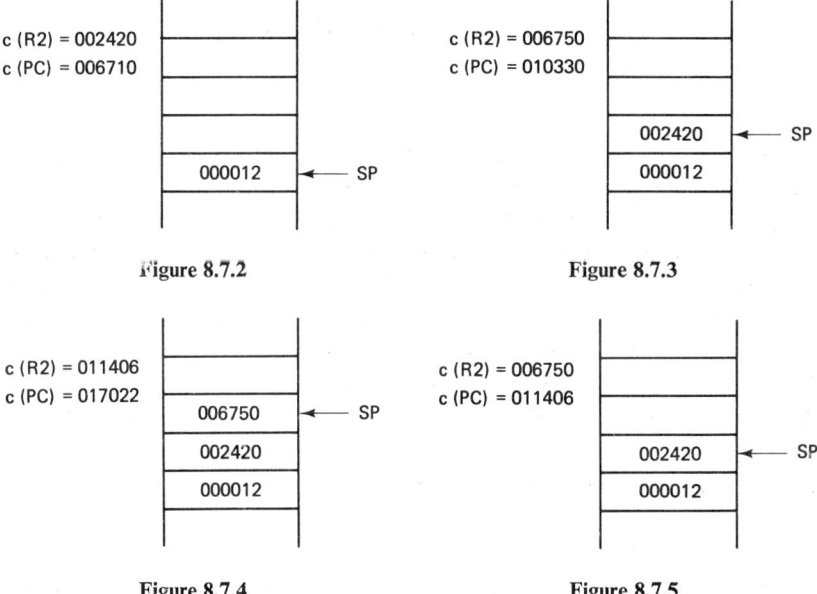

Figure 8.7.2   Figure 8.7.3

Figure 8.7.4   Figure 8.7.5

top of the stack is popped into R2 (Fig. 8.7.6). Execution picks up in SUBA at the instruction immediately following SUBA's call to SUBB (006750) and continues to the RTS   R2 instruction at 007204. Again the PC is given R2's value (002420) and the top of the stack is popped into R2, giving R2 its initial value, 12. Execution has finally returned to the mainline program where it left off, namely, at the mainline's call to SUBA, and the stack is once again empty.

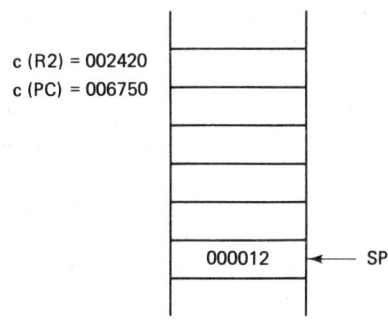

Figure 8.7.6

The reader who has followed the details of these nested subroutine calls will recognize that the reason the *returns* were handled correctly is that upon each return, R2 was given the *last* value it had—the returns occurred in the *reverse* order in which the calls took place. The stack, as a *last in–first out* structure, accomplished this—no other type of structure would do the job. Indeed, the situation is so automatic that we rarely need to concern ourselves with just what is taking place on the JSR and RTS because the CPU and the stack will generally manage matters nicely.

8.8 PASSING ARGUMENTS TO A SUBROUTINE

The only specific subroutine we have dealt with thus far, namely, the subroutine PRINT that displays the five rows of a 5 × 5 matrix, has the unusual feature that it *always* performs the *same* task on the *same* memory locations—it always prints the five numbers beginning at MATRIX, then the five numbers beginning at MATRIX + 12, and so forth. If some other matrix was present in this program, say a 4 × 7 matrix located at ARRAY, then we could certainly not use the subroutine PRINT to print its four rows, in a row-by-row fashion. While the routine PRINT may be useful in some program environments, it is far more typical for a subroutine to deal with different **parameters**, or **arguments**—values, addresses, counters, and so forth—*each* time it is called.

As an example of a subroutine that can operate on variable data, let us continue our matrix example and consider the task of finding the largest of a collection of numbers. (We have already programmed this job in a variety of ways.) For example, it may be desirable to know the largest number in the matrix, or perhaps the largest number in the fourth row of the matrix. (This is a frequent activity in that area of mathematics known as *linear programming*.) In order to perform this task the subroutine must know *how many* numbers are to be dealt with, along with the *address* of the *first* such number. Thus for the subroutine to calculate the largest number in the matrix, we would need to pass it the address of the first of these numbers, namely MATRIX, along with the number of the numbers, 25_{10}. Similarly, to find the largest number in the fourth row the subroutine requires the address MATRIX + 36 and the count 5. This section will describe some of the methods that might be used to pass these arguments to the subroutine. The methods are limited only by the programmer's imagination, so we can scarcely cover all of them. Rather, we present here some standard techniques; we give some others in the exercises. As the reader gains experience in these matters, he will invent other useful schemes.

In writing a maximizing subroutine to do the job at hand, we shall have to establish some conventions. Let us assume that R1 will be used as the subroutine transfer register, that R∅ contains the count of numbers to be maximized, and that R2 contains the address of the first of those numbers. Since the purpose of the subroutine is to calculate the largest of the numbers, the subroutine will somehow have to communicate that maximum number *back to* the mainline program that called it. We shall employ R5 for this purpose—by the time control has been returned to the mainline from the subroutine, the largest of the numbers in question will be in R5. We can now write a "skeleton" module to do this job. The programming segment in Fig. 8.8.1 will execute properly *provided that* R2 contains the address of the first number and R∅ contains the number of numbers. As we shall see, depending on how the arguments are passed to the routine, it may be necessary to "front end" this module with a few additional instructions to ensure that R2 and R∅ have the proper values. The purpose of the first program instruction, DEC R∅, is to give R∅ the number of *compares* that will have to be made, which is always one less than the number of numbers.

```
                         ;'SKELETON' MAXIMIZING ROUTINE
                         ;
                         ;C(R2) = ADDRESS OF 1ST NUMBER
                         ;C(R∅) = COUNT OF NUMBERS TO BE MAXIMIZED
                         ;
                         ;MAXIMUM RETURNED IN R5
                         ;
002460  005300           DEC    R∅           ;DECREMENT TO NUMBER
                                             ; OF COMPARES
002462  012205           MOV    (R2)+,R5     ;1ST NO. - TEMPMAX
002464  020522   LOOP:   CMP    R5,(R2)+     ;COMP. TEMPMAX WITH NO.
002466  002002           BGE    NEXT         ;TEMPMAX BIGGER -- SKIP
002470  016205           MOV    -2(R2),R5    ;REPLACE TEMPMAX
        177776
002474  077005   NEXT:   SOB    R∅,LOOP      ;PROCESS NEXT NUMBER
                         ;
002476  000201           RTS    R1           ;DONE -- RETURN
```

Figure 8.8.1

The easiest way for the mainline to pass the required information to the subroutine is for the mainline program *itself* to set registers ∅ and 2 prior to jumping to the subroutine. Thus if we simply label the first instruction of the skeleton module MAX: and execute the instructions

```
        MOV   #5,R∅
        MOV   #MATRIX+12,R2
        JSR   R1,MAX
```

then the subroutine will return in R5 the largest number in the second row of the matrix, and we do not need to make any additions to or changes in the skeleton routine.

While this scheme is certainly the most direct way to pass the necessary arguments to this subroutine, it may be impractical if a subroutine needs a great deal of information—we may simply not have enough registers to cover the required arguments. Thus we offer another scheme which, while it is a bit more complicated in the *handling* of the arguments, places no restriction on the *number* of arguments passed to the routine. The idea is to include the arguments to be passed, listed as .WORDs., immediately following the call to the subroutine. Thus our last example might be called as

        JSR   R1,MAX
        .WORD 5
        .WORD MATRIX+12

We show a program segment to implement this call in Fig. 8.8.2, and since it contains a number of new features, we examine it in detail. Note the use of "25." in the .BLKW at 001000. The assembler treats numbers followed by a decimal point as being decimal—base 10—rather than octal. In the remainder of the text we shall take advantage of this feature, implemented purely for programmer convenience, whenever it is useful to do so.

```
                              .
001000           MATRIX: .BLKW    25.              ;THE 5-BY-5 MATRIX
                              .
001724   004167         JSR      R1,MAX            ;MAXIMIZE
         000520
001730   000005         .WORD    5                 ; THE 5 NUMBERS
001732   001012         .WORD    MATRIX+12         ; BEGINNING AT MATRIX+12
001734                  (NEXT MAINLINE INSTRUCTION)

                        ;SUBROUTINE 'MAX'
                        ;
002450   010046 MAX:    MOV      R0,-(SP)          ;SAVE REGISTERS
002452   010246         MOV      R2,-(SP)          ; R0 AND R2 ON STACK
002454   012100         MOV      (R1)+,R0          ;GET COUNT
002456   012102         MOV      (R1)+,R2          ; AND ADDR OF 1ST NUMBER

                        ; 'SKELETON' MAXIMIZING ROUTINE
                        ;
                        ;C(R2) = ADDRESS OF 1ST NUMBER
                        ;C(R0) = COUNT OF NUMBERS TO BE MAXIMIZED
                        ;
                        ;MAXIMUM RETURNED IN R5
002460   005300         DEC      R0                ;DECREMENT TO NUMBER
                                                   ; OF COMPARES
002462   012205         MOV      (R2)+,R5          ;1ST NO. = TEMPMAX
002464   020522 LOOP:   CMP      R5,(R2)+          ;COMP. TEMPMAX WITH NO.
002466   002002         BGE      NEXT              ;TEMPMAX BIGGER -- SKIP
002470   016205         MOV      -2(R2),R5         ;REPLACE TEMPMAX
         177776
002474   077005 NEXT:   SOB      R0,LOOP           ;PROCESS NEXT NUMBER

002476   012602         MOV      (SP)+,R2          ;RESTORE REGISTERS
002500   012600         MOV      (SP)+,R0          ; R0 AND R2 FROM STACK
                        ;
002502   000201         RTS      R1                ;DONE -- RETURN
```

Figure 8.8.2

The call to the subroutine MAX is followed by two words which contain the count and the address. When the JSR R1,MAX is encountered, the PC will contain the value 001724. The destination address is calculated, c(R1) is stacked, and then R1 is given the *current* PC value, which by now is 001730. Then the PC is given the destination address, and thus control is passed to the subroutine MAX. The first instructions executed in MAX are the stacking of registers Ø and 2, the reason for which is quite important. The subroutine, as we know, needs to use these registers for the count and the address, respectively. However, there is now no assurance that the contents of these registers are not significant to the *mainline* program. In the preceding example, the mainline explicitly used these registers to pass values to the subroutine. In this case, however, those registers are *not* being used for this purpose, and thus there is no reason to believe that the mainline is not using them for some other purpose. Thus, to be on the safe side, the subroutine saves them on the stack before using them for its own internal purposes. We shall see that their mainline values will be restored before returning to the calling portion of the program.

The next instruction to be executed (at location 002454) is MOV (R1)+,R∅. What number is moved into R∅, and what is the purpose of the autoincrement mode? Recall that by the time control was passed to the subroutine MAX, c(R1) = 001730. Thus the contents of the memory location whose address is in R1, that is, the contents of memory location 001730, is moved into R∅. Hence the number moved into R∅ is 000005, the number count. Thus we have managed to place the count of numbers to be maximized into R∅ as required. At the same time, the autoincrementing has moved the contents of R1 up to 001732. The next instruction—MOV (R1)+,R2—moves the contents of the location whose address is in R1 into R2. Since c(R1) = 001732, c(001732) is moved into R2, namely, the address MATRIX + 12 (001012). Thus again R2 has been properly set to the address of the first number to be maximized, and c(R1) has been autoincremented to 001734.

Now that the proper number count and address have been established in R∅ and R2, respectively, the subroutine may proceed as before. Upon its completion, that is, when all the numbers have been compared, we are ready to return. But before doing so, the original mainline values of R∅ and R2 are restored from the stack. (Note that they are popped off the stack in reverse order.) The RTS   R1 instruction is now encountered. Its effect is to move the current contents of R1 into the PC and also to pop the top of the stack into R1 to restore its original mainline value. Since at this point c(R1) = 001734, we return to this location, namely, to the instruction *immediately following* the two .WORDs. And this is precisely where we *should* return. In returning to the mainline portion of the program, we have *skipped around* these two .WORDs, as desired. How was this accomplished? This was a result of using the *autoincrementing* addressing mode in the two MOV instructions at locations 002454 and 002456.

While a fair amount of activity occurred here that was essential to the proper handling of the subroutine, it was nonetheless peripheral to the actual subroutine instructions themselves. It will be worthwhile to review it briefly. Notice that the front end of the subroutine as written expects the calling program to have inserted two .WORDs after the subroutine call, and it should be clear that if those .WORDs are not there, or if they are there in the wrong order, the subroutine either will not return properly or will not do its job correctly. Next, observe that the subroutine saved the registers it used prior to using them. Since the subroutine may know little about register activity in the mainline program that calls it, this is simply sound programming practice. Finally, we noted that R∅ and R2 were restored from the stack prior to the subroutine return, but we glossed over the restoring of the transfer register R1. If R∅ and R2 had *not* been restored prior to the RTS R1, the RTS would have popped the top of the stack into R1, and this would have been the mainline value of R2, *not* the mainline value of R1. This failure to restore the mainline value of R1 properly could have serious consequences in the mainline.

If the reader is left with the impression that the passing of arguments to a subroutine requires much attention to detail, then he has not been misled. The calling program must have a fair amount of information concerning the subroutine's handling of these arguments, and the subroutine must know *how* it is being called by the mainline. The stack must be managed properly and the return address must take into account arguments that are being passed to the subroutine. In this regard the programming is quite painstaking, but exercising care in this area will result in properly functioning, useful routines.

We close this section with a final example of passing arguments to a subroutine. In this case, the arguments are passed *on the stack* (Fig. 8.8.3). And while this means of argument transmission is quite standard, we shall see that the necessary programming is considerably more involved than it was in the two schemes we have examined so far. The idea is simple: Prior to passing control to the subroutine, we stack the number count and the address of the first number. Thus

```
MOV   #5,-(SP)
MOV   #MATRIX+12,-(SP)
JSR   R1,MAX
```

Upon entering the subroutine we immediately encounter a difficulty: The two arguments that we pushed on the stack for transmission to the subroutine are no longer on the top of the stack, where they might be popped off. For the JSR instruction itself has pushed the current (mainline) contents of the transfer register R1 onto the stack. Thus when we are ready to execute the subroutine MAX, the stack will appear as in Fig. 8.8.4. (Here ML R1 stands for the mainline value of R1, which—in this example—is not known.) In fact, since we decided that it is good practice for a subroutine to save (on the stack) the contents of any registers the subroutine needs, R∅ and R2 should again be pushed onto the stack, and thus the number count and the address MATRIX + 12 sift even farther down into the stack (Fig. 8.8.5). The fact that the numbers we need are buried in the stack is of no real consequence, however, since any stack entry may be *accessed*, even though the only entry that can be *removed* is the one at the top of the stack. Since, for example, the number count (5) is 4 words down from the top of the stack, it can be accessed by referencing 10(SP). Thus in the subroutine MAX, the instruction MOV   10(SP),R∅ moves this count into R∅ without, of course, affecting the stack in any way. In a similar

```
                   .
001000         MATRIX: .BLKW    25.
                   .
001724   012746    MOV     #5,-(SP)            ;PUT COUNT AND
         000005
001730   012746    MOV     #MATRIX+12,-(SP)    ; ADDRESS ON STACK
         001012
001734   004167    JSR     R1,MAX              ;JUMP TO SUBROUTINE
         000504
001740             (NEXT MAINLINE INSTRUCTION)
                   .
                   ;SUBROUTINE 'MAX'
                   ;
002444   010046 MAX:  MOV  R0,-(SP)            ;SAVE REGISTERS
002446   010246    MOV     R2,-(SP)            ; R0 AND R2 ON STACK
002450   016600    MOV     10(SP),R0           ;GET COUNT
         000010
002454   016602    MOV     6(SP),R2            ; AND ADDR OF 1ST NUMBER
         000006
                   ;
                   ; 'SKELETON' MAXIMIZING ROUTINE
                   ;
                   ;C(R2) = ADDRESS OF 1ST NUMBER
                   ;C(R0) = COUNT OF NUMBERS TO BE MAXIMIZED
                   ;
                   ;MAXIMUM RETURNED IN R5
                   ;
002460   005300    DEC     R0                  ;DECREMENT TO NUMBER
                   ;                           ; OF COMPARES
002462   012205    MOV     (R2)+,R5            ;1ST NO. = TEMPMAX
002464   020522 LOOP: CMP  R5,(R2)+            ;COMP. TEMPMAX WITH NO.
002466   002002    BGE     NEXT                ;TEMPMAX BIGGER -- SKIP
002470   016205    MOV     -2(R2),R5           ;REPLACE TEMPMAX
         177776
002474   077005 NEXT: SOB  R0,LOOP             ;PROCESS NEXT NUMBER
                   ;
002476   012602    MOV     (SP)+,R2            ;RESTORE REGISTERS
002500   012600    MOV     (SP)+,R0            ; R0 AND R2 FROM STACK
002502   012666    MOV     (SP)+,2(SP)         ;MOVE ML R1 DOWN STACK
         000002
002506   005726    TST     (SP)+               ; AND ADJUST SP
                   ;
002510   000201    RTS     R1                  ;DONE -- RETURN
```

Figure 8.8.3

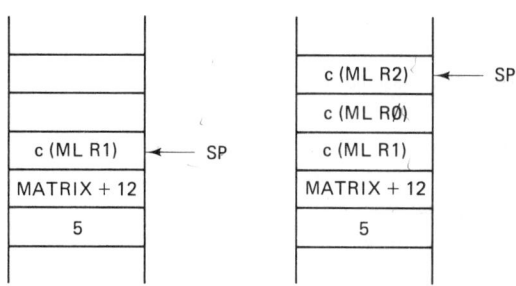

Figure 8.8.4   Figure 8.8.5

fashion, the entry MATRIX + 12 is put into R2, and we may now allow the subroutine to proceed as before.

The difficulties begin when we are ready to return to the mainline portion of the program. After R2 and R∅ are restored to their original mainline values, the stack contains the numbers shown in Fig. 8.8.6. At this point we could simply execute RTS R1 and the mainline value of R1 would be properly restored and control would be returned to the instruction following the JSR to MAX. But this would leave the two entries MATRIX+12 and 5 still on the stack. While this might be desired under some circumstances, normally when arguments are transmitted to a subroutine on the stack, the subroutine should "clean" the stack prior to returning, rather than leaving this task to the mainline program. We can do this with two instructions (Fig. 8.8.7).

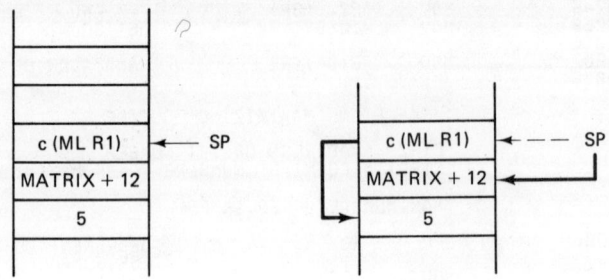

Figure 8.8.6   Figure 8.8.7

The first is MOV (SP)+,2(SP), which requires a little analysis. The reference to (SP)+ is to the top of the stack, namely, c(ML R1). *After* this reference, but *before* the reference to 2(SP), the stack pointer value is incremented by 2. Thus this MOV moves c(ML R1) into the location one word down from the *new* top of the stack, and hence c(ML R1) is MOVed into the location previously occupied by the number count, 5. This gives a stack containing two entries—MATRIX + 12 is on top of the stack, and c(ML R1) is one word down in the stack. The next instruction—TST (SP)+—gets the address in SP, *increments c(SP) by 2,* and then sets the condition codes N and Z according to the contents of that address. In fact, we do not care how the condition codes were set. The purpose of the instruction is not to test the word at the top of the stack, but rather to increment the stack pointer by 2. This is an easy, one-word scheme for incrementing the stack pointer, or any other register, for that matter, by 2. Thus we have managed to move the stack pointer down without having to pop the top of the stack, since in fact we were not interested in moving MATRIX + 12 anywhere. The stack now contains the single entry c(ML R1), and the RTS R1 then will restore R1 to its mainline value.

The reader could, with some justification, accuse us of "stack abuse" here. We have manipulated the stack and the stack pointer in ways that violate the "rules" of stack management if by these rules we mean that items are to be added and removed only at the top of the stack, and that the stack pointer moves only on pushes and pops. We counter such accusations with the claim that the end justifies the means. While it has been necessary to proceed with some care, these instructions have gotten the job done. (As Humpty Dumpty would have it, "The question is, which is to be master—that's all.")

Observe that the role played by the transfer register R1 in this example is much less active than it was in the preceding case. Here R1 was used only to save the return address, while the arguments came off the stack. In the preceding example, R1 was used directly to obtain those arguments from the mainline program.

8.9 USING THE PC AS A SUBROUTINE TRANSFER REGISTER

In our examples thus far we used one of the general-purpose registers, R$\emptyset$ to R5, as a transfer register for subroutine calls. However, there is no reason why the PC cannot be used for this purpose, as we shall show. Recall that the effect of the JSR instruction (page 167) is to calculate the destination address, stack the transfer register, give the transfer register the current PC contents, and then give control to the subroutine. If the transfer register is the PC, then the effect (diagrammatically) is

$$\text{TEMP} \longleftarrow \text{destination address}$$
$$\downarrow (\text{SP}) \longleftarrow c(\text{PC})$$
$$\text{PC} \longleftarrow c(\text{PC})$$
$$\text{PC} \longleftarrow c(\text{TEMP})$$

The third step in this process is somewhat wasted motion, but the key lies in the second step—the stacking of the *current* PC contents, which is the address of the instruction following the JSR. In a similar fashion, RTS   PC properly restores the PC for return to the mainline (page 168).

$$\text{PC} \longleftarrow c(\text{PC})$$
$$\text{PC} \longleftarrow (\text{SP}) \uparrow$$

Recall that when we transmitted arguments to a subroutine by means of .WORDs that immediately followed the subroutine call and when the transfer register was one of the general-purpose registers, then by the time control had been passed to the subroutine, that transfer register contained the address of the first of the arguments. We have already seen the ease with which the arguments can be obtained in this case, and this is why the hardware instruction JSR is constructed the way it is—it greatly simplifies subroutine argument transmission. If, on the other hand, the transfer register is the PC then the situation is not nearly so convenient, for the address of the first argument is on top of the stack, and it is more cumbersome for the subroutine to access the arguments in this case. Furthermore, if a mainline transmits, for example, three arguments in this fashion to a subroutine called via the PC, then we must make sure to adjust the number on top of the stack, by adding 6 in this case, before returning with RTS   PC.

If a mainline program passes arguments to a subroutine either directly through the general-purpose registers or on the stack, then the use of the PC as the transfer register yields a situation that is as easily managed as if a general-purpose register had been used. In fact, using the PC for these purposes frees up an additional register for subroutine use. The reader would be well served if he reviewed the three examples of the preceding section, in each case replacing the transfer register R1 by the PC, and determining what modifications, if any, need to be made.

8.10 RECURSIVE SUBROUTINES

In Sec. 8.7 we saw that subroutines could call other subroutines in the course of their execution, and even if several such nested routines used the same transfer register, the stack structure took care of proper subroutine returns automatically. In fact, a subroutine can even call *itself* in the midst of its processing. This concept is known as subroutine call **recursion**, and provided care is taken in the construction of the subroutine to avoid *infinite recursion*—the phenomenon in which a subroutine invokes itself continually, with no provision for terminating the recursion—the stack will once again manage the returns in a way that requires little programmer intervention.

As a simple and conceivably useful example, consider a situation in which we need to know the address in a block of memory where the first byte containing an *odd* (8-bit) number occurs. The subroutine assumes that the address of the first such byte to be tested is in R1, and since no other arguments need to be passed, the PC is used as a subroutine transfer register. The first instruction in the subroutine ODD is BITB   #1,(R1), which performs a logical *AND* of the number 001 and the contents of the byte whose address is in R1. The condition codes are set, and if the result of the *AND*ing was nonzero, then evidently bit 0 of the byte was a 1, and hence the contents of that byte is odd. A listing of the subroutine ODD and a sample mainline program that invokes it is shown in Fig. 8.10.1.

The reader should have little difficulty following the logic of this program, but it would be most instructive to monitor the stack each time it changes its state, as the result of the JSRs and RTSs, and in particular to note how the returns begin to "unravel" once a byte is found containing an odd value.

While the example above may be a bit contrived, the *concept* of recursion is by no means an oddity in computer science and mathematics. It is not unusual for mathematical functions to be *defined* recursively, and we offer one such familiar example.

```
 1                              ;MAINLINE PROGRAM -- CALLS SUBROUTINE 'ODD'
 2                              ; TO FIND POSITION OF FIRST ODD BYTE IN A
 3                              ; BLOCK OF MEMORY
 4                              ;
 5  000000  012701   START:  MOV     #BLOCK,R1       ;SET ADDR OF 1ST NUMBER
            000012'
 6  000004  004767           JSR     PC,ODD          ;CALL THE SUBROUTINE
            000016
 7  000010  000000           HALT                    ;STOP -- R1 CONTAINS
 8                                                    ; ADDRESS OF 1ST ODD
 9                                                    ; BYTE IN 'BLOCK'
10                              ;
11                              ;THE BLOCK OF NUMBERS
12                              ;
13  000012  000212   BLOCK:  .WORD   212,300,43552,177722,3,24
    000014  000300
    000016  043552
    000020  177722
    000022  000003
    000024  000024
14                              ;
15                              ;THE SUBROUTINE 'ODD'
16                              ;
17  000026  132711   ODD:    BITB    #1,(R1)         ;TEST BIT 0 OF BYTE
            000001
18  000032  001003           BNE     DONE            ;IF NONZERO, IT'S ODD
19  000034  005201           INC     R1              ; ELSE INCREMENT ADDR
20  000036  004767           JSR     PC,ODD          ; AND CALL THIS ROUTINE
            177764
21                              ;
22  000042  000207   DONE:   RTS     PC              ;RETURN
23                              ;
24          000000'           .END    START
```

Figure 8.10.1

Let n be a nonnegative integer, and define the function f as follows:

$$f(n) = 1 \text{ if } n = 0$$

$$f(n) = n \cdot f(n-1) \text{ if } n > 0$$

The reader may recognize this as the definition of the factorial function, whose value is usually written as $n!$. (To establish that in fact this *does* define $f(n)$ for all nonnegative integers n requires a technique such as the principle of mathematical induction.) The recursion, of course, lies in the second line of the definition, where the function invokes itself. The activity here is similar to what took place in the last example; in fact, in the exercises we give some suggestions for writing a program that calculates $n!$ by means of a recursive subroutine call. Such recursive definitions frequently lead to recursive programming procedures. We shall see other examples in the remainder of the text.

8.11 MULTIPLE SUBROUTINE ENTRY POINTS

The memory location to which processor control is passed from a mainline program executing a jump-to-subroutine is called a subroutine **entry point**—the point at which the subroutine is entered. In the two principal examples of subroutines in this chapter, those entry points were given the symbolic names PRINT and MAX. However, a subroutine need not have a *unique* entry point; it is quite possible and perhaps useful to enter a subroutine at a variety of places.

As a simple (if not useful) example of this idea, consider a subroutine that does multiple duty in that by entering it at the appropriate place, we may decrement $c(R4)$ by 6, by 4, or by 2.

```
DECBY6:   SUB   #2,R4
DECBY4:   SUB   #2,R4
DECBY2:   SUB   #2,R4
          RTS   PC
```

Since no arguments need to be passed, we assume here that the PC is the subroutine transfer register. It should be clear that if the routine is entered at the entry point named DECBY6, then three subtractions of 2 take place, giving a total decrement by 6. The actions at the other entry points are equally obvious.

As a more realistic example, consider again the subroutine MAX, which returns in R5 the largest of a specified collection of numbers. Specifically, we shall concern ourselves with the version of Fig. 8.8.2, in which the arguments— the number count and the address of the first number—are passed to the subroutine in .WORDs immediately following the subroutine call. By now the reader is quite familiar with the procedure. We let the first number be the maximum (temporarily) and then compare it with the remaining numbers. If a larger one is found, it is used to replace the temporary maximum in R5. This decision is made by a CMP instruction, followed by a BGE, at locations 002464 and 002466 in the listing of Fig. 8.8.2. It should be clear that if this BGE is replaced by a BLE, then the number returned in R5 will be the *minimum* of the numbers rather than the maximum. Thus we intend to write a subroutine with *two* entry points, called MAX and MIN, that returns the maximum or minimum of the numbers, depending upon which entry point was referenced in the subroutine call.

Since the only difference between the two routines is the conditional branch—BGE or BLE—we choose not to duplicate the code required to do these two tasks. Rather, at each entry point, MAX and MIN, we place just enough instructions to ensure that the proper conditional branch instruction is present at location 002466 before the body of the routine is executed. Note in Fig. 8.10.2 that at the symbolic location BRANCH (002466) we included the source code BR   NEXT. This is surely not what we want to have happen in either case. We placed this instruction here so that the assembler will calculate the correct word displacement in the low-order byte of the branch instruction. The high-order byte of that word is modified at the entry points MAX and MIN so that the instruction becomes BGE or BLE, respectively. Normally we tend to avoid such instructions, which modify other instructions. They often lead to programs that are difficult to read, understand, and maintain. Here, however, the ease of programming, savings in code, and resulting efficiency are so great

```
                          ;SUBROUTINE WITH ENTRY POINTS 'MAX' AND 'MIN'
                          ; RETURNS IN R5 THE MAXIMUM OR MINIMUM OF A
                          ; COLLECTION OF NUMBERS
                          ;
002432  112767   MAX:    MOVB    #004,BRANCH+1   ;MAKE BRANCH 'BGE'
        000004
        000027
002440  000403           BR      MAXMIN          ; AND SKIP AROUND
002442  112767   MIN:    MOVB    #007,BRANCH+1   ;MAKE BRANCH 'BLE'
        000007
        000017

                          ;
                          ;MAIN SUBROUTINE PROCESSING STARTS HERE
                          ;
002450  010046   MAXMIN: MOV     R0,-(SP)        ;SAVE REGISTERS
002452  010246           MOV     R2,-(SP)        ; R0 AND R2 ON STACK
002454  012100           MOV     (R1)+,R0        ;GET COUNT
002456  012102           MOV     (R1)+,R2        ; AND ADDR OF 1ST NUMBER
002460  005300           DEC     R0              ;MAKE NUMBER OF COMPARES
002462  012205           MOV     (R2)+,R5        ;1ST NO. = MAX OR MIN
002464  020522   LOOP:   CMP     R5,(R2)+        ;COMPARE WITH NEXT NO.
002466  000402   BRANCH: BR      NEXT            ;BECOMES 'BGE' OR 'BLE'
002470  016205           MOV     -2(R2),R5       ;REPLACE MAX OR MIN
        177776
002474  077005   NEXT:   SOB     R0,LOOP         ;PROCESS NEXT NUMBER
002476  012602           MOV     (SP)+,R2        ;RESTORE REGISTERS
002500  012600           MOV     (SP)+,R0        ; R0 AND R2 FROM STACK
002502  000201           RTS     R1              ; AND RETURN
```

Figure 8.10.2

that we cannot resist the temptation. This type of freestyle programming is by no means objectionable *provided* it is used only when it makes sense to do so and is well documented within the source code.

8.12 EXERCISES

8.1.1. Let LIST be the (symbolic) address of the first word of a block of 29 consecutive memory words, interpreted *by the programmer* as a vector named V, subscripted as follows:

$$V(1), V(2), \ldots, V(29)$$

(a) Write a few instructions that will put the contents of V(I) into R5, where the (integer) subscript I is assumed to be in R1.

(b) Determine what changes would have to be made if the subscripting began at 0 and ended at 28.

(c) Determine what changes would have to be made if the subscripting began at -14 and ended at 14.

8.1.2. Let ARRAY be the (symbolic) address of the first word of a block of 30_{10} consecutive memory words, interpreted *by the programmer* as a matrix named T of five rows and six columns, subscripted as follows:

$$T(1, 1) \ldots . T(1, 6)$$

$$T(2, 1) \ldots . T(2, 6)$$

$$\ldots \ldots \ldots \ldots$$

$$T(5, 1) \ldots . T(5, 6)$$

(a) Write a few instructions that will put the contents of T(I, J) into R5, where the (integer) subscripts I and J are assumed to be in R1 and R2, respectively.

(b) Determine what changes would have to be made if the subscripting began at $(-2, 0)$ and ended at $(2, 5)$.

8.1.3. A first in–first out structure that is a slight modification of a queue is a **silo**. In this case the **head** of the silo, where entries are removed (and which might better be called the **bottom** of the silo) always occupies a *fixed position*. As entries are added to the silo, they are added at the **tail** (better, the **top**). As entries are removed, all other entries in the silo *drop down one position* (hence the name silo).

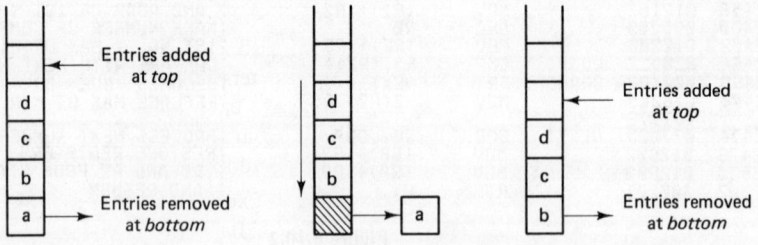

Figure 8.12.1

Explain why the supermarket checkout line is a better illustration of this structure than it is of a queue.

8.2.1. (a) If a stack can contain at most 50_{10} one-word entries at any one time, what is the minimum amount of storage that must be set aside for it?

(b) Suppose two stacks are required in a program, each of which can grow to 50_{10} one-word entries. What is the minimum amount of (combined) storage that must be set aside for them?

(c) Suppose two stacks are required in a program and that it is known that the total number of one-word entries in the two stacks at any given time will never exceed 50_{10}. What is the minimum amount of (combined) storage that must be set aside for them? Why? How are these two stacks managed?

8.2.2. Suppose a stack, whose stack pointer is R3, initially contains the following entries:

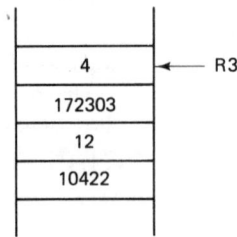

Figure 8.12.2

Determine what entries will be in the stack after execution of *each* instruction in the following sequence of instructions:

(a) MOV (R3)+,R5   (b) MOV #17,−(R3)
(c) NEG (R3)   (d) ADD 4(R3),(R3)
(e) ADD (R3)+,2(R3)   (f) MOV (R3)+,(R3)
(g) MOV (R3),−(R3)

8.2.3. Suppose a program uses a queue that we estimate will never contain any more than 60_{10} words at any one time. Suppose also that the queue area in the program is established as follows:

QUEUE: .BLKW 74
QUEND:

(a) How should the head and tail pointers be initialized?

(b) At any given time, how can it be determined if the queue is *empty* or *full*?

(c) Suppose that after the head and tail pointers are initialized, 40_{10} entries are added to the queue. Next, those same entries are removed from the queue. The queue is now clearly empty. What are the states of the head and tail pointers? Can another 40_{10} entries be added to the queue?

8.2.4. The reader who went through the details of Exercise 8.2.3 found that queue management is by no means a trivial matter. It is more complicated by far than stack management. For a task of intermediate difficulty, explain how to deal with a *silo*. (See Exercise 8.1.3 for the description of a silo.)

8.3.1. Suppose a program requires a stack that is estimated to contain a maximum of 60_{10} (one-word) entries. Space is allocated as follows, with the stack pointer initialized at the number STKEND:

STACK: .BLKW 74
STKEND:

(a) How can the programming determine that the stack is full, so that an additional push would result in a stack overflow?

(b) How can the programming determine that the stack is empty, so that an additional pop would result in a stack underflow?

8.3.2. One way to circumvent the problem of using a stack to hold both words and bytes is to assume that the stack is a *byte* stack. Pushing a *word*, then, would require *two* pushes, one for each byte of the word. Popping a word would be treated in an analogous fashion.

(a) If R2 is used as the stack pointer for such a byte stack, what instructions would be required to push the contents of the word whose symbolic address is DATA onto the stack?

(b) What would be required to pop the top of the stack into the *word* whose symbolic address is ADDR?

(c) How could the (word) contents of R4 be pushed onto the stack?

8.4.1. In the program of Fig. 8.4.2, suppose the counter, 4, is pushed onto the stack (MOV #4,−(SP)) instead of being put into R∅ (MOV #4,R∅). What program changes would then be required?

8.5.1. In transferring control to a subroutine, rather than using a general-purpose register to save the current contents of the PC we could as well *stack* the PC. The return-from-subroutine would then involve adjusting this stack item.

Show that the following scheme will properly return to the main portion of the program:

```
            MOV   PC,-(SP)
            JMP   SUBR
              .
              .
              .
  SUBR:       .
              .
              .
            ADD   #4,(SP)
            MOV   (SP)+,PC
```

8.5.2. What changes would have to be made in the scheme of Exercise 8.5.1 if the jump-to-subroutine is achieved by each of the following:

(a)
```
    MOV   #SUBR,R2
    MOV   PC,-(SP)
    JMP   (R2)
```

(b)
```
    MOV   PC,-(SP)
    MOV   #SUBR,R2
    JMP   (R2)
```

(c)
```
    MOV   PC,-(SP)
    MOV   #SUBR,-(SP)
    JMP   @(SP)
```

(d)
```
    MOV   PC,-(SP)
    MOV   #SUBR,-(SP)
    JMP   @(SP)+
```

(e)
```
    MOV   #SUBR-4,R2
    MOV   PC,-(SP)
    JMP   4(R2)
```

8.5.3. Consider two subroutines SUBR1 and SUBR2, where the instructions within SUBR1 include a jump to SUBR2, where each subroutine uses R1 to hold the current PC (return address).

```
            MOV   R1,-(SP)
            MOV   PC,R1
            ADD   #10,R1
            JMP   SUBR1
            MOV   (SP)+,R1
              .
              .
              .
  SUBR1:      .
              .
              .
            MOV   R1,-(SP)
            MOV   PC,R1
            ADD   #10,R1
            JMP   SUBR2
            MOV   (SP)+,R1
              .
              .
              .
            MOV   R1,PC
              .
              .
              .
  SUBR2:      .
              .
              .
            MOV   R1,PC
```

By keeping careful track of the entries on the stack and the value in R1, show that SUBR2 correctly returns to SUBR1, which in turn properly returns to the main portion of the program. What is it about this scheme that seems to make it work?

8.6.1. Suppose SUBR is a subroutine that uses R3 as its transfer register. The most straightforward way for the main portion of the program to reference SUBR is with JSR   R3,SUBR or possibly JSR   R3,@#SUBR. Another possibility, however, might be

```
MOV  #SUBR,R5
JSR  R3,(R5)
```

(This is not so curious as it may first appear—such constructions using register deferred mode are not uncommon.) Verify that this JSR, combined with the return instruction RTS   R3, will produce the desired result. But consider now the rather more bizarre construction

```
MOV  #SUBR,R3
JSR  R3,(R3)
```

By examining the details of the JSR and RTS instructions, determine if this will generate a proper jump-to-subroutine. If it does, will the RTS   R3 (in SUBR) correctly return to the main portion of the program? If so, what will be the contents of R3 by the time control has been returned to the main program?

8.6.2. Determine if the PC can be used as a subroutine transfer register by examining in detail the effects of the program segment

```
                        .
                        .
                        .
002066                  JSR  PC,SUBR
002072                  .
                        .
                        .
003644    SUBR:         .
                        .
                        .
004042                  RTS  PC
                        .
                        .
                        .
```

8.6.3. It was stated that the RTS   Rn instruction gives the PC the value currently in Rn, and then the top of the stack is popped into Rn. In effect, the CPU executes the "instructions"

```
MOV  Rn,PC
MOV  (SP)+,Rn
```

Show that the instruction RTS   Rn *cannot* be replaced by the *program* instructions

```
MOV  Rn,PC
MOV  (SP)+,Rn
```

or by the *program* instructions

MOV (SP)+,Rn
MOV Rn,PC

8.6.4. Assume that SUBR is a subroutine that returns by means of the instruction RTS R4. What would be the consequences of calling this routine with JSR R1,SUBR?

8.6.5. Suppose that instead of the JSR instruction that we have described, the PDP-11 implemented the hardware instruction *S*ave-*P*rogram-counter-and-*J*ump-to-*S*ubroutine, to which we temporarily assign the mnemonic SPJS. It behaves as follows: When SPJS SUBR is executed, the current PC is stored at SUBR—that is, the word whose symbolic address is SUBR—and control is passed to location SUBR+2: PC ← SUBR+2. Then a typical subroutine reference would be

```
     SPJS  SUBR
     (next mainline instruction)
        .
        .
        .
SUBR:    .BLKW  1       ;RETURN ADDRESS SAVED HERE
     (first SUBR instruction)
```

(This is more than a contrived exercise—some machines use precisely this jump-to-subroutine scheme.)

(a) Show that this effectively passes control to the subroutine and saves the return address.

(b) Show that no special RTS-type instruction is needed for subroutine return by stating a standard PDP-11 instruction with which the return to the main portion of the program can be accomplished.

(c) Show that this instruction will properly handle nested subroutine references and returns, as in Exercise 8.5.3.

8.8.1. Consider the following subroutine call:

```
026040     ADDR1:    .WORD  6
026042     ADDR2:    .WORD  142
                        .
                        .
                        .
030662               JSR  R4,SUBR
030666               .WORD  ADDR1
030670               .WORD  ADDR2
030672               (next mainline instruction)
```

The routine SUBR shown below does nothing but set the values of one or more of the registers R0 to R3, and then returns to the mainline program. In each case state what values the registers are given and whether the subroutine returns correctly to the next mainline instruction. If the return is not correct, suggest steps that might be taken to insure a proper return.

(a) SUBR: MOV (R4)+,RØ   (b) SUBR: MOV @(R4)+,RØ
           MOV (R4)+,R1   MOV @(R4)+,R1
           RTS R4   RTS R4

(c) SUBR: MOV (R4),RØ   (d) SUBR: MOV @(R4)+,RØ
           MOV @(R4)+,R1   MOV @(R4)+,R1
           MOV R4,R2   MOV @-2(R4),R3
           MOV (R4)+,R3   RTS R4
           RTS R4

(e) SUBR: MOV (R4)+,RØ   (f) SUBR: MOV (R4),RØ
           MOV @-(R4),R1   MOV @(R4)+,R1
           MOV @(R4)+,R2   RTS R4
           MOV @-2(R4),R3
           RTS R4

(g) SUBR: MOV @(R4),RØ
           MOV (R4),R1
           TST (R4)+
           MOV @(R4)+,R2
           RTS R4

8.8.2. Modify the program of Fig. 8.8.3 so that the maximum, instead of being returned in R5, is on top of the stack upon return to the mainline program. (Of course, this maximum should be the only thing on the stack upon return.)

8.8.3. In the program listing of Fig. 8.8.3, could the instruction TST (SP)+ at location 002506 have been replaced by TSTB (SP)+? Why, or why not?

8.8.4. In the discussion of the program of Fig. 8.8.3 we stated that the instruction TST (SP)+ was an easy way to increment SP by 2. We also implied that this scheme could be used to increment a general-purpose register by 2, as well. Show that this is not always the case. That is, determine the conditions under which TST (Rn)+ will increment Rn by 2 (n = Ø, 1, . . . , 5) and those under which this instruction is inappropriate for this purpose. Why should this *always* work for R6 (SP)?

8.9.1. We have seen that the PC (R7) can be used as a subroutine transfer register. What would be the effect of using SP (R6) for this purpose? Would it always work? Sometimes work? Never work?

8.9.2. We suggested that the use of the PC as a subroutine transfer register was somewhat inconvenient if the arguments needed by the subroutine were transmitted by means of .WORDs following the subroutine call. Consider the specific example

```
JSR   PC,SUBR
.WORD   ARG0
.WORD   ARG1
.WORD   ARG2
.WORD   ARG3
.WORD   ARG4
.WORD   ARG5
(next mainline instruction)
```

Show what instructions in SUBR would be required to assign Rn the value ARGn (n = 0, 1, . . . , 5), in such a way that the return instruction (RTS   PC) would correctly return control to the next mainline instruction.

8.9.3. An interesting way to transmit k arguments to a subroutine (used, for example, by some FORTRAN compilers) is the following:

```
          JSR  PC,SUBR
          BR   NEXT
          .WORD  ARG1
          .WORD  ARG2
               .
               .
               .
          .WORD  ARGK
NEXT:     (next mainline instruction)
```

(a) Show that the return-from-subroutine is correctly achieved by making *no* adjustments in the transfer register.

(b) Show how the subroutine SUBR can access the ith argument, ARGi.

(c) What limitation does this scheme place on the *number* of arguments that can be passed to the subroutine?

(d) There is an additional and useful aspect to this peculiar method of argument transmission. One of the problems inherent in calling subroutines lies in the fact that normally the subroutine expects a specific number of arguments to be passed to it. Generally, if the number of arguments transmitted by the mainline is different from this expected number, not only will the subroutine probably not function properly, but there may also be problems with the subroutine return. Show that in this case there will never be a problem with the return. Show also that it is possible for the subroutine to *determine* how many arguments have been passed to it and thus possibly to take corrective action if this number differs from what was expected. Finally, as a corollary of this, show that if arguments are transmitted in this fashion, we may be able to write the subroutine to handle a *variable* number of arguments.

8.9.4. Another method of argument transmission (also used by some FORTRAN compilers) is the following:

```
TABLE:    .WORD  n
          .WORD  ARG1
          .WORD  ARG2
               .
               .
               .
          .WORD  ARGn
               .
               .
               .
          MOV  #TABLE,R5
          JSR  PC,SUBR
```

Show how the subroutine can determine the number of arguments passed to it and how it can access the ith argument, ARGi.

8.9.5. If a subroutine that requires arguments from the mainline uses the PC as a transfer register, it is convenient to place the arguments on the stack for subroutine retrieval. For example, if two arguments, ARG1 and ARG2, are stacked (in that order) prior to the JSR, then the stack will appear as shown in Fig. 8.12.3 and we can reference ARG1 as 4(SP), ARG2 as 2(SP). While this is

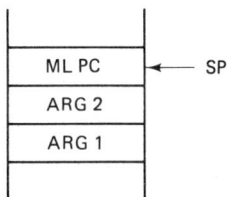

Figure 8.12.3

quite straightforward, upon the return (RTS   PC) the arguments will still be on the stack. And if we desire that the subroutine clean the stack prior to the return, this becomes a problem, although of course we can do it. Some models of the PDP-11 have an instruction, whose mnemonic is MARK, that is implemented *precisely* for the purposes of cleaning up the stack at subroutine return time. Investigate the description of MARK in Appendix A, noting in particular the role played by R5, and then explain in detail the output of the following program, including an explanation of what the stack looks like at each stage of execution. (This program is not intended to be in any way useful. It simply illustrates the action of the MARK instruction, but the reader should be able to imagine how MARK could be used to advantage in a more practical situation.)

```
 1 001000  012705  START:  MOV     #555,R5
            000555
 2 001004  010546          MOV     R5,-(SP)      ;SAVE ML C(R5)
 3 001006  012746          MOV     #1234,-(SP)   ;ARGUMENT 1
            001234
 4 001012  012746          MOV     #4321,-(SP)   ;ARGUMENT 2
            004321
 5 001016  012746          MOV     #006402,-(SP) ;'MARK 2'
            006402
 6 001022  010605          MOV     SP,R5
 7 001024  004767          JSR     PC,SUB
            000044
 8 001030  010567          MOV     R5,ADDR
            000036
 9 001034                  $OUT.OCT  #ADDR,#1
10 001070                  $EXIT
11                         ;
12 001072          ADDR:   .BLKW   1
13                         ;
14 001074  010667  SUB:    MOV     SP,ADDR
            177772
15 001100                  $OUT.OCT  ADDR,#5
16 001134  000205          RTS     R5            ;(NOT 'RTS   PC')
17                         ;
18          001000'        .END    START
```

Figure 8.12.4

8.10.1. In the recursive subroutine of Fig. 8.10.1, why would the following instructions yield an incorrect result?

```
ODD:      BITB   #1,(R1)+
          BNE    DONE
          JSR    PC,ODD
DONE:     DEC    R1
          RTS    PC
```

8.10.2. Write the subroutine ODD of Fig. 8.10.1 as a *nonrecursive* routine. (This is not really any more difficult than the subroutine as written.) What advantages or disadvantages are there to the two versions?

8.10.3. Consider the following subroutine:

```
FACT:     CMP    R2,#1
          BEQ    DONE
          MUL    R2,R1
          DEC    R2
          JSR    PC,FACT
DONE:     RTS    PC
```

Show that if prior to invoking FACT, the mainline routine sets R1 to 1 and R2 to n, then FACT will return in R1 the value $n!$. What limitations are placed on n in this procedure? How could those limitations be circumvented, or at least extended? How can this routine be written nonrecursively?

8.10.4. Consider the following recursive function definition:

Let n be a positive integer, and define the function F as follows:

$$F(n) = 1 \text{ if } n = 1 \text{ or } n = 2;$$

$$F(n) = F(n-1) + F(n-2) \text{ if } n > 2$$

$F(n)$ is called the nth *Fibonacci number*. Write a nonrecursive subroutine to generate the nth Fibonacci number and test the routine by calculating and printing (in decimal) the first 15 Fibonacci numbers. What would be involved in writing the subroutine *recursively*?

8.10.5. Show that the instruction SPJS, as described in Exercise 8.6.5, *cannot* be used for recursive subroutine calls. What would have to be done to accomplish recursion with this kind of jump-to-subroutine instruction?

8.10.6. As a variation on the concept of recursion, consider two subroutines, SUBR1 and SUBR2, each of which calls the *other*, that have some provision for terminating the nested subroutine calls. Show that once again the stack manages the calls and returns correctly by considering an example in which SUBR1 calls SUBR2, which in turn calls SUBR1, and so forth, with calls terminating and the returns beginning after, for example, SUBR1's third call to SUBR2. (Such routines are sometimes called **coroutines**.)

8.11.1. Exercise 7.7.6 gives some suggestions for the writing of a program to put a block of numbers into increasing order.

(a) Write this task as a subroutine that is passed its two arguments—the number of numbers to be ordered and the address of the first of the numbers—by means of .WORDs following the call to the subroutine.

(b) Write the routine in such a way that the arguments are passed to it on the stack.

(c) Write the routine with two entry points, INCR and DECR, the first of which results in the numbers in question being put in increasing order, the second in decreasing order.

8.11.2. Another method for putting numbers in increasing or decreasing order, called a **linear insertion sort**, is described below for the increasing case. Following the theme of Exercise 8.11.1 above, write subroutines to implement increasing and decreasing sorts by means of this technique.

Consider a collection of numbers in consecutive memory locations. We want to rearrange them so that they are in increasing order, and we approach the task as follows: For the moment, we consider the first number to be in its proper position, and we examine the second number. If the second number is at least as large as the first, we leave the situation alone and move on to the third number. If not, we exchange the first and second numbers. We now decide where the third number belongs, *relative to the first two numbers*. If the third number is smaller than the first, we move the second number to the location occupied by the third, move the first number to the second position, and insert the third number in the first position. (The first three numbers are now in increasing order.) If the third number is at least as big as the first but smaller than the second, we interchange the second and third. Finally, if the third number is at least as big as the second, we leave it where it is and move on to the fourth.

In general, the sorting proceeds as follows: Assume that the first k numbers have already been placed in increasing order. We determine where, among those first k numbers, the $(k + 1)$st number belongs. Suppose it belongs in the ith position. The numbers between the ith and kth positions inclusive are moved up one word, and the $(k + 1)$st number is then moved into the position vacated by the ith number. By the time all of the numbers have been dealt with, they will be in increasing order. (While the programming for this type of sort is a bit more involved than that required in Exercise 8.11.1, the rewards are correspondingly greater—the linear insertion sort is generally quite a bit more efficient than the technique of Exercise 8.11.1.)

9

External Symbols,
Relocation, and Linking

9.1 EXTERNAL SUBROUTINES

In the preceding chapter we looked at a number of examples of subroutines, some of them purely illustrative, others more realistically useful. Even of the useful subroutines, some were of a rather special-purpose type. For example, the subroutine to print the five rows of a matrix in a true matrix format was surely extremely useful within the program that manipulated the 5×5 matrix, but it is difficult to imagine how it might be used in other programs. On the other hand, the routines that found the largest or smallest of a collection of numbers, or those that sorted numbers in increasing or decreasing order, can conceivably be useful in a wide variety of programs. Thus we may loosely classify useful subroutines as either those that are significant only in a particular program environment, or those that are more generally useful. We shall investigate this second category of routines briefly in this section.

A general-purpose subroutine is an obvious boon to the programmer, especially if it is well-written—that is, it is independent of the program in which it resides, arguments are easily passed to it, and so forth. But our enthusiasm over such a routine's utility is tempered somewhat by the fact that we must include the *source code* for the subroutine in any program that requires its use. Admittedly, we need not concern ourselves with the *logic* of the subroutine; we simply copy the source code into the program knowing that the source code will assemble into a subroutine whose operation will be correct (provided that we have copied it correctly). Nonetheless, if such a subroutine is fairly long, or if a number of routines are needed, the task can become onerous, and the more code that needs copying, the more chances there are for human error.

There appear to be two ways to deal with this problem. We could supply our assembling clerk with copies of the source code for all of our useful subroutines and then when presenting him with a mainline program for assembly, tell him which subroutines will be called in the mainline and request that he "attach" the source code for those routines to the mainline program, at the end of the program, for instance, to keep them out of the mainstream of processing. This would do the job, and presumably the clerk could manage this task. Notice that this does not eliminate the reproduction of the source code; it merely transfers the burden from the programmer to the assembler. This is one way to cope with the situation and is sometimes (although infrequently) done in practice. But we are looking for something more efficient.

Suppose we present our clerk with a copy of the source code for one of these useful subroutines, with the request that he assemble it and keep a copy of the *object code* that he generated. Next we give him the source code for a mainline program, again requesting that he assemble it, but also that he append to the object code of the mainline the object code for the subroutine called by the mainline. Thus the clerk has needed to assemble the subroutine *just once*, rather than each time the source code for the subroutine was included in a mainline program, and the improvement in efficiency is obvious. Such a subroutine is referred to as an **external subroutine**, since its source code is no longer internal to the mainline's source code.

Despite the desirability of this scheme, the number of problems that it creates almost (but not quite) makes it unworkable. To see what these problems are, consider a simple example. We write a subroutine named EXSUB (by which we mean that its entry point has the symbolic address EXSUB). This is assembled, and its object code is saved (somewhere). Next we write a mainline program that contains the instruction

JSR   R2,EXSUB

This reference is going to give the assembling clerk problems, for since EXSUB is an external subroutine, the symbol EXSUB will *not* be defined within the mainline program. Thus the clerk would have to announce that EXSUB is an *undefined symbol*. But even if we notified the clerk *in advance* that EXSUB is an external routine, he would still not be able to complete the job we want done. Recall that EXSUB's object code has to be appended to the object code of the mainline. Even if the clerk could identify the collection of object code that represents this subroutine, he would be unable to determine the entry point EXSUB. For after he assembled the subroutine, he saved the object code as we desired, but discarded the source code—and presumably with it, the *symbol table* for the subroutine. And of course it is precisely in the symbol table that the value of the entry point EXSUB is maintained. Finally, even putting all of these difficulties aside, we are clearly expanding the clerk's (assembler's) role far beyond what was originally intended. The situation is apparently quite complex and the details are becoming somewhat confusing. It would be wise to handle these problems one at a time.

9.2 EXTERNAL SYMBOLS

It should be clear from the discussion above that if the assembler is *not* informed in advance that a particular symbol (in our example, the symbol EXSUB) is external to the main program—that it is an **external symbol**—then the assembler is going to treat it as an *undefined* symbol and will flag with an error any line of source code that references it. We can so notify the assembler with the directive .GLOBL—in this particular case, .GLOBL EXSUB. The directive .GLOBL is an abbreviation of the word **global** which, in this context, is taken as the opposite of the word **local**. A **local symbol** is one that is *local* to the program itself, that is, is defined within the program. Thus a **global symbol** is one that is *not* locally defined. We prefer the term *external* for this concept and would even suggest the directive .EXT, but .GLOBL is the directive recognized by the PDP-11 assembler.

Now that the assembler is aware that EXSUB is externally defined, how will it deal with a reference such as JSR R2,EXSUB? Suppose for the sake of definiteness that this subroutine call occurs at 001044. The assembler can manage the JSR R2 portion of the instruction, assembling it as 004267. The next word is to be the displacement to the memory location whose symbolic address is EXSUB, but of course the assembler does not know that address and thus cannot complete the assembly of this instruction. The best it can do is recognize that the displacement *should* go in the next word and therefore make provision for it—leave a word in the object code in the anticipation that it will (somehow) be filled in later with the appropriate displacement. Thus the object code generated here will be

001044	004267	JSR R2,EXSUB
001046	000000*G*	
001050	------	(next mainline instruction)

Note that the assembler has placed the number 000000 in location 001046. On the program listing, that location has also been flagged with the letter G, to indicate that its contents is the result of a global, or external, reference. Since the assembler has no way of determining the value EXSUB and thus cannot calculate the proper displacement to be filled in at 001046, we might conclude that the assembler has put the value 000000 here *merely* to ensure that a word has been reserved in the object code for that displacement and that the value itself—000000—is of no significance. However, we would be only partially correct. To be sure, the assembler cannot calculate the displacement, and a word does need to be left in the object code. But leaving an "open" word, whose value is of no consequence, could more easily be handled by the assembler simply by advancing its location assignment counter by 2—as if a .BLKW   1 had been encountered.

To see the significance of the number placed here by the assembler for the unknown displacement, we must anticipate what will happen when the module containing EXSUB is ultimately appended to this mainline module. (We shall cover this topic in detail in Sec. 9.6.) When the value EXSUB later becomes known, (so that the proper displacement *can* be calculated), that displacement is not simply placed in location 001046. Rather, the displacement is *added* to the *contents* of 001046. Of course, in this example the effect is the same, since $c(001046) = 000000$. But now consider the following example:

```
001044        004267        JSR   R2,EXSUB-6
001046        177772
001050        ------        (next mainline instruction)
```

Here the assembler has filled in location 001046 with $177772 = -6$. When the value EXSUB is ultimately known, the displacement to EXSUB will be calculated and then added to the contents of 001046. This will yield the displacement to EXSUB−6, as desired.

The symbol EXSUB, even though external to the program, will appear in the assembly's symbol table as

$$EXSUB = ****** \ G$$

The asterisks, of course, mean that the symbol has not been defined, as we expected. The G simply indicates that the symbol has been specified as global. We have seen this symbol table entry once before, in the listing of Fig. 6.7.1, where the symbol $.... was shown to be undefined and global. The symbol $.... is the name of an external subroutine entry point invoked by the macroinstruction $OUT.OCT.

We have managed to prevent the assembler from displaying its displeasure with undefined symbols, but this has scarcely achieved any progress toward our ultimate goal—the ability to *append* the *object code* of a subroutine to that of a mainline program in such a way that the mainline may make references to that external subroutine. Before advancing in that direction, we need to know something of the *environment* within which assemblies and program executions take place.

9.3 THE OPERATING SYSTEM

In Chapter 5 we stated the *possibility* of loading main memory with the executable machine instructions for a program, setting the PC to the program's start (or transfer) address, and then beginning execution of the machine code. The loading of memory might take place at the computer's console terminal or through front-panel switches on a word-by-word basis, but by now the

reader must be aware that because of the size of the programs with which we
have been dealing—and they are still quite small by most standards—this
scheme is hardly practical. Instead, we take advantage of a program written
specifically for this purpose, called a **loader**, that is one segment of a collection
of programs known as an **operating system**.

In the most general terms, an operating system is a collection of programs
which perform useful tasks for the programmer, not only for the purposes of
programmer convenience but also to achieve an overall efficient use of the
hardware. The programmer communicates with this collection of utility programs by means of a routine charged with the servicing of requests and management of the entire system. Such a routine is typically called a **supervisor**, **monitor**,
or **executive routine**. Thus, for example, when the programmer requests the
assembly of a source program, the request is made to the supervisory routine,
whose job it is then to pass control to the appropriate operating system utility
program, in this case the assembler. Similarly, when a machine-executable
program is to be run (executed), it is the responsibility of the operating system
to see that the machine code is loaded into main memory and that control of
the processor is passed to it at the correct location. In discussing the program
listing of Fig. 6.7.1, we mentioned the fact that the macroinstruction $EXIT
had the effect of returning control *to the operating system* when program execution had been completed. We now know that control should be returned to the
operating system so that it can accept another programmer command—for
another assembly, execution, or whatever.

Throughout the remainder of the present chapter we shall say more about
the individual modules that make up an operating system. However, we shall
say no more about the system itself—the supervisor, how it invokes system
utilities, and how these interact with one another. Operating systems come in
such a variety of shapes and sizes that it would be neither useful nor possible
to describe them here.

9.4 OBJECT FILES AND EXTERNAL SYMBOLS

The purpose of the assembler is to build an *object* program—a collection of
16-bit words that when loaded into main memory, can be interpreted (decoded)
by the CPU as executable instructions. But having generated the object code,
what does the assembler do with it? The answer is that this code is *saved* (somewhere) in a file, called the **object file**. A **file** is simply some collection of related
data. An **assembler object file** is thus the collection of 16-bit words made up of
the object code generated by the assembler that corresponds to a given source
program. This file is *stored* (or *saved*) somewhere after assembly by the assembler—usually working in conjunction with other operating system utilities (a
file processor, for example)—for future reference. The *where* is not of real
concern to us at this point—in typical modern computing systems, files are

saved on magnetic disks or tapes, and in fact the file can simply be saved in main memory. What is of consequence is that the file is *named* and can later be referenced by that name. The name itself is of no real importance, as long as it uniquely distinguishes the file to which it refers. In Sec. 9.7 we shall see the significance of the name associated with an object file.

We reiterate that the function of the assembler is to accept as input a source (or mnemonic) program, to generate 16-bit object code for that program, and to save that object code in an object file under some specified name. But note that once the program has been assembled, the only thing that requires saving is the pure object code—the programmer mnemonics and programmer symbols are no longer of any use *unless* the source program contains a reference to an *external symbol*. In this case, if that reference is ever to be resolved, the assembler must save a bit more in its object file. Consider again the example of Sec. 9.2, in which the reference JSR   R2,EXSUB was assembled as

$$001044 \qquad 004267$$
$$001046 \qquad 000000$$

It would surely do no good to save this code *without* some indication of how the entry 000000 is ultimately to be adjusted. What information is required to make this adjustment? We must know just *where* this reference is (001046), to *what* it is a reference (EXSUB), and *how* the reference is made—in this case, the reference is to the *displacement* from the current PC to the entry point EXSUB, although EXSUB might also have been referenced by its actual *address*. Thus information of the nature

$$\text{EXSUB} \qquad 001046 \qquad \text{displacement}$$

would have to be passed along with the pure object code in order to resolve this reference later. Of course, if other references to EXSUB (or other external symbols) were made, they would also be included, for example,

EXSUB	001046	displacement
	001220	displacement
	002004	address
	002020	displacement

Thus the assembler, in building the object file, will have to include with it an **external reference table**, whose entries are similar to those shown above. Just how a particular assembler, working within a given operating system, might handle the saving of this external reference information can vary greatly, but this is the *minimal* information that it must pass along with the object code, however it might do so in a specific case.

One other piece of information available to the assembler that will be needed later is the **start**, or **transfer**, **address** as specified in the .END directive—the address at which execution is to begin if and when the machine-language program is executed. This information is passed along in the object file, which

Object file
MAIN

| Transfer address |
| External reference table |
| Object (machine) code |

Figure 9.4.1

now appears as shown in Fig. 9.4.1, where we arbitrarily chose the name MAIN for the file.

Having dealt with the mainline program, we now move on to the subroutine EXSUB which, as we noted, is going to undergo a *separate* assembly. There is no reason to believe that the assembler will handle the subroutine differently from the mainline and in fact it does not. However, there is an important idea involving the transfer address that must be treated here. At what address do we want execution of the subroutine to "start"? The question is really meaningless, since the subroutine is not started anywhere—it owes its existence to a mainline program that *itself* will start, somewhere pass control to the subroutine, and then regain control when the subroutine has completed execution. Thus the concept of start, or transfer, address for a subroutine simply does not apply, and therefore *no* transfer address will be included in the .END directive which ends a subroutine's source code. How does the assembler treat this situation? There are a number of ways it might deal with it, but typically the assembler assigns a *default* transfer address to indicate that there is in fact *no* transfer address. An easy way to do this is to give subroutines the transfer address 000001 which, since it is *odd*, could *never* be a legitimate start address. Why does the assembler even bother assigning a transfer address to a subroutine? There are two reasons, the first of which is *consistency*. By assigning a transfer address to *every* programming module it assembles, the assembler will then *always* generate object files that contain a transfer address, whether that address is valid or not. We shall discuss the second reason in Sec. 9.7.

Upon completion of its processing of the subroutine EXSUB and the building of an object file for it, as shown in Fig. 9.4.1 and named SUBR, the assembler once again discards the subroutine's source code and symbol table. But this is going to be disastrous to the mainline program's reference to EXSUB, the subroutine entry point. For if that reference is ever to be resolved, and we already made provisions when assembling the mainline to maintain enough information to resolve it, then the *value* EXSUB must be known. That value is kept in the subroutine's symbol table, and if that table is discarded at the completion of the assembly, then we shall lose some vital information. Somehow we must notify the assembler to save enough symbol table information so that the mainline reference to EXSUB can be resolved. That is, we must indicate that the subroutine symbol EXSUB will be used in a *global* fashion, not just *locally* within the subroutine. There are two ways in which we can do this. The first involves the use of the directive .GLOBL—.GLOBL EXSUB. Evidently this directive is serving double duty. If a symbol name appears in a .GLOBL directive and if that symbol is *not* defined within the programming module, then the symbol is apparently global in the sense of being *external*. If the symbol *is* defined within the module, then the symbol is global in that it is used globally rather than merely locally. This dual use of the directive .GLOBL can cause confusion, and for this reason we prefer the second method of declaring a symbol as being global: When the symbol is *defined*, by using it as a label, it will be declared as a global symbol if its definition is followed by *two* colons rather than one; thus

EXSUB: :

The effect of declaring global symbols is that the assembler, in building the object file, will also include these symbols and their values in a **global symbol table**. The object file built by the assembler appears in Fig. 9.4.2, which is a slight expansion of Fig. 9.4.1. It is important to understand that the assembler will generate this object file structure regardless of the *type* of programming module it is assembling —mainline or subroutine—for a subroutine may contain external references (to other external subroutines, for example), and a mainline may specify some symbol as being global. In brief, the assembler generates files as shown in Fig. 9.4.2. It has no way of knowing whether it is dealing with a mainline or subroutine module.

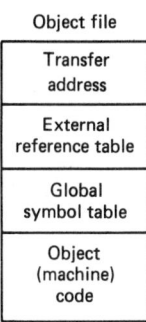

Object file

| Transfer address |
| External reference table |
| Global symbol table |
| Object (machine) code |

Figure 9.4.2

9.5 OBJECT MODULE RELOCATION

When we first discussed the concept of mnemonic program assemblies, we observed that if our clerk returned to us a listing of object code that he had assumed, by default, was to be loaded at address 000000, and if instead we decided to load that code into main memory beginning at location 001000, for instance, then we were flirting with disaster. (See page 103.) Specifically, in the example of Sec. 6.5, we had

```
000004      012702              MOV   #DATA,R2
000006      000032

                                  .
                                  .
                                  .

000032      000403      DATA:    403
```

The clerk correctly filled in the address 000032 (DATA) at location 000006, but if the object code is moved to 001000 then of course the symbolic address DATA will move with it, taking on the value 001032. Thus the word (address) at location 000006 will no longer be correct and some repairs to the relocated object code will have to be made prior to execution. We observed that the assembler can quite easily detect which words in the object code are sensitive to relocation of this sort. For the convenience of the programmer it will flag all such words on the program listing with an apostrophe (see page 109) and indicate relocation-sensitive symbols in the symbol table by the notation R.

To see how object code relocation can be accomplished, we need to introduce the following terminology: The **assembly load address** (ALA) is the address assigned by the assembler to the first word of object code of a program module. The **physical load address** (PLA) is the address in physical memory in which the first word of object code of a program module is loaded. (In our example above, ALA = 000000, whereas PLA = 001000.) The relocation problem is now almost trivial. To any word that is relocation sensitive, we need only to add the number PLA — ALA. In the example at hand, PLA — ALA = 001000 — 000000 = 001000, and thus relocation of the word 000032 at 000006 would result in its being adjusted to 001032 which in the relocated module is the physical address of the first of the five data numbers.

In order to accomplish this relocation of an *object* module, however, that module must carry with it two pieces of information. The first is the ALA so that the calculation above (PLA — ALA) can be made once a decision has been made as to where in physical memory the module is to be loaded. And in order to repair relocation-sensitive words we must, of course, know which words these are. Thus some kind of table, called the **relocation table**, that indicates which words need adjustment upon relocation must also be included in the object module. Finally, then, our object files contain the information shown in Fig. 9.5.1. Note that when an object module is relocated, its *transfer address*, along with the values of the symbols in the *global symbol table* that are sensitive to relocation, must be adjusted accordingly.

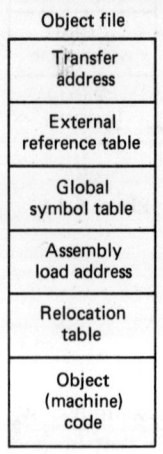

Object file

| Transfer address |
| External reference table |
| Global symbol table |
| Assembly load address |
| Relocation table |
| Object (machine) code |

Figure 9.5.1

9.6 THE APPENDING OF OBJECT MODULES

We can now deal with the problem that initiated this rather lengthy investigation—the ability to append to the object code of a mainline program the object code of a subroutine in such a way that a mainline reference to the subroutine can properly be placed in the mainline's object code. As an example of the various procedures and calculations involved, we shall use the subroutine of Fig. 8.10.2, which finds the maximum or minimum of a block of numbers. The subroutine is assembled as a separate programming module that is to be called by a mainline program. As an appropriate mainline, we offer an example (Fig. 9.6.1) that simply reads some numbers, finds their maximum and minimum, and then prints these.

There is nothing here that we have not already discussed, but a few things are noteworthy. Observe that in line 3, the symbols MAX and MIN appear in a .GLOBL directive to indicate that they are external. In line 9 (JSR R1,MIN) the assembler inserted the code 004167 at 000160. This is the JSR, but the next

word was assembled as 000000G. This, of course, is the (unknown) displacement
to MIN. A similar construction is found at line 13. Note also that in the symbol
table the symbols MAX and MIN appear as undefined (******) and global (G),
although a better term would be *external*.

MAINLINE PROGRAM

```
 1                                    .TITLE   MAINLINE PROGRAM
 2                                    ;
 3                                    .GLOBL   MAX,MIN         ;EXTERNAL SYMBOLS
 4                                    ;
 5  000000            BLOCK:  .BLKW   40.             ;STORAGE FOR 40. NOS.
 6  000120            ANSWER: .BLKW   2               ;MIN AND MAX GO HERE
 7                                    ;
 8  000124            BEGIN:  $IN.DEC #BLOCK,#35.     ;READ IN 35. NUMBERS
 9  000160  004167            JSR     R1,MIN          ;FIND MINIMUM
            000000G
10  000164  000043            .WORD   35.             ; OF 35. NUMBERS
11  000166  000000'           .WORD   BLOCK           ; STARTING AT 'BLOCK'
12  000170  010567            MOV     R5,ANSWER       ;SAVE MINIMUM
            177724
13  000174  004167            JSR     R1,MAX          ;FIND MAXIMUM
            000000G
14  000200  000043            .WORD   35.             ; OF 35. NUMBERS
15  000202  000000'           .WORD   BLOCK           ; STARTING AT 'BLOCK'
16  000204  010567            MOV     R5,ANSWER+2     ;SAVE RESULT
            177712
17  000210                    $OUT.DEC #ANSWER,#2     ;PRINT MIN AND MAX
10  000244                    $EXIT                   ; AND EXIT
19                                    ;
20            000124'         .END    BEGIN           ;('START' ADDRESS)
```

SYMBOL TABLE

```
ANSWER  000120R          BLOCK    000000R          MIN   = ****** G
BEGIN   000124R          MAX   = ****** G          $.... = ****** G
```

Figure 9.6.1

Figure 9.6.2 shows what the object file contains, other than the object code
itself. (Compare this with Fig. 9.5.1.) The subroutine containing the entry
points MAX and MIN is shown in Fig. 9.6.3 and is also quite straightforward.

Table		Contents	
Transfer address		000124	(relocation sensitive)
External references	MAX	000176	(used as displacement)
	MIN	000162	(used as displacement)
Global symbols	none		
Assembly load address		000000	
Relocation table		000166	(relocation sensitive
		000202	references to 'BLOCK')

Figure 9.6.2

SUBROUTINE -- FINDS MAX OR MIN

```
 1                                    .TITLE  SUBROUTINE -- FINDS MAX OR MIN
 2                                 ;
 3 000000   112767   MAX::  MOVB    #004,BRANCH+1  ;MAKE BRANCH 'BGE'
           000004
           000027
 4 000006   000403          BR      MAXMIN         ; AND SKIP AROUND
 5 000010   112767   MIN::  MOVB    #007,BRANCH+1  ;MAKE BRANCH 'BLE'
           000007
           000017
 6 000016   010046   MAXMIN: MOV    R0,-(SP)       ;SAVE REGISTERS
 7 000020   010246          MOV     R2,-(SP)       ; R0 AND R2 ON STACK
 8 000022   012100          MOV     (R1)+,R0       ;GET COUNT
 9 000024   012102          MOV     (R1)+,R2       ; AND ADDR OF 1ST NO.
10 000026   005300          DEC     R0             ;MAKE NO. OF COMPARES
11 000030   012205          MOV     (R2)+,R5       ;1ST NO. = MAX OR MIN
12 000032   020522   LOOP:  CMP     R5,(R2)+       ;COMPARE WITH NEXT NO.
13 000034   000402   BRANCH: BR     NEXT           ;BECOMES 'BGE' OR 'BLE'
14 000036   016205          MOV     -2(R2),R5      ;REPLACE MAX OR MIN
           177776
15 000042   077005   NEXT:  SOB     R0,LOOP        ;PROCESS NEXT NUMBER
16 000044   012602          MOV     (SP)+,R2       ;RESTORE REGISTERS
17 000046   012600          MOV     (SP)+,R0       ; R0 AND R2 FROM STACK
18 000050   000201          RTS     R1             ; AND RETURN
19                                 ;
20          000001          .END                   ;(NO 'START' ADDRESS)


SYMBOL TABLE

BRANCH   000034R          MAX      000000RG       MIN      000010RG
LOOP     000032R          MAXMIN   000016R        NEXT     000042R
```

Figure 9.6.3

Notice the use of the double colon at lines 3 and 5, which declares MAX and MIN as global symbols. Observe also that they appear in the symbol table flagged as both global and relocation-sensitive. The information carried in this module's object file is shown in Fig. 9.6.4.

Table	Contents		
Transfer address	000001	(relocation insensitive)	
External references	none		
Global symbols	MAX	000000	(relocation sensitive)
	MIN	000010	(relocation sensitive)
Assembly load address	000000		
Relocation table	none		

Figure 9.6.4

We now have all the information required to load the mainline program into main memory, load the subroutine, and to patch the mainline object code at the locations referencing MAX and MIN—locations 000162 and 000176 in the mainline listing of Fig. 9.6.1. The first decision that must be made concerns the PLA for the mainline object code. Any physical memory location will do, and since the ALA for this module is 000000, it might seem that 000000 would also be a natural choice for the PLA, since then PLA − ALA = 000000 and thus no relocation would be required. We choose instead PLA = 001000 for two reasons. First, as simple as it is, it will be useful to demonstrate in a non-trivial way the relocation process. And second, a popular operating system running on many of the PDP-11 computer systems frequently uses 001000 as the PLA. Thus the first word of the mainline object code will be loaded at 001000, the next at 001002, and so forth, with the last word of that module finally being loaded at 001244.

Next, some of the words just loaded must be adjusted. First, this module's transfer address is now no longer 000124—the relocation moved it to 001124. A look at the mainline's relocation table indicates that the words at 000166 and 000202, which because of the relocation are now at 001166 and 001202, respectively, need to be adjusted. We do this by adding PLA − ALA = 001000 to their contents. In each case, these words become 000000 + 001000 = 001000, the relocated value of the symbol BLOCK. The mainline object code has now been loaded into memory and the relocation-sensitive words have been repaired. The only remaining task for the mainline is the calculation of the displacements to MAX and MIN. That these calculations are required is indicated by the fact that references exist in the external symbol table. To manage these displacements, the module containing the entry points MAX and MIN will have to be loaded into memory so that the physical addresses MAX and MIN will be known.

Once again any memory location will do for the PLA for the subroutine's object code (except, of course, those locations currently occupied by the main-line). Since the last location taken up by the mainline has address 001244, it seems natural to begin the loading of the subroutine at the next available position, namely, 001246, and this is what we shall do. We note that in the subroutine itself there is no relocation table (more properly said, the relocation table is *empty*), and thus there are no adjustments of object code required because of the relocation. However, the values of MAX and MIN in the global symbol table will have to be modified. In particular, the physical locations represented by the symbols MAX and MIN are now

$$MAX = 000000 + (PLA - ALA)$$
$$= 000000 + 001246 - 000000$$
$$= 001246$$
$$MIN = 000010 + (PLA - ALA)$$
$$= 000010 + 001246 - 000000$$
$$= 001256$$

We can now insert the references to MAX and MIN in the mainline. The external reference table indicates that there is a reference to MIN at 000162, which because of the mainline's relocation is now 001162. By the time the CPU has fetched this (as yet unknown) displacement upon execution, the PC will have the value 001164. Thus the displacement that belongs at 001162 is (value of MIN) — (current PC) + (current contents of 001162) = 001256 — 001164 + 000000 = 000072. In a similar fashion we determine that the displacement to MAX in the second subroutine call should be 000046. Now that both modules have been loaded into main memory and the necessary repairs have been made, execution can begin at the transfer address, namely, 001124.

A couple of items remain to be tidied up, but they are not really in the mainstream of the discussion. When the subroutine object module was loaded into main memory at location 001246, no mention was made about adjusting its transfer address, 000001. So that all modules are treated consistently, we shall also adjust it, to 000001 + 001246 = 001247. Since the result is odd, it is still invalid. As we shall see, this address will be of no consequence to the final program execution, but this is not to say that it is not significant. The second item concerns the reference in the mainline program to a routine named $...., a subroutine called in the macroinstructions $IN.DEC and $OUT.DEC. Presumably that reference would also appear in the external reference table, the module containing that entry point would have to be loaded and relocated, and the mainline's reference to $.... would have to be inserted once the physical addresses were known.

9.7 THE LOADER-EDITOR-LINKER AS AN OPERATING SYSTEM UTILITY ROUTINE

While the procedures of the preceding section may have appeared to be somewhat complex, the real difficulties were brought on by the necessity for attention to the details—the calculation of displacements and relocation factors—rather than the concepts themselves. To see that the process involved in this task is really fairly simple, it will be useful to break the job down into three separate phases.

The simplest phase of the procedure is the **loading** of object code into main memory. The PLA for this module is all that has to be known here, in addition to *what* object code is to be loaded. In our example we took the PLA for the *first* object module to be loaded as 001000, and subsequent modules were loaded at the *next available* locations. This is about all that we need to or can say about loading.

The next phase involves the adjustment of relocation-sensitive words in the various object modules. Since words in the object code are actually changed in the process, this phase is frequently referred to as object module **editing**. To accomplish this editing, the module's ALA, its PLA, and the locations of the words in the module that are sensitive to relocation need to be known. Since this information *is* available, editing amounts simply to adding a *fixed* number (PLA − ALA) to each such word.

Now that the various modules have been loaded and edited, the only remaining task is the phase called **linking** of the object modules. This involves the determination of the addresses of or displacements to locations in one module that are referred to in another module. The information required for this job is *where* in one module an external reference is made, and the *location* in the other module of that referenced symbol. As we know, this information is carried in the external reference table and global symbol table, respectively.

Given the tasks to be done, the information available to do them, and the procedures required to accomplish the three phases described above, it seems reasonable that operating system utility routines could be written to perform these jobs. Such routines are written and supplied with most operating systems, although it is not unusual for a *single* program, frequently called a **linker** (or **linkage editor**), to take on all three of these jobs. (In this case the linker is doing more than just providing intermodule links.)

What information is needed by such a program (or programs) to build the executable module as in the preceding section? It needs only to be given the *names* of the object files that enter into the linking process. For once these file names are known, each file may be loaded, one after the other at an appropriate physical load address as described above. When all the files have been loaded (with their corresponding tables), the relocation-sensitive words can be edited and the linkages required by external references can be set up. Thus for the principal example of this chapter, we would need only to inform the linker of the object file names, MAIN and SUBR. The linker would load MAIN (as we suppose, at 001000), load SUBR immediately behind it, and then edit both files—although SUBR requires no editing, as we have seen—and set up the links required by the external subroutine calls in MAIN.

What if, in this example, the linker was supplied with the names of the object files in the order SUBR, MAIN rather than MAIN, SUBR? In this case SUBR would be loaded at 001000, with MAIN being loaded in main memory immediately behind it. In one of the exercises the reader is asked to show that while this *does* produce a *different* final collection of object code in main memory, it does *not* substantially affect the executable *program*.

We now know the input to the linker—named object files—and we also know its output—a machine-executable program. This program—collection of object code—we shall call an **absolute load module**. We use the word *absolute* here in the sense that the addresses at which the object code now resides are *absolute* (physical) addresses, as opposed to their addresses in the object files, which were taken *relative* to the assembly load address and which are generally changed upon loading and relocation. There are now a number of things the linker might do with this absolute load module. It might simply pass control back to the supervisory program, leaving the load module in main memory for the programmer's use. The linker might even begin program execution of the load module, since it knows the program's transfer address. This is the so-called **load-and-go** mode of loading, editing, and linking, which would be accomplished simply by MOVing the program's transfer address into the PC.

A third action frequently taken by a linker is to *save* the load module in a file. Here some care must be taken, for not only must the object code making up the executable program be saved, but the program's transfer address also must be saved along with it. This leads to another question. If the linker has been presented with a number of object files for loading, editing, and linking, and if *each* of those files has in its table a transfer address for that module, how does the linker know which is the transfer address for the load module? The answer is quite simple. If the object files have been built properly, then *one and only one* of them will have a *valid* transfer address, namely, the module we think of as the mainline program. If *no* module, or *more than one*, has a valid transfer address, the linker will be unable to determine the load module's transfer address. The only other piece of information that requires saving in the load module file is the actual load address itself. The running of the executable program then amounts to loading the object code in this load module file into main memory and beginning execution at the transfer address.

The final way in which the linker might manage the load module is to save it and its transfer address in a file, but in a *relocatable* format. That is, upon loading of the file for execution, the PLA is determined (somehow) and then any relocation-sensitive words are edited. Clearly, if this is the form in which the load module is to be saved, then in addition to the object code and the relocation-sensitive transfer address, a master relocation table for the entire module must also be saved. While this may not seem to be a very efficient way to manage the load module, some comments in Sec. 9.9 suggest why such a scheme might be desirable or even necessary.

9.8 LOAD MODULE EXECUTION

We noted in the preceding section that if the linker leaves the absolute load module in main memory upon completion of its task, then execution amounts simply to setting the PC to the module's transfer address. In practice, however, at least one more thing is done—a value is assigned to the *stack pointer* (R6). A utility routine called the **run processor** sets the SP and does so in such a way that the amount of available stack space is sufficient for most purposes. (See Sec. 8.4, in which two possible schemes are described.) This action of the run processor explains the rather cavalier attitude we took where we simply assumed in Chapter 8 that the hardware stack had been established in main memory with an appropriately initialized pointer.

If the absolute load module has been saved in a file, then the run processor must be informed of the name of that file. It can then load the module into main memory (using the saved load address), set the stack pointer, and begin execution at the (saved) transfer address. Finally, if the load module has been saved as a relocatable load module, then the run processor must decide or be told what load address to use, load the module at that address, and prior to execution *edit* the relocation-sensitive words. This process, in which the relative addresses in the module are made absolute, is frequently referred to as **absolute loading**.

9.9 POSITION-INDEPENDENT CODE

In our investigation in Chapter 7 of the various program counter addressing modes (see, in particular, page 136), we indicated that the *effects* of modes 3 and 6 were identical—the effective location was the memory location whose address was specified in the instruction. (The example used there was INC   BUFFER and INC @#BUFFER—in both cases the contents of the memory location whose symbolic address is BUFFER is incremented.) In mode 3, the actual address referenced becomes part of the instruction, whereas in mode 6, the address itself is not used in the instruction, but rather the *displacement* from the current PC to that address. The distinction is now seen to be significant to our discussion of relocation. If the actual address of a memory location is used as a part of an instruction, then that word is sensitive to program relocation. On the other hand, if the displacement to the address from the current PC is used, then that displacement is *not* relocation sensitive. In general, an instruction with no relocation-sensitive words is called **position independent**, since any relocation of it in main memory will have no effect upon its proper execution. The subroutine of this chapter, with entry points MAX and MIN and whose object file we named SUBR, is such a case. None of its instructions are relocation sensitive—the subroutine consists exclusively of position-independent code. (The *values* of the *symbols* MAX and MIN, however, *are* sensitive to relocation; the code making up the module's instructions is not.) In writing that subroutine, no conscious effort was made to ensure that it would be position independent; it just turned out that way. But there are occasions in which we might specifically desire that a module's code be insensitive to relocation. While it would be far from the mainstream of the development of topics in this chapter to go into much detail on this subject, we shall indicate some circumstances under which position-independent code can be most desirable.

A typical operating system consists of a large number of utility programs to do a variety of tasks for the programmer. The assembler and linker are two of these, and we also alluded to a file-processing routine. The run processor mentioned above is another example of an operating system utility. Since these routines are generally quite large and since many of them are required only occasionally, in order to conserve main memory (one of its most limited resources), an operating system will frequently *not* keep these routines permanently resident in main memory. Rather, it will save them (on disk, for example) and bring them into main storage when a programmer request requires their use. Complicating this situation is the fact that in many operating systems, the available (free) main memory is *not static*; the amount of free storage grows as modules are released from it (perhaps saved on a disk) and shrinks, for example, as utility routines are brought into it to perform some task. Thus when a routine needs to be brought into main memory, an operating system routine (which *is* permanently resident), called a *storage manager*, is usually invoked to determine where that utility can reside at that time. Since available memory is a *dynamic* concept, a given system utility routine may not always be loaded *at the same memory locations* each time it is brought into memory. If that is the case, then the executable module making up that routine *cannot* be an *absolute* load module—it must be *relocatable*. Of course if that module is **naturally relocatable**—consists exclusively of position-independent code—then the module can be brought into memory and executed immediately; no editing of relocation-sensitive words is required, since there are no such words. In large modules invoked frequently by an operating system, this elimination of editing can result in substantial savings in time.

We make no claim that the writing of position-independent code is a trivial matter. In many cases it is quite difficult, if possible at all, requiring what most programmers would view as rather unnatural program constructions. To see this the reader might take one of the programs he has already written and try to recast it, insofar as possible, into position-independent code. In an operating system environment the writing of naturally relocatable programs can have significant rewards. In a normal programming situation, with which we are mainly concerned here, this type of coding is usually unnecessary and, if it results in programs that are obscure and difficult to read and maintain, is undesirable.

9.10 SOME CLOSING REMARKS

Before leaving this chapter we want to clear up any possible misconceptions the reader might have as a result of our discussions. We described the loading-editing-linking process as being fairly simple, both conceptually and in practice. In this regard we were not misleading. But commercially supplied linkers, as operating system utilities, may give to the programmer capabilities which extend far beyond the simple load-edit-link procedure mentioned here. In these cases such utilities can be extremely complex, even requiring the programmer to learn a fairly sophisticated language just to be able to communicate with them.

The principal example of this chapter dealt with the linking *of* a subroutine *to* a mainline program. The reader may infer from this that some mainline program is always at the heart of the linking process, with some collection of subroutines consisting of executable code being attached to this mainline. Indeed, this is frequently what happens in practice but from the linker's point of view, the situation is by no means so mainline oriented. Recall that the assembler, in building object files, *always* generates precisely the same *type* of file, regardless of what the source code looks like or what its intent may be. The linker, then, rather than linking some object files *to* a central (mainline) object file, instead looks upon its task as the linking of structurally identical object files *together*. There is no reason why such files must be subroutines, or even why they must contain any executable code at all. As long as the assembler can build an object file, that is, as long as the source code can be assembled, those object files can be loaded, edited, and linked. In fact, in several of the exercises, one of the object modules consists exclusively of *data*—a collection of .WORDs.

9.11 EXERCISES

9.2.1. If EXSUB is an externally defined symbol, explain the difference between the assembler's handling of JSR   R2,EXSUB and JSR   R2,@#EXSUB.

9.2.2. If EXSUB is an externally defined symbol, explain how the assembler will handle the construction

```
          MOV   #EXSUB,R3
          JSR   R2,(R3)
```

9.2.3. Suppose EXBUFR is an externally defined symbol. Explain how the assembler will generate code for the following instructions:
  (a) MOV   #4,EXBUFR
  (b) CLR   @#EXBUFR+4
  (c) MOV   EXBUFR−2,R2

9.2.4. We stated in Sec. 8.8 that if a subroutine made use of one or more of the general-purpose registers, then it was good programming practice to save the contents of these registers prior to their use, and then to restore their values before returning to the mainline (calling) portion of the program. Explain why the saving and restoring of registers used by an *external* subroutine is *essential*, rather than merely good programming practice.

9.4.1. Consider the following mainline program:

```
                  .GLOBL   COUNT,BUFFER
          START:  MOV   #BUFFER,R2
          LOOP:   INC   (R2)+
                  DEC   COUNT
                  BNE   LOOP
                  HALT
                  .END  START
```

  (a) Construct the symbol table for this program.
  (b) Construct the external reference table for this module's object file.

9.4.2. Consider the following "program."

```
DAYS::     .WORD   31.,28.,31.,30.,31.,30.
           .WORD   31.,31.,30.,31.,30.,31.
           .END
```

(The data consist of the number of days in the months of a non–leap year.)

(a) Can the assembler assemble this "program" into an object file? Explain.

(b) If the answer to part (a) above is yes, what will be the transfer address, external reference table, and global symbol table?

9.5.1. Construct the relocation table for the program of Exercise 9.4.1.

9.5.2. Referring to Exercise 9.4.2, write a mainline program that will print the number of days in a month when that month is specified as a number between 1 and 12 inclusive. Input the month number in decimal (using $IN.DEC) and output the number of days in decimal ($OUT.DEC). (At this point, do not attempt to deal with invalid months, such as −3 or 14.) Specify the symbol DAYS as external (with the .GLOBL directive).

(a) Write and assemble the mainline program.

(b) Describe the transfer address, external reference table, global symbol table, assembly load address, and relocation table, all of which are constructed as part of the object file.

(c) Expand on this programming example by writing a mainline program that will determine the number of days in a month based on the month *and year*. (Clearly the only modification required involves dealing with February in leap years. Thus the input 2,1985 should result in the number 28 as output, while 2,1928 should generate 29.)

9.6.1. (*Continuation of Exercise 9.5.2.*) Name the object file built in Exercise 9.5.2(a) MONTHS and the object file of Exercise 9.4.2 NODAYS. If the object code of NODAYS is appended to that of MONTHS, and if MONTHS is loaded at physical location 004204, answer the following questions.

(a) What is the physical load address of NODAYS?

(b) How are the references to DAYS in the mainline program resolved— explicitly, what are the ultimate contents of the words in the mainline that could not be supplied by the assembler?

(c) How are relocation-sensitive words in the mainline adjusted?

9.6.2. In the subroutine of Fig. 9.6.3, the entry point MAX could have been removed and then referred to as MIN − 10. In the mainline (Fig. 9.6.1) line 3 could then have been changed to .GLOBL MIN and line 13 to JSR R1,MIN−10. What would be the effects of these changes on the mainline and subroutine assemblies and on the process to resolve external references when the subroutine object module is appended to that of the mainline?

9.7.1. (*Continuation of Exercise 9.6.1.*)

(a) Load, edit, and link the files MONTHS and NODAYS of Exercise 9.6.1. Execute the resulting module and test it.

(b) Do the same as in part (a) above for the mainline program of Exercise 9.5.2(c).

9.7.2. Explain carefully and completely how the load module will appear if the linker loads the object module SUBR (containing the entry points MAX and MIN) at 001000 with MAIN immediately behind it. (See Sec. 9.6 for the definitions of the modules MAIN and SUBR.) Specifically, determine where each object module is loaded, how relocation-sensitive words in each module are adjusted, how the mainline references to MAX and MIN are completed, and what the load module's transfer address is. Finally, verify that the resulting load module is the "same" executable program, in the sense that for given input, it will generate the same output as the load module constructed in Sec. 9.6.

9.7.3. Let MOD1 be the name of the object file for the program

```
              .GLOBL  DATA1
DATA2::       .WORD   101242
START:        MOV     @DATA1,R3
              HALT
              .END    START
```

and MOD2 the name of the object file for

```
              .GLOBL  DATA2
DATA1::       .WORD   DATA2
              .END
```

Assume MOD1 is loaded at physical location 001000 and that MOD2 is loaded immediately behind it.

(a) What will be the PLA for MOD2?

(b) What will be the load module's transfer address?

(c) What editing of relocation-sensitive words will be required, if any?

(d) State explicitly what the object code for the load module will be.

(e) If the load module is executed, what number will be MOVed into R3?

10

Character Codes

10.1 CHARACTER PROCESSING

The programs and subroutines that we have seen so far have been concerned exclusively with the task of manipulating *numbers*—finding a maximum or minimum, sorting in some particular order, and so forth. Historically, the early computers were explicitly designed to do this type of number manipulation—to find the numerical solutions of differential equations, for example. But with the possible exception of very special purpose machines, or computers in a scientific environment, the general-purpose computer of today (and the PDP-11 is one of these) spends a substantial amount of its time manipulating *text*—strings of *characters*. Indeed, in some commercial establishments, the vast majority of processor time is devoted to such character processing. The developing, maintaining, and printing of mailing lists is an example of such an activity, as is the currently popular application known as *word processing*.

If a character, such as *Q*, or even a string of characters, for example, MADE IN USA, is to be *processed*—somehow manipulated by the CPU— then that character or string of characters will have to reside in main memory. Since we know that only 16-bit signed or unsigned integers can occupy a main memory word, evidently we must *convert* characters to *numbers*, called **character codes**, in order to store and process text in main memory.

10.2 CHARACTER CONVERSION

There is only one guideline to which we *must* adhere in converting characters to numbers: The conversion scheme must assign *distinct* numbers to different characters. Thus, for example, if we decided to assign the integer 143 to the character *Q and* to the character @, then there would be no problem in the *assignment* of a number to either of these characters. But the reverse operation— the *assignment* of a *character* to the number 143—would not be well defined. We would have no way of knowing whether the number 143 stood for the character *Q* or the character @. In the mathematician's terminology, the function that assigns numbers to characters must be *invertible*, or *one-to-one*.

Provided that we recognize this one constraint of the *uniqueness* of the assignment of characters to numbers, there is no *theoretical* reason for preferring one scheme to any other. However, there are a number of *practical* considerations that will guide our thinking in the development of character code assignments. For example, whatever number we assign as a code for the *character* 0 (not to be confused with the *number* 0), it may prove to be convenient to assign to the character 1 the number that is one greater than the code for 0. Similarly, we assign to the character 2 a number one greater than the code for 1, and so forth, up to the character 9.

In dealing with nonnumerical characters, we might decide that the code for *B* should be one greater than the code for *A*, the code for *C* one greater than the code for *B*, and so forth. We could handle the lower case alphabetical characters, *a*, *b*, . . . , *z* in an analogous way, The management of the special characters—$, #, ¢,), :, and so forth—presents more of a problem, since there is no natural or lexicographic order to guide us.

In deciding what numerical code to assign a given character, we should proceed in a rational fashion, partly in the hope that the decisions we make will ease the burden of *programming* for text manipulation later (a topic that we will touch on briefly but that for the most part we leave to the exercises). But there are three other considerations that come into play here. The first of these involves the "overhead" of main memory involved with character processing. There are about 100 characters in common use in the English language, even if we include such "nonprinting" characters found on computer terminals as line feed, carriage return, back space, and so forth. Thus if we begin the conversion scheme at the number 0 (regardless of what character might be assigned to 0), we find that we can use the numbers between 0 and 100 or so to convert any character in a unique way. The significance of this choice lies in the fact that any such number may be held in a single main memory *byte* rather than in a full *word*. And lest the reader attach no importance to this, consider the following example: In a mailing list, a typical name and address takes up about 50 or 60 characters. If these characters were to be stored in a one-character-per-word fashion, then even a small mailing list of 100 names and addresses would consume 5000 words of main memory. On a one-character-per-byte basis, only 2500 words would be required. This is still a substantial amount of storage, but surely it is an improvement over the other, more wasteful scheme.

The second consideration that plays a role in the assigning of codes to characters involves *standardization*. We can assign character codes any way we choose, but if our assignment of these codes differs from the assignments used by other computer installations, we are going to have some severe problems if interinstallation communication becomes necessary. For this reason a commonly accepted coding scheme is most useful. While no universal coding among computer users has yet been achieved (and in some cases, for good reason), neither is the situation chaotic—there are only a few widely accepted coding schemes, and for the most part the conversion between these is not too complex a task. The third consideration in selecting a character coding procedure, in part influenced by standardization concepts, concerns the actual computer *hardware* and will be discussed in the next section.

10.3 ASCII CODE

We shall mention a few of the commonly used coding schemes before moving on to the conversion that is of primary interest to the PDP-11 user. One of these is the so-called *Binary-Coded-Decimal* (or BCD) code. This code can be useful when a string of numeric characters, for example the string of *three* characters "198", must be converted to the *number* 198, which can then be manipulated *arithmetically*. An extension of this code, called EBCDIC, which stands for *Extended-Binary-Coded-Decimal-Interchange-Code* and which converts alphabetical as well as numerical strings, is currently widely used in some installations.

The coding we shall be concerned with throughout the remainder of the text is ASCII—*American-Standard-Code-for-Information-Interchange*. We concentrate on this code for two reasons. First, ASCII code is the conversion most widely used at present for general-purpose computers, and the coding has a number of features that makes it fairly easy to use from the programmer's point of view. A more compelling reason involves the hardware. Some of the devices common to many PDP-11 systems actually *generate* ASCII code. Thus, for example, when we depress the *S*-key on a terminal the result (as we shall see in Chapter 12) is that the ASCII code for the character *S* is transmitted to the computer. In a similar fashion, when a card reader reads the card punches in a column that represent the character *$*, the card reader converts those punches to the ASCII code for the *$* character, which is then transmitted to the computer. Finally, if a message such as OUT OF DATA is to be printed on a line printer, the ASCII code for these 11 characters must be sent to the printer, the embedded blanks being characters as well as those that actually print on the printer.

The ASCII codes for the various characters are given in Appendix C, in their octal codings. While we shall say little more now about the specific coding to be found in that table, the reader might find it profitable to browse through it, making whatever observations about the coding scheme that he might come across.

10.4 THE .BYTE, .BLKB, AND .EVEN DIRECTIVES

Suppose we wish to include in a program the ASCII code for some text, for example, MADE IN USA, for ultimate transmission to a terminal, line printer, or some other ASCII-coded device. How can we accomplish this? We know that the ASCII code is to be placed in individual bytes, and therefore the most convenient form for such a message is to have the character codes in *consecutive* bytes. Thus this text will appear in main memory as shown in Fig. 10.4.1, if we assume that its first character is located at memory location 020466. We have used the symbol ƀ here to indicate a blank or space character.

This, of course, is simply a symbolic representation of memory. What actually resides in these bytes is the ASCII codes for the characters displayed,

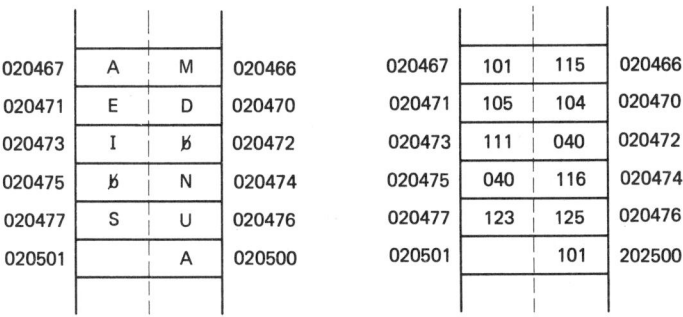

Figure 10.4.1   Figure 10.4.2

so the reality of the situation is shown in Fig. 10.4.2. In order to form the two bytes making up the codes for the characters M and A, with the code for M in the low-order byte and that for A in the high-order byte, we need to put these bytes together into a word that we can then insert in the program in the form of a .WORD. Putting the bytes 101 and 115 together yields the word 040515, so placing the directive .WORD   40515 at location 020466 will take care of the first two characters in the message. Notice that we are again being plagued by a problem that first appeared in Chapter 4—the difficulty, *in octal*, of putting bytes together to form words because the byte boundary does not coincide with an octal digit boundary. In a similar fashion we can form the words that represent, in their high- and low-order bytes, the ASCII codes for the next four pairs of characters. We encounter some difficulty with the last character (the A in USA) that occupies the low-order byte at location 020500; the question is what to do with the high-order byte, which does not contain a character code. Since that byte presumably will not be used, we may as well fill it in with 0s, that being the easiest number with which to deal. So the collection of words that represent this text, in locations 020466 to 020500, inclusive, is

```
020466      .WORD   040515
020470      .WORD   042504
020472      .WORD   044440
020474      .WORD   020116
020476      .WORD   051525
020500      .WORD   000101
```

All of these computational aggravations are quite unnecessary, for if the assembler has the capability to generate a specified word (signalled by the .WORD directive), then it should certainly be able to form a specified byte. In fact the assembler directive .BYTE, followed by one or more byte values separated by commas, will do precisely this. We could simply have included the directives

```
020466      .BYTE   115,101,104,105,040,111
            .BYTE   116,040,123,125,101
```

to generate the ASCII codes for the characters in this text. A little counting will show that the last byte, 101, is in fact loaded at 020500 and this leads to a minor problem. In generating these bytes, the assembler moved its location assignment counter up by *one* for each byte generated, and now that the text is completed, this counter has the value 020501. This *odd* value is going to cause a problem if the next thing to be assembled is a *word-type* construction, which would have to be assembled at an even (word) address—for example, an instruction or a .WORD. Since the number of bytes generated is odd, evidently we need some means of forcing the assembler's location assignment counter up to an even value, even at the expense of a wasted byte. We can do this with the assembler directive .BLKB   n which, analogous to .BLKW   n reserves n *bytes* of storage. Therefore in order to ensure that the location counter is back to an even address, we need only include the directive .BLKB   1. Thus

```
020466      .BYTE   115,101,104,105,040,111
200474      .BYTE   116,040,123,125,101
020501      .BLKB   1
020502      (next word to be assembled)
```

There are two undesirable aspects of the scheme as thus far presented. First, even though we can direct the assembler to generate individual bytes, we must still look up the ASCII code for the characters that must be encoded. And while perhaps this is not very burdensome for a short message such as we have been dealing with here, for text of any length this chore would soon become very annoying. We shall cope with this problem in the next section. The second difficulty is of a bookkeeping nature. If we are going to insert character codes in a program, on a byte-by-byte basis, and if what is to be assembled immediately after this text requires assembly at a word address, then we must decide whether to include a .BLKB   1 after this text or not, the decision being based on our ability correctly to count the number of bytes in the text. While such counting is more tedious than challenging, it is another potential area for error. But even assuming that we correctly counted the bytes and did or did not make the appropriate .BLKB   1 adjustment for the assembler's location assignment counter, we may on subsequent assemblies of the program decide to make a few changes in this text—add a character here, delete two characters there, and so forth. This text manipulation can alter the byte count, and on each such modification we shall have to take care to recount the bytes to make certain the proper .BLKB adjustment was made. We can deal with this entire problem much more easily simply by issuing the assembler the following command: If the location assignment counter is currently *odd*, move it up 1 to the next even number (address), leaving a wasted byte in the program; if it is currently *even*, leave it alone—ignore this directive. We do this with the directive .EVEN which, unlike most of the other directives, has no argument. There is also a directive .ODD which ensures the location counter has an odd value, but it is rarely used.

We can now place the bytes for the message MADE IN USA in the program in such a way that the next address is even with the directives

```
020466    .BYTE   115,101,104,105,040,111
020474    .BYTE   116,040,123,125,101
020501    .EVEN
020502    (next word to be assembled)
```

where the effect of the .EVEN directive is to insert .BLKB   1. If, instead, the text had been MADE IN USA! then no such one-byte block would have been inserted, since the last byte of the text—the ASCII code for !—would have been generated at location 020501, leaving the assembler's location assignment counter at the even address 020502.

10.5 THE .ASCII AND .ASCIZ DIRECTIVES

Since the assembler is already looking up quite a bit in tables (to find mnemonics, for example), we should be able to pass along to it the task of looking up the ASCII codes for characters, provided only that we inform it of the characters whose codes we want generated. This we do by means of an assembler directive, .ASCII, whose general form is

$$\text{.ASCII} \quad \#\text{text}\#$$

Here the number sign is used as a **delimiter,** indicating to the assembler where the string of text characters begins and where it ends. The delimiter # is *not* considered to be part of the text. Any printing character will serve as a delimiter except, of course, a character that appears in the text string itself. Thus

```
.ASCII    #MADE IN USA#
.ASCII    /THE QUICK BROWN FOX/
.ASCII    QMADE IN USAQ
```

are all acceptable uses of the .ASCII directive, although the use of the delimiter Q in the third example is to be discouraged, simply because it makes the text a bit difficult to read. We prefer delimiters such as #, /, \$, & and so forth, since these characters do not frequently occur in text strings, but almost any character will do. Notice that the directive

```
.ASCII  SMADE IN USAS
```

would not assemble as desired. The assembler would take the character S as the delimiter, would begin generating ASCII code, but would *stop* code generation when it encountered the S in USA. Thus the effect is the same as the directive

```
.ASCII  SMADE IN US
```

(which generates code for the string MADE IN U), and the assembler would not know how to deal with the extraneous characters AS in the source code.

Sometimes it is desirable to insert into a string of text the ASCII code for a *nonprinting* character or characters. A frequent example is a string of text that contains an embedded carriage return/line feed combination. Since these are printer *control* characters, there is no way to include them directly in a .ASCII directive. There are two ways to insert these into text. First, we can construct *three* directives, as follows:

```
TEXT:    .ASCII   /ALAS,/
         .BYTE    015,012
         .ASCII   /ALACK!/
```

(015 and 012 are the ASCII codes for carriage return and line feed, respectively.) The second scheme involves inserting these two codes directly into the .ASCII directive, but *not* within the directive's delimiters, enclosed in angle brackets. Thus

```
TEXT:     .ASCII  /ALAS,/⟨015⟩⟨012⟩/ALACK!/
```

Fig. 10.5.1 shows the code generated by the assembler for this text string. Note the use of the .EVEN directive to ensure an even address for the word following the text. In a similar fashion, on a terminal which has the capability of physically backspacing, if the text

```
.ASCII   /ANGLE O/⟨010⟩/-=30/
```

was transmitted, the resulting printed output would be

$$\text{ANGLE } \Theta = 30$$

```
020442    101    TEXT:    .ASCII    /ALAS,/<015><012>/ALACK!/
020443    114
020444    101
020445    123
020446    054
020447    015
020450    012
020451    101
020452    114
020453    101
020454    103
020455    113
020456    041
                            .EVEN
020460                      (NEXT PROGRAM WORD)
```

Figure 10.5.1

(010 is the ASCII code for the backspace character, which has resulted in the hyphen's overstriking the character O.)

The .ASCIZ directive is identical with .ASCII in all respects *except* that after the assembler has generated the requested ASCII code, it inserts *one additional byte* containing the number 000. The "character" whose code is 000 is called NUL; it is nonprinting. This is a feature of the assembler implemented for the use of the programmer, who could as well have inserted .BYTE 0 after a .ASCII directive. We shall see in the next section and in Chapter 12 how it can be used to advantage.

10.6 READING AND PRINTING ASCII TEXT

The ability to print ASCII text can greatly enhance the appearance and readibility of the printed output of our programs. For example, the inclusion of the short messages

THE NUMBERS IN THEIR ORIGINAL ORDER:

and

THE NUMBERS IN INCREASING ORDER:

would surely improve the appearance of the output of a program or subroutine that sorts numbers. (In the exercises we shall see some other uses for such printed text.) Messages such as these may be printed using the macroinstruction $OUT.ASC. Thus, for example, the instructions

```
            $OUT.ASC   #TEXT,#13.
              .
              .
              .
    TEXT:    .ASCII   /ALAS,/<015><012>/ALACK!/
              .
              .
              .
```

would result in the printed output

ALAS,
ALACK!

When we deal with a collection of numbers (structured as a vector, for instance), we are normally very much aware of precisely *how many* such numbers are under consideration, since this frequently influences the processing—the controlling of loops, for example. However, when printing messages as those shown above, we are normally not concerned with just how many characters there are in the message—these characters require no processing other than printing. Thus it is a nuisance when using $OUT.ASC to have to count the number of characters to be output, to supply the second argument to this macroinstruction. If we count incorrectly, or if modifications are made in the text, we may find that we are printing a truncated message or a message that contains bytes that are not intended to be in the text. $OUT.ASC allows an option in which *no* character count is specified. The only information passed to it is the address of the first byte of the text, and $OUT.ASC will continue printing ASCII characters *until it encounters a NUL*, at which time it returns control to the user program. Thus in the last example we could take advantage of this feature by writing

$OUT.ASC   #TEXT
.
.
.

TEXT: .ASCIZ   /ALAS,/⟨015⟩⟨012⟩/ALACK!/

In a similar fashion, if we issue the command

$IN.ASC   #BUFFER,#17

the routine will accept characters, byte by byte, putting them successively in locations BUFFER, BUFFER+1, BUFFER+2, and so forth, until it receives the fifteenth character, which it will put in BUFFER+16, at which time the routine will return control to the user program. Again, this requires that the programmer know in advance how many characters are to be read, and in many cases this is either of no consequence or not possible. Thus $IN.ASC has a mode analogous to $OUT.ASC in which no count is passed to the macroinstruction. Thus, for example,

$IN.ASC   #BUFFER

will read characters and put them in the locations BUFFER, BUFFER+1, and so forth, until it encounters the *end-of-line* character (carriage return). The routine does *not* put this character in the next main memory byte, but rather inserts a NUL byte (000). Thus the consecutive bytes of main memory generated by the use of this version of $IN.ASC will appear exactly as if they had been generated by a .ASCIZ directive. In using this mode the programmer must ensure that the block of bytes set aside for these characters is sufficiently large to hold the longest such input, including the NUL, to avoid the possible overlaying of other code in the program.

10.7 THE APOSTROPHE CONSTRUCTION

There is one further way we may have the assembler generate ASCII code, this time on a *single* character basis. If a character is preceded by an *apostrophe*, the assembler will convert the source code construction to the one-byte ASCII code for that character. Thus the effect of

MOVB   #'W,R4

is to move the code for the character W—namely 127—into R4. This instruction could as well, but perhaps not as conveniently, have been written as

MOVB   #127,R4

In a similar way,

.BYTE   'P,'D,'P,'-,'1,'1

is equivalent to

.ASCII   #PDP-11#

but is scarcely as easily written. We shall see a number of uses of this construction in the remainder of the text.

10.8 EXERCISES

10.3.1. Determine the five words whose consecutive bytes contain the ASCII code for the 10 characters in the text TIME FLIES.

10.3.2. Write a subroutine that locates the first occurrence of a specified character in a string of characters. Specifically, suppose R$\emptyset$ contains the address of the first byte of the string to be searched, R1 contains the ASCII code for the character to be searched for (in its low-order byte), and let the subroutine leave the address of the specified character in R$\emptyset$ upon return to the calling routine. Thus, for example, if the first byte of the string A$\emptyset$LOAF$\emptyset$OF$\emptyset$BREAD is located at 002401 and if R1 contains the code for the character F, then upon return R$\emptyset$ will contain 002406. (Here $\emptyset$ represents a single blank or space character.) The only error possible is the *absence* of the character being searched for in the specified string. We shall not attempt to deal with this potential problem here.

10.3.3. What is the relationship between the ASCII codes for upper-case and lower-case alphabetical characters?

10.3.4. Locate a table of EBCDIC code and find the relationship (if any) between the codes for upper-case and lower-case alphabetical characters.

10.3.5. We stated in Section 10.3 that a card reader, by means of its internal hardware, may convert the punches in a card column to the ASCII code for the corresponding character prior to passing the card column information to the computer. Some card readers, however, do not do this conversion; rather, they transmit to the computer a *reflection* of the punches in the 12 rows of each column, which represents a 16-bit word, each bit being a 1 to indicate a punch, or a 0 to indicate no punch. (Only 12 of the 16 bits are used.) For example, if a card column contains punches in the top, the third from the top, and the bottom (twelfth) rows, then the 16-bit word passed to the computer would be

$$1\ 0\ 1\ 0\ 0\ 0\ 0\ 0\ 0\ 0\ 0\ 1\ 0\ 0\ 0\ 0$$

or 120020 (in octal). Find a table of card codes (sometimes called *Hollerith code*) and try to determine how easy or difficult it would be to write a program to convert this card code to ASCII.

10.5.1. Write a routine that will remove all the blanks (ƀ's) from a string of ASCII text that is assumed to end in a NUL.

10.5.2. Write a routine that will convert any lower-case alphabetical characters in a string (that ends in a NUL) to upper case.

10.5.3. If R2 contains in its low-order byte the ASCII code for one of the *characters* $0, 1, \ldots, 7$, what instruction will convert the contents of R2 to the *number* represented by that character?

10.5.4. Suppose R1 contains the address of the first byte of a string, ending in a NUL, consisting of one, two, or three numerical *characters*, each of which ranges between 0 and 7. Write a subroutine that converts this string, considered as an *octal* number, to a binary number and leaves the result in RØ. (See Exercise 10.5.3. The ASH instruction may be useful here.)

10.5.5. Consider a string of from one to four characters, each of which is one of the numerical characters $0, 1, \ldots, 9$. Assume the string ends in a NUL. Convert this string, considered as a *decimal* number, to a binary number.

10.5.6. Write a subroutine which, given the addresses of two strings (each of which ends in a NUL), will determine which string is the *first* in lexicographic order. (There are a number of ways in which this information can be returned by the subroutine.)

10.5.7. Write a program to put a collection of strings, each of which is assumed to end in a NUL, in lexicographic order. (This is a nontrivial exercise. *Suggestion:* To avoid the overhead involved in moving strings about in main memory to put them in order, construct a *vector* whose entries are the *addresses* of the first byte of the strings. Thus if

```
        ADDR1:      .ASCIZ    /string₁/
        ADDR2:      .ASCIZ    /string₂/
                      .
                      .
                      .
        ADDRN:      .ASCIZ    /stringₙ/
```

then the vector will be of the form

```
    POINTR:     .WORD     ADDR1, ... , ADDRN
```

If we must interchange string$_I$ and string$_J$, we interchange ADDRI and ADDRJ in the vector instead.)

10.5.8. Convert a 16-bit binary number to a string of six octal digits that is the number's octal representation.

10.5.9. In BCD code, a decimal digit (0, 1, . . . , 9) is coded in *four* bits as 0000, 0001, . . . , 1001. Thus a PDP-11 16-bit word can hold four such BCD representations. (These 4 bits are sometimes referred to as *half-bytes*, although the term *nybble* also seems to be creeping into the literature.) Thus the decimal number 1987 would be encoded in a single word as

$$\underbrace{0001}_{1} \quad \underbrace{1001}_{9} \quad \underbrace{1000}_{8} \quad \underbrace{0111}_{7}$$

The reason for using BCD code is that it is relatively easy to convert from a string of numerical decimal ASCII characters to this internal BCD format, and conversely. (The situation is very little different from the ease with which octal representations are managed.)

(a) Convert four-character ASCII strings to internal BCD format. (In testing this routine, it will probably be most useful to print the resulting numbers in binary, using $OUT.BIN.)

(b) Convert a 16-bit BCD-coded number to a string of four decimal ASCII characters.

(c) Notwithstanding the ease of conversion between ASCII and BCD code, a heavy price is paid when arithmetic is attempted on BCD-coded integers. Consider the following simple example:

$$
\begin{array}{ll}
0001\ 0010\ 0101\ 0011 & 1253 \\
+\ 1000\ 0001\ 0001\ 0101 & +\ 8115 \\
\hline
1001\ 0011\ 0110\ 1000 & 9368
\end{array}
$$

As we see, the *binary* addition resulted in a correct BCD representation. But now consider

$$
\begin{array}{ll}
0001\ 0010\ 0101\ 1001 & 1259 \\
+\ 1000\ 0010\ 0111\ 1000 & +\ 8278 \\
\hline
1001\ 0100\ 1101\ 0001 & 9537
\end{array}
$$

Clearly much went wrong here, for two reasons. First, there was a carry from bit 3 into bit 4 that was not dealt with. And second, there *should* have been a carry from bit 7 into bit 8, but there was none. As a nontrivial exercise, implement BCD addition of 16-bit words, assuming for convenience that the BCD-coded numbers are in some general-purpose registers.

(This task is difficult at best. Computers that rely on such BCD arithmetic—typically the microprocessors—frequently have **half-byte carry** indicators in their processor status words, so that carries from bit 3 into bit 4, for instance, can be detected. Some of these machines even have special hardware instructions, called **decimal adjust** instructions, that will make the appropriate adjustments to a BCD-coded word after addition or subtraction.)

10.6.1. Tell what will be printed when the program of Fig. 10.8.1 is executed. This example suggests the possibility of using computers to *decode* hidden messages. It is also possible for them to *encode* English-language text, and in fact the .WORDs in the listing above were generated by such an encoding

```
000000  110256  BLOCK:  .WORD   110256,124202,110100,124202
000002  124202
000004  110100
000006  124202
000010  040220          .WORD   040220,117216,040210,122256
000012  117216
000014  040210
000016  122256
000020  125236          .WORD   125236,110216,077250
000022  110216
000024  077250
                        ;
000026  012700  START:  MOV     #BLOCK,R0
        000000'
000032  000241  LOOP:   CLC
000034  006020          ROR     (R0)+
000036  020027          CMP     R0,#START
        000026'
000042  001373          BNE     LOOP
000044                  $OUT.ASC  #BLOCK,#START-BLOCK
000100                  $EXIT
                        ;
        000026'         .END    START
```

Figure 10.8.1

program. An analysis of the scheme used here will reveal that it is so simple that it would scarcely give even a novice cryptographer much of a struggle. The reader might wish to investigate more elaborate and complex encoding schemes and corresponding decoding techniques.

10.6.2. Consider a name written as a string in the form

last, first, initial

such as JONES,JOHN,J and suppose that each such string ends in a NUL (000) byte.

(a) Build from this string a second string in the form

firstþinitial.þlast

thus JOHNþJ.þJONES where, as usual, þ represents a blank or space character. The subroutine of Exercise 10.3.2 will be useful here. We assume every such string contains precisely two commas and a one-character middle initial. Assume that no name will be longer than 40_{10} characters. Input the string using $IN.ASC, with no character count, and output the resulting modified string using $OUT.ASC, again with no character count.

(b) Modify the program of part (a) to deal with names that contain *no* middle initial. Thus, for example, JONES,JOHN, should give as output the string JOHNþJONES.

10.6.3. Suppose a string is input using $IN.ASC in its no-character-count form, so that the resulting string ends in a NUL. Write a subroutine to find the number of characters in such a string.

10.6.4. Write a program that inputs a string (of no more than 20_{10} character length) and then substitutes that string for the character ? in the string

THEþ?þBROWNþFOX

(This is a common task performed by text editors and word processors.)

10.6.5. Consider the string of characters

BYþTHEþDAWN'SþEARLYþLIGHT

Write a program that will locate the first instance of a specified character in this string and will then delete a specified number of characters from the string, beginning with the given character. Thus, for example, if the program is given the input H,14 the routine should output the string

BYβTRLYβLIGHT

What will be the output for D,0? For A,72?

10.6.6. (*Continuation of Exercise 9.5.2.*) Write a program that prints the number of days in a specified month, given the month entered as its first three characters, such as JAN, FEB, and so on.

10.6.7. (*Continuation of Exercise 10.6.6.*) Write a program that prints the number of days in a specified month, given the month (entered as its first three characters) *and* the year. (See Exercises 10.3.1 and 10.5.5.) Thus the string FEB,1928 input by means of $IN.ASC should generate the output 29.

10.6.8. (*Continuation of Exercise 10.6.7.*) Expand upon Exercise 10.6.7 so that the output for APR,1942, for example, is

APRIL,β1942,βCONTAINSβ30βDAYS

11

The TRAP Instruction

11.1 SUBROUTINES REVISITED

In Chapter 8 we examined the subroutine concept in some detail, and in that and subsequent chapters we found that subroutines can be extremely useful, either written internally as a part of the main programming module or written externally, later being linked to the mainline program. We give a brief review of some of these ideas before proceeding with the main topic of this chapter.

The activity that underlies the subroutine concept is the saving and restoring of the PC—prior to relinquishing control to the subroutine, the mainline saves the PC somewhere so that the subroutine, upon the completion of its processing, can restore this value of the PC in order to return control back to the mainline. Just *where* the PC is saved does not concern us in this general discussion. It might, for example, always be saved in some *fixed* location in main memory, although the consequences of such a scheme would be to place severe restrictions on the programmer. In Exercise 8.6.5 we suggested a design, in actual use on some machines, in which the PC was saved in the first word of the subroutine itself. On the PDP-11, as we are aware, the PC is saved in a general-purpose register or perhaps on the stack, while in other machines that have a hardware stack but perhaps do not have these general-purpose registers, the PC is simply stacked prior to giving control to the subroutine. The PDP-11 hardware stack plays an important role in the *uses* of subroutines— nested subroutine calls, subroutines that call one another, and recursive sub- routine calls—and we took advantage of it on numerous occasions. But the stack does not directly enter into the subroutine *concept*.

Another topic of some interest in Chapter 8 was the transmission of arguments to a subroutine, and we saw a number of ways in which that can be done. If arguments are passed to a subroutine through the general-purpose registers or on the stack, then there is no apparent advantage to using one of the general-purpose registers as the subroutine transfer register—we may just as well stack the PC, which is the effect of the JSR   PC,SUBR construction. If, on the other hand, arguments are placed immediately after the JSR instruction in .WORDs—a useful and popular method of argument transmission—then the use of a general-purpose register as the transfer register is most helpful in the "picking up" of those arguments by the subroutine, and in this case the use of the PC as the transfer register is something of a nuisance, although obtaining the arguments is certainly still possible. Thus on a machine whose JSR instruction *always* pushes the PC onto the stack—that is, whose JSR instruction comes in this form *only*—the transmission of arguments to a subroutine is usually done by some means *other* than placing the arguments in .WORDs following the subroutine call.

11.2 THE HYPOTHETICAL JTZ INSTRUCTION

Consider a hypothetical computer (and certainly *not* the PDP-11) that implements the following instruction: JTZ, which is the mnemonic for the hardware instruction *J*ump-*T*hrough-*Z*ero. Its effect is described as follows:

$$\downarrow (SP) \longleftarrow c(PC)$$
$$PC \longleftarrow c(000000)$$

We see that when JTZ is executed, the current contents of the PC is pushed onto the stack, and the PC obtains a new value from location 000000. That is, execution resumes at the memory location whose address is in 000000. It is important to realize that the jump that occurs here is not *to* 000000, but rather *through* 000000.

This is certainly a peculiar instruction when compared with those with which we are already familiar. However, because of the saving (stacking) of c(PC), it appears that this instruction might be usable for a jump-to-subroutine type construction, and we shall pursue that idea briefly. For the moment let us assume that the PDP-11 *does* implement the JTZ instruction, and for the purposes of program listings, we even assign it a dummy op–code—007200. For illustrative purposes we take as a subroutine one that replaces the contents of R∅ with it absolute value (Fig. 11.2.1). All that we need to do is to test c(R∅). If this number is nonnegative we simply return; otherwise we replace c(R∅) with its negative and return. A few preliminaries are required before executing the JTZ instruction.

Since the JTZ instruction will place in PC the contents of memory location 000000, we must first ensure that the *address* of the subroutine is in location 000000. This is done at line 43, where ABS is the symbolic address of the

```
  1              000000          ZERO = 0                ;'JUMP-THROUGH' ADDR
                                 .
  2 000000   172335  DATA:   .WORD   172335
                                 .
 43 000556   012767  START:  MOV     #ABS,ZERO       ;SET UP ROUTINE ADDR
             001266'
             000000
                                 .
 55 000610   016700          MOV     DATA,R0         ;PUT NUMBER IN R0
             177164
 56 000614   007200          JTZ                     ; AND JUMP-THRU-0
 57 000616                                           ;(NEXT INSTRUCTION)
                                 .
 89 001266   005700  ABS:    TST     R0              ;CHECK SIGN
 90 001270   100001          BPL     RETURN          ;NONNEGATIVE -- OK
 91 001272   005400          NEG     R0              ; ELSE CHANGE SIGN
 92 001274   012607  RETURN: MOV     (SP)+,PC        ;RESTORE ML PC
                                 .


SYMBOL TABLE

ABS      001266R            RETURN  001274R          ZERO  = 000000
DATA     000000R            START   000556R
```

Figure 11.2.1

subroutine entry point. And, of course, prior to executing the JTZ, we must have in R0 the number whose absolute value is to be found (line 55). When the JTZ instruction is *fetched* by the CPU, c(PC) will be moved up to 000616. This number (address) is then stacked, and the PC is given the contents of memory location 000000, namely, 001266 = ABS. The subroutine then executes and upon completion, needs only to pop the top of the stack (which contains 000616) into the PC to achieve the proper return. That is, we really need no special kind of return-from-JTZ instruction, since as opposed to RTS, the return is completely straightforward. The situation is so simple that little more can be said about it. However, we should note line 1: ZERO = 0. Here we created a symbol, ZERO, but instead of using it somewhere in the program as a *label* (such as DATA or START) and thus having the *assembler* assign it a value, we *directly assigned* its value (0) by means of the equal-sign construction— a so-called **direct assignment statement**. Notice that ZERO appears in the symbol table with the value 000000, although the *form* of the entry is a bit different, the equal sign indicating that its value was directly assigned rather than calculated. The symbol ZERO was used in line 43—MOV   #ABS,ZERO, the instruction that set the contents of 000000 in preparation for the JTZ. This instruction could just as well have been MOV   #ABS,@#0. Our motivation for using this construction is to emphasize that ZERO is an *address*, to whose memory location we are MOVing the number (address) ABS, a device that somewhat improves the understandability of the program listing. (In the next chapter, for example, we shall make direct assignments such as LF = 12, the ASCII code for the line feed character. Then in the program listing a reference to the symbol LF will be substantially more meaningful to the reader than would be a reference simply to the number 12.)

In the program segment of Fig. 11.2.1 we transmitted the argument to the subroutine ABS through RØ. If instead we had decided to transmit that argument by following the JTZ instruction with a .WORD containing the address of the number whose absolute value is to be found, the processing in ABS would be far more complicated, as is shown in the listing of Fig. 11.2.2.

```
 1        000000            ZERO = 0                    ;'JUMP-THROUGH' ADDR
                                                        ;
 2 000000 172335   DATA:    .WORD    172335
                            .
35 000556 012767   START:   MOV      #ABS,ZERO          ;SET UP ROUTINE ADDR
          001226'
          000000
                            .
57 000614 007200            JTZ                         ;JUMP-THRU-0
58 000616 000000'           .WORD    DATA               ;ADDR OF NUMBER
59 000620                   .                           ;(NEXT INSTRUCTION)
                            .
81 001226 017646   ABS:     MOV      @(SP),-(SP)        ;PUT ADDR ON STACK
          000000
92 001232 005776            TST      @(SP)              ;CHECK SIGN
          000000
93 001236 100002            BPL      RETURN             ;NONNEGATIVE -- OK
94 001240 005476            NEG      @(SP)              ; ELSE CHANGE SIGN
          000000
95 001244 005726   RETURN:  TST      (SP)+              ;MOVE SP UP BY 2
96 001246 062716            ADD      #2,(SP)            ;ADJUST RETURN ADDR
          000002
97 001252 012607            MOV      (SP)+,PC           ; AND RESTORE ML PC
```

Figure 11.2.2

By now the reader should have little difficulty in following the details of the programming, although some scrutiny will be required to see just what numbers are being manipulated, since several instructions are doubly deferred. In particular, the instruction at line 91 puts the number (address) DATA on top of the stack; at line 95 the stack pointer is adjusted to remove the number DATA on top of the stack, since it has served its purpose; and at line 96 the return PC—on top of the stack—is adjusted to skip around the .WORD   DATA in the mainline portion of the program. The processing required by the subroutine here is clearly more involved than in the preceding example, but the reader should be aware that this is *not* specifically the fault of the JTZ instruction—the same problems would have occurred if instead we had used JSR   PC,ABS. Rather, the difficulty occurs because the return address is on the stack, rather than in some register.

The problems encountered in using this method for the transmission of arguments to a subroutine by means of the JTZ instruction are overshadowed by a far more severe difficulty. If JTZ uses location 000000 to pick up the address of the subroutine—to jump through—then how could we ever reference *more than one* subroutine in a program? Location 000000 can hold only *one* subroutine address, or at best, only one at a time, and thus if two or more subroutines were to be referenced by means of JTZ then the only way in which this could be accomplished would be to change the contents of 000000 to the appropriate subroutine entry point address each time JTZ was executed. Since a JSR-type instruction *does* exist on the PDP-11 (and almost every other machine as well), it appears that the JTZ instruction, if it was implemented at all, would almost never be used.

11.3 THE TRAP INSTRUCTION

The reader may justifiably wonder why we devoted an entire section of this chapter to an instruction that is hypothetical, is not implemented in the PDP-11 hardware, and that turns out not to be very useful from the programmer's standpoint anyway. The reason is that the PDP-11, while in fact it does not implement such a JTZ instruction, *does* have an instruction that is almost identical in its operation to JTZ—the instruction TRAP. The effect of TRAP is to stack c(PC) and then to load the PC with the contents of a *fixed* memory location. Thus TRAP does exactly what the hypothetical JTZ does, although the fixed location in the case of TRAP is 000034, not 000000; however, TRAP actually does a bit more—it also stacks c(PSW) and obtains a *new* PSW, again from a *fixed* memory location. The effect of the instruction TRAP is described as follows:

$$\downarrow (SP) \longleftarrow c(PSW)$$
$$\downarrow (SP) \longleftarrow c(PC)$$
$$PC \longleftarrow c(000034)$$
$$PSW \longleftarrow c(000036)$$

Notice that the PSW is stacked *first*, followed by the PC. Thus after execution of the TRAP instruction, the return PC will be on top of the stack, with the "old" PSW one word down in the stack. This order of stacking these registers is of some consequence to programming with the TRAP instruction, as we shall see shortly. The memory locations 000034 – 000036 are referred to as the **TRAP vector**.

Recall that to return from a JTZ-type jump, the only thing required was the popping of the top of the stack back into the PC. In the case of TRAP, however, the situation is a bit more complex, since TRAP has pushed *two* things on the stack. Thus a special PDP-11 instruction *is* needed here to restore the PC and PSW. The instruction is RTT, which stands for *Re*Turn-from-*T*rap, and it can be described as follows:

$$PC \longleftarrow (SP) \uparrow$$
$$PSW \longleftarrow (SP) \uparrow$$

Some models of the PDP-11 do not implement the instruction RTT. For these the instruction RTI will do just as well, and a glance at the descriptions of these two instructions in Appendix A will reveal that with one exception, their behaviors are identical. (The difference between RTT and RTI lies in their reaction relative to the state of a bit in the PSW—the *trace-trap* bit, or T-bit. If this bit is set, a trap through the vector at 000014 – 000016 will occur after execution of each instruction, *including* the RTI instruction, but *excluding* the instruction RTT. But this T-bit is normally used only by operating-system-supplied debugging aids, and thus the distinction between RTT and RTI will be of no consequence to us in this text.)

Since the TRAP instruction is structurally the same as the hypothetical JTZ, with the exception of the stacking of the PSW, we should be able to use TRAP as we used JTZ in the preceding section. Figure 11.3.1 is a listing of a

```
 1            000034     ..     TRAPPC = 34            ;TRAP VECTOR PC
 2            000036            TRAPPS = 36            ; AND PSW
 3                              ;
 4  000000    172335     DATA:  .WORD   172335
                                .
35  000556    012767     START: MOV     #ABS,TRAPPC    ;SET UP ROUTINE ADDR
            001226'
            000034
36  000564    005067            CLR     TRAPPS         ; AND PSW
            000036

                                .
57  000614    104400            TRAP                   ;TRAP TO 'ABS' ROUTINE
58  000616    000000'           .WORD   DATA           ;ADDR OF NUMBER
59  000620                      .                      ;(NEXT INSTRUCTION)

                                .
91  001226    017646     ABS:   MOV     @(SP),-(SP)    ;PUT ADDR ON STACK
            000000
92  001232    005776            TST     @(SP)          ;CHECK SIGN
            000000
93  001236    100002            BPL     RETURN         ;NONNEGATIVE -- OK
94  001240    005476            NEG     @(SP)          ; ELSE CHANGE SIGN
            000000
95  001244    005726     RETURN: TST    (SP)+          ;MOVE SP UP BY 2
96  001246    062716            ADD     #2,(SP)        ;ADJUST RETURN ADDR
            000002
97  001252    000006            RTT                    ;RESTORE PC AND PSW
```

Figure 11.3.1

program segment that is simply the last example of the preceding section with JTZ replaced by TRAP. There are also a couple of other minor noteworthy changes. Again (lines 1 and 2) we used a direct assignment statement to assign the values 34 and 36 to the symbols TRAPPC and TRAPPS. (We remind the reader that this is by no means necessary—we could as well have used 34 and 36—the symbolic names are simply a bit more meaningful when reading the listing.) Line 35 moves the address of the ABS routine into location 000034 to set up the PC word of the TRAP vector. Now the question is what to do with location 000036—the PSW word of the TRAP vector. Recall that when the TRAP takes place, this word will become the new PSW. It is difficult to see how any *particular* value in this word will influence the processing that takes place in the routine ABS once it is TRAPped to, and thus we might be inclined simply to ignore location 000036 = TRAPPS—to let its value be whatever it happens to contain and not bother loading it with anything special. For a variety of reasons, most of which will not become clear until the next chapter, it is best that we *know* what the contents of the PSW will be once we begin executing the TRAP routine ABS because the PSW contains some bits other than the condition codes that can influence the actions taken by the CPU. It turns out that a value of 0 will always be safe in the cases we are examining here, so at line 36 the second word of the TRAP vector is cleared. The only other modification that we need to make is to replace the return statement in the routine ABS. The instruction MOV (SP)+,PC will no longer do, since that will not restore the PSW—the PSW from the main portion of the program will be left on the stack. Thus we use RTT (or RTI) instead. Aside from these changes the program proceeds exactly as before, since as with JTZ, the return PC is on top of the stack.

11.4 TRAPPING TO MULTIPLE ENTRY POINTS

We commented in Sec. 11.2 that since the action of the JTZ instruction is always to give to the PC the value of the contents of 000000, then if the JTZ was to be used to transfer control to *more than one* routine entry point, the contents of 000000 would have to be modified prior to the execution of each JTZ. Since the architecture of the TRAP instruction is not substantially different from that of the JTZ and thus cannot overcome this problem, it appears that the same comment applies to TRAP. In fact, if we do a little additional programming, we *can* transfer control to a number of different entry points using TRAP, *without* changing the PC word of the TRAP vector.

The op-code for the TRAP instruction is 104400, which in binary is

$$1 \quad 000 \quad 100 \quad 1 \quad 00 \quad 000 \quad 000$$

The low-order byte, 00 000 000, is in fact *unused* by the CPU. That is, the high-order byte contains enough information for the decoder to recognize the TRAP instruction; it then simply ignores the contents of the low-order byte. Thus the op-codes 104400, 104401, 014477, 104720, and so forth, *all* represent the TRAP instruction. If the assembler is given the instruction TRAP to assemble, it will generate the code 104400, as we expect. However, if it is asked to assemble the instruction TRAP   n, where n is an (unsigned) integer between 0 and 377 inclusive, it will generate a word whose high-order byte contains the code for TRAP and whose low-order byte contains the integer n. Thus, for example, TRAP   12 will result in the code 104412, whereas TRAP   104 will be assembled as 104504. (Keep in mind that *all* of these still represent *the* TRAP instruction.) The significance to the programmer of the number in the low-order byte is seen in the next example, a listing of which is shown in Fig. 11.4.1 and which contains some features that warrant discussion.

```
1        000034        TRAPPC = 34           ;TRAP VECTOR PC
2        000036        TRAPPS = 36           ; AND PSW

14 000142 012767 START: MOV    #XFER,TRAPPC  ;SET UP TRAP PC
          001016'
          000034
15 000150 005067        CLR    TRAPPS        ; AND PSW
          000036

49 000436 104404        TRAP   4             ;TRAP WITH CODE 4
50 000440               .                    ;(NEXT INSTRUCTION)

64 000512 104401        TRAP   1             ;TRAP WITH CODE 1
65 000514               .                    ;(NEXT INSTRUCTION)

88                                           ;ROUTINE TRANSFERS CONTROL TO SPECIFIED MODULE
89                                           ;
90 001016 011603 XFER:  MOV    (SP),R3       ;GET RETURN ADDRESS
91 001020 116303        MOVB   -2(R3),R3     ;GET TRAP CODE
          177776
92 001024 006303        ASL    R3            ; AND DOUBLE IT
93 001026 000173        JMP    @DSPTCH-2(R3) ;JUMP 'THROUGH' VECTOR
          001110'
94                                           ; TO SPECIFIED ROUTINE

126                                          ;VECTOR TO DISPATCH CONTROL TO ROUTINE
127                                          ;
128 001112 001266' DSPTCH: .WORD  MOD1
129 001114 001344'        .WORD  MOD2
130 001116 001410'        .WORD  MOD3
131 001120 001436'        .WORD  MOD4

153 001266        MOD1:                      ;MODULE #1 ENTRY POINT

167 001342 000006        RTT                 ;RETURN
168                       ;
169 001344        MOD2:                      ;MODULE #2 ENTRY POINT

181 001406 000006        RTT                 ;RETURN
182                       ;
183 001410        MOD3:                      ;MODULE #3 ENTRY POINT

195 001434 000006        RTT                 ;RETURN
196                       ;
197 001436        MOD4:                      ;MODULE #4 ENTRY POINT

212 001470 000006        RTT                 ;RETURN
```

Figure 11.4.1

In this example we assume that the program segment contains four routines, the entry points of which are labeled MOD1, MOD2, MOD3, and MOD4. We wish to be able to enter any of these modules by means of the TRAP instruction, but *without* having to modify the first (PC) word of the TRAP vector. In line 14 the address XFER (001016) is placed in the first word of the TRAP vector (location 000034) and the second word of that vector is cleared at line 15, for lack of anything better to do with it. Let us examine in detail the effect of the instruction TRAP 4 at line 49.

When the PC contains 000436, the CPU will fetch the TRAP instruction (namely, 104404) and move c(PC) up to 000440. TRAP will stack the contents of the PSW (whatever that might be) and the contents of the PC (000440), put the contents of 000034 (001016) in the PC and the contents of 000036 (000000) in the PSW. Thus execution picks up at the location labeled XFER. The instruction MOV (SP),R3 will move—but not pop—the contents of the word at the top of the stack into R3, so then c(R3) will be 000440. The *source* of the MOVB −2(R3),R3 instruction is the contents of the memory byte whose address is c(R3) − 2 = 000440 − 2 = 000436, namely, the low-order byte of the TRAP 4 instruction. Since that byte contains the number 004 and since the *destination* of the MOVB instruction is R3, by the time the instruction will have completed execution, c(R3) will be 000004. The next instruction (at line 92) doubles this value, so then c(R3) will be 000010. In the JMP instruction at line 93, the address of the EL (the destination) is calculated as follows: The index, DSPTCH-2 (001110), is added to c(R3) (000010) and the result is the value 001120. Since the JMP instruction is *deferred* (@), the address of the destination is the contents of 001120, namely, 001436 = MOD4. Thus the number 4, which we have referred to as the **trap code**, has passed control to the routine whose entry point address is the *fourth* entry in the vector DSPTCH—the so-called **dispatch vector**. Once the routine at MOD4 executes, it ends with RTT. The top of the stack, namely, the number 000440, is popped off the stack into the PC, as is the "old" contents of the PSW, and thus execution resumes at 000440, the next instruction in the mainline portion of the program. The reader would do well to do a similar analysis of the TRAP 1 instruction at line 64.

While this example does seem to accomplish what it set out to do and does contain some interesting and new types of programming, the question remains why one would choose to use the TRAP instruction under any circumstances, when the far more convenient JSR is available. We shall not be able to give a completely satisfactory answer to this question, except to say that on machines that have this kind of trap-type instruction, it is frequently used to advantage in *system programming*, that is, in writing the various modules that make up the operating system. In brief, TRAP was never intended for general, everyday programming use.

11.5 THE ALTERNATE GENERAL REGISTER SET

By now the reader probably has the impression that the TRAP instruction is peculiar at best. Possibly its most puzzling aspect is the saving of the PSW (and its subsequent restoration upon execution of RTT or RTI). So far we have not been able to find anything to do with this PSW that is picked out of location 000036 except to clear it to 0. In this section we offer an example that illustrates that it may actually be useful to obtain a *new* PSW upon a TRAP and then to restore the PSW to its *original* value when returning to the portion of the program that executed the TRAP. We confess that as a justification for the action taken by the TRAP/RTT combination—the stacking and unstacking of the PSW—the example is a bit thin. However, it does introduce another idea that is of considerable interest for some machines and in some environments.

Throughout the text we referred to *the* set of general-purpose registers, R∅ to R5. On *some* models of the PDP-11 there are in fact *two* such sets of general registers. However, there is no *notational* difference between these— regardless of which set is being referenced, the third register in the set is *called* R2, for example. But then how does the CPU know *which* register 4 is to be incremented when executing an instruction such as INC   R4—op-code 005204? The answer lies in bit 11 of the PSW. If this bit is on, the CPU selects one of the general-register sets; if it is off, the CPU selects the other set. Thus the CPU, in processing an instruction that involves a general-purpose register, will first examine the PSW to determine *which* of these registers is being referenced— the register from set 0 or that from set 1. (We informally name the register sets 0 and 1 to correspond to bit 11 of the PSW.)

The program segment of Fig. 11.5.1 illustrates how the programmer can take advantage of this alternate register set when using the TRAP instruction to transfer control to a routine, which here is named ENTPT. After the address ENTPT is put in location 000034 for the purpose of jumping to the routine, the second word of the TRAP vector—the PSW word—is set to 004000. This sets bit 11 to 1 and sets all other bits to 0. The next instruction (line 8) sets the *current* PSW to 0. The only purpose for this instruction is to ensure that bit 11

```
1              000034         TRAPPC = 34
2              000036         TRAPPS = 36
3              177776         PSW    = 177776
4
5  000000      012767   START: MOV    #ENTPT,TRAPPC   ;SET UP TRAP PC
               000226'
               000034
6  000006      012767         MOV    #4000,TRAPPS    ;SETS BIT 11 IN PSW
               004000
               000036
7                                                    ; WORD OF TRAP VECTOR
8  000014      005067         CLR    PSW             ;MAKE SURE USING
               177776
9                                                    ; REGISTER SET 0

41 000116      104400         TRAP                   ;TRAP TO 'ENTPT'
42 000120                      .                     ;(NEXT INSTRUCTION)

74 000226             ENTPT:   .                     ;ROUTINE ENTRY POINT
75                             .                     ;ROUTINE USES GENERAL
76                             .                     ; REGISTER SET 1

93 000252      000006         RTT                    ;RESTORE PC AND PSW
94                                                   ;(RETURNS TO REGISTER
95                                                   ; SET 0)
```

Figure 11.5.1

of the PSW—the register-set bit—is 0 so that mainline processing will proceed with general register set 0. Main processing now begins and presumably uses a number of the general register set 0 registers. When the TRAP occurs at line 41, control is passed to the address labeled ENTPT, the current contents of the PSW and PC having been stacked, and a new PC and PSW having been obtained from the TRAP vector. By the time processing begins in the routine ENTPT, the PSW will have a value in which bit 11 is 1, and thus ENTPT will execute with general register set 1. Any register R∅ to R5 may now be used *without* saving and restoring because ENTPT is executing with a register set that is *different* from that used by the mainline; therefore those mainline register values will be unaffected by whatever is done in ENTPT. When the RTT is executed, the original (mainline) PSW will be restored, and processing will continue with general register set 0 and with it, the mainline values of those registers. Thus the TRAP instruction may be used to switch between the two general register sets on models that implement this feature. Indeed, there are easier ways to switch register sets, and in fact register-set swapping is rarely used in day-to-day programming.

11.6 THE LINKAGE EDITOR REVISITED

This section may be omitted since it deals with matters that do not influence the subsequent material in the text and do not affect the user's ability to assemble, link, and execute programs. On the other hand, the reader who is seeking a slightly deeper understanding of the loading-editing-linking process may find it profitable to devote some time to the principal topic involved here.

The perceptive reader may have noticed what appear to be incorrectly calculated displacements generated by the assembler in each of the program listings of this chapter. Specifically, consider the program segment listing of Sec. 11.3 (Fig. 11.3.1). Line 35 appears as

```
000556      012767      START:        MOV  #ABS,TRAPPC
000560      001226'
000562      000034

000564                                (next instruction)
```

The MOV instruction, assembled correctly as 012767, indicates that the source is referenced as mode 2 PC addressing—immediate mode—and thus that the relocation-sensitive word 001226 is to be moved to the destination. The destination is specified as being mode 6 PC addressing (PC relative), and thus the address of the destination is calculated at follows: We take the current contents of the PC, which upon execution would be 000564, and add to it the displacement 000034. The resulting destination address is 000564 + 000034 = 000620. But this can scarcely be correct, since the destination of this MOV is *supposed* to be 000034, the address of the first word of the TRAP vector. On the other hand, suppose the assembler *had* correctly calculated the displacement: $000564 + disp = 000034$, so the displacement is 177250 and the MOV instruction is assembled as

000556	012767	START:	MOV	#ABS,TRAPPC
000560	001226'			
000562	177250			

000564   (next instruction)

While this *appears* to be correct, it will not do for the following reason: Suppose the object module represented by this listing is now loaded at memory location 001000. Then the word 177250 at location 000562 as shown above will be relocated to location 001562. With a displacement of 177250 as specified, the reference will then be to memory location 001034, not 000034 as desired.

The problem should be fairly clear. An *absolute* (that is, *fixed*) address was referenced by a module that is subject to *relocation*, and the reference was made by the *displacement* to that absolute address. When a relocatable module makes reference by displacement to an address within that module that *also* is moved by the relocation, the displacement to the reference does not change and thus does not need to be adjusted, as we saw in Chapter 9. But if a reference is made to a *fixed* address—an address that will *never* move—in a module that is later relocated, then the displacement to that fixed address will have to be repaired when the referencing statement is moved (relocated). If the problem is clear, the solution may not be, but it is nonetheless manageable.

In generating the object file from a source file such as that under consideration, the assembler recognizes such mode 6 (or 7) PC addressing references to absolute addresses. Because of the potential problem caused by object module relocation, the assembler cannot correctly calculate a displacement that will be valid under relocation. Thus instead it places the absolute address itself (000034, in this case) in what should be the displacement word and records that it has done so at this word (that is, at 000562) in still another table, called the **absolute reference table**, that is built as part of the object file. In the editing phase of the load-edit-link process, the editor can find these absolute references, and since it knows the PLA, and consequently the physical address of such absolute references, *and* the absolute address being referenced, it can easily calculate the appropriate displacement and insert it into the load module, overlaying the absolute address placed there by the assembler. Thus, for example if the module in question was loaded at 001000, so that the absolute reference to 000034 occurred at 001562, the editor would use an assumed PC of 001564 and calculate the displacement to 000034: $000034 - 001564 = 176214$. This number would replace the absolute reference at 001562 in the load module, and upon execution the instruction would correctly refer to location 000034.

As a final comment we note that if the source instruction MOV #ABS,TRAPPC had been written as MOV #ABS,@#TRAPPC, which would have been assembled as

000556	012737	START :	MOV #ABS,@#TRAPPC
000560	001226'		
000562	000034		

000564   (next instruction)

then all of the recording of locations and subsequent adjustments by the linkage editor would have been unnecessary, since in *absolute* PC addressing mode, the absolute address 000034 would *not* have to be adjusted upon relocation of the object module.

11.7 EXERCISES

11.1.1. What would be the consequences of a jump-to-subroutine instruction that always saved the PC in some *fixed* location (such as 00000, for example), as suggested in Sec. 11.1? In particular, how would called subroutines that call other subroutines be managed?

11.2.1. The hypothetical JTZ instruction was described as stacking c(PC) and then loading the PC with the contents of memory location 000000. Is the pair of instructions

```
MOV  PC,-(SP)
MOV  0,PC
```

an exact replica of JTZ? Explain.

11.2.2. How does the hypothetical JTZ instruction differ from the construction JSR PC,@0?

11.2.3. Would RTS   PC serve to return from a routine entered by means of a JTZ instruction?

11.3.1. TRAP has three close relatives: EMT, BPT, and IOT. (Of these, EMT is almost identical.) Look up their descriptions in Appendix A and compare them with TRAP.

11.3.2. Explain why the TRAP instruction is or is not *exactly* emulated by the sequence of instructions

```
MOV  PSW,-(SP)
MOV  36,PSW
MOV  PC,-(SP)
MOV  34,PC
```

11.3.3. Explain why the TRAP instruction is or is not *exactly* emulated by the sequence of instructions

```
MOV  PSW,-(SP)
MOV  36,PSW
JSR  PC,@34
```

11.3.4. Explain why the RTT instruction is or is not *exactly* emulated by the sequence of instructions

```
                              MOV   2(SP),PSW
                              MOV   (SP)+,(SP)
                              MOV   (SP)+,PC
```

11.3.5. By carefully examining the stack activity that takes place in lines 66 to 73, show that the program segment of Fig. 11.7.1 successfully TRAPs to MAX (the routine that finds the maximum of a specified number of numbers), leaves the maximum on the stack, and correctly returns to the mainline portion of the program (by means of an RTT instruction).

```
  1           000034       TRAPPC = 34              ;ADDR OF TRAP VECT PC
  2           000036       TRAPPS = 36              ;ADDR OF TRAP VECT PSW
                                    .
 25  001232         DATA:          .               ;(NUMBERS TO BE
 26                                                 ; MAXIMIZED HERE)
                                    .
 38  001730   012767  START: MOV   #MAX,TRAPPC      ;SET UP TRAP VECTOR PC
              003024'
              000034
 39  001736   005067         CLR   TRAPPS          ; AND PSW
              000036
 40  001742   104400         TRAP                  ;GO DO THE TRAP
 41  001744   000005         .WORD 5               ;NUMBER COUNT
 42  001746   001232'        .WORD DATA            ; AND ADDRESS
 43  001750                                        ;(NEXT ML INSTRUCTION)
                                    .
 66  003024   011646  MAX:   MOV   (SP),-(SP)      ;MOVE ML PC AND
 67  003026   016666         MOV   4(SP),2(SP)     ; PSW UP IN STACK
              000004
              000002
 68  003034   010046         MOV   R0,-(SP)        ;SAVE REGISTERS
 69  003036   010246         MOV   R2,-(SP)        ; R0 AND R2
 70  003040   017600         MOV   @4(SP),R0       ;GET NUMBER COUNT
              000004
 71  003044   062766         ADD   #2,4(SP)        ; AND ADJUST ML PC
              000002
              000004
 72  003052   017602         MOV   @4(SP),R2       ;GET DATA ADDRESS
              000004
 73  003056   062766         ADD   #2,4(SP)        ; AND ADJUST ML PC
              000002
              000004
                                    ;
 74  003064   005300         DEC   R0              ;ADJUST NUMBER COUNT
 75  003066   012266         MOV   (R2)+,10(SP)    ;PUT 1ST NO. IN STACK
              000010
 76                                                ; AS (TEMP) MAXIMUM
 77  003072   026622  LOOP:  CMP   10(SP),(R2)+    ;CHECK AGAINST NEXT NO.
              000010
 78  003076   002003         BGE   NEXT            ;BIGGER -- SKIP AROUND
 79  003100   016266         MOV   -2(R2),10(SP)   ;REPLACE TEMP MAX
              177776
              000010
 80  003106   077007  NEXT:  SOB   R0,LOOP         ;PROCESS NEXT NUMBER
 81  003110   012602         MOV   (SP)+,R2        ;RESTORE REGISTERS
 82  003112   012600         MOV   (SP)+,R0        ; R0 AND R2
 83  003114   000006         RTT                   ;RETURN FROM TRAP
                                    .
```

Figure 11.7.1

11.3.6. By monitoring the state of the stack during the recursive TRAPs that take place at line 18, show that when the program of Fig. 11.7.2 is executed, the (decimal) number that will be printed is 720 (6!).

```
 1              000034            TRAPPC = 34
 2              000036            TRAPPS = 36
 3                                ;
 4  000000                ANSWER: .BLKW    1
 5                                ;
 6  000002      012767    START:  MOV      #RECURS,TRAPPC
                000070'
                000034
 7  000010      005067            CLR      TRAPPS
                000036
 8  000014      012700            MOV      #6,R0
                000006
 9  000020      012701            MOV      #1,R1
                000001
10  000024      104400            TRAP
11  000026      010167            MOV      R1,ANSWER
                177746
12  000032                        $OUT.DEC #ANSWER,#1
13  000066                        $EXIT
14                                ;
15  000070      070100    RECURS: MUL      R0,R1
16  000072      005300            DEC      R0
17  000074      001401            BEQ      RETURN
18  000076      104400            TRAP
19  000100      000006    RETURN: RTT
20                                ;
21              000002'            .END     START
```

Figure 11.7.2

11.3.7. Suppose c(000034) = SUB, where SUB is the entry point of some routine that exits by means of an RTT instruction. When the following program segment is executed, can it be determined whether the conditional branch instruction BEQ will in fact generate a branch to NEXT? Explain.

```
            .
            CLR   R4
            TRAP
            BEQ   NEXT
            .
```

How, if at all, does this situation differ from

```
            .
            CLR   R4
            JSR   PC,SUB
            BEQ   NEXT
            .
```

where SUB is a subroutine that returns by means of RTS   PC?

11.4.1. Referring to the program of Fig. 11.4.1, we see that it would certainly be possible to have a large number—hundreds, perhaps—of routine entry points in the dispatch vector DSPTCH, routines that could be accessed through the program segment at XFER, which transfers control to a specified entry point based on the TRAP code—the integer in the low-order byte of the TRAP instruction.

(a) Show that the program segment at XFER, as written, will *not* properly handle a reference such as TRAP 206 or, for that matter, TRAP n, where n is greater than 177_8.

(b) How can the deficiency uncovered in part (a) be repaired?

(c) What is the limit on the number of routines to which control can be passed using the scheme of this programming example?

(d) One other minor deficiency exists in the routine XFER, namely, the use, without saving and restoring, of R3 to determine the offset from the beginning of the dispatch vector DSPTCH, which is used in the JMP instruction at line 93 (Fig. 11.4.1). How, if at all, can this be corrected? Can R3 be saved and restored later? Can the JMP be accomplished *without* the use of a general-purpose register?

11.5.1. In Sec. 11.5 we saw that the TRAP instruction may be used to change general register sets because it obtains a new PSW from location 000036. Explain how this can complicate the transmission of arguments to the routine to which TRAPping takes place.

11.5.2. What, if anything, is the difference between MOV #4000,TRAPPS and BIS #4000,TRAPPS? (See the program listing of Fig. 11.5.1.) These instructions are not identical, of course, but is there any difference in their net *effect*, as far as the program segment is concerned?

11.5.3. What would be the effect of the switching of the general register sets, as discussed in Sec. 11.5, if TRAPs were used in a *recursive* or *nested* fashion?

11.5.4. Discuss a method of changing register sets that does not require replacing the PSW (as occurs on a TRAP), and thus can be used by a JSR-type subroutine.

11.6.1. How can the assembler recognize a reference to an absolute number? It must be able to do so in order to build the absolute reference table.

11.6.2. Why does the @# construction (for example, CLR @#TRAPPS) require *no* adjustment upon linkage editing?

11.6.3. If the ALA of a relocatable object module is 000000 and the instruction

JSR PC,@0

is located at 000464 relative to the ALA, how will this instruction be assembled? If the PLA of the module is ultimately 003442, how, if at all, will the code generated for this JSR be modified by the linkage editor?

12

Interrupts and
Input/Output Processing

12.1 INTRODUCTION

The preceding chapter was devoted to a study in some depth of the instruction TRAP, and the reader might well wonder why so much time was invested in an instruction that, by our own admission, is not frequently used in day-to-day programming. Possibly one of the more puzzling aspects of the instruction is the saving of the PSW and the picking up of a new PSW at location 000036. There seemed to be little need to save and restore the processor's status, except for the one example in which we used this feature to switch general register sets—a task that we could have handled quite as easily in other ways. And if saving the PSW is of little or no consequence, then TRAP could be replaced by JSR   PC,XXX, an instruction that is far more flexible and easily managed.

In fact, we are *not* particularly interested in the specific instruction TRAP (or its close relatives EMT, IOT, and so forth). Rather, our concern lies with the trap *concept*—that under certain circumstances, the contents of the PSW and PC are stacked, and a new PC and PSW are taken from some *fixed locations* in main memory. The "certain circumstances" may, as we have seen, result from program execution of the instruction TRAP. On the other hand, they may also result from an *external event* over which we—more properly, our program— have no control, which can *force* the CPU to execute a trap-type instruction while our program is executing. Indeed, such external events occur relatively frequently, as we shall see in the remainder of this chapter. It will shortly become evident that the save-the-current-PSW/fetch-a-new-PSW/restore-the-old-PSW sequence is absolutely essential to the proper execution of our programs.

Thus we shall see that the PSW, which played an almost insignificant role in the preceding chapter, is of utmost importance. Our study of the TRAP instruction has laid some important foundations that will serve us well as we investigate the numerous phenomena associated with **hardware interrupts**.

12.2 INTERRUPTIONS

To gain some insights into the types of interruptions to which a computing system is subjected and the ways in which it might deal with them, we look at some of the interruptions with which *people* must cope in their daily lives—there are some interesting analogies here. Each day we are constantly bombarded with interruptions. The simple act of walking from one class to another is frequently interrupted by stopping to talk with a friend. In driving to the store we are interrupted by a traffic light changing from green to red or by a pedestrian stepping off the curb. We examine below a number of real-life events, that will give us some direction in our investigation of analogous computer events and the hardware and corresponding programming necessary to deal with them in an efficient manner.

  • *Scenario 1*   Suppose we are sitting at home in the living room, reading, when the dog barks at the back door, asking to be let in. We put down the book, walk to the back door, let the dog in, return to the living room, pick up the book, and continue reading.

This is surely a common and especially simple event; it is an example of an **interruption** and we have dealt with it in the obvious way. A brief analysis of this situation shows that a fair amount of activity has occurred, but because we have dealt with situations of this nature so often, the processes necessary for the successful treatment of this simple type of interruption are no longer at a conscious level—we have managed to cope with the interruption without really thinking about it.

First, we must be made *aware* that an interruption has occurred, which was done by our hearing the dog bark. (If the dog had merely gone to the back door and sat down, it is unlikely that he would have been admitted until perhaps sometimes later when we actively looked for him.) Next, we must recognize the sound as that made by a barking dog, and not the telephone or the doorbell. (This is not quite so silly as it sounds. We actually do go through some kind of process to determine the *source* of the interruption so that we can properly treat it—when the dog barks, it will do no good to pick up the phone, any more than opening the back door will be a meaningful response to a ringing phone.) We must also recognize the bark as belonging to *our* dog and that it came from the back door and not from the front yard. Finally, we must somehow distinguish our dog's "let me in" bark from other kinds of barks.

Having determined the nature of this interruption, we recognize that we have a well-defined procedure for dealing with it. However, before implementing that procedure, we make a note of what we were doing at the time the interruption occurred. That is, we note (mentally) that we were reading in the living room when interrupted. We might even put a bookmark in the book to assist us further in picking up where we left off. Without this note we could surely let the dog in, but we would never be able to return to what we were doing. Thus we put down the book, walk to the back door, let the dog in, and then ask, Now, where were we? A (mental) glance at our note indicates that we were reading when the interruption occurred, so we return to the living room, pick up the book, and continue reading where we left off.

The reader may rightfully complain that we have *overanalyzed* a situation so simple that it scarcely deserves the time devoted to it. But the processes that we went through in this example are most significant and worth summarizing, as follows:

1. In the course of doing something (reading), we were interrupted.
2. We determined what caused the interruption (dog at the back door) and determined that it should be dealt with.
3. We made a note of what we were doing when interrupted.
4. We processed the interruption (let the dog in).
5. We looked at our note to determine how to return to what we had been doing.
6. We returned to what we were doing before being interrupted (reading).

We diagram this situation in Fig. 12.2.1.

In the remaining examples we shall not make such a detailed analysis. But the reader should be aware that all of these processes are brought into play

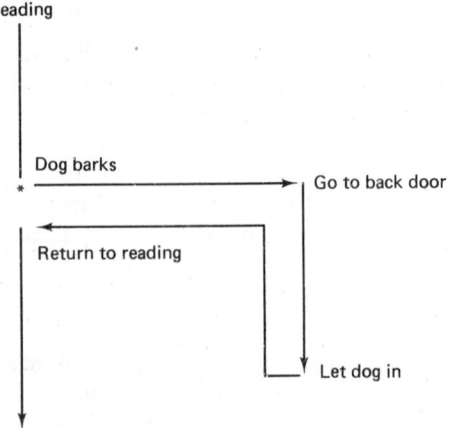

Figure 12.2.1

whenever we deal with any kind of interruption, although for the most part they lie at a subconscious level. Nonetheless almost every day-to-day mundane interruption that we deal with involves the six steps summarized above.

- *Scenario* 2   Suppose next that while we are reading, the phone rings. We put down the book, answer the phone, hang up at the end of the conversation, and return to reading.

The sequence of events here is virtually identical with that in Scenario 1. The differences lie in the *source* of the interruption—the phone rather than the dog—and the *process* involved in dealing with the interruption—a phone conversation rather than the opening of the back door.

- *Scenario* 3   Assume now that we are reading when we hear the dog barking at the back door. We put down the book, get up, and start for the back door. On the way, we hear the phone ringing. That is, in the process of dealing with *one* interruption we have been interrupted a *second* time. We might take the following approach to this slightly more complicated situation: Since it will take only a second or two to reach the back door and let the dog in, we shall continue dealing with the dog's interruption. Having completed that task, there will still be time to answer the phone and manage its interruption. That is, we have decided to treat these two interruptions *in sequence*, in the order in which they occurred. Similarly, if we had answered the phone and were in the midst of a conversation when the dog began barking, we might have let him bark until we had hung up the phone. Again, we would have dealt with the interruptions in sequence.

Because of the complexity introduced by the second interruption, we shall briefly analyze this situation. When the dog first barks we make a mental note of what we are doing (reading) and begin to process the dog's interruption. That is, we *start* for the back door. When the phone begins to ring, we consciously decided that for the moment, we are going to *ignore* that interruption, and thus we continue to the door and let the dog in. Having completed the processing of the dog's interruption, we now look at our mental note to determine how to return to what we were doing when the dog first interrupted us. However, we recognize that there is a second interruption (the phone) that must be coped with before we can return to our reading. Thus we answer the phone, deal with the caller, and hang up. *Now* we look at our note and return to reading. A diagram of this situation is shown in Fig. 12.2.2.

- *Scenario* 4   In this scenario we suppose, as in Scenario 3, that we are reading when the dog barks. On the way to the back door, the phone rings. Assume, however, that we have been expecting an important call. We will probably let the dog wait this time and answer the phone. When we have

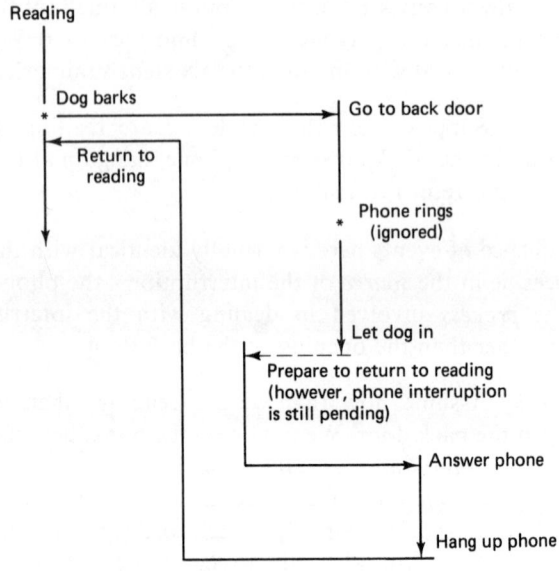

Figure 12.2.2

completed the conversation, we will continue to the back door, let the dog in, and resume our reading.

This situation is quite similar to that of Scenario 3, but the chief difference—the temporary abandonment of the processing of the dog's interruption—involves an idea of sufficient importance that again an in-depth analysis will be worthwhile.

When the dog begins barking, we put down our book and make a mental note, which we shall call note A, of what we were doing at the time the interruption occurred. Thus note A refers to the fact that we were reading. Next, we begin processing the dog's interruption. But as we are on the way to the back door, the phone rings, and for the reasons explained above, we decide that we should answer it. How do we handle this interruption? In the same way we treated the first; that is, we make a note, note B, of what we were doing when the interruption occurred—walking to the back door to let the dog in—and go answer the phone. Having completed the conversation and hung up the phone (that is, having processed the phone interruption), we now ask, Where were we? The answer is on our note. But which note? We have "written" *two* notes, A and B; to which should we refer? The answer, of course, is that we should look at the *last* note that we wrote, note B. Doing so will return us to the task of letting the dog in. Finally, we will look at note A and resume reading. Again, a diagram will aid our understanding of the sequence of events that have taken place (Fig. 12.2.3).

We noted above, that having completed the handling of the phone inter-

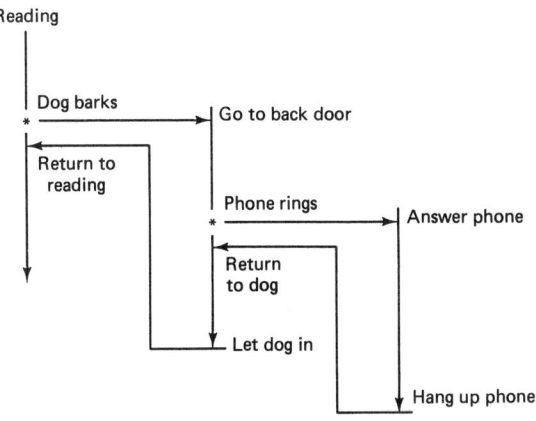

Figure 12.2.3

ruption, we should look at note B to determine where to resume. If, instead, we had looked at note A, and thus gone back to our reading immediately, the processing of the dog's interruption would never have gone to completion; the dog would remain indefinitely at the back door waiting to be let in. Thus it is essential that as we write these mental notes to remind us where to return after treating an interruption, that we look at the notes *in reverse order*. That is, the *last* note written should be the *first* note we look at after completing the processing of an interruption. If the reader finds this last-note-written–first-note-read sequence reminiscent of the last-in–first-out structure of the stack, then he has anticipated some concepts to be discussed in the remainder of the chapter.

In each of the last two examples, both interruptions were ultimately dealt with. In the first case, they were treated sequentially. In the second, the processing of the interruptions was *nested*; that is, the processing of the first interruption was initiated but then suspended temporarily while the second interruption was handled. For people, this nesting of interruptions can cause some problems if the nesting becomes fairly *deep*. Thus if the processing of an interruption is itself interrupted, and this phenomenon occurs several times, we start to lose track of the mental notes we have written to effect a proper return to what we were doing, or we begin to process these notes in the wrong order—forgetting which was the *last* note we had written. Fortunately, computers do not have this problem, since nothing is ever written "mentally" and some sort of stack structure will always keep things in proper order.

We offer a final scenario that is a bit different from its predecessors in that it involves the **suppression** of an interruption.

- *Scenario 5* Suppose now that instead of doing some casual reading, we are involved with studying for a final examination. Indeed, we place such importance on this task that we decide to disable the bell on the phone. The phone is still usable for outgoing calls, but if there is an incoming call, the bell will not ring—we will be unaware that the call is being made. Assume that while we are studying, the dog barks to come in. In a sense, this is an interruption. However, because of the importance of the task at hand, we simply *ignore* it—we let the dog bark. We continue studying despite the dog's request. Similarly, if someone attempts to call us on the phone, we ignore that interruption also. But observe that these two interruptions are conceptually different. In the case of the dog, we recognize that he is requesting service of some kind, but we simply elect not to provide it. In the case of the incoming phone call, we are not even *aware* that there is a request for service.

In addition to the concepts of interruptions and their treatments, another notion has crept into this discussion—that of a hierarchy of importance, or **priority** scheme. For instance, in Scenario 3 we seemed not to give any particular preference to the barking dog or the ringing phone—we handled their interruptions in sequential order. On the other hand, in Scenario 4 even though we were dealing with the dog at the time, we gave priority to the phone when it began ringing. Finally, in Scenario 5 we assigned *ourselves* (more properly, our task of studying) a higher priority than the dog's barking. (Recall that in that example the phone was in such a state that it could not even generate interruptions.) But even in this last case, the priority assigned to our studying is probably not the highest possible; it is unlikely that in spite of the importance of the job of studying we are apt to ignore an interruption such as the house's catching on fire.

To summarize the results of this section, we have seen that each of us is frequently subjected to interruptions, we treat those interruptions in some reasonable fashion, and we do so in such a way that we can continue with the job at hand after we have handled the interruption. In the case of multiple interruptions we sometimes deal with these in a sequential manner, and in other cases, as a result of our assignment of priorities to the interruptions, we manage them in a nested fashion. In fact, it is not unusual for us to alter the priorities of events from time to time—as we saw, a phone call does not *always* take precedence over letting the dog in. Finally, we observe that many of these activities take place at a subconscious level as a result of many years of experience in dealing with these matters. It is only in this regard that we differ from computers in processing interruptions.

12.3 PROCESSOR INTERRUPTS

The interruptions and their features described in the preceding section are remarkably analogous to the kinds of interruptions to which a computing system is subject. The CPU rarely enjoys the opportunity of executing user programs from start to finish—it is interrupted frequently by a variety of external events, most often a peripheral device requesting some kind of service. Some simple activities that may cause the CPU's processing to be interrupted are the striking of a key on a terminal, a line printer running out of paper, the completion of the task of writing a block of memory to a disk, or a card reader encountering a special end-of-file card. In each of these cases a device has arrived at a state wherein it requires some servicing from the CPU, and it requests that service by interrupting the CPU's current activity. To introduce some of the concepts and features involved in the interruption of CPU processing, we shall look at an especially simple device, the **external clock**.

All computers contain a "clock," namely, some device that is capable of ticking off some fixed time interval. Such a timer is necessary for a number of reasons. For example, when input signals are applied to a circuit made up of several gates, we cannot expect the output of that circuit to be *immediately* available; the electronic components require some time to react to those signals. The delays involved are not great; usually they are measured in billionths of a second. But nonetheless some delay is involved, and one of the purposes of the internal clock is to tick off these delays to ensure that valid data is present at the output of such a circuit. Likewise, the fetching of the contents of a memory location is a relatively slow operation, since the memory units that make up physical words typically react to signals somewhat sluggishly, and of course they must react in order to be read or written.

But this clock that helps control the internal flow of information within the computing system has nothing to do with real-world time—there is no way to use this clock to indicate that it is midnight or 3:12 P.M. For this reason, many computing systems also contain an *external* clock (external to the CPU) with which it *can* keep track of real time. This clock is typically used for a number of things, such as keeping track of the amount of time a particular user has utilized the system, indicating on printed listings the time at which a source file was assembled, and in the case of timesharing computers, to let the CPU know that a particular user has exhausted his or her "time-slice" and that the CPU should now move on to the next user. While there are a number of different types of clocks that can be found on a PDP-11 system, the simplest one, and the one we shall investigate, is the **line-time clock**.

As the reader is doubtless aware, most electric devices operate on **alternating current** supplied by a power company. In an alternating current power supply the voltage at one terminal is always at 0 volts, while the voltage at the other terminal alternates between $+110$ volts and -110 volts. In contrast, in a steady voltage supply, such as a 9-volt transistor battery, we can assume that one terminal is always at 0 volts and the other is always at $+9$ volts. (We shall not go into the reasons for the desirability of alternating current as opposed to **direct current**.) The rate at which this change from positive to negative to positive occurs is called the **frequency** of the current source and is measured in cycles per second. In most parts of the United States and Canada, alternating current has a frequency of 60 cycles per second, or 60 *hertz*, as is more commonly said. (Alternating current in many European countries has a frequency of 50 hertz.) It is possible for a fairly simple electronic device to detect this swing of the power source from positive to negative and each time such a swing occurs, to *interrupt the CPU*. We shall investigate this phenomenon at some length.

Each peripheral device can be considered as being made up of two units, the **device** itself (in our case, the line-time clock; other examples are terminals, printers, and the like) and a **device controller**, the electronics that actually communicates with the CPU or other peripherals via the address, data, and control buses.

Figure 12.3.1 is an expansion of Fig. 1.2.1. and it reveals a few new features. First, note that we indicated that the CPU contains **interrupt flags**—some bits internal to the processor whose role will shortly be evident. The controller itself contains a **status register**—a 16-bit word whose individual bits give information about the status of the device, as the name implies. The layout of the clock's status register is shown in Fig. 12.3.2. Generally, each device controller has associated with it a status register, but most devices are sufficiently complex

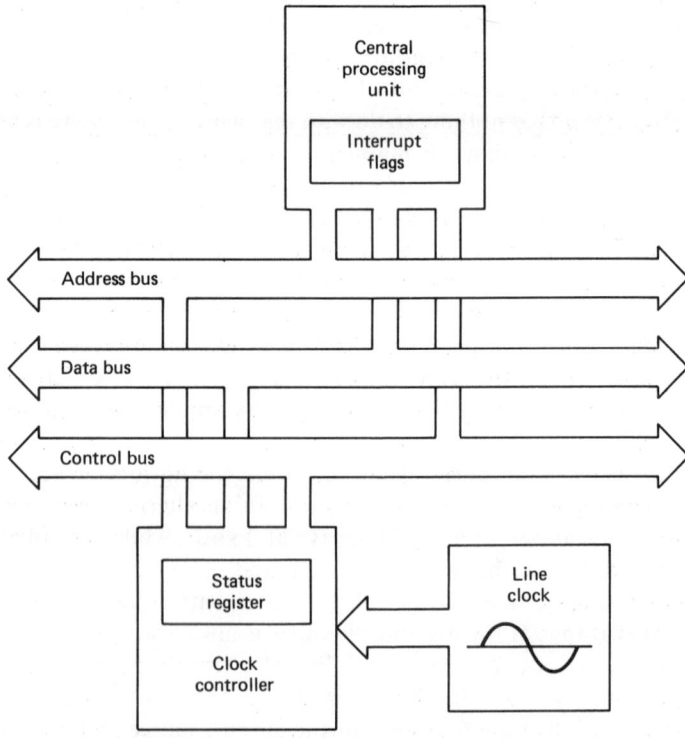

Figure 12.3.1

that additional registers are required. These might include a **data register** (a 16-bit word through which data is exchanged between the device and the CPU or main memory), an **error register** (whose bits are used to determine what kind of error is involved if one occurred), a **word count register**, and so forth. The line-time clock, on the other hand, is so simple that it requires only a status register, and indeed only 2 of the 16 bits in that register are even of any significance. The line clock status register does *not* reside in main memory, and yet it *is* addressable. That is, it has an address and can thus be manipulated by any of the standard PDP-11 instructions, a situation we have already encountered with the PSW. The clock's status register is located at address 777546.

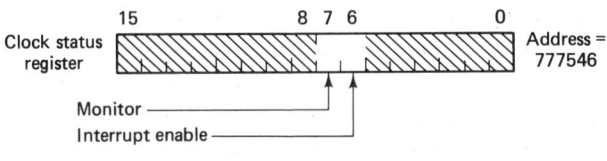

Figure 12.3.2

Now recall that the line clock is "ticking" at the rate of 60 times per second, and thus a tick occurs every $16\frac{2}{3}$ milliseconds. (A **millisecond**, abbreviated **msec** or **ms**, is $\frac{1}{1000}$ second.) What happens when the clock ticks? The answer depends in part on the state of bit 6, the **interrupt enable bit**, in the status register. If this bit is off, nothing happens. (This is not exactly true, but for our present purposes, in which we are concerned with the effect on the CPU, that answer is quite correct.) Thus let us suppose bit 6, the interrupt enable bit, is *on* when a clock tick occurs. A number of things happen as a result of this event, and we shall look at them in some detail.

First, the clock notifies the clock controller that it has ticked—that a $16\frac{2}{3}$ millisecond time interval has elapsed. The controller responds to this information in two ways. First, it *sets* (that is, makes equal to 1) bit 7 of its status register, the monitor bit. And second, it notifies the CPU of the event by sending an **interrupt signal** down one of the lines on the control bus. What happens to this signal when it reaches the CPU? It is possible that the CPU is not even in a position to react to it. For example, the CPU may be in the midst of processing an instruction, and disaster would surely strike if it was not allowed to complete its operation. In fact, the process by which the clock controller notifies the CPU that a clock tick has occurred is a bit less direct than we have led the reader to believe. When the clock ticks and the controller sends an interrupt signal down the control bus, the CPU is not notified of this event immediately. Rather, an **interrupt flag**, which we can think of as a 1-bit register in the CPU, is set to 1.

It is time to be somewhat more specific about how the CPU executes instructions in sequence. We have been saying that whenever the CPU has completed the execution of a program instruction, it examines the PC to obtain the address of the next instruction, fetches that instruction from main memory, executes it, and so forth. In fact, the sequence of events is as follows: Having completed execution of an instruction, the CPU first examines the interrupt flag. If that flag is *off*, it proceeds as usual—fetches the next instruction being pointed at by the PC, and so on. But if the interrupt flag is *on*, the CPU executes a *trap*, that is, it takes an action almost identical to its response to the *program* instruction TRAP. Specifically, it pushes the current c(PSW) and also the current c(PC) onto the stack. Notice that this PC that has been stacked contains the address of the instruction that *would* have been executed next, had the interrupt flag *not* been on. Next, new PC and PSW values are picked up from fixed locations in main memory, as in any trap-type instruction. These fixed locations are 000100 (the PC) and 000102 (the PSW).

Thus when the clock ticks, the clock controller sets the monitor bit in the status register and sends an interrupt signal down the control bus—more briefly, the clock **generates an interrupt**. The CPU responds by stacking the PSW and PC (in that order) and getting a new PC and PSW from locations 000100 and 000102, respectively. Execution continues, of course, at whatever address is in 000100, since now c(PC) = c(000100). Some small routine to respond to the clock's interrupt, called the clock's **interrupt handling routine** or **interrupt handler** will probably be executed here. We offer below an especially simple routine to do this job. (Fig. 12.3.3).

We assume that we have four memory locations to keep track of real time. One, called HOURS, contains the number of hours that have passed since midnight. Two others, MINUTS and SECS, keep track of the minutes and seconds within the hour specified in HOURS. And the fourth, SPLITS, counts the number of split seconds (that is, clock ticks) since the last second was recorded. Thus every time c(SPLITS) = 60_{10}, we increment c(SECS) by 1 and reset c(SPLITS) back to 0. Likewise, every time c(SECS) becomes 60_{10}, we clear it and increment c(MINUTS) by 1. We treat HOURS similarly. We also assume that these four locations were set initially to their appropriate time values. The reader will see that the interrupt handling routine is quite easily managed.

Since the reader should have no difficulty following the logic of the interrupt handler at location TICK, we shall concentrate on some of the other features of this programming segment. First, we gave the symbolic name CLKINT to memory location 000100, the first word of the **interrupt vector** (analogous to the term **TRAP vector**) and the first of the two words from which the CPU will obtain a new PC and PSW in the event of a clock interrupt. Similarly, we assigned the name CLKSTS to the clock's status register address. The next four bytes shown are simply the locations where the time is kept. The instruction MOV #TICK,CLKINT sets up the address TICK in the first word of the interrupt vector. (Notice that we did nothing with the *second* word of that vector; we shall say more about that later.) The next instruction, MOV #100,CLKSTS, enables the clock interrupt—turns on bit 6 in the

```
          CLKINT = 000100              ;CLOCK INT VECTOR ADDR
          CLKSTS = 177546              ;CLOCK STATUS REG ADDR
          .
          .
HOURS:    .BLKB    1                   ;KEEP TRACK OF HOURS,
MINUTS:   .BLKB    1                   ;  MINUTES,
SECS:     .BLKB    1                   ;  SECONDS AND
SPLITS:   .BLKB    1                   ;  1/60TH SECONDS
          .
          .
          MOV      #TICK,CLKINT        ;SET UP CLOCK INTERRUPT
                                       ;  HANDLER ADDRESS
          MOV      #100,CLKSTS         ;ENABLE INTERRUPTS
                                       ;(BEGIN USEFUL PROCESSING)
          .
          .
TICK:     INCB     SPLITS              ;COUNT ANOTHER TICK
          CMPB     SPLITS,#60.         ;FULL SECOND?
          BNE      RETURN              ;NO -- EXIT
          CLRB     SPLITS              ;YES -- RESET
          INCB     SECS                ;  AND ADJUST SECONDS
          CMPB     SECS,#60.           ;FULL MINUTE?
          BNE      RETURN              ;NO -- EXIT
          CLRB     SECS                ;RESET SECONDS
          INCB     MINUTS              ;  AND ADJUST MINUTES
          CMPB     MINUTS,#60.         ;FULL HOUR?
          BNE      RETURN              ;NO -- EXIT
          CLRB     MINUTS              ;YES -- RESET
          INCB     HOURS               ;  AND ADJUST HOURS
RETURN:   RTI                          ;RESUME PROCESSING
          .
          .
```

Figure 12.3.3

status register. At this point we presumably begin some useful processing. One-sixtieth of a second later, the clock ticks and an interrupt is generated. Wherever the CPU happens to be in the course of program execution, when it completes its current instruction it will notice that the interrupt flag is on and will execute a trap. The current contents of the PSW and PC will be stacked, and a new PC and PSW will be obtained from locations CLKINT and CLKINT +2, respectively. Since c(CLKINT) = TICK, processing will now pick up in the interrupt handling routine. There the time, in the form of numbers of clock ticks, will be updated, and finally the RTI instruction will be executed. As we know, the effect of RTI is to pop the top of the stack twice, into the PC and PSW, respectively. The popping of the PC causes execution to resume at the point where the CPU was interrupted. Thus useful processing picks up again until the next clock interrupt, at which time the above process is repeated.

There are a number of questions surrounding this process, a few of which have been with us for some time. We shall answer these in this chapter; in fact, we shall deal with two of them immediately. The reader may be somewhat bothered by the fact that the clock is interrupting meaningful processing every $16\frac{2}{3}$ milliseconds, at which time the interrupt handling routine must be executed. It might appear that most of the CPU's time will be spent processing the clock interrupts rather than doing useful processing. This problem seems further complicated by the fact that the interrupt handling routine as shown on the program listing is not very efficient. The tasks done there could have been written in fewer instructions and without the numerous time-consuming main memory fetches. (The interrupt handler was written for clarity and ease of understanding, not for efficiency.) But in fact, even in the *worst* case, when the time is such that each of the memory bytes must be cleared and the next incremented, the total time spent in the interrupt handler is substantially less than 50 microseconds (which is 50 millionths of a second, or 0.05 milliseconds). Thus we see that the time spent in handling the interrupts is really quite insignificant when compared with the time spent in program execution.

Another question involves the PSW. We commented in the last chapter that there appeared to be no need to save c(PSW) when the TRAP instruction was executed, and in fact it is difficult even to contrive an example in which saving the PSW is necessary when a TRAP instruction is performed. And since what takes place during an interrupt is almost identical to what happens on a TRAP, the reader might be led to believe that the same would be true for the CPU's processing of an interrupt—that the saving and restoring of the PSW would not be required. But we must be aware that there are two significant differences between the processing of TRAP and the processing of an interrupt. First, TRAP is a *program* instruction, whereas an interrupt is not. And second, the *precise place* within program execution at which an interrupt will take place cannot be predicted; in some sense, interrupts—even clock interrupts—are *random* events. It is this fact that makes the saving of the PSW essential to proper program execution. To see this, consider the following example.

Suppose a program contains the pair of instructions

DEC   R4
BNE   LOOP

which are evidently designed to control a program loop of some sort. Consider the situation in which just prior to execution, c(R4) = 1. Then DEC   R4 will decrement c(R4) to 0, and as a result, the Z-bit in the PSW will be set to 1. Because of this, BNE   LOOP will *not* be executed, and the processor will simply fetch the next instruction for processing. But now suppose that during execution of the DEC   R4 instruction, a clock interrupt occurs.

DEC   R4
* clock interrupt occurs here
BNE   LOOP

Once again, because c(R4) was decremented to 0, the Z-bit in the PSW has been set and now, because of the interrupt the CPU must execute a trap. Suppose however, the PSW is *not* saved prior to passing control of the CPU to the interrupt handler. A look at our proposed clock interrupt handling routine reveals that regardless of which instructions are executed there, the last instruction processed in the handler will always result in a *nonzero* number, and hence upon return from this routine and resumption of main processing, the Z-bit in the PSW will be *off*. We return, of course, to the BNE   LOOP instruction, and that branch *will* take place, even though in this case it *should not* have. Thus we see that if c(PSW) is not saved and later restored when an interrupt occurs, there is little hope of maintaining control of program processing.

12.4 MEMORY ADDRESSING REVISITED

The perceptive reader may have noted an apparent inconsistency in the preceding section. We stated (correctly) that the address of the clock status register is 777546, and yet in the program listing of that section we see that the symbol CKLSTS, which was to stand for the address of this status register, was given the value 177546, not 777546. But notice that the direct assignment statement

CLKSTS = 777546

would have been nonsense, since the number 777546 requires an 18-bit representation and thus could not be held in a main-memory 16-bit word. Thus we did the best we could and assigned CLKSTS the value 177546, with the two most significant bits simply missing. But if this is the case, then how could a statement such as MOV   #100,CLKSTS, which assembles as

$$012767$$
$$000100$$
$$177546$$

possibly reference the clock's status register?

The answer to this question lies with the hardware itself and how it deals with addresses. In fact, the addressing on the PDP-11 is 18-bit addressing, not 16-bit addressing.* Thus each addressable word—main memory words, device registers, the PSW—has an 18-bit address, even though *program* references to such addresses are always expressed as 16-bit words. Apparently, then, the *hardware* must convert such a 16-bit address to an 18-bit address. It does so in the following way: To construct an 18-bit address from a 16-bit word, bits 15, 14, and 13 of the address are *AND*ed together. The result (either 0 or 1) is used as bits 17 and 16 of the 18-bit address (Fig. 12.4.1). Thus the status register's address, 177546, is converted by the hardware to the configuration of Fig. 12.4.2. An address such as 142307 is converted again to 142307, as shown in Fig. 12.4.3. This hardware scheme implies that memory addressing on the PDP-11 has the following appearance:

*Some models of the PDP-11 use 22-bit addressing, and on these the generation of full addresses from 16-bit addresses is handled somewhat differently from what is described in this section. However, the differences in no way affect the *programming* of devices.

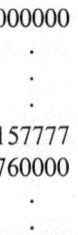

000000
.
.
.
157777
760000
.
.
.
777777

and that the addresses between 160000 and 757777, inclusive, can never be generated. In fact, some models of the PDP-11 contain optional hardware, called a **memory management unit**, that converts addresses in a more complex way, so that physical memory can be placed in this "gap."

On most PDP-11 systems, the addresses between 000000 and 157777 are addresses of bytes in main memory, while the addresses from 760000 to 777777 represent, for example, various device registers, which do not reside in main memory.

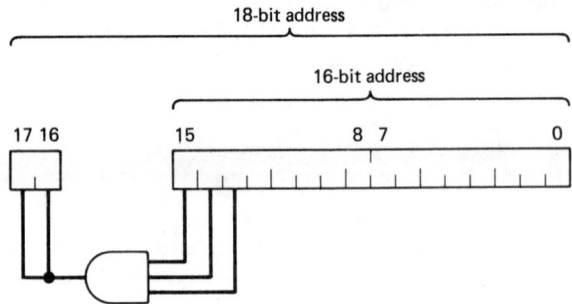

Figure 12.4.1

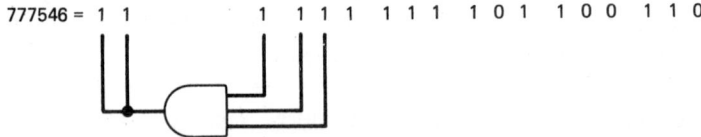

Figure 12.4.2

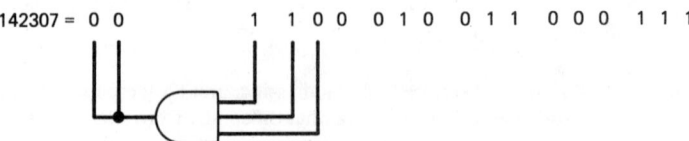

Figure 12.4.3

12.5 NONINTERRUPT MODE

In Sec. 12.3 we saw that if the clock requested service—ticked—while the CPU was processing a user program, for example, an interrupt signal was sent down the control bus to the CPU, control of the processor was passed to a clock interrupt routine, the real-world time was updated, and then, since sufficient information had been saved (namely, the PC and PSW), execution of the user program was able to be resumed. This is certainly a useful scheme for keeping track of the time of day, but it is not limited to the line-time clock. *Any* device— a keyboard, line printer, card reader—when in need of service can so notify the CPU by generating this interrupt signal. Therefore it is somewhat puzzling that there is a bit in the clock's status register, and the status register of most other devices, called the *interrupt enable* bit. We saw that if that bit is *on*, each clock tick will cause an interrupt. What we infer from this, however, is that if the interrupt enable bit is *off*, then when the device needs service—the clock ticks, or whatever—*no* such interrupt signal is generated. In fact, that is quite correct. But that being the case, how does the CPU become aware that service is required by the device? The answer is, It does not.

But the situation is not quite so hopeless as it might first appear. To gain some insight into this matter, let us return for a moment to Sec. 12.2. Recall that we were examining the various ways in which we handle personal interruptions in our daily lives, and in Scenario 5 we turned off the bell on the phone. In effect, we disabled that device's ability to generate interrupts—to call our attention to the fact that service was required by ringing its bell. It is important to note that we did *not* disable the device itself—it was still capable of all the functions of a phone *except* the ability to generate interrupts. Thus it was still possible for the phone to accept an incoming call, but since we were not aware that such a call existed, we did not process it.

Does all of this mean that it is *impossible* for us to detect an incoming call? Not at all. Even though the bell is disconnected, we can service incoming calls as follows if we assume that an incoming call will stay on the line for 10 seconds before hanging up: We pick up the receiver. If we detect a dial tone, we hang up the phone, wait 10 seconds, and pick up the phone again. If we detect a dial tone, we hang up, and keep repeating this process. If a call comes in, then sooner or later we will pick up the phone and detect the *absence* of a dial tone. We are now ready to talk to the calling party. Unlikely as it may seem that we would actually carry out such a process, we sketch an algorithm to show how the "program to detect an incoming call" operates.

1. Wait 10 seconds.
2. Pick up receiver.
3. If dial tone detected, go to step 1.
4. If dial tone not detected, say "hello" and begin conversation.

Of course, we would never try to manage incoming calls in this fashion. We are tying up our time completely with this simple task, and there seems little hope that we can be doing anything else useful while we are waiting for an incoming call. Answering the phone is best handled on an interrupt basis, and this is precisely why there are bells on telephones (and doorbells on doors, and why football referees have whistles). But the point we are making here is that despite the fact that it would be absurd to do so, it is *possible* to process this device (phone) on a noninterrupt basis.

A computing system may be able to deal with one or more of its devices on a noninterrupt basis by a process that is remarkably analogous to the procedures in the example above. To see how it can do this, we return to our ticking clock, but this time we assume that the interrupt enable bit (bit 6) in the clock's status register is *off*. How can the CPU detect that a clock tick has occurred? To answer this question we examine in more detail the so-called monitor bit (bit 7) in the status register. Recall from Sec. 12.3 that whenever the clock ticks off $\frac{1}{60}$ second, it notifies its controller and the latter device takes two actions: It sets the monitor bit and sends an interrupt signal to the CPU. The interrupt handler of Fig. 12.3.3 does nothing with the monitor bit, however, as a glance at the program segment shows. In fact, in that example, the monitor bit behaves in the following way: The instruction MOV #100,CLKSTS turns on the interrupt enable bit, the action we are actually interested in, and turns *off* the monitor bit, which we do not really care about. One-sixtieth of a second later, the clock ticks and the controller turns the monitor bit *on* and also generates an interrupt. Since there is no program instruction in the clock interrupt handler to reset (turn off) that bit, it simply stays on. One-sixtieth of a second later, the clock ticks again. The controller once more turns the monitor bit on, but since it is already on, it simply stays on—that is, it does not become more on than it was before. This monitor bit, which we have neglected, will play a key role when we handle the clock on a noninterrupt basis.

Even if the clock interrupt is disabled, an executing program can keep track of the number of clock ticks in the following way: The program tests the state of the clock's status register. If the monitor bit is off, it immediately goes back to test the state of the monitor bit *again*. If it finds it still off, it repeats the process until it determines that the monitor bit has come on. At this point the program can increment a tick counter, for instance; *turn the monitor bit off;* and go back into the loop to test the state of that bit. In this way the program can count clock ticks, and since the clock is ticking (but not interrupting) 60 times per second, the program can keep track of elapsed time. This process of constantly or frequently testing the status of a device to determine, on a noninterrupt basis, if it requires service is referred to as **polling** the device.

But notice that the effect of this procedure is to *tie up* the CPU with the single task of counting clock ticks (it can really do nothing else at this point), and the reader may wonder why we would ever want to do this. One answer is that for a variety of reasons, we might want a program (perhaps more exactly, the CPU) to *delay* for a fixed length of time, that is, in effect to stop processing for some time interval. Of course, counting clock ticks *is* still processing, but it is natural to think of the computer as being in a sort of stall state for that interval. For instance, in a program that generates a graphic display on a television screen, we may want to display a figure, delay for perhaps ½ second, generate another figure, delay, and so forth, to give the appearance that the display is moving on the screen. We assume that after the first picture has been displayed, there is no useful processing that can be done until the next picture is displayed, so the delay that is necessary for the desired effect is not really "costing" us anything in processor time.

As another example, consider a user program that, in the course of execution, requires some information from the computer operator. At that point, it might send a message to the operator's terminal and wait for a response, without which it cannot proceed. It is not unusual for programs of this nature to go into a **keyboard wait**, that is, to wait for the operator's response for a fixed time interval—15 or 30 seconds, for example. If no response comes during that time, the program might prompt the operator with another message, or it might simply assume that in the absence of a reply, a *default* response is to be used.

Figure 12.5.1 shows a program segment that marks time for 15 seconds by polling the clock and counting off 900 ticks. We assume that the clock interrupt is disabled. Given the preceding discussion, the reader should encounter no difficulty in analyzing these few program instructions.

```
        CLKSTS = 177546        ;CLOCK STATUS REGISTER
        .
        MOV     #900.,R2       ;TO COUNT 900 'TICKS'
                               ; (= 15 SECONDS)
CHECK:  TSTB    CLKSTS         ;CHECK STATUS REGISTER
        BPL     CHECK          ;BIT 7 OFF -- CHECK AGAIN
        CLRB    CLKSTS         ;BIT 7 ON -- TURN IT OFF
        DEC     R2             ; AND DECREMENT COUNTER
        BNE     CHECK          ;MORE TICKS -- DO AGAIN
        .                      ; ELSE DONE -- CONTINUE
        .
```

Figure 12.5.1

Thus we see that the line-time clock can be used in interrupt mode and in noninterrupt mode. In the former case, it can easily be used as a true clock to maintain the time of day. In the latter case, the time of day cannot reasonably be kept, and in fact the clock is used as an **interval timer** much like the familiar kitchen timers that can be preset to a fixed number of minutes. But the clock is not peculiar in this regard—almost any peripheral device can be handled on an interrupt or noninterrupt basis, and we shall see another example of this. In dealing with a noninterrupting device, however, we must be aware that we shall probably be devoting the CPU exclusively to the task of device management in the same way and for the same reasons that the noninterrupting clock required the processor's undivided attention.

12.6 FURTHER DETAILS OF THE INTERRUPT SEQUENCE

Our discussion so far reveals that the sequence of events that takes place when a device interrupts for service is fairly straightforward. The device signals the CPU that it requires service, and when the CPU is able to do so, it stacks c(PSW) and c(PC), and traps to the device's service routine (interrupt handler). When service is completed, an RTI restores the CPU's status, and execution is resumed where it was left off. But the picture is far more complicated than we have painted it, as the next example will show.

Suppose a computing system supports four peripheral devices, A, B, C, and D. (Fig. 12.6.1). Assume further that all of these devices are capable of

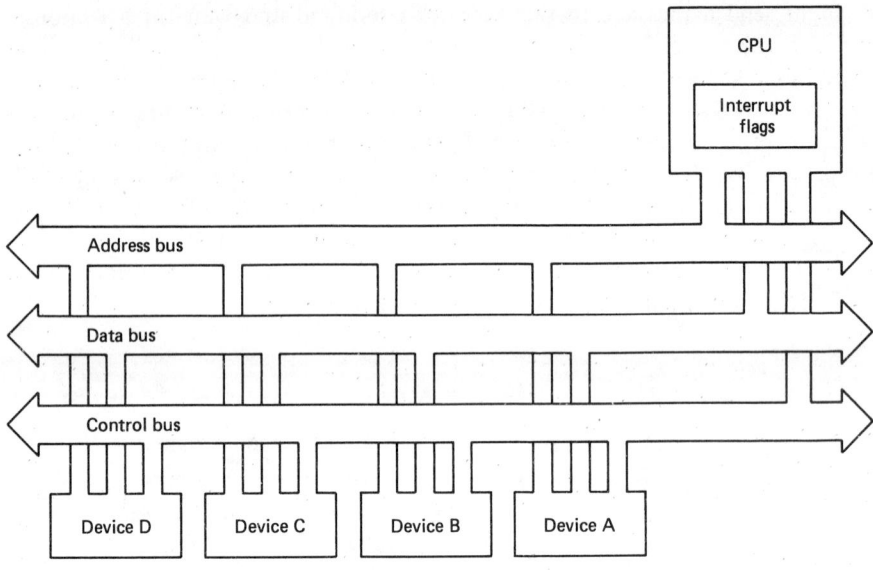

Figure 12.6.1

generating interrupts and that in fact device B and device D do generate interrupts *virtually simultaneously.* This situation is by no means impossible or even unlikely. We know that a certain short time interval is required for the CPU to execute a given instruction, and it is clearly possible that within that interval, a key will be struck on a terminal *and* the clock will tick, for example. Both of these events will cause the interrupt flag to be set, and this situation raises the following questions:

1. How does the CPU know which device or, in this instance, devices caused the interrupt?
2. How can the CPU determine the address of the interrupt vector to be used when trapping?

3. If device D, for example, is serviced, will device B's interrupt ever be acknowledged? If so, when? Both devices cannot be serviced at the same time.
4. Once the interrupt flag is set, how and when is it cleared?

We shall answer these questions in this section and in so doing we shall raise other questions with which we shall deal in subsequent sections. To understand how this apparent conflict of interrupting devices is managed, we shall have to take a more detailed look at the interrupt process itself and, in particular, at the various signals that pass along the control bus between the CPU and the device. In the discussion to follow we shall not look at *all* of the details of the interrupt sequence; some of these are irrelevant to a resolution of the problem at hand and would unnecessarily obscure an already complicated situation. We note also that what we say here applies to the PDP-11; other machines handle interrupts in somewhat different ways. Nonetheless, the various request, grant and acknowledge signals; the preserving of the CPU's status; the raising and lowering of interrupt flags; and so forth are tasks most computers must handle in one way or another. A sound understanding of how the PDP-11 deals with interrupts will serve the reader well in understanding concepts and will be a good starting point in an examination of interrupt handling for architecturally different machines.

When a device capable of generating interrupts requests service, the following events and communication between the CPU and the device's controller take place:

1. The device controller turns on a line of the control bus, called a **bus request** (BR) line. We say that the controller **asserts BR**. The effect of this is to raise the interrupt flag in the CPU.
2. When the CPU is able to do so, that is, when it has completed its current instruction, it asserts a signal called **bus grant** (BG) on the control bus.
3. *Each* device on the control bus responds to BG in the following way: If the device had *not* asserted BR, that is, if the device was not requesting service from the CPU, it simply passes the BG signal on to the next device on the bus. But if the device *had* requested service, it takes the following three actions:
   a. It *blocks* BG from going further down the bus.
   b. It asserts an **acknowledge signal** back to the CPU. In effect, this notifies the CPU that its BG signal was picked up by some device.
   c. It *clears* the BR signal.
4. The CPU receives the device's acknowledge signal and responds by *clearing* BG.
5. The device controller places the address of the first word of the device's interrupt vector on the *data bus* and sends still another signal down the

control bus to the CPU. In the PDP-11 literature, this last signal is referred to as **interrupt request** (INTR).

6. The CPU responds to INTR by using the address on the data bus as a trap (interrupt) vector address and performs a standard trap sequence.

All of this may seem to be a complex way of passing control to an interrupt routine, but we shall see that this is really a minimal scheme that will allow the proper handling of interrupts, especially in the event that two or more interrupts are pending at the same time, as we assume to be the case here. Let us return to the four questions we stated earlier and see how many we can now answer.

Question 1 asked how the CPU knows which device is interrupting. We see that in fact it does *not* know; however, it *need not* know. The device is, in some sense, uniquely defined by its interrupt vector address. That address is a part of the controller's hardware and thus is *fixed* for each device. At an appropriate time the controller asserts that address on the data bus. Thus question 2 is answered. We postpone question 3 for a moment and note that question 4, which asked how and when the interrupt flag is cleared, is answered: The controller itself clears BR after the CPU has recognized the device with its BG signal.

To answer question 3, let us examine the particular situation in detail. Recall that we assumed that device B and device D had interrupted simultaneously. We assume also that these devices reside on the bus in the configuration shown in Fig. 12.6.1. When the CPU detects that the interrupt flag is on, it sends a BG signal down the control bus. The first device controller to see that signal is that of device A because it is closest to the CPU. Since that device is not requesting service, it simply passes the BG signal farther along the control bus. The next device to see the signal is device B, and since it is requesting service, it blocks further propagation of the signal and, among other things, *clears* the BR signal that it *and* device D had originally asserted. Is the BR signal actually cleared? Yes, but only momentarily. For device D is still asserting the signal, since it has not seen the BG signal from the processor. Thus, although the interrupt flag that is set by the BR signal goes off, it comes right back on again. Consequently, even though device B has obtained the processor's services and a trap takes place through device B's interrupt vector, the interrupt flag is still set.

12.7 DEVICE PRIORITIES

To continue with the example of the preceding section, we saw that device B was given control of the CPU and that device D still has a pending interrupt. To be more precise, since device B is closer (physically) on the bus to the CPU than is device D, the CPU responded to device B and loaded the PC and PSW with the contents of device B's interrupt vector. Thus as execution is about to be resumed, the PC contains the address of the first instruction of the device B interrupt service routine. (Recall that the original PSW and PC values were placed on the stack.) But the CPU does not fetch and execute that first instruction immediately. Before doing so, it examines the interrupt flag—an action the CPU *always* takes before fetching the next instruction—and it detects that the flag is *set*—it is being asserted by device D. As before, the CPU responds by sending a bus grant signal. Again, device A is not requesting service, so it passes the signal farther down the bus to device B. But device B is *also* not requesting service—recall that it cleared its bus request signal. Thus device B passes the signal to device C, which in turn passes it to device D. Device D *is* requesting service, acknowledges the BG signal, places its interrupt vector address on the data bus, and the CPU does another trap. As a result of the trap, the c(PSW) and c(PC) are put on the stack. Notice that this PSW and PC are those that correspond to the first instruction (as yet uenexecuted) of the device B interrupt handler. The CPU then fetches the PC and PSW corresponding to the device D interrupt routine, and commences execution there. Thus while the device B interrupt handling routine had control of the CPU, that control was short-lived. In fact, before the first instruction could be executed, control was transferred to the device D routine.

Assuming no further interrupts, the device D service routine will run to completion and execute an RTI, which will pop a new PC and PSW from the stack. Since these are the PC and PSW corresponding to the beginning of the device B routine, execution of the device B handler picks up, runs to completion, and another RTI will provide resumption of whatever was executing at the time the two interrupts occurred. A diagram of this situation is shown in Fig. 12.7.1. Thus even though device B is closer to the CPU than is device D,

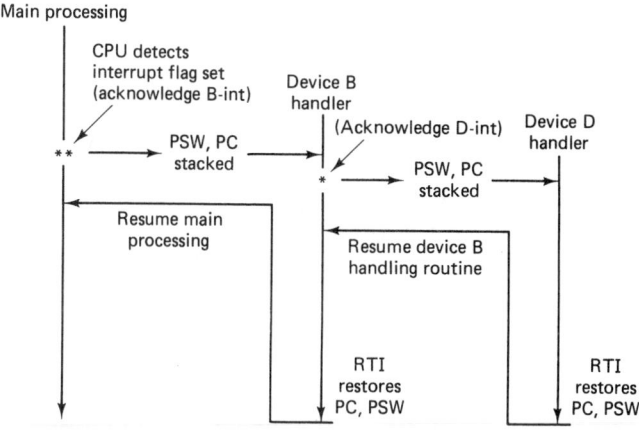

Figure 12.7.1

and device B was serviced by the CPU first, nonetheless it was device D's service routine that completed execution first.

Recall from our examples of Section 12.2 that in dealing with real-life interruptions, we frequently impose (perhaps subconsciously) a system of **priorities** or hierarchy of importance to these interruptions. If two interruptions occur simultaneously, we might choose to process them in a particular order. Or if we are dealing with an interruption when another occurs, we may temporarily suspend what we are doing to cope with the second interruption. In a similar fashion, PDP-11 peripheral devices are assigned priorities to reflect the fact that, in effect, some devices are more important than others. For example, a clock that is keeping real-time would likely be assigned a fairly high priority. For when the clock ticks, we want to be certain that the tick is recorded fairly quickly. If the clock had a low priority, it is possible that it would tick, but because we were tied up with a higher priority interrupt, enough time would pass that a second tick (and consequently a second interrupt) would occur before we got around to processing it. However, there would be no way of determining that *two* ticks had occurred; we would increment a counter by *one*, thereby losing one clock tick. Admittedly, the loss of $\frac{1}{60}$ second is nothing to become particularly upset about, *unless* it occurs frequently. And conceivably, it could.

A PDP-11 **priority level** is an integer between 0 and 7, inclusive. The larger the number, the higher the priority level, in a sense that we shall shortly make clear. Peripheral devices are usually assigned priorities between 4 and 6, inclusive. Priority level 7 is a special case, reserved for a purpose that need not concern us in the present discussion. Priorities 0 to 3 are typically not used for peripheral devices, which is not to say that they are of no use as we shall see in the next section. Generally, if two devices request CPU service, the device with the higher priority will receive the CPU's attention first. For the details of how priorities work, we need to examine the hardware further.

We stated in the last section that when a device requests interruption of the CPU, it asserts *the* bus request line BR, and that the CPU responds by asserting *the* bus grant signal BG. In fact, there are *four* BR and BG lines: BR4 to BR7 and BG4 to BG7. Each device on the control bus is attached to *one* of these bus request lines and to the corresponding bus grant line. The line-time clock, for example, is interfaced to the control bus via BR6 and BG6. Thus when the clock interrupts, it does so at priority level 6, its controller asserts BR6 and receives the CPU's acknowledge signal on BG6. This scheme has several implications. First, each device apparently has a *hardware-fixed* priority level, which is determined at the time the device is attached to the bus. Generally speaking, the only way to change a device's priority is physically to rewire it. Second, there is no *single* interrupt flag—there is one for each of the priority levels 4 to 7, which is set when a device *on that priority level* requests service. And finally, when the CPU asserts BGn, only the devices on that line, that is, at priority level n, will see the signal—devices at other levels are unaffected by it.

How does this hardware scheme achieve what we normally think of as prioritizing? The answer is quite straightforward. When the CPU completes execution of its current instruction, it examines its interrupt flag. We know now that there are *four* such flags, and in fact the CPU examines them in a highest-flag-first order. Thus, for example, if two devices, one with priority 4 and the other with priority 6, are both requesting service, the CPU will examine flag 7 first. Seeing that it is off, the CPU will move down to flag 6. Since this flag is set, the CPU will assert BG6, thereby leaving the priority level 4 *unserviced*, at least for the time being. Thus in this way the higher priority devices get service from the CPU first.

The priority scheme *should* have the following effect: If two devices of different priority levels interrupt simultaneously, then the device of higher priority should be given service first, and its interrupt handling routine should *execute to completion* before the lower priority device is given service. Likewise, if a higher priority device has interrupted and the CPU is executing its service routine when a lower priority device interrupts, the latter interrupt should be *ignored* until the higher priority device has been completely serviced. Finally, if the CPU is dealing with the service routine for a lower priority device when a higher priority device interrupts, execution of the lower priority device's interrupt routine should be suspended, the higher priority device serviced, and then processing of the lower priority device's interrupt handler should be resumed. Unfortunately, the scheme as described so far does not achieve this; in fact, in most cases it handles devices in *exactly the wrong order*. This is not really a fault of the scheme as we have developed it. Rather, we need to *expand* the priority system somewhat, and we shall do this in the next section. To see why matters do not quite work out as desired, we consider a simple example.

Let A and B be two devices, with priority levels 4 and 6, respectively. Suppose that these devices have interrupted simultaneously, that is, within the same CPU instruction execution cycle. If the reader wants some physical devices to have as specific examples, he might take A to be a terminal keyboard and B to be the line clock. Thus we assume that a key on the terminal has been struck at essentially the same time that the clock has ticked. Device A asserts BR4, and device B asserts BR6. When the CPU completes its current instruction, it examines its interrupt flags in the order 7, 6, 5, 4. Since flag 6 is on, it asserts BG6. Device B captures this BG6 signal, sends back an acknowledge signal to the CPU, and clears its BR6 signal, thus *clearing* flag 6. Next, the CPU clears BG6 as a response to the acknowledge signal. Then the device controller for device B places that device's interrupt vector address on the data bus, and the CPU executes a trap using that vector. Thus by the time the smoke clears, the original c(PSW) and c(PC) have been stacked, PC contains the address of the first instruction in the device B interrupt handling routine, and the level 6 interrupt flag has been *cleared*. The CPU is now ready to fetch this first instruction, but before doing so, it examines its interrupt flags, again in the order 7, 6, 5, 4. It sees that flags 7, 6, and 5 are *clear*, but flag 4 is still *set*—nothing happened in the process described above to clear it. Thus the CPU begins *another* interrupt sequence—it sends out a BG4 signal, device A acknowledges it and clears BR4 (also clearing the level 4 interrupt flag), device A's interrupt vector address is placed on the data bus, and the CPU executes another trap. Now the current c(PSW) and c(PC) are stacked. But in this case the stacked PC contains the address of the first instruction of the device B service routine. The new PC that is picked up on the trap contains the address of the device A service routine. Once again the CPU is prepared to execute an instruction, namely, the first device A handler instruction. Before doing so, it once more examines its interrupt flags. *This* time it finds all flags cleared, so it can begin actual program execution. But note that the CPU is processing the interrupt handling routine for device A, the *lower priority* device. If no further interrupts occur, that routine will go to completion, and an RTI instruction will pop the stack into the PC and PSW. What is being executed now? The answer is, The device B interrupt routine has been resumed (recall that it never really got started). Presumably it runs to completion, and a final RTI will pass control back to whatever was being done when these two interrupts first occurred. Thus we see that even though device B had a higher priority than device A, it was device A's service routine that was completed first. This is not the result we were looking for in establishing a priority scheme; in fact, it is just the reverse of the desired effect. We leave it to the reader to verify that the results of the next two examples are as described.

Suppose now that while some program is being executed, device B interrupts on priority level 6. If no other interrupts are pending, control will be passed to the device B interrupt handling routine. Suppose next that while the CPU is dealing with this service routine, device A interrupts at level 4. The CPU will *stop* processing the level 6 handler and *start* processing this level 4 handler. The latter will run to completion, the device B handler will be resumed and completed, and finally the main program will be picked up at the point of (device B) interruption. But again, this result is not consistent with our concept of priorities: A level 4 device should not be allowed to interrupt the processing of a level 6 interrupt.

Finally, assume that in the course of main program execution, device A interrupts at level 4 and device A servicing commences. Suppose that in the midst of that processing, device B interrupts at level 6. As above, control will be passed to the device B handler, which will go to completion, device A handling will again be resumed, and finally main processing will continue. In this case, a higher priority device (device B) has interrupted the servicing of a lower priority device (device A). In this instance, the desired result *was* achieved.

Thus the priority scheme proposed—that of having the CPU examine the interrupt flags on a highest-priority-first basis—while it appeared promising early on has proven to be most disappointing in practice. However, the situation is salvaged in a most simple and elegant fashion—in addition to the peripheral devices, we also assign the CPU *itself* a priority level which is *adjustable*.

12.8 THE CPU PRIORITY

The CPU's priority, like that of the devices, is a number between 0 and 7, inclusive, and it is determined by bits 7 to 5 of the PSW, as shown in Fig. 12.8.1. This priority may be set under program control in one of two ways. First, a

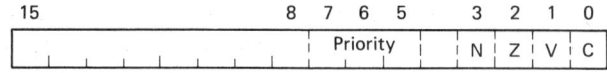

Figure 12.8.1

standard PDP-11 hardware instruction, such as MOV, BIS, or CLR, can affect these bits. Thus, for example, MOV #300,PSW will set the CPU's priority to 6, since bits 7 and 6 were set, but note that all other bits were cleared by this instruction. There is also a special instruction whose only function is to set these bits. The instruction is SPL—*Set Priority Level*—and its format is SPL n. Execution of the instruction will set bits 7 to 5 in the PSW to *n*. (*Note:*   Not all models of the PDP-11 will decode the instruction SPL.)

The second way in which the CPU priority can be set is as a result of any kind of *trap*—either execution of an instruction such as TRAP or EMT, *or* the trap associated with a device interrupt. We shall see in a moment how we can take advantage of this action. We note first that the priority concept for the CPU differs from that for a peripheral device in the following way: A peripheral device is assigned a priority by being wired to the control bus on one of the bus request and bus grant levels. Thus device priority cannot be altered by programming; it can be varied only with some hardware changes. The CPU's priority, on the other hand, is *not* hardware-fixed—it *can* be altered by programming.

We are finally in a position to reveal *all* that takes place during the interrupt sequence. Recall that when the CPU completes an instruction, prior to beginning the next instruction it looks at the interrupt flags. If it sees none of them set, it proceeds with the next instruction. But suppose it detects that one of the interrupt flags *is* set. Contrary to the impression we have given so far, the processor does *not* automatically begin the interrupt sequence (sending BG, stacking the PSW and PC, trapping, and so forth). Rather, it first checks the priority level of the interrupting device, that is, the level of the requesting BR line, against *its own* priority. If the priority level of the interrupting device is *higher than* the processor's priority, the CPU initiates the interrupt sequence as described above. However, if the requesting device has a priority that is *less than or equal to* the CPU's priority, the CPU *ignores* the request and begins execution of the next instruction. These two simple concepts—that the CPU's priority may be set under program control, and that devices interrupting at levels that do not exceed the priority of the CPU are essentially ignored or unseen by the processor (we frequently say that such interrupts are **masked out**) —make the device priority scheme work. Not only does the scheme work, but how, when, and if devices interrupt main processing or one another's service routines is under the complete control of the programmer.

We shall illustrate these ideas in some detail with two examples. Each of them will deal with two devices that generate interrupts at different levels. One of the devices will be the familiar line-time clock, which interrupts at level 6. The other will be the console keyboard, about which we need to say a few words. Like any other interrupting device, the console keyboard has an interrupt vector, at locations 000060 and 000062. It also has a status register, which is very much like the clock's status register, at location 777560. Bit 6 of the status register is again the interrupt enable bit. There are some other bits in this register that are of significance, but for the purposes of this example, we shall not need to be concerned with them. If the interrupt enable bit is set, then the keyboard controller will generate an interrupt each time a key is struck on the keyboard. And if conditions are right—if the CPU's priority is low enough—then the interrupt sequence will be entered and processing will transfer to the keyboard's interrupt handling routine. We shall not be explicit about just what that service routine does because that is not really our concern here; we are more interested in the interrupt structure of the situation. Likewise, although we do have an example of a suitable interrupt routine for the clock, we shall not show it here.

In Fig. 12.8.2 we assume that a clock interrupt occurs during main processing. Control is transferred by the usual interrupt sequence to the clock service routine. While that routine is executing, a keyboard interrupt occurs. But in this case, unlike the example of the last section, processing of the clock service routine *continues*, the keyboard interrupt having been effectively masked out. When the clock routine finishes, the keyboard service routine is dealt with, and finally main processing resumes. This is precisely the action we want if we consider the clock to be more important than the keyboard—the latter device has been prevented from interrupting the higher priority clock. We look at this programming segment in detail.

The first few instructions shown ensure that various locations are properly initialized before main processing commences. In particular, the address of the clock's service routine, TICK, is put in the first word of the clock's interrupt vector (000100) and the number 300 is put in the second word (000102). Notice that this action sets bits 7 to 5 of that word to 110. In a similar fashion, the address KEY is moved into 000060 and the word at 000062 gets the number 200, thus setting bits 7 to 5 of that word to 100. We then ensure that the CPU's

```
                000100          CLKINT  =  000100
                177546          CLKSTS  =  177546
                000060          KBINT   =  000060
                177560          KBSTS   =  177560
                                ;
                                ;INITIALIZE INTERRUPT VECTORS
                                ;SET PROCESSOR PRIORITY
                                ;ENABLE DEVICE INTERRUPTS
                                ;
001000          012767          MOV     #TICK,CLKINT      ;SET SERVICE ADDR
                006342'
                000100
001006          012767          MOV     #300,CLKINT+2     ; AND PRIORITY
                000300
                000102
001014          012767          MOV     #KEY,KBINT        ;KEYBOARD SERVICE ADDR
                007404'
                000060
001022          012767          MOV     #200,KBINT+2      ; AND PRIORITY
                000200
                000062
001030          000230          SPL     0                 ;SET CPU PRIORITY = 0
001032          012767          MOV     #100,KBSTS        ;ENABLE KB INTERRUPTS
                000100
                177560
001040          012767          MOV     #100,CLKSTS       ;ENABLE CLK INTERRUPTS
                000100
                177546
                                ;
                                ;BEGIN MAIN PROCESSING
                                ;
001046                          .
001050                          .
001052                          .
001054                          .
                                   <--- (Clock interrupt occurs)
001056                          .
001060                          ;
                                ;CLOCK INTERRUPT HANDLER
                                ;
006342          TICK:           .
006344
                                   <--- (Keyboard interrupt occurs)
006346                          .
006350
006352          000002          RTI                       ;RETURN FROM CLOCK INT
006354                          .
006356
                                ;
                                ;KEYBOARD INTERRUPT HANDLER
                                ;
007404          KEY:            .
007406                          .
007410                          .
007412
007414          000002          RTI                       ;RETURN FROM KB INT
007416                          .
007420                          .
```

Figure 12.8.2

priority is 0 (SPL 0) and enable the keyboard and clock interrupts. Main processing can now begin.

While the CPU is processing, we suppose that a clock interrupt occurs as shown on the listing. When the CPU completes execution of its current instruction at 001054, it examines the interrupt flags in the order 7, 6, 5, 4. It sees that flag 7 is clear, but that flag 6 is set, since the clock interrupts on BR6. Comparing the priority 6 with its own priority, which is 0, the CPU sees that the request is at a *higher* level than its own, and thus it enters the interrupt sequence. Specifically, it responds to BR6 by asserting BG6. The clock detects BG6 and acknowledges it, at the same time clearing BR6. The CPU then clears BG6, and the clock places the address of the first word of its interrupt vector, 000100, on the data bus and so notifies the CPU with the INTR signal on the control bus. The CPU pushes the current c(PSW) (whose value is immaterial to this discussion) on the stack, and then pushes the current c(PC), whose value is 001056, on the stack. Next, the PC gets the contents of memory location 000100, namely, 006342 = TICK. The PSW gets the contents of memory location 000102 (000300). Thus processing continues in the clock's service routine.

We assume now that during the course of the execution of the instruction at 006344, a key is struck on the console terminal. An interrupt is generated by the keyboard's controller at priority level 4. When the CPU completes execution of its current instruction, it examines the interrupt flags. It sees that flags 7, 6, and 5 are clear, but that flag 4 is *set*. The CPU compares that interrupt level with its own, and finds that its priority level is 6. This is a result of having picked up a new PSW with the value 000300 from location 000102. The priority bits, bits 7 to 5, are set to 110, and thus the CPU is currently running at priority level 6. Since 4 is not greater than 6, the CPU ignores the request for service from the keyboard and continues in the clock service routine. This examination of the interrupt flags and the ignoring of the level 4 request takes place prior to each of the remaining instructions in the clock service routine.

Finally the clock service routine executes RTI. The top of the stack is popped into the PC—recall that the address 001056 was on top of the stack—and the original PSW is also popped off the stack. Thus main processing is about to resume at 001056. However, prior to executing the instruction at that address, the CPU examines the interrupt flags and determines that flag 4 is set. Since its own priority is now 0, having been restored to that value when the old PSW was retrieved from the stack, the CPU again enters the interrupt sequence. Without going into all the details, we know that the current c(PSW) (again, whose value is of no concern, except for the fact that the priority bits are 000) is pushed on the stack, the current c(PC) (001056) is pushed on the stack, a new PC is obtained from 000060 (which contains 007404 = KEY), and a new PSW (with priority bits 100) from 000062. Thus the CPU is now executing the keyboard service routine, and it is running at priority level 4. Since no further interrupts occur, the service routine goes to completion, executes RTI, and the original PC (001056) and PSW are restored. Thus main processing finally resumes, in the absence of further interrupts.

Our next example (Fig. 12.8.3) is a variation of the preceding one, and while it is equally interesting and illuminating, we shall treat it in a somewhat more cursory fashion. We assume the same initial conditions as before, but this time a keyboard interrupt occurs during main processing. Control is

```
        000100              CLKINT = 000100
        177546              CLKSTS = 177546
        000060              KBINT  = 000060
        177560              KBSTS  = 177560
                            ;
                            ;INITIALIZE INTERRUPT VECTORS
                            ;SET PROCESSOR PRIORITY
                            ;ENABLE DEVICE INTERRUPTS
001000  012767              MOV     #TICK,CLKINT    ;SET SERVICE ADDR
        006342'
        000100
001006  012767              MOV     #300,CLKINT+2   ; AND PRIORITY
        000300
        000102
001014  012767              MOV     #KEY,KBINT      ;KEYBOARD SERVICE ADDR
        007404'
        000060
001022  012767              MOV     #200,KBINT+2    ; AND PRIORITY
        000200
        000062
001030  000230              SPL     0               ;SET CPU PRIORITY = 0
001032  012767              MOV     #100,KBSTS      ;ENABLE KB INTERRUPTS
        000100
        177560
001040  012767              MOV     #100,CLKSTS     ;ENABLE CLK INTERRUPTS
        000100
        177546
                            ;
                            ;BEGIN MAIN PROCESSING
                            ;
001046                      .
001050                      .
001052                      .
001054                      .
                              <--- (Keyboard interrupt occurs)
001056                      .
001060                      .
                            ;
                            ;CLOCK INTERRUPT HANDLER
                            ;
006342          TICK:       .
006344                      .
006346                      .
006350                      .
006352  000002              RTI                     ;RETURN FROM CLOCK INT
006354                      .
006356                      .
                            ;
                            ;KEYBOARD INTERRUPT HANDLER
                            ;
007404          KEY:        .
007406                      .
                              <--- (Clock interrupt occurs)
007410                      .
007412                      .
007414  000002              RTI                     ;RETURN FROM KB INT
007416                      .
007420                      .
```

Figure 12.8.3

transferred to the keyboard service routine, and while execution is taking place in that routine, a clock interrupt occurs. As we shall see, at that time control is passed to the clock's interrupt routine, which executes (presumably capturing the clock tick and updating the time) and then returns control to the keyboard service routine. Finally, main processing is resumed after the keyboard has been serviced. Observe that once more this is the desired effect. Even though the keyboard interrupt had caused keyboard servicing to commence, the clock interrupt was honored immediately—the more important device has been allowed to interrupt a less important device.

As in the preceding example, the device interrupt vectors and status registers are initialized, and the processor's priority is set to 0. Main processing begins, and we assume that just prior to execution of the instruction at 001056, a keyboard interrupt occurs. This interrupt is acknowledged by the CPU, which stacks the currents c(PSW) and c(PC) (001056), gets a new PC (007404 = KEY) from location 000060 and a new PSW (000200) from location 000062. Processing thus picks up at the beginning of the keyboard service routine, and since the CPU's current PSW has the value 000200, it is running at priority level 4. While the CPU is executing this routine, the clock generates an interrupt just prior to the instruction at location 007410. Before it fetches the instruction at 007410, the CPU examines its interrupt flags and detects that flag 6 is set. Comparing this level with its own priority (4), it determines that this new interrupt *should* be honored, since that priority level exceeds its own. Thus the current keyboard service routine c(PSW) is stacked, and the current c(PC) (007410) is also stacked. A new PC and PSW are obtained from 000100 and 000102, with values 006342 and 000300, respectively, and processing of the clock service routine begins. The reader should have no difficulty in seeing that in the absence of further interrupts, when the clock routine goes to completion, keyboard service is resumed and, upon its completion, main processing picks up where it was interrupted, at 001056.

We need to comment about the numbers we assigned to the *second* word of these devices' interrupt vectors. When a device interrupts and that interrupt is honored by the CPU, whatever integer is in the second word of the interrupt vector will determine, among other things, the priority with which the CPU will execute the device's service routine. The contents of that word becomes the CPU's processor status word, and bits 7 to 5 of that word determine CPU priority. The reader will note that for the clock vector, those bits were set to 6, which happens to be the level at which the clock interrupts. Similarly, for the keyboard, a priority 4 device, bits 7 to 5 of its vector word at KBINT + 2 were set to 4. Was this merely accident or whim? No. It was also not *necessary* to set the priority bits in the second word of a device's interrupt vector to the priority of the device itself. We could have set those bits for either device any way we wanted. But we shall show that they were set in a reasonable way.

When a device service routine is executing, the CPU is running at a priority level that was determined by the priority bits of the second word of the interrupt vector for the device. The philosophy is that when a device is being serviced, higher priority devices *should* be allowed to interrupt this servicing, and lower priority devices should *not* be allowed to interrupt. What about devices attempting to interrupt at the *same* priority level? There seems to be no compelling reason to give them immediate service since in a sense they are no *more* important than what is currently taking place, so we let them wait until the device at hand has been serviced.

Some computers do not have this rather elaborate hardware priority structure, and in these cases assigning priorities to devices must be handled in some other fashion. Suggestions in this direction will be found in several of the exercises. For those computers that do, like the PDP-11, if the priority of a device is hardwired, then we have no choice about the level at which a device interrupts—this has been predetermined by the computer manufacturer. In some cases, these preassigned priorities might not serve our purposes. As a simple example, consider a PDP-11 system that supports a console keyboard and a paper tape reader, *both* of which are wired to interrupt at level 4. For a variety of reasons we might place more importance on the paper tape reader—perhaps, because it is a relatively slow device and that it is reading data needed by our program, we never want it to be delayed, preferring rather to hold up the keyboard if necessary. But if we follow the scheme just described for determining the number in the second word of each device's interrupt vector—that is, make that word 200—then when either device's interrupt service routine is executing, the CPU will be running at priority level 4, and the other device will not be able to interrupt it. And while we do not want the keyboard to interrupt paper tape processing, we *do* want to allow the paper tape reader to interrupt keyboard interrupt handling.

A simple way to accomplish this—in a sense overriding the manufacturer's intent—is to put the number 000200 in the second word of the paper tape reader's interrupt vector. Thus processing of its service routine will take place at priority level 4. But in the keyboard's interrupt vector, we set the second word to 000140. Thus implies that the keyboard's interrupt routine will execute at priority level 3. In doing this we are *not* changing the levels at which the devices interrupt, since in fact we *cannot* change these. Rather, we have established that their service routines will execute with CPU priorities 4 and 3, respectively.

Suppose now that the paper tape routine is executing when the keyboard interrupts at level 4. Since the CPU has priority 4 also, the interrupt will be masked, as desired. On the other hand, if the keyboard service routine is executing, with the CPU at priority 3, and the paper tape interrupts at level 4, the interrupt will be honored—control will be passed to the paper tape routine, again as desired. Thus while we may not be able to alter the actual hardware priorities of the various devices, we still have a great deal of control over which devices can even generate interrupts, and for those that do so, we may be able to force execution of their service routines in whatever order we choose.

If two devices interrupt *simultaneously*, and if they interrupt at *different* levels, then of course the device with the higher priority obtains the service of the CPU first. If, however, they interrupt at the *same* level, then the device that gets service first is the first device to see the CPU's BG signal, that is, the device that is physically closest to the CPU on the control bus.

12.9 THE CONSOLE TERMINAL

The present section has no bearing on the remainder of the text and thus can be omitted. On the other hand, the conscientious reader may wish to look at some of the details of the console terminal to enhance his understanding of and facility with computer peripheral devices. The terminal is more representative of devices than is the line clock, and it exhibits some features that we have not yet discussed.

The typical terminal device in use today is in fact *two* devices: a keyboard (input device) and a printer (output device). They bear a resemblance to an electric typewriter, but there is no mechanical or electrical connection between these two devices. The only reason we think of them as a unit is that they are usually housed in the same cabinet, and they frequently share a common device controller that is in fact actually two separate controllers. Despite all this, the keyboard and printer are frequently quite closely associated through *software* (programming), and their behavior relative to their respective controllers is quite similar. For this reason, we use a common figure (Fig. 12.9.1) to represent them. This figure should thus be interpreted as corresponding to either the keyboard or the printer (but not both simultaneously). The double arrow

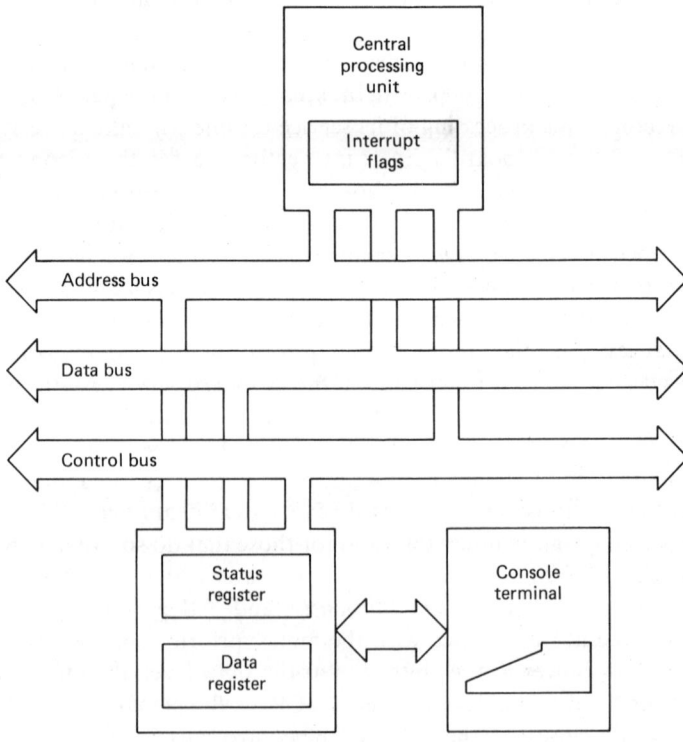

Figure 12.9.1

between the terminal and the controller indicates that data can flow either *from* the keyboard *to* the controller and thence to the various buses, or *from* the controller *to* the printer.

In the preceding section we mentioned the keyboard's controller, and in particular its status register. We now examine this controller in a bit more detail. The keyboard has associated with it *two* 16-bit registers, a **status register** and a **data register,** sometimes called a **data buffer.** These are shown in Fig. 12.9.2, along with their address assignments. Depending on the type of terminal device, the keyboard's status register might also contain a few more significant bits, but for our purposes we can safely ignore them. The data register is a simple structure: its low-order byte contains the ACSII code for the character that corresponds to the last key that was struck on the keyboard. The status register also appears to be quite simple, especially in light of our experience with the clock status register. One suspects that the data available bit will be on whenever valid data is present in the data register. This is quite correct, but there are some special considerations here that warrant our investigation.

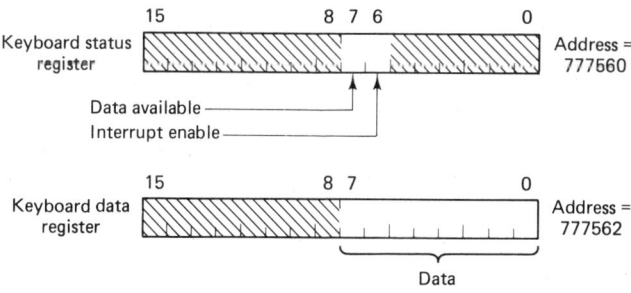

Figure 12.9.2

When a key is struck on the keyboard, the following events occur: The keyboard logic generates the ASCII code for the character in question, and sends this 8-bit (or sometimes 7-bit) code to the controller's data register. When the data register is filled, the controller detects this fact and turns on the data available bit on the status register. If the interrupt enable bit in the status register is on, the controller will send a BR signal (interrupt) down the BR4 line of the control bus. If the interrupt enable bit is off, no such interrupt will be generated.

Suppose that the interrupt enable bit in the keyboard status register is set when a key is struck on the keyboard. Then the code will be transferred to the data register, the data available bit will come on, and an interrupt will be generated. Since that interrupt will ultimately be acknowledged (unless the processor's priority is held at 4 or greater), a keyboard service routine will execute. But suppose that routine makes no provision for *turning off* the data available bit. What will happen when another key is struck? The code for that key will be transferred to the data register, overlaying what was formerly there, and the data available bit will be turned on. However, that bit was already on, so it simply stays on. Is another interrupt generated? The answer, curiously enough, is no. To understand why, we must examine what triggers the interrupt. The interrupt is *not* triggered by the interrupt enable and the data available bits' both being on. Rather, an interrupt occurs when the interrupt enable bit is on and the data available bit *changes its state from* 0 *to* 1. This low-to-high **transition** of the data available bit, in the presence of a set interrupt enable bit, causes the interrupt to occur. Thus if the data available bit was *not* cleared after a character was typed, then the *next* keystroke will *not* generate an interrupt.

How is the data available bit of the keyboard status register cleared? Any reference to the keyboard data register will clear this bit. Typically, when the programming detects a keyboard interrupt, a keyboard service routine will *get* the code for the character typed and put it somewhere, perhaps on a stack. Thus the service routine might contain an instruction such as MOVB KBDATA,−(R5), where KBDATA = 177562. Let us examine what happens when such an instruction is executed. The CPU wants to read the contents of this register so that it can stack it. To do so it places the given address, namely, 177562, on the address bus and sends a READ signal down the control bus. *Each* device on the bus sees this control signal and examines the address on the address bus. The device then asks the question, Is this address the address of one of my registers? If the answer is no, that device will ignore the READ signal. Only one device, namely, the keyboard, will answer yes to the question. The controller will place the *contents* of the register in question (KBDATA) on the data bus and send an acknowledge signal back to the CPU to indicate that the requested data is available on the data bus. At the same time, the controller *clears* bit 7 of the status register, the data available bit. This is precisely the effect we want in order properly to manage this device.

Could we just as well have turned bit 7 off with an instruction such as MOV #100,KBSTS or BIC #200,KBSTS (where KBSTS = 177560), and at the same time left the interrupt enable bit (bit 6) on? Interestingly enough, the answer is no. While we can certainly *read* this bit—we do so each time we read the status register—that bit can only be *written* (set to 0 or 1) by the controller. For this reason, bit 7 is referred to as a **read-only bit,** as opposed to bit 6, which is called a **read-write bit.**

While we shall use the printer in the next example, we shall not say much about it now. Its registers are shown in Fig. 12.9.3. Since we shall be handling the printer on a noninterrupt basis, we need only to determine *how* to print a character, and that task is especially simple. To print a given character, we need only to move the ASCII code for that character into the printer's data register. This starts the printing process, and at the same time turns *off* the "ready" bit in the status register. Thus on a noninterrupt basis, to print a character we can examine the ready bit until we see that it is on—that is, the printer is ready to accept another character—and then move the ASCII code for the desired character into the data register.

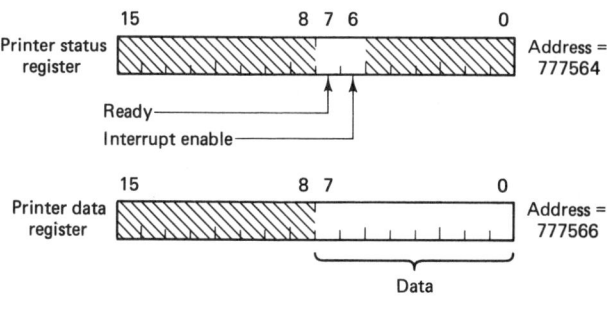

Figure 12.9.3

The idea behind the program segment of Fig. 12.9.4 is quite simple. We assume that a user program is executing, but that in the course of that execution one or more keys are struck on the keyboard. While perhaps we can do nothing with this input at the moment, we can at least save it for later processing. The characters are saved in a 256_{10}-byte area called BUFFER. Recall that the keyboard and printer, as devices, have nothing to do with one another; the mere striking of a key will not cause the character to appear on the printer. Thus our keyboard service routine makes provision for accepting a character, placing it in BUFFER, and then sending the code for the character to the printer, which is managed as a noninterrupting device. This process is called **character echoing.** We must also be aware that when the carriage return key is struck on the keyboard and echoed to the printer, the type element will return to the left margin but, unlike an electric typewriter, the paper will not feed up one line. Thus we have made provision in the keyboard handler to detect a carriage return and to supply the missing line feed.

With this background the reader should have little difficulty following the example. The first few lines set R3 as a pointer to the buffer where characters will be stored, initialize the keyboard's interrupt vector, enable keyboard interrupts and disable printer interrupts, and set the processor's priority to $\emptyset$. (The instruction CLR   PSW could as well have been SPL   0.) Interrupts from the keyboard pass control to the routine KEY, where the character is echoed and saved in the buffer. We remind the reader that this is not a complete program, so a number of things have not been provided for. For example, we see no instructions to examine the buffer and act on its contents and no provision to handle a possible buffer overflow. But it does accomplish its principal objective: showing how keyboard interrupts can be dealt with in some reasonable way.

Our final example (Fig. 12.9.5)—again a program segment rather than a

```
            000015           CR    = 15              ;ASCII CARRIAGE RETURN
            000012           LF    = 12              ;ASCII LINE FEED
            000060           KBINT = 60              ;KB INT VECTOR ADDR
            177560           KBSTS = 177560          ;KB STATUS REG ADDR
            177562           KBDATA = KBSTS+2        ;KB DATA REG ADDR
            177564           PTRSTS = 177564         ;PRINTER STAT REG ADDR
            177566           PRDATA = PTRSTS+2       ;PRINTER DATA REG ADDR
            177776           PSW   = 177776          ;PSW ADDRESS
001000              BUFFER:  .BLKB  256.             ;KEYBOARD INPUT BUFFER

001400      012703          MOV    #BUFFER,R3        ;INITIALIZE BUFFER ADDR
            001000'
001404      012767          MOV    #KEY,KBINT        ;SET UP VECTOR ADDR
            004726'
            000060
001412      012767          MOV    #200,KBINT+2      ; AND PSW
            000200
            000062
001420      012767          MOV    #100,KBSTS        ;ENABLE KB INTERRUPT
            000100
            177560
001426      005067          CLR    PTRSTS            ;DISABLE PRINTER INT
            177564
001432      005067          CLR    PSW               ;CPU PRIORITY = 0
            177776
                            ;
                            ;BEGIN MAIN PROCESSING
                            ;
                             .
                             .
                             .
                            ;
                            ;KEYBOARD SERVICE ROUTINE
                            ;
004726      116723  KEY:    MOVB   KBDATA,(R3)+      ;PUT CHAR IN BUFFER
            177562
004732      105767  ECHO:   TSTB   PTRSTS            ;PRINTER BUSY?
            177564
004736      100375          BPL    ECHO              ;YES -- CHECK AGAIN
004740      116367          MOVB   -1(R3),PRDATA     ;ECHO CHARACTER
            177777
            177566
004746      126327          CMPB   -1(R3),#CR        ;WAS IT CARR RETURN?
            177777
            000015
004754      001006          BNE    RETURN            ;NO -- RETURN
                                                     ; ELSE END-OF-LINE
004756      105767  EOL:    TSTB   PTRSTS            ;PRINTER BUSY?
            177564
004762      100375          BPL    EOL               ;YES -- CHECK AGAIN
004764      112767          MOVB   #LF,PRDATA        ; ELSE SEND LINE FEED
            000012
            177566
004772      000002  RETURN: RTI                      ;RETURN TO MAIN PROC
                             .
                             .
```

Figure 12.9.4

complete program—deals with the handling of the console printer on an interrupt basis. We assume that in the course of executing a program it becomes necessary to send a message of some kind, perhaps an error indication or an informational message (for example, the current time). Conditions may be such that processing can continue even while the message is being printed. Thus we start the printer by sending the first message character and go back to main

```
        000015          CR     = 15            ;ASCII CARRIAGE RETURN
        000012          LF     = 12            ;ASCII LINE FEED
        177564          PTRSTS = 177564        ;PRINTER STATUS REG
        177566          PRDATA = 177566        ;PRINTER DATA REG
        000064          PTRINT = 64            ;INT VECTOR ADDR
                               ;
001000  012767'         MOV    #PRINT,PTRINT   ;SET INTERRUPT ADDR
        010226'
        000064
001006  012767          MOV    #200,PTRINT+2   ; AND INTERRUPT PSW
        000200
        000066
001014  000230          SPL    0               ;SET CPU PRIORITY
                               ;
                               ;BEGIN MAIN PROCESSING
001016                  .

003406  012700'         MOV    #TEXT,R0        ;SET MESSAGE ADDR
        016442'
003412  012767          MOV    #100,PTRSTS     ; AND START PRINTING
        000100
        177564
003420                  .                      ;CONTINUE PROCESSING
                        .
                        .
010226  105710  PRINT:  TSTB   (R0)            ;DONE WITH MESSAGE?
010230  001402          BEQ    RETURN          ;YES -- SKIP AROUND
010232  112067          MOVB   (R0)+,PRDATA    ;SEND ANOTHER CHARACTER
        177566
010236  000002  RETURN: RTI                    ;RETURN TO PROCESSING
                        .
016442     124  TEXT:   .ASCIZ /TEST MESSAGE/<CR><LF>
016443     105
016444     123
016445     124
016446     040
016447     115
016450     105
016451     123
016452     123
016453     101
016454     107
016455     105
016456     015
016457     012
016460     000
                        .EVEN
016462                  .
                        .
```

Figure 12.9.5

processing. After the first character has been sent, the printer will interrupt processing, we send the next character and resume processing, and so forth, until the entire message has been transmitted.

The first few instructions in the example initialize a few things as usual, and then main processing begins. When it is determined that the message is to be sent (at location 003406), we put the address of the first byte of the message into R∅, which will be used as a pointer to step through the message characters. But the next instruction, at 003412, namely MOV #100,PTRSTS, requires some explanation. While it should be clear that this instruction enables printer interrupts—turns on bit 6 of the status register—the associated comment indicates that this instruction actually *starts* the printing process. In fact it does, but to determine why, we must examine the device and its controller in more detail.

With the interrupt enable bit set, the printer behaves similarly to the keyboard. When the ready bit goes through a low-to-high transition, an interrupt will occur (Fig. 12.9.3.) The difference between these two devices lies in their *normal* state. The normal state of the keyboard is "data not available." That is, unless a key has been struck and not processed, the data available bit (bit 7) will be off, and this is its usual state. Bit 7 in the printer's status register, however, is a ready bit, and ready (to accept another character for printing) is the normal state for the printer. Indeed, in the example, since the printer was presumably not in use prior to our decision to use it, it was in this ready state. The effect of the MOV #100,PTRSTS instruction is to set the low-order byte of the status register to the bit configuration 0 1 0 0 0 0 0 0. But since the printer is not in use, the controller is constantly asserting bit 7 of this register. This bit comes on, and now, since the interrupt enable bit (bit 6) is set, an interrupt is generated. While this may seem to be rather bizarre device behavior, as long as we are aware of it, we can cope with it and even take advantage of it, as we have here.

The interrupt handling routine itself is fairly straightforward. The character about to be sent to the printer is first checked to see if it is a NUL, which indicates "end of message." If not, the character is sent, the message pointer (R∅) is incremented by 1, and control is immediately returned to main processing. Some time later (typically, $\frac{1}{30}$ second, depending on the type of terminal device) the printer will again come ready, generate another interrupt, and so forth. Ultimately, when the printer service routine detects the NUL, it simply returns. Since no new character was put in the printer's data register, no further interrupts will be generated.

Two conclusions we can draw from this section are that not all devices are alike with regard to data transmission, nor are they alike in their interrupt structure. For example, recall that the keyboard would not generate interrupts so long as its data available bit was left on, and yet the clock had no difficulty interrupting the CPU even though its monitor bit had never been cleared. And while on the PDP-11 a conscious effort was obviously made at some standardization (of status registers, for example), different devices are constructed to perform different functions, so each has to be treated to some extent as a special case. In short, if we wish to use and program for a specific device, we shall have to become acquainted with all of that device's peculiarities.

Device handling is a nontrivial matter that requires much care and attention to details and potential timing problems—device interrupts at unexpected times. This is one of the reasons why we have supplied the macroinstructions $IN. DEC, $OUT.ASC, and so forth. It is unrealistic to expect the beginning assembly language programmer to be able to manipulate the complexities of devices before he or she has developed the level of sophistication in hardware and software implicit in this chapter. There is another reason for our use of these macroinstructions. Some computer operating systems, especially timesharing systems, are highly protective of their integrity. For example, upon execution of a program, before the CPU references an address, the system may check to make sure that the address about to be referrenced is not out-of-bounds, so to say. If it is, the system will frequently abort the offending instruction, and in fact may simply termimate the entire program execution. The device registers typically have such out-of-bounds addresses. The macroinstructions described in Appendix B work very closely with the operating system, making sure to execute only acceptable instructions.

Despite the obvious complexities involved with the management of devices at this hardware level, we should note that the PDP-11 is a machine whose architectural structure makes this management especially *simple*. In some other machines, the situation ranges from slightly less convenient to almost intolerable. Device handling in the PDP-11 is relatively easy because the device registers have *addresses* and thus can be manipulated by the standard PDP-11 instructions. But we pay for this convenience by tying up a fair amount of address space that could otherwise be used for main memory.

12.10 EXERCISES

12.3.1. What is the difference between the action taken by the CPU on an interrupt and on execution of the instruction TRAP?

12.3.2. Write a clock interrupt handling routine that updates real time as in the example of Sec. 12.3, but that does so in a more sophisticated fashion, preferably with fewer program instructions.

12.3.3. The following device service routine simply keeps track in two locations, COUNT and COUNT+1, of the number of device interrupts. It could potentially cause programming errors. Why? Find two distinct ways to fix it in order to avoid these potential problems.

```
DEV:    MOV   #COUNT,R2
        INCB  (R2)+
        INCB  (R2)
        RTI
```

12.4.1. *Kilo* (K) is the prefix meaning 1000, but relative to computers we normally take kilo to mean 1024_{10}, the power of 2 closest to 1000. Thus 1024 words is referred to as 1 kiloword (Kw), and 1024 bytes is 1 kilobyte (Kb). Given the addressing scheme discussed in Sec. 12.4, how many kilowords of memory are devoted to user memory, and how many are reserved for device registers, that is, addresses on the buses rather than in main memory?

12.4.2. In Fig. 12.4.1 there appears the symbol

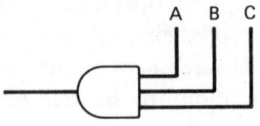

Figure 12.10.1

How is a three-input *AND* gate to be interpreted? That is, what is its output for given inputs A, B, and C?

12.5.1. In Sec. 12.5 we saw that the line-time clock could be used to keep track of real time (in interrupt mode) or as an interval timer (in noninterrupt mode). We could not use the clock as a timekeeper and then when it was needed as an interval timer, *disable* its interrupt temporarily for this purpose, without losing some real time. One solution to this dilemma is to use *two* clocks, one for each purpose, and some computing systems do just that. As another solution, write a program segment that uses the time-of-day clock as a timer to delay 10 seconds, for instance, *without* disabling its interrupting capabilities and thus without losing real time. The WAIT instruction (Appendix A) may be found to be useful here.

12.8.1. **(a)** The instruction SPL   0 will set the CPU's priority level to 0, and so will CLR   PSW. What (if anything) is the difference between these instructions?

(b) What is the difference between SPL   6 and MOV   #300,PSW?

(c) Why will BIS   #300,PSW *not necessarily* set the CPU's priority to 6?

12.8.2. **(a)** Consider two devices, A and B, with interrupt vectors at DEVA and DEVB, respectively, interrupting at priority levels 4 and 5, respectively. As the program segment of Fig. 12.10.2 executes, explain carefully and completely the contents of the stack each time the stack changes state. Assume the stack to be initially empty.

(b) As in part (a) above, except now assume that devices A and B interrupt at levels 5 and 4, respectively. Assume *no* changes in the programming itself.

12.8.3. We have seen that the PDP-11 has a rather elaborate interrupt structure. Consider now a computer that is much less sophisticated in this regard. We assume that its peripheral devices have status registers so that we can detect the state of the device, but when *any* device interrupts, control is *always* vectored to the *same* service routine. (Several of the popular microcomputers have this simple structure.)

(a) If control is always passed to a common service routine, how can that routine determine the device or devices requesting service?

(b) Assuming that the question in part (a) has been answered, how can the common service routine pass control to a routine that will then service the interrupting device?

(c) Assuming satisfactory answers to the questions in parts (a) and (b), how can a *priority* scheme be imposed upon the devices? This is by no means a trivial task, but it can be done through programming. (*Suggestion:* The

```
                000320              DEVA = 320
                000364              DEVB = 364
001000          000230    START:    SPL    0
001002          012767              MOV    #INTA,DEVA
                002240'
                000320
001010          012767              MOV    #200,DEVA+2
                000200
                000322
001016          012767              MOV    #INTB,DEVB
                002406'
                000364
001024          012767              MOV    #240,DEVB+2
                000240
                000366
001032          005001              CLR    R1

                          <--- (device A interrupt occurs)

001034          005201              INC    R1
001036          000000              HALT
                                    .
                                    .
                                    .
002240          005201    INTA:     INC    R1

                          <--- (device B interrupt occurs)

002242          000002              RTI
                                    .
                                    .
002406          005201    INTB:     INC    R1
002410          000002              RTI
                                    .
                                    .
```

Figure 12.10.2

common service routine might keep track of which device service routine, if any, is currently executing.)

This situation can be partially emulated on the PDP-11, as follows: Consider three devices, all of which interrupt at level 4. Put the address of the *common* service routine in the first word of the interrupt vector for *each* device.

12.9.1. State how the keyboard could be handled on a noninterrupt basis by polling the device, that is, by constantly testing the keyboard status register. What are reasonable conditions under which the polling would cease?

12.9.2. The first example of Sec. 12.9 had the feature that a carriage return was detected as a special case and the programming inserted a line feed to provide paper movement. Add sufficient program instructions to the service routine to deal with one or more successive RUBOUT (or DELETE) characters (ASCII code = 177).

12.9.3. Look up the concept of *terminal fill count* and adjust the two programs of Sec. 12.9 accordingly.

12.9.4. Even though the ASCII code for a character requires only 7 bits, some terminal controllers will always assert bit 7 in the data register. Thus, for example, the code for the character A will appear in the data register as 301, rather than the expected 101. How can this easily be coped with, regardless of whether the controller asserts bit 7 or not?

12.9.5. Transmission of 8-bit data between a terminal and its controller's data register can take place in two ways. In one, called **parallel transmission**, the 8 data bits are directly connected to the data register through 8 lines, one for each bit. In the other, called **serial transmission**, a byte in one device is disassembled into its separate bits, and each bit is transmitted to the other device, where it is reassembled into an 8-bit byte, referred to as **serialization** and **deserialization** respectively. Locate an appropriate reference and determine the meanings of the following terms:

(a) mark **(b)** space **(c)** start bit **(d)** stop bit **(e)** parity **(f)** baud rate.

12.9.6. If a PDP-11 contains a line printer as a high-speed output device, the printer will have to be dealt with by the system software. In the appropriate manual, look up the details of line printer operation and write service routines to handle this device on an interrupt and noninterrupt basis.

12.9.7. In light of our experience with computer hardware interrupts, review the real-life scenes of Sec. 12.2. In particular, state which hardware concepts are involved in each of these—interrupts, stacking of c(PSW) and c(PC), priorities, and so on.

12.9.8. Write a program that prints a message containing 10 or so characters on the console printer on an interrupt basis. The clock is also interrupting, and just as printing begins, the clock time is observed. When printing is completed, the clock time is again observed, and the elapsed time (in some suitable units) is printed.

13

Macroinstructions and Conditional Assemblies

13.1 INTRODUCTION

Consider the following simple problem: Suppose we have a string of ASCII characters located in a block of contiguous bytes, the first of which is in the byte whose symbolic address is TEXT. We wish to find the location (address) of the *first* occurrence in the string of a specific character, for instance, X. The reader should have no difficulty in establishing that the program segment of Fig. 13.1.1 will do the job.

Such a task is by no means unusual, for programs that request information from a user may have to scan the text that the user entered for certain key characters in order to interpret the response. In fact, such string scanning would quite likely occur with sufficient frequency that we would scarcely code this program segment in line as shown in Fig. 13.1.1. Rather, we would write a short subroutine to do this job. An example of such a subroutine is given in Fig. 13.1.2; we assume that the ASCII code for the character being searched for is in R∅ and that PC is the subroutine transfer register. We have also made the following improvement over the program segment shown in Fig. 13.1.1: Assuming that the text string ends in a NUL (ASCII code = 000), we can detect the error that occurs when the specified character is *not* present in the string. In that case, we set the carry bit in the PSW. If the character *is* found, we clear the carry bit. Thus upon return from the subroutine, the main portion of the program can execute

BCS   ERROR

to deal with the fact that an expected string character was not found. (Setting or clearing the carry bit is a most convenient and efficient way to pass yes-no-type information between programming modules. Provided that we exercise some care we may also use the other PSW condition code bits in a similar fashion.)

```
        MOVB    #'X,R0          ;PUT CHAR CODE IN R0
        MOV     #TEXT,R1        ;TEXT ADDR IN R1
LOOP:   CMPB    R0,(R1)+        ;CHARACTER SOUGHT?
        BNE     LOOP            ;NO -- TRY AGAIN
        DEC     R1              ;YES -- ADJUST POINTER
        ......                  ;(CONTINUATION
                                ; OF PROGRAM)
```

Figure 13.1.1

```
GETCHR: MOV     #TEXT,R1        ;TEXT ADDR IN R1
LOOP:   TSTB    (R1)            ;CHECK FOR END-OF-TEXT
        BEQ     EOT             ;END-OF-TEXT -- ERROR
        CMPB    R0,(R1)+        ;CHARACTER SOUGHT?
        BNE     LOOP            ;NO -- TRY AGAIN
        DEC     R1              ;YES -- ADJUST POINTER
        CLC                     ;SET 'NO ERROR' FLAG
        BR      DONE            ; AND SKIP AROUND
EOT:    SEC                     ;ERROR -- SET FLAG
DONE:   RTS     PC              ;RETURN
```

Figure 13.1.2

Suppose next that we are dealing with a program in which it is frequently necessary to push three registers on the stack—for example, R1, R3, and R5—to save their contents so that they might be used temporarily for other purposes. (Presumably we would also want to restore them after they were no longer needed.) Again, since we would not want to include these three pushes directly in line every time they were needed, we might be inclined to write a subroutine such as that shown in Fig. 13.1.3. But a moment's reflection will reveal that this

```
SAVE:   MOV     R1,-(SP)        ;SAVE
        MOV     R3,-(SP)        ; THREE
        MOV     R5,-(SP)        ; REGISTERS
        RTS     PC              ; AND RETURN
```

Figure 13.1.3

routine will not do the job. While the RTS   PC will pop the top of the stack into the PC, the top of the stack is now c(R5), *not* the value of the PC at the time the corresponding JSR   PC,SAVE was executed. (The situation can actually be salvaged, and a suggestion in that direction will be found in the exercises.) Thus it would seem that we have little choice but to code these three push instructions in line each time they are required.

13.2 MACROINSTRUCTIONS

We should probably quickly tire of having to insert these same instructions over and over again in a program, so we might consider this mundane chore a likely task for the assembling clerk. (We realize that our clerk has long since been replaced by the PDP-11 assembler, but for the moment it will be useful to bring him back onto the scene.) Thus, in submitting this program to the clerk for assembly, we might include the following note: In this program we make numerous references to the term SAVE, which is neither an instruction mnemonic nor one of your directives. Each time you see the word SAVE, insert in the program the following instructions:

```
MOV   R1,-(SP)
MOV   R3,-(SP)
MOV   R5,-(SP)
```

There is no reason why the clerk cannot handle this job, although he must be careful to avoid a few problems that we shall discuss shortly.

We have created here, with the term SAVE and our directions to the assembling clerk, a kind of "superinstruction," a package of PDP-11 instructions that has been *named*, in particular, named SAVE. Such a superinstruction is called a **macroinstruction**. The set of instructions that makes up the macroinstruction is called the **macroinstruction definition**, or **macro definition**, for short. Thus in the present case, the name of the macroinstruction is SAVE, and its definition is given by the three MOV instructions shown above. When the clerk replaces the macroinstruction by its definition, that is, replaces the reference to SAVE by the three MOV instructions and places these in the source code, he is said to be **expanding** the macroinstruction. And finally, when the programmer makes reference to the macroinstruction SAVE in the source program, he or she is said to **invoke**, or **call**, the macroinstruction.

Since the macroinstruction SAVE may be invoked numerous times in a program, we may decide that even though the clerk would have to expand it, we do not choose to see the expanded code on the listing of the source program. In other cases, it may be useful to see the expansion. Thus we should have some means of directing the clerk to list these expansions or to suppress such listings. For example, if the source code

```
SAVE
INC   R2
```

was assembled at location 002404 for instance, and we chose to see the listings of the macro expansions, the clerk should produce the following:

002404		SAVE	
002404	010146	MOV	R1,-(SP)
002406	010346	MOV	R3,-(SP)
002410	010546	MOV	R5,-(SP)
002412	005202	INC	R2

On the other hand, if we had specified that this expansion not be listed, we should see

002404		SAVE
002412	005202	INC R2

Of course the clerk would have placed the machine code for the three MOV instructions in the object file at locations 002404, 002406, and 002410, regardless of whether he actually wrote them on the listing or not.

The process that the clerk goes through in expanding an instance of this macroinstruction is quite simple, but it is worth looking at in some detail. Recall that in assembling a program, the clerk (or assembler) makes two passes through the source code. On the first of these, he determines the addresses of the various instructions by means of the location assignment counter and establishes values for the symbolic addresses that he encounters. When on this first pass he comes across the pseudomnemonic SAVE, he realizes that it *may* refer to a special programmer-defined macroinstruction. Thus he examines the current macrodefinitions—there may well be more than one such definition— and locates one named SAVE. He then writes down the definition as specified, paying no attention to what might be the *meaning* of what he is writing. Finally, he continues the first-pass assembly process by examining the lines of source code that he has just written down in place of SAVE, assigns addresses to the instructions and values to the symbols, and so forth. He then completes the translation process on the second pass.

13.3 THE PDP-11 MACROINSTRUCTION ASSEMBLER

Most commercially supplied assemblers can handle macroinstructions just like our clerk, and the PDP-11 assembler is no exception. Figure 13.3.1 is the assembler's listing of a program segment in which the macroinstruction SAVE is defined and then invoked. Line 1, .LIST   ME, is an assembler directive that we have used to request a *LIST*ing of the *M*acro *E*xpansion. Note that we are not referring to the listing of the macro *definition*, which is also listed, but rather to the listing of the instructions that make up the macroinstruction each time the

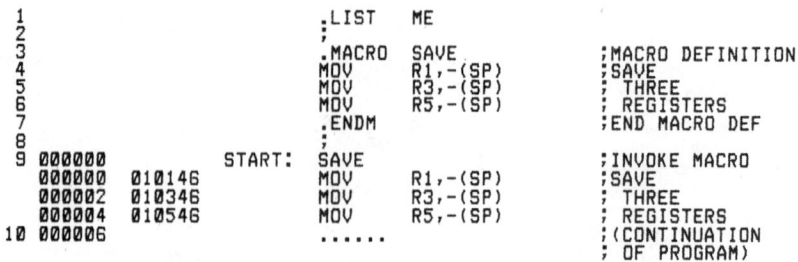

Figure 13.3.1

macroinstruction is *invoked*. In line 3 the directive .MACRO informs the assembler that a macro definition follows, and that the name of this macro-instruction is SAVE. Lines 4, 5, and 6 are, of course, the definition of SAVE. Line 7, .ENDM, is another assembler directive, this time informing the assembler that it has come to the *END* of the *M*acro definition. Observe that no addresses or object code has been assigned to these instructions, as expected—lines 3 through 7 are, after all, simply a *definition* of the macroinstruction, and that macroinstruction has not yet been invoked. It is useful to view this definition as a *reference* statement that the assembler simply puts in a table of macro-instruction definitions under the name SAVE. At line 9 the macroinstruction is actually invoked. The three lines of source code are listed, including comments, along with their addresses and object code. These lines are listed as a result of the .LIST   ME directive at line 1. If instead .NLIST   ME—do *N*ot *LIST M*acro *E*xpansions—had been used, these three lines would not be shown, although of course the corresponding machine code would have been placed in the object file.

13.4 SOME WORDS OF CAUTION

Figure 13.4.1 is the listing of a program segment in which the macro SAVE is defined *after* it is invoked for the first time. Apparently all is well. Even though the macro itself is not defined until lines 5 through 9, because of the reference to SAVE at line 3, the assembler inserted the three MOV instructions, with their proper machine code, in the expected locations—000000, 000002, and 000004. The assembler also correctly located the CLR   R4 instruction at 000006. We might conclude from this example that just *where* in the source program a macro is defined is immaterial. But a moment's thought about the process the assembler (or assembling clerk) must go through to handle the macro call will lead us to conclude just the opposite—that the assembler could *not* have properly handled this situation. To resolve this dilemma and gain some insights into

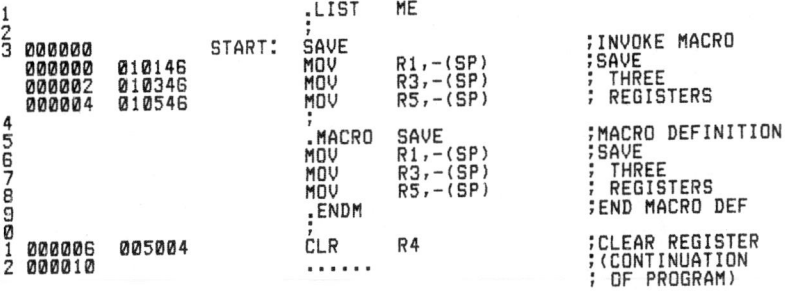

Figure 13.4.1

what the assembler has actually done here, we modify this program segment simply by placing the label ADDR on the **CLR   R4** instruction (Fig. 13.4.2).

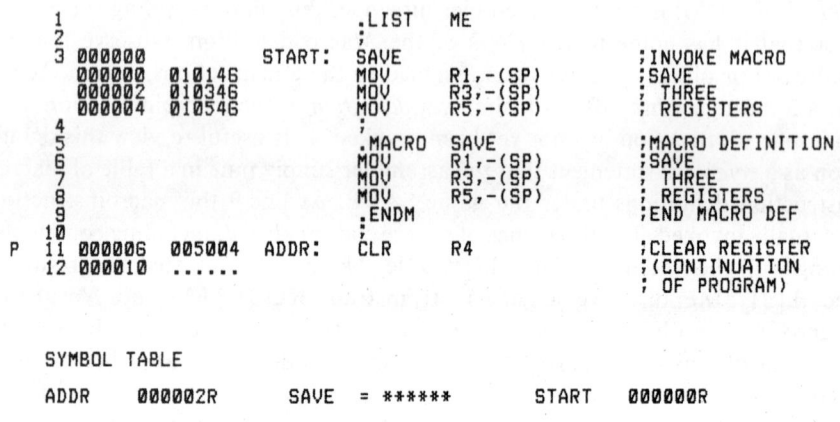

```
 1                           .LIST   ME
 2                           ;
 3  000000          START:   SAVE                    ;INVOKE MACRO
    000000  010146            MOV     R1,-(SP)        ;SAVE
    000002  010346            MOV     R3,-(SP)        ; THREE
    000004  010546            MOV     R5,-(SP)        ; REGISTERS
 4                           ;
 5                           .MACRO  SAVE            ;MACRO DEFINITION
 6                            MOV     R1,-(SP)        ;SAVE
 7                            MOV     R3,-(SP)        ; THREE
 8                            MOV     R5,-(SP)        ; REGISTERS
 9                           .ENDM                   ;END MACRO DEF
10                           ;
P11  000006  005004  ADDR:   CLR     R4              ;CLEAR REGISTER
12  000010  ......                                   ;(CONTINUATION
                                                     ; OF PROGRAM)


SYMBOL TABLE

ADDR    000002R      SAVE  = ******      START   000000R
```

Figure 13.4.2

Again the macro call at line 3 seems to have been handled properly, but there are three peculiarities. First, line 11, which makes reference to the label ADDR, has been flagged with the letter P. This stands for a **phase error**, a term with which we shall deal presently. Next notice that in the program listing, ADDR has the value 000006, while in the symbol table its value is given as 000002. Finally, the symbol table contains the *symbol* SAVE, which is evidently undefined, as the six asterisks in the value field indicate. A careful examination of the assembler's action on the first *and* second passes will resolve all three of these anomalies.

On its first pass through the source code, the assembler encounters (at line 3) the word SAVE. It recognizes that this is not a PDP-11 assembler mnemonic, nor is it an assembler directive. A look at its table of macroinstruction definitions reveals that there are no such definitions, and thus the assembler concludes that SAVE is not a macro name. The only way the assembler can resolve this reference to SAVE is by assuming that SAVE *must* be a symbolic address that has not yet been encountered—a forward reference—and that what the programmer intended by default was

.WORD   SAVE

Thus the assembler puts SAVE in its symbol table with the notation ******, meaning that the value of SAVE is not yet known. Since in fact SAVE is *never* defined in this program segment, we have now accounted for the appearance of SAVE in the symbol table with the "value" ******. Assuming that this .WORD is intended here, the assembler will move its location assignment counter up to 000002 to allow for the as yet unknown .WORD and continue scanning the lines of source code.

The assembler next encounters line 5, the definition of the macro SAVE. The assembler puts away the source code between lines 5 and 9 for future reference, and next sees the line

ADDR: CLR   R4

It now comes upon the definition of the symbol ADDR. It puts that symbol in its symbol table, and gives it the value corresponding to the current value of the location assignment counter, namely, 000002. This accounts for that value's showing up in the symbol table. The assembler now completes its first pass on the remainder of the source program.

As the assembler begins its second pass through the source code, it again encounters the word SAVE. Here we must pay particular attention to the *order* in which the assembler attempts to resolve this reference. Again it realizes that this is neither a mnemonic nor a directive, and we might be inclined to think that it would go immediately to its symbol table for the value of SAVE. However, when the assembler encounters a construction that could be *either* a symbol reference or a macro call, it searches its table of macro definitions *first*. In so doing, it now *does* find the definition of the macroinstruction SAVE. It inserts the code for the macroinstruction and then processes that code—that is, the assembler generates the machine code for each of the three MOV instructions, being careful to advance its location assignment counter by 2 for each instruction. Thus upon the assembler's completion of its handling of the macro SAVE, its location assignment counter has the value 000006, and it is ready to assemble the next line of source code, namely, the INC R4 instruction, labeled ADDR. At this point the assembler does a little checking and uncovers a problem. Its location assignment counter is 000006, which should then be the value of the symbol ADDR. But the value as specified in the symbol table is 000002. Somehow (and we know why, of course) the value to be assigned to ADDR has *gotten out of phase* between the two assembly passes. There is no hope of repairing the situation, and the assembler flags this line with a phase error.

The difficulty described here has clearly resulted from our invoking a macro prior to its definition. This will almost always cause problems, and the reader is cautioned to make certain that macros are defined before they are called. Most programmers tend to place all macroinstruction definitions at the very beginning of the source program for easy reference (by the programmer, not the assembler), and while this is considered good programming practice, it is not necessary—as long as the assembler has the definition *prior to* any reference to the macro, all will be well.

As a second example of things that can go wrong, consider a program that uses the *same name* for a symbol and a macroinstruction. The program of Fig. 13.4.3 illustrates the problem. It reads 16_{10} numbers (in decimal) and then invokes a subroutine, named SORT, to put these numbers in (some unspecified) order. The routine SORT needs to know the address of the first number and

```
  1                                .LIST   ME
  2                                ;
  3                                .MACRO  SAVE             ;MACRO DEFINITION
  4                                MOV     R1,-(SP)         ;SAVE
  5                                MOV     R3,-(SP)         ;  THREE
  6                                MOV     R5,-(SP)         ;  REGISTERS
  7                                .ENDM                    ;END MACRO DEF
  8                                ;
  9 000000            SAVE:        .BLKW   20               ;NUMBERS TO BE SORTED
 10                                ;
 11 000040            START:       $IN.DEC #SAVE,#20        ;READ 16 NUMBERS
 12 000074                         SAVE                     ;INVOKE MACRO
    000074   010146                MOV     R1,-(SP)         ;SAVE
    000076   010346                MOV     R3,-(SP)         ;  THREE
    000100   010546                MOV     R5,-(SP)         ;  REGISTERS
 13 000102   004567                JSR     R5,SORT          ;SORT THE NUMBERS
             000210
 14 000106                         SAVE                     ;PARAMETERS FOR
    000106   010146                MOV     R1,-(SP)         ;SAVE
    000110   010346                MOV     R3,-(SP)         ;  THREE
    000112   010546                MOV     R5,-(SP)         ;  REGISTERS
 15 000114   000020                20                       ;  SUBROUTINE
 16 000116   ......                                         ;(CONTINUATION
                                                            ;  OF PROGRAM)
```

Figure 13.4.3

the count of numbers, and these two parameters are passed to the subroutine by placing them in .WORDs immediately following the subroutine call. We make two unfortunate choices here. First, the name we give to the block of storage that holds the numbers (SAVE) is also the name of a macroinstruction defined in the program. Second, we rely on the assembler to default SAVE to .WORD SAVE.

Line 12 of the listing is a conscious call to the macro SAVE, that is, we want to save the three registers at this point. The source code at lines 13, 14, and 15 is

```
JSR  R5,SORT
SAVE
20
```

What we intend here, of course, is that SAVE and 20 are to be .WORDs, parameters needed by the routine SORT. However, the assembler, upon encountering SAVE (without the .WORD) has expanded the *macro* SAVE, since it has again come upon a construction that *could* be a macro call and thus has searched its table of macro definitions *before* searching its symbol table. The program is now clearly in serious trouble.

This problem could have been avoided if we had explicitly used .WORD SAVE instead of SAVE. Since .WORD SAVE is a construction that cannot be a macro call, the assembler will search its symbol table immediately for the value of SAVE. As we see from Fig. 13.4.4, the use of .WORD does in fact get us out of this difficulty. But once again the reader should recognize a caution here—the programmer who uses the same name for a symbol and a macro-instruction will very likely get what he deserves.

```
 1                          .LIST   ME
 2                          ;
 3                          .MACRO  SAVE            ;MACRO DEFINITION
 4                          MOV     R1,-(SP)        ;SAVE
 5                          MOV     R3,-(SP)        ;  THREE
 6                          MOV     R5,-(SP)        ;  REGISTERS
 7                          .ENDM                   ;END MACRO DEF
 8                          ;
 9 000000          SAVE:    .BLKW   20              ;NUMBERS TO BE SORTED
10                          ;
11 000040          START:   $IN.DEC #SAVE,#20       ;READ 16 NUMBERS
12 000074                   SAVE                    ;INVOKE MACRO
   000074  010146           MOV     R1,-(SP)        ;SAVE
   000076  010346           MOV     R3,-(SP)        ;  THREE
   000100  010546           MOV     R5,-(SP)        ;  REGISTERS
13 000102  004567           JSR     R5,SORT         ;SORT THE NUMBERS
           000204
14 000106  000000'           .WORD  SAVE            ;PARAMETERS FOR
15 000110  000020           .WORD   20              ;  SUBROUTINE
16 000112  ......                                   ;(CONTINUATION
                                                    ;  OF PROGRAM)
```

Figure 13.4.4

13.5 PASSING ARGUMENTS TO A MACROINSTRUCTION

The macroinstruction SAVE of the preceding four sections has done what it was designed to accomplish, but one of its deficiencies is that while it saves three registers on the stack, it can be used to save *only* the specific registers R1, R3, and R5. If in the course of a program we need to save R1, R2, and R4, we could not use the macro SAVE to do so. We would either have to code the appropriate instructions in line or possibly write a second macroinstruction to deal with this new situation.

Evidently we need a variable macroinstruction definition, one that saves *unspecified* registers. We could then specify the registers to be saved whenever the macro was called. That is, we need a definition like

MOV   RA,-(SP)
MOV   RB,-(SP)
MOV   RC,-(SP)

in which we give specific values to the letters A, B, and C—for example, A = 1, B = 2, and C = 4—each time the macro is invoked. It will be necessary to inform our clerk (or the assembler) that the letters A, B, and C are **dummy arguments** that are to be replaced by **real arguments** that will be specified each time the macro is invoked. We can accomplish this quite simply in the macro-instruction's "naming" statement. For example,

.MACRO   SAVE   A,B,C

will tell the assembler that the macro whose definition follows is named SAVE, and that A, B, and C are dummy arguments that are to be replaced by real arguments when the macro is called. The modified macroinstruction definition now looks like

```
        .MACRO   SAVE   A,B,C
        MOV   RA,-(SP)
        MOV   RB,-(SP)
        MOV   RC,-(SP)
        .ENDM
```

Now when we invoke the macro with the statement SAVE   1,2,4, for example, we shall expect the assembler to expand the macroinstruction as defined above and then to make the specified replacements, so the finished product will be

```
        MOV   R1,-(SP)
        MOV   R2,-(SP)
        MOV   R4,-(SP)
```

How should the assembler handle a macro call such as SAVE   1,2,4? The naming statement in the macro definition,

```
        .MACRO     SAVE   A,B,C
```

is called the **macroinstruction prototype statement**, and it serves a number of purposes. First, of course, it names the macroinstruction. Second, it implies that each time this macro is invoked, three real arguments will be supplied after the macro name, separated by commas. (Actually, spaces will also do as separators.) Finally, it indicates—by *naming* the dummy arguments A, B, and C— which letters in the definition of the macroinstruction are to be replaced by the real arguments. Notice that the replacement is *positional*—SAVE   1,2,4 will give A the value 1, B the value 2, and C the value 4, whereas SAVE   2,1,4 will yield A = 2, B = 1, and C = 4. With this background, we are ready to define and invoke this macro. As the listing of Fig. 13.5.1. indicates the results are far from satisfactory.

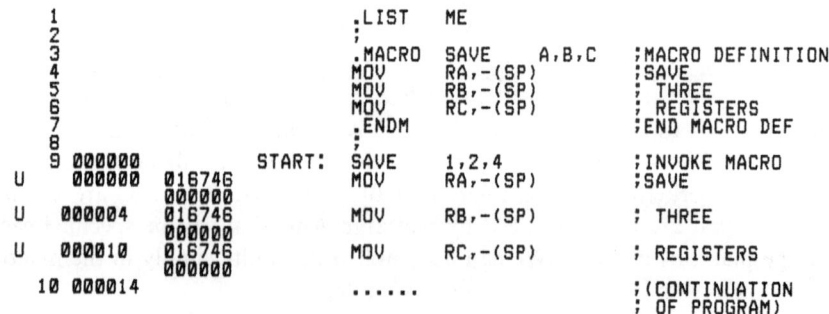

Figure 13.5.1

The U's flagged in the left margin indicate that some symbols are un- defined. To see why, we examine in detail the action taken by the assembler in expanding the macro. Evidently the assembler found no difficulties with the macro prototype at line 3 or with the definition in lines 4 to 6. When the macro was invoked at line 9, the assembler took the following action: It looked in its table of macro definitions, found the definition of SAVE, and expanded it as follows:

```
MOV   RA,-(SP)
MOV   RB,-(SP)
MOV   RC,-(SP)
```

Since the macro prototype indicates three dummy arguments, and since the macro call also specified three real arguments, the assembler assigned the values A = 1, B = 2, and C = 4. Now the assembler goes through the source code it has just generated and is prepared to make replacements for A, B, and C as specified. That is, it is to replace each instance of A by 1, each B by 2, and each C by 4. However, it finds *no instance* of A. To be sure, it sees the term RA, but it does not treat the A part of that term as an instance of A. Rather, it takes RA to be an indivisible term and makes no replacement. In a similar fashion, it makes no replacements in RB and RC. Now it is clear why these symbols have been flagged as undefined—the assembler thinks RA, RB, and RC are *symbols* of the program, but it can find no definition of them.

As disappointed as we might be with the assembler's inability to handle what appears to be a simple task, our disappointment should be tempered with a certain amount of gratitude. For suppose the assembler *had* dealt with this macro expansion as we had desired. To see what the disastrous consequences might be, consider the following simple macroinstruction that merely pops the top of the stack into a specified register. (Of course, this one-line macro would normally just be coded in line, not written as a macro.)

```
.MACRO   POP   P
MOV   (SP)+,RP
.ENDM
```

If the assembler had expanded the preceding example "correctly," then when the macro POP was invoked with argument 3—POP 3, for instance—the expansion would be

```
MOV   (S3)+,R3
```

which is obviously nonsense and would be flagged with an error.

There are two ways to cope with the present problem, one of which we defer until the next section. A straightforward means of coaxing the assembler into making the desired replacement involves redefining the macro.

```
.MACRO   SAVE   A,B,C
MOV   A,-(SP)
MOV   B,-(SP)
MOV   C,-(SP)
.ENDM
```

Then instead of invoking the macro as SAVE 1,2,4, we call it by SAVE R1,R2,R4. When the macro is expanded, the source code shown above is generated, and then the assembler makes the requested replacements. This time it *does* find an occurrence of the term A and replaces it with its value, namely R1. In a similar fashion, it deals with B and C as expected (Fig. 13.5.2).

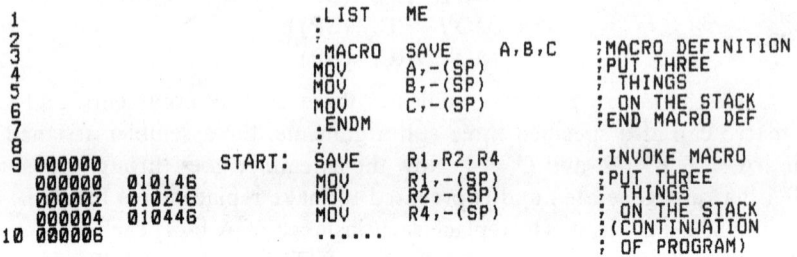

Figure 13.5.2

Actually this is a far more general-purpose macroinstruction than we originally intended. For not only will it put the contents of three specified registers on the stack, it will put *anything* on the stack. For example, if we wish to save R1 and R5, and also the contents of the memory location whose symbolic address is ADDR, we can invoke the macro as shown in Fig. 13.5.3. In a similar fashion we could save these two registers and also stack the *address* ADDR, rather than the contents of that location (Fig. 13.5.4).

Passing arguments to a macroinstruction is a far more powerful concept than perhaps the reader realizes. Almost *anything* can be passed as an argument because of the way the assembler deals with these arguments. Let us review the macro expansion process. When the assembler encounters a reference to a macro, it finds the macro name in the macro definition table and simply replaces the call with the definition. The assembler does so by inserting the source lines— strings of ASCII-coded character—that make up the definition. Next it searches

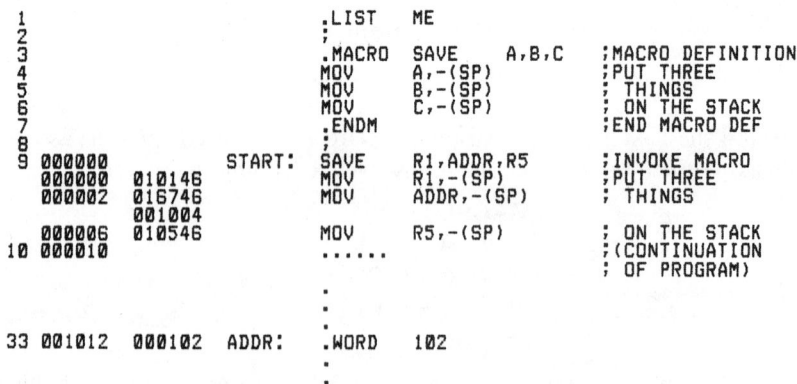

Figure 13.5.3

```
1                          .LIST   ME
2                          ;
3                          .MACRO  SAVE      A,B,C    ;MACRO DEFINITICN
4                          MOV     A,-(SP)            ;PUT THREE
5                          MOV     B,-(SP)            ; THINGS
6                          MOV     C,-(SP)            ; ON THE STACK
7                          .ENDM                      ;END MACRO DEF
8                          ;
9  000000         START:   SAVE    R1,#ADDR,R5        ;INVOKE MACRO
   000000  010146          MOV     R1,-(SP)           ;PUT THREE
   000002  012746          MOV     #ADDR,-(SP)        ; THINGS
           001012
   000006  010546          MOV     R5,-(SP)           ; ON THE STACK
10 000010                  ......                     ;(CONTINUATION
                                                      ; OF PROGRAM)
                                  .
                                  .
                                  .
33 001012  000102  ADDR:   .WORD   102
                                  .
                                  .
```

Figure 13.5.4

for the dummy arguments and when it finds them, replaces them with their real argument counterparts, which again are just strings of ASCII characters. Finally, the assembler returns to the beginning of the macro expansion and starts its first-pass processing on this code. To give some indication of the power of this concept, we show next a macro that passes an entire PDP-11 instruction mnemonic as an argument. In this way we can customize macroinstructions for a variety of purposes (Fig. 13.5.5). (We do not claim any particular merit for this macro except as an illustrative example.) Notice that the assembler has properly replaced the dummy argument INS with SEC and has correctly generated the machine code for the set-carry-bit instruction.

```
1                          .LIST   ME
2                          ;
3                          .MACRO  CUSTOM  REG,INS    ;MACRO DEFINITION
4                          CLR     REG                ;CLEAR REGISTER
5                          INS                         ;(CUSTOM INSTRUCTION)
6                          .ENDM
7                          ;
8  000000         START:   CUSTOM  R2,SEC             ;INVOKE MACRO
   000000  005002          CLR     R2                 ;CLEAR REGISTER
   000002  000261          SEC                         ;(CUSTOM INSTRUCTION)
9  000004                  ......                     ;(CONTINUATION
                                                      ; OF PROGRAM)
```

Figure 13.5.5

We look at another program segment in which the same macro CUSTOM is invoked, but this time the argument MOV   #3,R4 is passed to it in place of the dummy argument INS (Fig. 13.5.6). As we see, things have gone badly. The problem arises from the assembler's interpretation of MOV   #3,R4 as *three* real arguments, namely MOV, #3, and R4. Thus as far as the assembler is concerned, REG is to be replaced by the string R2, INS is to be replaced by the string MOV, and #3 and R4 are unneeded arguments. (Recall that the blanks between MOV and #3 are considered by the assembler as valid separat-

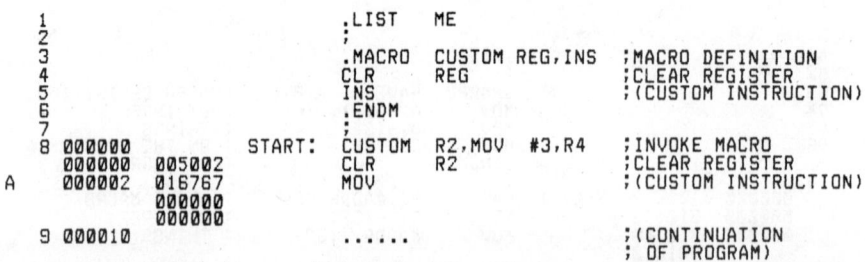

```
1                          .LIST   ME
2                          ;
3                          .MACRO  CUSTOM REG,INS   ;MACRO DEFINITION
4                          CLR     REG              ;CLEAR REGISTER
5                          INS                      ;(CUSTOM INSTRUCTION)
6                          .ENDM
7                          ;
8  000000        START:    CUSTOM  R2,MOV  #3,R4    ;INVOKE MACRO
   000000  005002           CLR     R2             ;CLEAR REGISTER
A  000002  016767           MOV                     ;(CUSTOM INSTRUCTION)
           000000
           000000
9  000010                   ......                  ;(CONTINUATION
                                                    ; OF PROGRAM)
```

Figure 13.5.6

ing characters in the argument list.) Evidently we need some means of telling the assembler to treat MOV #3,R4 as a *single* real argument to be substituted for the dummy argument INS. We do this by enclosing the string in angle brackets (⟨and⟩), as shown in Fig. 13.5.7.

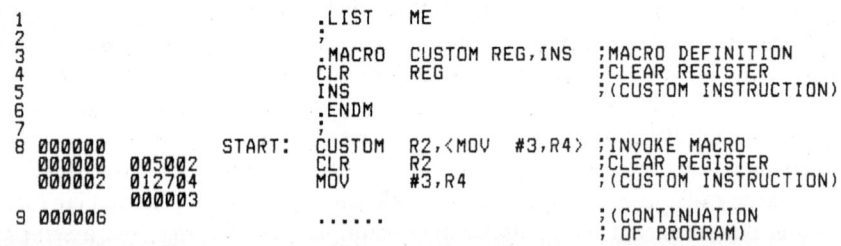

```
1                          .LIST   ME
2                          ;
3                          .MACRO  CUSTOM REG,INS   ;MACRO DEFINITION
4                          CLR     REG              ;CLEAR REGISTER
5                          INS                      ;(CUSTOM INSTRUCTION)
6                          .ENDM
7                          ;
8  000000        START:    CUSTOM  R2,⟨MOV  #3,R4⟩  ;INVOKE MACRO
   000000  005002           CLR     R2             ;CLEAR REGISTER
   000002  012704           MOV     #3,R4          ;(CUSTOM INSTRUCTION)
           000003
9  000006                   ......                  ;(CONTINUATION
                                                    ; OF PROGRAM)
```

Figure 13.5.7

We close this section with a final look at the assembler's process of replacing dummy arguments with real arguments. Recall the definition of our ultimately successful macroinstruction SAVE.

```
.MACRO  SAVE  A,B,C
MOV   A,-(SP)          ;PUT THREE
MOV   B,-(SP)          ; THINGS
MOV   C,-(SP)          ; ON THE STACK
.ENDM
```

Suppose we had changed the *comments* in these lines of source code to read

```
;PUT A
; FEW THINGS
; ON THE STACK
```

Observe what happens when the macro of Fig. 13.5.8 is invoked. In the first line of the expansion of the macro, the assembler correctly replaced the term A with the string R1, to yield

```
MOV   R1,-(SP)
```

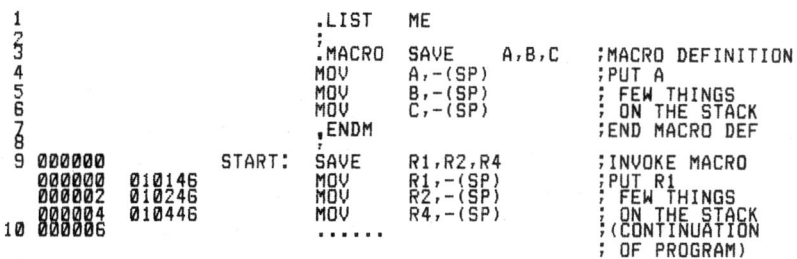

```
 1                          .LIST   ME
 2                          ;
 3                          ;MACRO  SAVE     A,B,C    ;MACRO DEFINITION
 4                          MOV     A,-(SP)           ;PUT A
 5                          MOV     B,-(SP)           ; FEW THINGS
 6                          MOV     C,-(SP)           ; ON THE STACK
 7                          .ENDM                     ;END MACRO DEF
 8                          ;
 9   000000        START:   SAVE     R1,R2,R4         ;INVOKE MACRO
     000000  010146         MOV     R1,-(SP)          ;PUT R1
     000002  010246         MOV     R2,-(SP)          ; FEW THINGS
     000004  010446         MOV     R4,-(SP)          ; ON THE STACK
10   000006                 ......                    ;(CONTINUATION
                                                      ; OF PROGRAM)
```

Figure 13.5.8

But it did not stop there; it also replaced the A in the *comment* with the string R1, making the comment

;PUT   R1

While this may be somewhat amusing and surely does no harm in this instance, it does point out just how literally the assembler treats this task. We must be aware of the assembler's slavish approach to this job in order to avoid unexpected problems.

13.6 PASSING MACROINSTRUCTION ARGUMENTS BY CONCATENATION

Recall one of our failures early in the last section. We included in a macro definition the "instruction"

MOV   RA,-(SP)

and then upon invoking the macro, we passed the real argument 1 in place of the dummy argument A. Of course the A was not replaced with the 1, and by now we probably consider these early attempts as somewhat simplistic. Nonetheless we can salvage something here.

In examining what went wrong, we decided that the assembler did not treat the A in RA as a recognizable instance of the character A; rather, it treated RA as a single, indivisible term. We need some scheme to split the A off from the R. We could try

R,A

or

R A

but the assembler would simply generate

R,1

and

R 1

respectively, and neither of these would do what we desire. We require some punctuation that will notify the assembler that the term in question (in our case, the A) *is* a separate entity and that will tell the assembler to *remove the punctuation* when making the replacement. The PDP-11 assembler uses the apostrophe for this purpose, and the replacement process in this case is called **concatenation** because the real argument string is chained onto whatever else is in the source code. An example will clarify this idea.

Consider a macroinstruction that increments the *high-order* byte of a specified register. (Recall that the high-order byte of a register cannot be referred to directly.)

```
.MACRO    INCHIGH   X
SWAB  R'X
INCB  R'X
SWAB  R'X
.ENDM
```

When the macro is invoked, INCHIGH 3, for example, each instance of the term X will be replaced with the real argument 3, and the 3 will be concatenated onto the preceding R, giving as the macro expansion

```
SWAB    R3
INCB    R3
SWAB    R3
```

This is precisely the action in which we are interested. We can now successfully write the principal example of the preceding section as listed in Fig. 13.6.1.

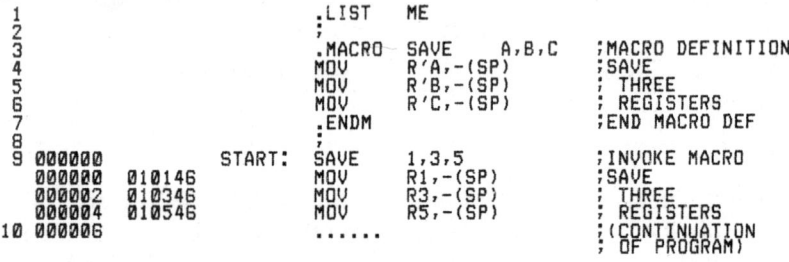

Figure 13.6.1

As another example, consider a program in which we desire to have the ASCII code for a particular character in R∅. (Once again, the required instruction would doubtless be coded in line rather than written as a macroinstruction, but this simple example will illustrate one of the features of concatenation.) We write a macroinstruction to do this job that contains only one line of instruction.

```
.MACRO   SETCODE   CHAR
MOVB   #'CHAR,R∅
.ENDM
```

In the line that moves the ASCII code for the character into R∅ we are taking advantage of the assembler apostrophe construction to which the assembler responds by generating the ASCII code for the specified character. When we invoke this macro to place the code for the character H in R∅ we encounter some difficulties as we see from Fig. 13.6.2. The problem is clear. Instead of merely substituting an H for the dummy variable CHAR, the assembler performed a *concatenation* of the H, and in the process swept off the apostrophe. To resolve the dilemma, we need to look more closely at how the assembler deals with the apostrophe construction.

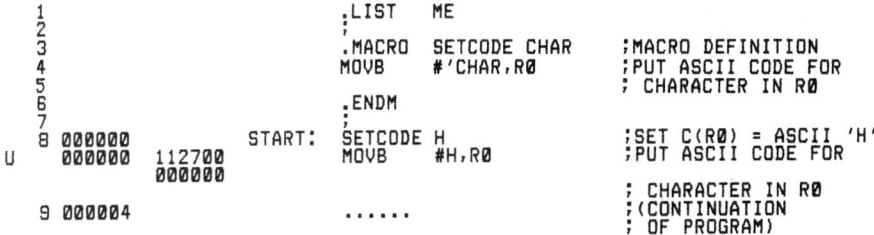

Figure 13.6.2

When, in the process of expanding a macro definition, the assembler encounters an apostrophe *immediately preceding* a dummy argument, it removes that apostrophe and replaces the dummy argument with the real argument corresponding to it. If, in addition, the dummy argument is *followed by* an apostrophe, the assembler removes that second apostrophe also. Thus in making replacements, the assembler removes the apostrophe or apostrophes *immediately preceding or immediately succeeding* the dummy variable to be replaced, but *only those* apostrophes. The solution to our present problem is now clear. Instead of MOVB   #'CHAR,R∅ we use a double apostrophe, MOVB   #''CHAR,R∅. When the macro is expanded, the apostrophe immediately preceding the dummy variable CHAR will cause concatenation but will also be removed, leaving one apostrophe to indicate the generation of the ASCII code for the specified character. The listing of Fig. 13.6.3, the repaired version of the program segment, shows that the modification handles the problem.

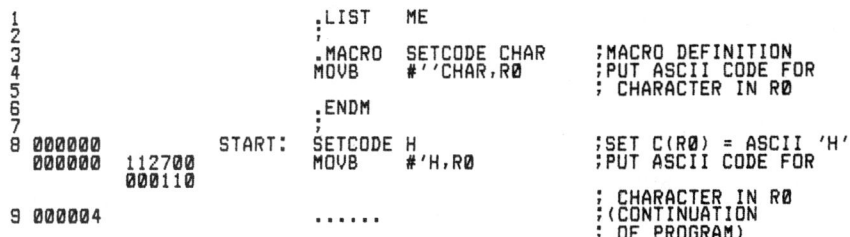

Figure 13.6.3

13.7 LOCAL SYMBOLS

In the course of assembling a user program, the assembler divides the source code into *blocks,* which are defined as follows: The first block consists of the lines of source code from the beginning of the program to the first line containing a normally formed symbol definition, that is, a symbol followed by a colon— a label—as opposed to a direct assignment of a value to a symbol, The next block extends to the next normally formed symbol definition, and so forth. The last block starts at the last symbol definition and ends with the .END statement. There are also a few other ways in which these blocks can be begun and ended, but they will be of little consequence to us here. The interested reader is referred to the appropriate assembler manual.

Within each of these blocks it is possible for the programmer to define **local symbols,** which behave in all respects just like any other symbol (START, ADDR, and so on), with two exceptions. First, the *name* of a local symbol is always an *integer n,* in the range from 1 to 65535, followed by a dollar sign. Thus 1$, 57$, and 32768$ are local symbol names. Second, a local symbol has a value *only* within the block in which it is defined. This feature has two consequences. One is that a reference in one block to a local symbol in another block will be flagged as an error, since the reference will be treated as *undefined.* The second consequence is that the same local symbol can be used repeatedly in the same program without resulting in multiply defined symbol errors, provided we ensure that any two such local symbol definitions do not occur in the same block.

Since the blocks into which the assembler divides source code are defined specifically for the purposes of these local symbols, they are referred to as **local symbol blocks.** The following example will clarify these ideas. We are not concerned with the function of the program shown in Fig. 13.7.1; we are more interested in the local symbol blocks and how the local symbols are treated. The interested reader may want to follow the logic of the program to see what it does—note that we did not supply comments to assist in this task, but the line of ASCII text at the bottom indicates that the program puts numbers in some order. In fact, this is a solution to Exercise 7.7.7.

We see that there are two local symbol blocks here, consisting of lines 2 to 15 and lines 17 to 21. In the first of these blocks, the symbols 29$, 12$, and 62$ are defined and referenced. In the second block, only the symbol 12$ is defined. Notice that although the symbol 12$ is defined twice, the assembler did not report the conflict that would normally be caused by a multiply defined symbol, since the definitions of 12$ occurred in different local symbol blocks. Incidentally, the symbol PRINT is not referred to anywhere in the program— its only purpose was to end the first local symbol block and start the second. Finally, observe that the symbols 29$, 12$, and 62$ do *not* appear in the symbol table, even though they are user-defined symbols.

```
 1 000000              START:  $IN.DEC  #BLOCK,#1
 2 000034      016746          MOV      BLOCK,-(SP)
              000200
 3 000040              $IN.DEC  #BLOCK,(SP)
 4 000072      011600          MOV      (SP),R0
 5 000074      005300          DEC      R0
 6 000076      010001  29$:    MOV      R0,R1
 7 000100      012702          MOV      #BLOCK,R2
              000240'
 8 000104      022212  12$:    CMP      (R2)+,(R2)
 9 000106      003405          BLE      62$
10 000110      011246          MOV      (R2),-(SP)
11 000112      016212          MOV      -2(R2),(R2)
              177776
12 000116      012662          MOV      (SP)+,-2(R2)
              177776
13 000122      077110  62$:    SOB      R1,12$
14 000124      077014          SOB      R0,29$
15
16 000126              PRINT:  $OUT.ASC #12$
17 000156              $OUT.DEC #BLOCK,(SP)+
18 000210              $EXIT
19
20 000212      124     12$:    .ASCIZ   /THE NUMBERS IN ORDER:/
   000213      110
   000214      105
   000215      040
   000216      116
   000217      125
   000220      115
   000221      102
   000222      105
   000223      122
   000224      123
   000225      040
   000226      111
   000227      116
   000230      040
   000231      117
   000232      122
   000233      104
   000234      105
   000235      122
   000236      072
   000237      000
21                     .EVEN
                       ;
22 000240      BLOCK:  .BLKW    20
23                     ;
24      000000'        .END     START


SYMBOL TABLE

BLOCK   000240R          START    000000R      $.... = ****** G
PRINT   000126R
```

Figure 13.7.1

Now that we see that we *can* use local symbols, the question is, *Would* we? That is, in day-to-day programming, would we typically use these local symbols instead of normally formed symbols? The answer is, Probably not. There is nothing the local symbols do for us that normally formed symbols do not, so there is little to compel us to use them. There are occasions in which we might use them, but these are rare. We shall see the real utility of local symbols in the next section, where we show that under some circumstances we can direct the assembler to *generate* these local symbols *automatically*.

13.8 AUTOMATICALLY GENERATED LOCAL SYMBOLS

Consider a program in which we frequently need to determine which of two registers contains the larger number. More accurately, we are interested in knowing what that larger number is. This situation naturally suggests the writing of a macroinstruction.

```
        .MACRO  BIGGER  A,B,C  ;MACRO DEFINITION
        MOV     R'A,R'C        ;ASSUME 1ST LARGER
        CMP     R'A,R'B        ;COMPARE
        BGE     DONE           ;ASSUMPTION CORRECT
        MOV     R'B,R'C        ; ELSE OTHER LARGER
DONE:                          ;(.ENDM CAN'T BE
                               ; LABELED)
        .ENDM
```

The macro works as follows: The register *numbers* A, B, and C are passed to the macro. The first two are the registers to be tested, and the larger of the two numbers will be put in the third register. The logic is quite simple. The first register is assumed to be the larger, and its contents is moved into the third register. Then the first is compared with the second. If the first register is larger than the second, the assumption was correct, and there is nothing more to do. If the second is larger than the first, the second is moved into the third.

The reader might be somewhat puzzled at the label DONE: on a line with no source code. DONE is to label the next line of the program, and where else could it go? If it were to be used as a label for the .ENDM statement—DONE: .ENDM—we would be in trouble, for upon expanding the macro, the assembler does not expand the .ENDM statement—.ENDM is simply a directive signaling the end of the macro definition. We shall see from the program of Fig. 13.8.1 that DONE does have the proper value, that is, the address of the next instruction in the program. For similar reasons, the .MACRO statement also should not be labeled.

In this program segment the macro BIGGER is invoked twice, and in each case it is expanded correctly, as we see. However, the symbol DONE is multiply defined. When the macro is expanded the first time DONE is given the value 002112. In the second expansion, DONE is assigned the value 003254. Since the assembler finds this situation intolerable, it flags these lines with an M-error—multiply defined symbol. It flags some other instructions with errors also, as a result of the multiple definition of DONE.

If we had thought about this problem in advance, we might have been able to anticipate it. Now that we know it exists, how do we cope with it? One

```
  1                     .LIST   ME
  2                     ;
  3                     .MACRO  BIGGER  A,B,C   ;MACRO DEFINITION
  4             MOV     R'A,R'C          ;ASSUME 1ST LARGER
  5             CMP     R'A,R'B          ;COMPARE
  6             BGE     DONE             ;ASSUMPTION CORRECT
  7             MOV     R'B,R'C          ; ELSE OTHER LARGER
  8     DONE:                            ;(.ENDM CAN'T BE
  9                                      ; LABELED)
 10                     .ENDM
 11                     ;
 12 001000   START:                     ;(START OF PROGRAM)

         .
         .
 44 002102             BIGGER  1,2,5    ;INVOKE MACRO
    002102  010105     MOV     R1,R5    ;ASSUME 1ST LARGER
    002104  020102     CMP     R1,R2    ;COMPARE
    002106  002001     BGE     DONE     ;ASSUMPTION CORRECT
    002110  010205     MOV     R2,R5    ; ELSE OTHER LARGER
 M  002112   DONE:                      ;(.ENDM CAN'T BE
                                        ; LABELED)

         .
         .
 73 003244             BIGGER  2,4,1    ;INVOKE MACRO AGAIN
    003244  010201     MOV     R2,R1    ;ASSUME 1ST LARGER
    003246  020204     CMP     R2,R4    ;COMPARE
 AD 003250  002377     BGE     DONE     ;ASSUMPTION CORRECT
    003252  010401     MOV     R4,R1    ; ELSE OTHER LARGER
 M  003254   DONE:                      ;(.ENDM CAN'T BE
                                        ; LABELED)

         .
         .
```

Figure 13.8.1

way is to pass a *fourth* argument to the macro to be used as a label in place of
DONE (Fig. 13.8.2). This takes care of the problem quite nicely. The first time
the macro is invoked, we pass it the value DONE to be used in place of the
label D. The second time we use the value DONE1 for the label, and as we
see from the listing, no conflict in symbol names now exists. Notice that,
provided we were careful, we could have passed *local* symbols such as 1$ or
54$ to the macro in place of DONE and DONE1.

While we have discovered a means of skirting the multiply defined symbol
problem, we are not completely out of the woods yet. All of the macroinstructions that we defined in this chapter are exceedingly short and simple—they are,
after all, illustrative examples, not necessarily real-world programming. Suppose
that a macro required 6 unique labels because of its logic and that this macro
was called 30 times in a single program. Invoking the macro would require
the programmer to construct 180 different symbol names that, of course, would
have to be distinct from *other* symbol names used in the program. While this
situation may be an extreme case, it is clear that naming the symbols passed
to a macro could become an excessive burden on the programmer. Fortunately,
the PDP-11 macroinstruction assembler comes to our aid once more.

If one or more of the dummy arguments in the macroinstruction prototype statement is *preceded by* a *question mark*, then the assembler takes the fol-

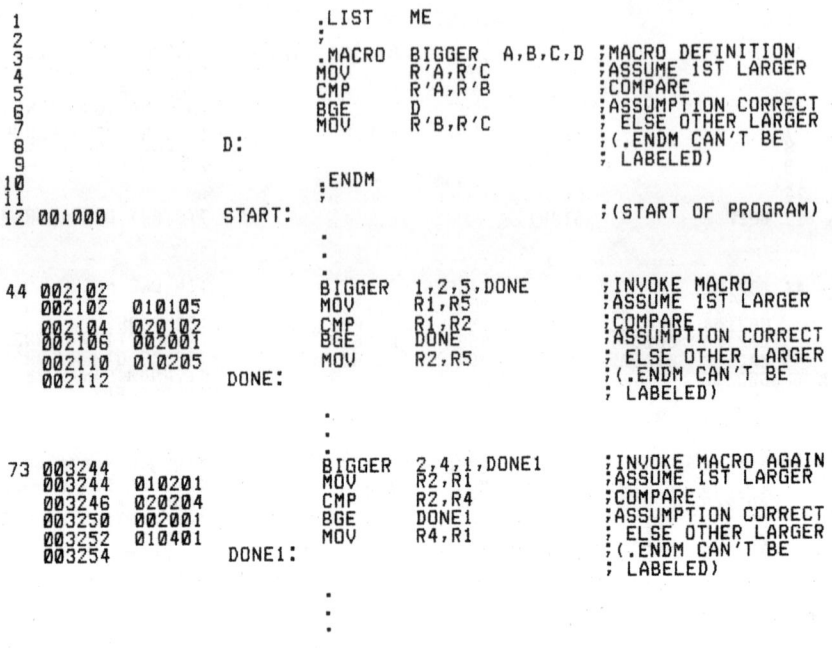

```
  1                     .LIST    ME
  2                     ;
  3                     .MACRO   BIGGER   A,B,C,D   ;MACRO DEFINITION
  4                     MOV      R'A,R'C            ;ASSUME 1ST LARGER
  5                     CMP      R'A,R'B            ;COMPARE
  6                     BGE      D                  ;ASSUMPTION CORRECT
  7                     MOV      R'B,R'C            ; ELSE OTHER LARGER
  8             D:                                  ;(.ENDM CAN'T BE
  9                                                 ; LABELED)
 10                     .ENDM
 11                     ;
 12 001000     START:                              ;(START OF PROGRAM)
                          .
                          .
                          .
 44 002102             BIGGER   1,2,5,DONE         ;INVOKE MACRO
    002102   010105    MOV      R1,R5              ;ASSUME 1ST LARGER
    002104   020102    CMP      R1,R2              ;COMPARE
    002106   002001    BGE      DONE               ;ASSUMPTION CORRECT
    002110   010205    MOV      R2,R5              ; ELSE OTHER LARGER
    002112     DONE:                               ;(.ENDM CAN'T BE
                                                   ; LABELED)
                          .
                          .
                          .
 73 003244             BIGGER   2,4,1,DONE1        ;INVOKE MACRO AGAIN
    003244   010201    MOV      R2,R1              ;ASSUME 1ST LARGER
    003246   020204    CMP      R2,R4              ;COMPARE
    003250   002001    BGE      DONE1              ;ASSUMPTION CORRECT
    003252   010401    MOV      R4,R1              ; ELSE OTHER LARGER
    003254     DONE1:                              ;(.ENDM CAN'T BE
                                                   ; LABELED)
                          .
                          .
                          .
```

Figure 13.8.2

lowing action when the macro is expanded: If a real argument *is* supplied for one of the dummy arguments preceded by a question mark when the macro is invoked, then the assembler will treat it in the usual way—make the substitution of the real argument for the dummy argument. However, if a real argument is *not* supplied for one of these special dummy arguments, then the assembler will supply the *next available local symbol* for that dummy argument.

Consider the macro prototype .MACRO TEST A,?B,C. If the macro is invoked as TEST 1,2,3, for example, then each of the dummy arguments is supplied with a real counterpart. On the other hand, if the macro is called with TEST 1,,3, then A will be given the value 1, C will be given the value 3, but B will be *given no value*. As another example, consider .MACRO DUMMY X,?Y. The call DUMMY 5,ADDR will supply values as usual: X = 5, Y = ADDR. But DUMMY 5 will supply X with the value 5 and Y with *no* value. It is in this sense that we mean that a dummy argument is or is not supplied with a value.

If a dummy argument is supplied with no value in the sense explained above, how the assembler handles it depends on what type of dummy argument it is. If it is a "normal" dummy argument, that is, one *not* preceded by a question mark, the assembler will assign the *empty string* of characters to it. Thus, for example, the macro TEST, defined as

```
.MACRO   TEST   A,B,C
CLR    R'A
CLR    R'B
CLR    R'C
.ENDM
```

invoked by TEST   1,,4 will be expanded as

```
CLR    R1
CLR    R
CLR    R4
```

If the dummy argument supplied with no value *is* preceded by a question mark, then the assembler will give it the next available local symbol as a value, in the following sense: In generating these local symbols, the assembler *begins with* the local symbol 64$. The assembler gives the value 65$ to the next such symbol it encounters, and so forth. This automatic generation of distinct local symbols continues until one of two things happens. When the assembler enters a new local symbol block, it starts the local symbol generation over again with 64$, since in a new local symbol block no symbol definition conflicts can exist. When and if the assembler has generated local symbols up to 127$, it will *start over again* with 64$, and this *does* imply multiply defined symbols. Thus the assembler will generate local symbols automatically within each local symbol block, in the range from 64$ to 127$; this range is normally much more generous than we would ever require. If problems should arise, they can be taken care of by the simple device of inserting a normally formed label somewhere in the program to force a new local symbol block, whether or not that symbolic address is referred to in the program.

We can now modify our macroinstruction BIGGER to take advantage of the assembler's ability to generate local symbols. Notice that each time the macro is invoked, the dummy variable D is *not* supplied with a value (Fig. 13.8.3).

It is suggested that dummy arguments be placed at the *end* of the argument list in the macroinstruction prototype statement when defining macroinstructions that use automatic local symbol generation. For example, if the three arguments X, Y, and Z are to be given automatically generated local symbol values, and if the macro is defined by

```
.MACRO   TEST   A,?X,?Y,B,?Z,C
```

then to give A the value 1, B the value R3, and C the value MOV, we would have to invoke the macro by

```
TEST   1,,,R3,,MOV
```

On the other hand, if the macro prototype were

```
.MACRO   TEST   A,B,C,?X,?Y,?Z
```

```
 1                                  ;LIST   ME
 2                                  ;
 3                                  .MACRO  BIGGER A,B,C,?D ;MACRO DEFINITION
 4                                  MOV     R'A,R'C         ;ASSUME 1ST LARGER
 5                                  CMP     R'A,R'B         ;COMPARE
 6                                  BGE     D               ;ASSUMPTION CORRECT
 7                                  MOV     R'B,R'C         ; ELSE OTHER LARGER
 8                          D:                              ;(.ENDM CAN'T BE
 9                                                          ; LABELED)
10                                  .ENDM
11                                  ;
12 001000           START:                                 ;(START OF PROGRAM)
                                       .
                                       .
44 002102                           BIGGER  1,2,5           ;INVOKE MACRO
   002102   010105                  MOV     R1,R5           ;ASSUME 1ST LARGER
   002104   020102                  CMP     R1,R2           ;COMPARE
   002106   002001                  BGE     64$             ;ASSUMPTION CORRECT
   002110   010205                  MOV     R2,R5           ; ELSE OTHER LARGER
   002112                  64$:                             ;(.ENDM CAN'T BE
                                                            ; LABELED)
                                       .
                                       .
73 003244                           BIGGER  2,4,1           ;INVOKE MACRO AGAIN
   003244   010201                  MOV     R2,R1           ;ASSUME 1ST LARGER
   003246   020204                  CMP     R2,R4           ;COMPARE
   003250   002001                  BGE     65$             ;ASSUMPTION CORRECT
   003252   010401                  MOV     R4,R1           ; ELSE OTHER LARGER
   003254                  65$:                             ;(.ENDM CAN'T BE
                                                            ; LABELED)
                                       .
                                       .
```

Figure 13.8.3

it would suffice to call the macro by

TEST   1,R3,MOV

13.9 REPEAT BLOCKS

A **repeat block** is a type of macroinstruction that differs significantly in a number of respects from those we have already studied. First, a repeat block is not *named* in the same way as is as an ordinary macroinstruction. Thus it cannot be invoked by its name and its definition is not set aside in a table of macro definitions. Rather, each time a repeat block is required in a program, it is defined at the point at which it is needed, and the assembler expands it when and where it encounters its definition. Second, a repeat block *always* contains *one and only one* dummy argument, and the real argument substitutes are listed along with the definition of the repeat block. Finally, the assembler expands the code that represents the definition of the repeat block not just *once,* but rather it expands it *once for each real argument.* The specifics of how a repeat block is formed should clarify these ideas.

The assembler directive to signal the beginning of an **indefinite repeat block**, used in place of .MACRO, is .IRP. On the same line with the .IRP directive is the name of *the* dummy argument (X, ARG, or whatever), followed by a comma, followed by a list of real arguments enclosed in angle brackets and separated from one another by commas or spaces. Thus, for example, a typical .IRP directive would look like

.IRP   Q,⟨1,2,MOV,R3⟩

The line or lines of source code instructions making up the definition of the repeat block then follow. The directive .ENDM follows the definition to indicate the end of the macro definition, just as before.

When the assembler encounters a .IRP directive, it inserts the source code making up the definition of the repeat block into the program *at that point* and then replaces the dummy argument in this source code with the *first* real argument in the list, following all the rules for argument replacement—concatenation, direct substitution, and so forth. Having expanded the repeat block, the assembler then expands it *again* and replaces the dummy argument with the *second* real argument in the list. Thus we now have *two* copies of the definition, one after the other. In the first copy, the first real argument replaced the dummy argument, while in the second copy, the second list argument replaced it. This process of expanding the definition and replacing the dummy argument continues until the real argument list is exhausted. The repeat block is now completely expanded.

The name *indefinite repeat block* is clearly appropriate. The definition— that is, the *block* of instructions making up the definition—is *repeated indefinitely*; the number of repeats are dependent upon the number of real arguments in the argument list. As a simple example, but one that is highly useful, we consider a one-line indefinite repeat block that saves on the stack the current values of registers 0, 2, 3, and 4.

.IRP   X,⟨0,2,3,4⟩
MOV   R'X,-(SP)
.ENDM

The source code making up the definition of the repeat block, namely MOV R'X,-(SP), will be inserted in the program four times, once for each of the arguments 0, 2, 3, and 4. Figure 13.9.1 shows how the PDP-11 assembler treats this repeat block.

```
1                        .LIST   ME
2                        ;
3  000000      START:    .IRP    X,<0,2,3,4>     ;INVOKE REPEAT BLOCK
4                        MOV     R'X,-(SP)       ;PUSH REGISTER
5                        .ENDM                   ;END REPEAT BLOCK DEF
   000000  010046       MOV     R0,-(SP)        ;PUSH REGISTER
   000002  010246       MOV     R2,-(SP)        ;PUSH REGISTER
   000004  010346       MOV     R3,-(SP)        ;PUSH REGISTER
   000006  010446       MOV     R4,-(SP)        ;PUSH REGISTER
6                        ;
7  000010                ......                 ;(CONTINUATION
                                                ; OF PROGRAM)
```

Figure 13.9.1

Since an indefinite repeat block is not named, its definition must be inserted in the program each time it is needed. If this occurs frequently and thus becomes an annoyance, we can eliminate the problem by constructing a normally formed macroinstruction (with a name, of course) whose definition consists of the desired repeat block. Thus the preceding example could be rewritten (Fig. 13.9.2) and then when needed, invoked *by name*. How much source code can be included within the definition of a repeat block? There are no restrictions in this regard, so as much code as the programmer might want can go in the block, and that code will be expanded once for each real argument. In fact, the code making up the definition of a repeat block can even contain another repeat block, as the next example shows. However, a certain amount of care is required, since a real argument currently being used for the outer repeat block can affect the code generated in the inner block.

```
 1                          .LIST   ME
 2                          ;
 3                          .MACRO  SAVE    A,B,C,D  ;MACRO DEFINITION
 4                          .IRP    X,<A,B,C,D>      ;INVOKE REPEAT BLOCK
 5                          MOV     R'X,-(SP)
 6                          .ENDM                    ;END REPEAT BLOCK DEF
 7                          .ENDM                    ;END MACRO ('SAVE') DEF
 8                          ;
 9  000000         START:   SAVE    0,2,3,4          ;INVOKE MACRO
                            .IRP    X,<0,2,3,4>      ;INVOKE REPEAT BLOCK
                            MOV     R'X,-(SP)
                            .ENDM                    ;END REPEAT BLOCK DEF
    000000  010046         MOV     R0,-(SP)
    000002  010246         MOV     R2,-(SP)
    000004  010346         MOV     R3,-(SP)
    000006  010446         MOV     R4,-(SP)
10  000010                 ......                   ;(CONTINUATION
                                                     ; OF PROGRAM)
```

Figure 13.9.2

The following example has no real merit except to show how repeat blocks can be nested and what happens as a result. This program segment merely generates the ASCII code for pairs of characters, the first character being taken from the set {A,B,C} and the second from the set {X,Y}. The reader will find it instructive to follow through the listing of Fig. 13.9.3 in detail, paying particular attention to which dummy variables have what values at the time each block is expanded.

Since spaces are taken as legal separators in the argument list of a repeat block, some care must be exercised in writing the arguments. The repeat block of Fig. 13.9.4 is *supposed* to generate the instruction CLR   R1, followed by an instruction specified in the argument list. As we see, the assembler evidently saw *four* arguments in the list—INC, R1, DEC, and R1. The problem is repaired as before, by using angle brackets as grouping symbols (Fig. 13.9.5).

There is a modification of the indefinite repeat block in which the argument list is a *string of characters* (Fig. 13.9.6). The format for the assembler directive for this block is

.IRPC   ARG,string

```
1                        .LIST   ME
2                        ;
3                        .IRP    P,<A,B,C>
4                        .IRP    Q,<X,Y>
5                        .ASCII  /'P''Q/
6                        .ENDM
7                        .ENDM
                         .IRP    Q,<X,Y>
                         .ASCII  /A'Q/
                         .ENDM
000000  101              .ASCII  /AX/
000001  130
000002  101              .ASCII  /AY/
000003  131
                         .IRP    Q,<X,Y>
                         .ASCII  /B'Q/
                         .ENDM
000004  102              .ASCII  /BX/
000005  130
000006  102              .ASCII  /BY/
000007  131
                         .IRP    Q,<X,Y>
                         .ASCII  /C'Q/
                         .ENDM
000010  103              .ASCII  /CX/
000011  130
000012  103              .ASCII  /CY/
000013  131
```

Figure 13.9.3

```
1                        .LIST   ME
2                        ;
3                        .IRP    A,<INC  R1,DEC  R1>
4                        CLR     R1
5                        A
6                        .ENDM
   000000  005001        CLR     R1
A  000002  005267        INC
           000000
   000006  005001        CLR     R1
   000010  000001        R1
   000012  005001        CLR     R1
A  000014  005367        DEC
           000000
   000020  005001        CLR     R1
   000022  000001        R1
```

Figure 13.9.4

```
1                        .LIST   ME
2                        ;
3                        .IRP    A,<<INC  R1>,<DEC  R1>>
4                        CLR     R1
5                        A
6                        .ENDM
   000000  005001        CLR     R1
   000002  005201        INC     R1
   000004  005001        CLR     R1
   000006  005301        DEC     R1
```

Figure 13.9.5

where again ARG is the dummy argument. The block is repeated once for each character in the string; for each repetition ARG is replaced by a string character. Thus, for example, when the assembler encounters

.IRPC   X,A4R

it will expand the macro definition once by replacing X with the character A, again with the character 4, and once more with the character R. Notice that angle brackets around the argument string are *not* required here. Thus the repeat block developed earlier in this section to save four registers on the stack could have been written as

```
1                                    .LIST   ME
2                                    ;
3                                    .IRPC   X,0234
4                                    MOV     R'X,-(SP)
5                                    .ENDM
     000000   010046                 MOV     R0,-(SP)
     000002   010246                 MOV     R2,-(SP)
     000004   010346                 MOV     R3,-(SP)
     000006   010446                 MOV     R4,-(SP)
```

Figure 13.9.6

While angle brackets need not be used around the argument string, they may be used, in which case they are taken as grouping symbols and are *not* interpreted as characters in the string, as the program segment of Fig. 13.9.7 indicates.

```
1                                    .LIST   ME
2                                    ;
3                                    .IRPC   X,<0234>
4                                    MOV     R'X,-(SP)
5                                    .ENDM
     000000   010046                 MOV     R0,-(SP)
     000002   010246                 MOV     R2,-(SP)
     000004   010346                 MOV     R3,-(SP)
     000006   010446                 MOV     R4,-(SP)
```

Figure 13.9.7

There are cases in which these angle brackets *are* required. Consider the task of generating the ASCII codes for the characters in the string OH, BOY! on a character-by-character basis. We might try to handle this (obviously contrived) problem with the construction

.IRPC   X,OH, BOY!
.ASCII /X/
.ENDM

but as we see from Fig. 13.9.8, the assembler evidently took the comma in this string to be a string delimiter, and assumed that the string passed to the IRPC was simply OH. Conceding defeat and deleting the comma from the string will

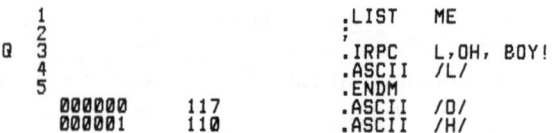

Figure 13.9.8

do us no good either, for now the assembler will treat the *blank* as a delimiter (Fig. 13.9.9). We solve the problem by enclosing the string in angle brackets, which the assembler will interpret as grouping symbols and not as being part of the string (Fig. 13.9.10).

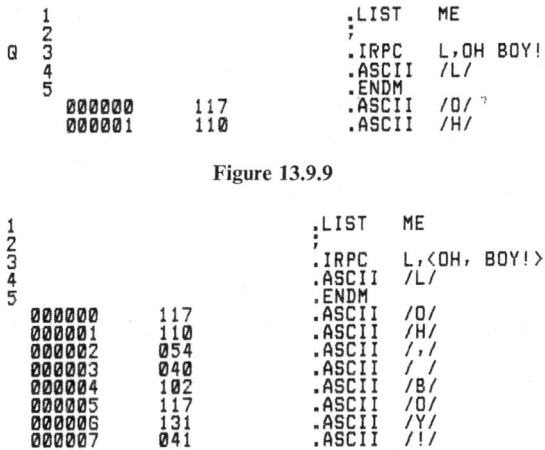

```
        1                            .LIST  ME
        2                            ;
   Q    3                            .IRPC  L,OH BOY!
        4                            .ASCII /L/
        5                            .ENDM
          000000        117          .ASCII /O/ ⌐
          000001        110          .ASCII /H/
```

Figure 13.9.9

```
        1                            .LIST  ME
        2                            ;
        3                            .IRPC  L,<OH, BOY!>
        4                            .ASCII /L/
        5                            .ENDM
          000000        117          .ASCII /O/
          000001        110          .ASCII /H/
          000002        054          .ASCII /,/
          000003        040          .ASCII / /
          000004        102          .ASCII /B/
          000005        117          .ASCII /O/
          000006        131          .ASCII /Y/
          000007        041          .ASCII /!/
```

Figure 13.9.10

There is a final form of the repeat block that is not often used but that comes in handy on occasion. The form of the assembler directive is .REPT n, and the code making up the definition of the repeat block is simply repeated n times. Notice that there is no dummy argument and consequently no argument replacement. It is difficult to invent a useful example, but consider the problem of generating a block of 14_{10} consecutive words of main memory, each containing a 0. One way to handle this job would be by the .WORD directive

.WORD   0,0,0,0,0,0,0,0,0,0,0,0,0,0

but it would be easier to use the type of repeat block shown in Fig. 13.9.11.

```
        1                            .LIST  ME
        2                            ;
        3             000016         .REPT  14.
        4                            .WORD  0
        5                            .ENDM
          000000       000000        .WORD  0
          000002       000000        .WORD  0
          000004       000000        .WORD  0
          000006       000000        .WORD  0
          000010       000000        .WORD  0
          000012       000000        .WORD  0
          000014       000000        .WORD  0
          000016       000000        .WORD  0
          000020       000000        .WORD  0
          000022       000000        .WORD  0
          000024       000000        .WORD  0
          000026       000000        .WORD  0
          000030       000000        .WORD  0
          000032       000000        .WORD  0
```

Figure 13.9.11

13.10 A BIT-SHIFTING MACROINSTRUCTION

The reader is doubtless familiar with, and may already have used, the PDP-11 instruction ASL—*A*rithmetic *S*hift *L*eft. The effect of the instruction is to shift each bit of the destination one position to the left. The high-order bit (bit 15) is shifted out into the carry bit, and the vacated low-order bit is filled with a 0. In some programming environments it is necessary to shift the bits of a word left not by just 1 bit but by several—shift left by 5 bits or by 8 bits, for example. Of course, we could simply include enough copies of the ASL instruction to achieve this, but if much shifting was involved, we would very likely write a macroinstruction to do the job. We offer an example in Fig. 13.10.1.

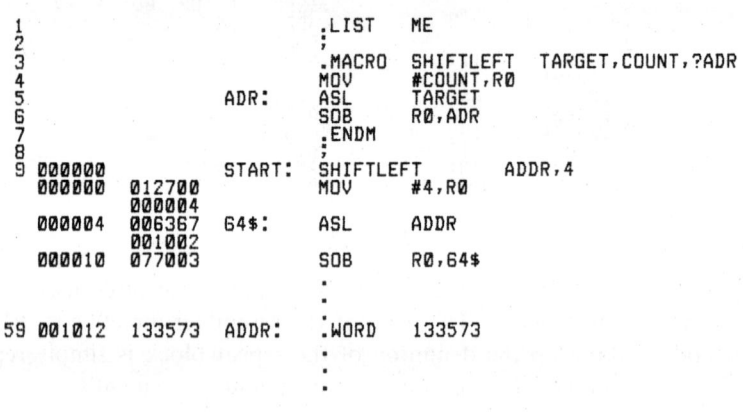

Figure 13.10.1

Here TARGET is the address of the 16-bit word to be shifted, and COUNT is the shift count. This count is placed in R∅, which is then used to control an SOB loop, the body of which is simply a left shift on TARGET. Notice the use of the automatically generated local symbol ?ADR. There are two potential problems here. First, R∅ is used as a loop-controlling counter, but it is possible that R∅ is currently in use for some other purpose when the macro is invoked. Second, it is conceivable that the macro might inadvertently be passed a *nonpositive* count, the result of which would probably not be what the programmer had intended. Neither of these problems is particularly difficult to fix, but we postpone repairs until Sec. 13.12. However, there is still another difficulty hidden here that is perhaps less obvious. We defer its discussion to Sec. 13.13.

The instruction set in Appendix A contains a PDP-11 instruction called *A*rithmetic *SH*ift (ASH) that does more than our macro SHIFTLEFT: It shifts either left or right according to a specified shift count. Nonetheless, SHIFT-LEFT serves two purposes. First, it is useful for illustrating a number of macro-assembler features, and as such it will be the principal example in the remainder of this chapter. Second, not all models of the PDP-11 implement the instruction ASH, so SHIFTLEFT or something like it is actually quite useful in practice. The reader is asked in an exercise to modify this macroinstruction to give a more realistic emulation of the instruction ASH.

13.11 CONDITIONALLY ASSEMBLED INSTRUCTIONS

Consider as examples two source programs that implement similar tasks: One places numbers in increasing order; the other puts numbers in decreasing order. Suppose that the jobs are sufficiently closely related that the source programs differ only in a few instructions, with the bulk of the two programs being identical. To execute them, of course, each program would have to be assembled, but we might be put off by the prospect of writing two versions of a perhaps lengthy procedure, which differ in at most a handful of instructions. Our aim in this section is to devise a means of writing only *one* version of the program containing some *optional* instructions, and then to inform our clerk (or the PDP-11 assembler) which options to use in assembling the *two* versions of the program. Thus we need to write the bulk of the instructions only once, and the clerk will selectively assemble one set of optional instructions or the other. The reader might claim that we are inclining toward laziness here: we prefer to think of it as programmer efficiency.

The principal example of Chapter 6 dealt with finding the maximum of a collection of numbers, and the program that ultimately did that job contained the instruction BGE   NEXT as source code. The purpose of this instruction was to skip around an instruction that replaced the temporary maximum. If we were concerned with writing a program to find the *minimum* of a collection of numbers, the *only* programming change we would have to make would be to replace BGE   NEXT with BLE   NEXT. We would like to be able to write the code for this program (programs?) once and then inform the clerk which version we wish assembled. In the following discussion it will be useful to refer to the program listing of Fig. 6.6.1.

Our clerk should certainly be able *selectively* to assemble source code, *provided* we inform him of just what code is to be assembled and the *conditions* under which it is or is not to be assembled. The lines of source code from which we want the clerk to select are BGE   NEXT and BLE   NEXT, but what condition should we use to let him know which code to insert and assemble? A simple but effective scheme is to tell him that *if* the symbol FLAG (or any other symbol not used in the program) *is defined* in the program, to assemble BGE NEXT. But if FLAG is *not defined* in the program, to assemble BLE   NEXT instead. Now we can select which version we want assembled by defining the symbol FLAG early in the program—the direct assignment statement FLAG = 0 would do—or by leaving FLAG undefined. Notice that the symbol FLAG is serving no purpose in the program other than to tell our clerk which branch instruction to assemble. The source program presented to the clerk could now be written as follows:

```
        (FLAG = 0)
            .
            .
            .
        CMP   R5,(R2)
```
**If the symbol* FLAG *is* defined, assemble
    the following instruction:
```
        BGE   NEXT
```
**If the symbol* FLAG *is* not *defined,*
    assemble the following instruction:
```
        BLE   NEXT
        MOV   (R2),R5
NEXT:   DEC   RØ
            .
            .
            .
```

Thus if the first line (FLAG = 0) is included in the source program, the clerk will put this symbol in his symbol table, and when he encounters the ** *If* statements in the source program, a look at the table will tell him FLAG is defined and thus that BGE   NEXT should be assembled here. Otherwise he will assemble BLE   NEXT if we leave FLAG undefined.

     In a similar fashion, the PDP-11 assembler can handle such **conditional assemblies**. The general form of a **conditional block** is

```
        .IF       conditional     argument(s)
        (The line or lines
        of source code to be
        assembled provided
        the condition tests
        as true)
        .ENDC
```

Notice that since more than one line of source code might be included in the conditional block, we had to inform the assembler of the end of the conditional block with the directive .ENDC—*END* Conditional block. The program just described can now be presented to the assembler, and we see what is assembled when the symbol FLAG *is* defined (Fig. 13.11.1). If, on the other hand, we had *failed* to define FLAG in the program, the result would be as shown in Fig. 13.11.2. As we see from the first program segment, since FLAG was defined, the instruction BGE   NEXT was assembled, and BLE   NEXT was *not* assembled. In the second case, the situation was reversed, since FLAG was *not* defined.

     The reader has probably deduced that the PDP-11 assembler uses the abbreviations DF and NDF for the conditional phrases *defined* and *not defined*,

```
 1            000000           FLAG = 0
                               .
                               .
 7 000016    020512           CMP     R5,(R2)
 8                            .IF     DF      FLAG
 9 000020    002001           BGE     NEXT
10                            .ENDC
11                            .IF     NDF     FLAG
12                            BLE     NEXT
13                            .ENDC
14 000022    011205           MOV     (R2),R5
15 000024    005300    NEXT:  DEC     R0
                               .
                               .
                               .
```

Figure 13.11.1

```
                               .
                               .
 6 000016    020512           CMP     R5,(R2)
 7                            .IF     DF      FLAG
 8                            BGE     NEXT
 9                            .ENDC
10                            .IF     NDF     FLAG
11 000020    003401           BLE     NEXT
12                            .ENDC
13 000022    011205           MOV     (R2),R5
14 000024    005300    NEXT:  DEC     R0
                               .
                               .
                               .
```

Figure 13.11.2

respectively. These are referred to as **complementary conditionals**. There are also a number of other conditionals used by the PDP-11 assembler. The details of each are given in the table of Fig. 13.11.3.

At the very best, the writing of conditional assembly blocks is a tricky business that requires much care if the results are to be as expected. Two things need to be remembered: First, the programmer must be aware of precisely *what* the assembler is testing when it processes a conditional directive; and second, the programmer must be cognizant of just what information is available *to the assembler*. A simple example will illustrate some of the pitfalls to which the novice might be subject.

Suppose ADDR is a user-defined symbol used as a label for the memory location whose address is 000622. Consider the sequence of instructions

                    CLR   ADDR
                    .IF   EQ   ADDR
                    (conditional block)
                    .ENDC

The uninitiated might be amazed to find that the conditional block was not assembled, since clearly ADDR has a 0 in it. Two major errors, or at least misinterpretations, were made here. First, the programmer assumed that what

PDP-11 Assembler Conditionals

Cond.	Name	Argument(s)	Block Assembled If
EQ	Equal to 0	Value*	Value = 0
NE	Not equal to 0	Value*	Value $\neq$ 0
GT	Greater than 0	Value*	Value > 0
LE	Less than or equal to 0	Value*	Value $\leq$ 0
LT	Less than 0	Value*	Value < 0
GE	Greater than or equal to 0	Value*	Value $\geq$ 0
DF	Defined	Symbol	Symbol is defined
NDF	Not defined	Symbol	Symbol is not defined
B	Blank	String	Arg is a blank string
NB	Nonblank	String	Arg is a nonblank string
IDN	Identical	String$_1$, String$_2$	String$_1$ is identical to String$_2$
DIF	Different	String$_1$, String$_2$	String$_1$ is different from String$_2$

*By *value* we mean any expression to which the assembler can assign a *numerical value*. Thus expressions such as ADDR, 7, START$-$ADDR, $\langle$START$-$ADDR$+2\rangle/2+14$, are all values, whereas R3, PC$+4$, and so forth, are not.

Figure 13.11.3

was being tested was the *contents* of ADDR, not the *value* of ADDR. In fact, the value of ADDR is 000622, which is certainly not 0. Second, even putting the first mistake aside, the programmer took the contents of ADDR to be 0 (since its contents were cleared), but he or she overlooked the fact that this clearing of the contents of ADDR takes place at *execution time* not at *assembly time*. The assembler knows nothing of what occurs when a program executes, and in general it knows nothing of the contents of various memory locations.

In the remainder of the chapter we shall illustrate a number of conditional assemblies using various conditional directives. In each case we shall give detailed explanations of how the assembler treated them. In the meantime we offer a few simple examples of some of the assembler's peculiarities and of what can go wrong. First, consider the following simple situation: The symbol ADDR was *assigned* the value 0 in a direct assignment statement, and subsequently a conditional tests ADDR to see if it is equal to 0. The condition tests as true and the conditional block is assembled, as we would expect (Fig. 13.11.4).

The program segment of Fig. 13.11.5 also assigns the value 0 to the symbol ADDR, but this time the conditional directive is flagged as an error. Again, ADDR was given the value 0, since it is a label on memory location 000000, so the conditional .IF EQ ADDR should test as true. In fact it

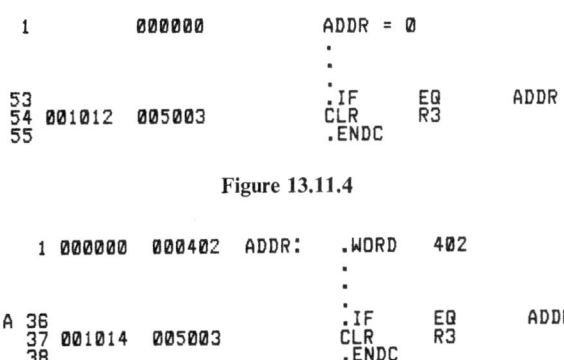

```
   1            000000            ADDR = 0
                                  .
                                  .
  53                              .IF      EQ       ADDR
  54  001012    005003           CLR      R3
  55                             .ENDC
```

Figure 13.11.4

```
   1  000000   000402   ADDR:   .WORD    402
                                  .
                                  .
A  36                             .IF      EQ       ADDR
   37  001014   005003           CLR      R3
   38                            .ENDC
```

Figure 13.11.5

did, and we see that the CLR   R3 instruction was assembled. The problem lies in *how* ADDR was given its value. In this second case, ADDR is a label having the value 0 because it was *assembled* at 000000. But ADDR is a relocation-sensitive symbol: If this program were relocated to some other memory location (001000, for instance), then the value of ADDR would no longer be 0, and hence the conditional block should *not* have been assembled. Thus this error can be taken as a warning—the assembling of this conditional block is correct *only* if the program is *loaded* in such a way that ADDR is given the value 0. In the first case, no such problem exists because the direct assignment ADDR = 0 gives ADDR the *absolute value* 0, which is insensitive to program relocation.

Having resolved this matter and gained some insights into how and why the assembler treats such constructions, the reader may be puzzled by the program segment of Fig. 13.11.6. START and ADDR clearly are symbols

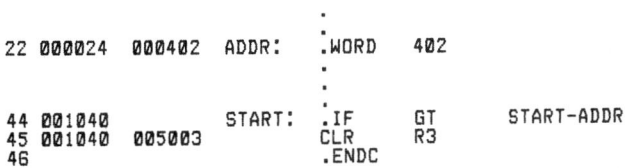

```
  22  000024   000402   ADDR:   .WORD    402
                                  .
                                  .
  44  001040            START:  .IF      GT       START-ADDR
  45  001040   005003           CLR      R3
  46                            .ENDC
```

Figure 13.11.6

whose values are dependent upon the program's load address, as in the preceding example, and yet the assembler appears to have been undisturbed by this conditional construction. But observe that even though both symbols are sensitive to relocation, their *difference*—START − ADDR = 001040 − 000024 = 001014—is *not*. That difference is always 001014, regardless of where the program might be located in main memory. For this reason the assembler was able to assert with confidence that START − ADDR is greater than 0 and thus assemble the conditional block.

As a final example consider the consequences of referencing a symbol in a conditional directive *prior to* the symbol's definition (Fig. 13.11.7). (This example should be reminiscent of the program segment of Sec. 13.4 in which a phase error was generated for substantially the same reason.) We see from the symbol table that the value of ADDR is 000002, while the value of START is 000000. Since START − ADDR is *negative*, the conditional block (which depends on the conditional GE) should not be assembled, and in fact it was not. But again we must carefully follow the assembler's handling of the conditional. When the assembler first encountered the .IF construction on the first pass through the source code, the assembler had *no* value for ADDR. Thus it treated START − ADDR as if it were START, whose value (0) was greater than or equal to 0. Consequently, *on the first pass*, the assembler recognized that the code for CLR   R3 would be inserted here *on the second pass*, and thus it moved its location assignment counter up by 2. Thus when the definition of ADDR was encountered, the location counter had already been moved up to 000002,

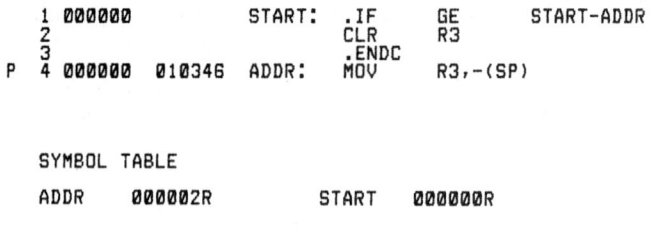

Figure 13.11.7

thereby accounting for ADDR's value in the symbol table. But on its *second* pass, the assembler found that START − ADDR was *not* greater than or equal to 0, and thus did *not* assemble the CLR   R3 instruction. When the definition ADDR: was again encountered, the location assignment counter had the value 000000, which was inconsistent with ADDR's symbol table value. This caused the phase error.

As before, we can only admonish the programmer to ensure that, in this environment, symbols are well defined before they are used. A thorough understanding of how the assembler handles these various constructions will eliminate the vast majority of programming errors, but experience is still the best teacher.

13.12 THE ASSEMBLER DIRECTIVE .MEXIT

When the assembler encounters the directive .MEXIT in the course of *expanding* a macroinstruction, it will *stop the macroexpansion*. That is, it behaves as if it had encountered the .ENDM directive. Thus, for example, the expansion of

```
.MACRO  PUSH  A,B
MOV  A,-(SP)
.MEXIT
MOV  B,-(SP)
.ENDM
```

when invoked with PUSH   R1,R2, would assemble only the instruction

```
MOV  R1,-(SP)
```

The instruction MOV   R2,-(SP) would be *listed*, but because of the
.MEXIT, it would never be *assembled*. Of course, it would be pointless to write
such a macroinstruction. The principal use of the .MEXIT directive is to halt
the macroexpansion assembling *conditionally*. That is, under certain circumstances, we want the assembler to stop the assembling process and pick up after
the macroexpansion. In other cases, we want the assembling to continue. As
an example of the use of this directive, we offer an improved version of a
macroinstruction defined earlier in this chapter.

Recall that in Sec. 13.9 we defined a macroinstruction named SAVE,
which contained an indefinite repeat block, the purpose of which was to save
four registers on the stack.

```
.MACRO  SAVE  A,B,C,D
.IRP    X,⟨A,B,C,D⟩
MOV     R'X,-(SP)
.ENDM
.ENDM
```

Because of the dummy argument list in the macro prototype, we can specify
which registers we want stacked. But this macroinstruction is still not as useful
as it might be, for we see from the definition that it can be used to save only
four registers, never more and never fewer. However, with a conditional use of
.MEXIT, we can modify this example to make it as general-purpose as possible.
The modification is shown in Fig. 13.12.1, where we assume that it would never
be required to save more than six registers on the stack.

The changes involve lines 3 and 4, where six arguments are passed from
the macro to the repeat block, and lines 5, 6, and 7, where we inserted a conditional block: Exit from the macro if the argument X is *blank*. It will be useful
to examine what happens when this macro is invoked. Keep in mind that the
repeat block will be expanded six times each time the macro SAVE is called,
since the repeat block is always passed six arguments.

The first time the repeat block is expanded, the conditional is

```
.IF    B    1
```

Since the string 1 is *nonblank*, the body of the conditional block—namely,
.MEXIT—is not acted on, and the instruction

```
MOV  R1,-(SP)
```

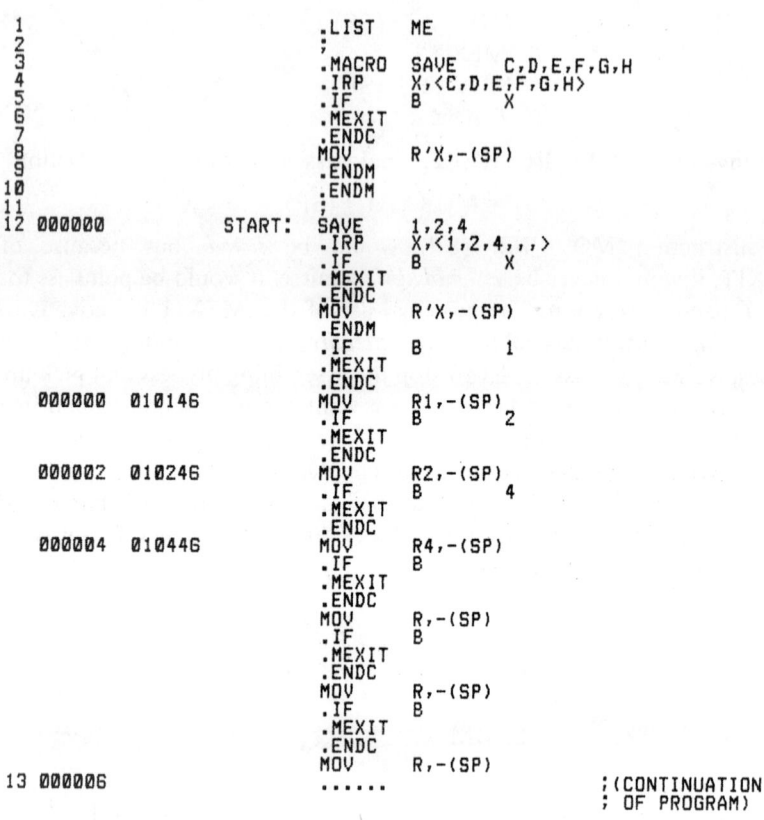

```
 1                         .LIST   ME
 2                         ;
 3                         .MACRO  SAVE    C,D,E,F,G,H
 4                         .IRP    X,<C,D,E,F,G,H>
 5                         .IF     B       X
 6                         .MEXIT
 7                         .ENDC
 8                         MOV     R'X,-(SP)
 9                         .ENDM
10                         .ENDM
11                         ;
12 000000         START:   SAVE    1,2,4
                           .IRP    X,<1,2,4,,,>
                           .IF     B       X
                           .MEXIT
                           .ENDC
                           MOV     R'X,-(SP)
                           .ENDM
                           .IF     B       1
                           .MEXIT
                           .ENDC
   000000  010146          MOV     R1,-(SP)
                           .IF     B       2
                           .MEXIT
                           .ENDC
   000002  010246          MOV     R2,-(SP)
                           .IF     B       4
                           .MEXIT
                           .ENDC
   000004  010446          MOV     R4,-(SP)
                           .IF     B
                           .MEXIT
                           .ENDC
                           MOV     R,-(SP)
                           .IF     B
                           .MEXIT
                           .ENDC
                           MOV     R,-(SP)
                           .IF     B
                           .MEXIT
                           .ENDC
                           MOV     R,-(SP)
13 000006          ......                          ;(CONTINUATION
                                                   ; OF PROGRAM)
```

Figure 13.12.1

is assembled. In the next two expansions of the repeat block, the assembler takes a similar action, since neither of the strings 2 or 4 is blank. However, in the fourth expansion of the repeat block, the dummy argument X is replaced with the empty string " ", and the conditional test becomes

.IF   B   " "

(We inserted the symbol " " here to indicate that the empty, or blank, string is being tested.) In this case, even though the assembler *listed* the expansion, namely,

MOV   R,-(SP)

it did not assemble it. Notice that it correctly took the dummy argument X to be an empty string and concatenated it onto the symbol R. In a similar fashion the remaining two expansions of the repeat block are listed, but not assembled.

Thus we have constructed a highly useful "superinstruction" to save as many registers as we want, and the conditional block has relieved us of the responsibility of counting arguments. In a similar fashion the reader will find it useful to construct a companion macro, for example, RESTORE, that will pop registers from the stack.

We return now to the macroinstruction SHIFTLEFT of Sec. 13.10. Recall that we detected two potential problems, one involving the possibly volatile contents of the "counting" register, R$\emptyset$, the other concerning the possibility of being passed a nonpositive shift count. We can now deal quite easily with both of these (Fig. 13.12.2). The first is handled simply by pushing R$\emptyset$ on the stack before its use and then restoring it later. The second is managed by inserting a conditional block that exits from the macro in the event the count is nonpositive. While this latest version of the listing is quite straightforward, the reader might profit from an examination of it.

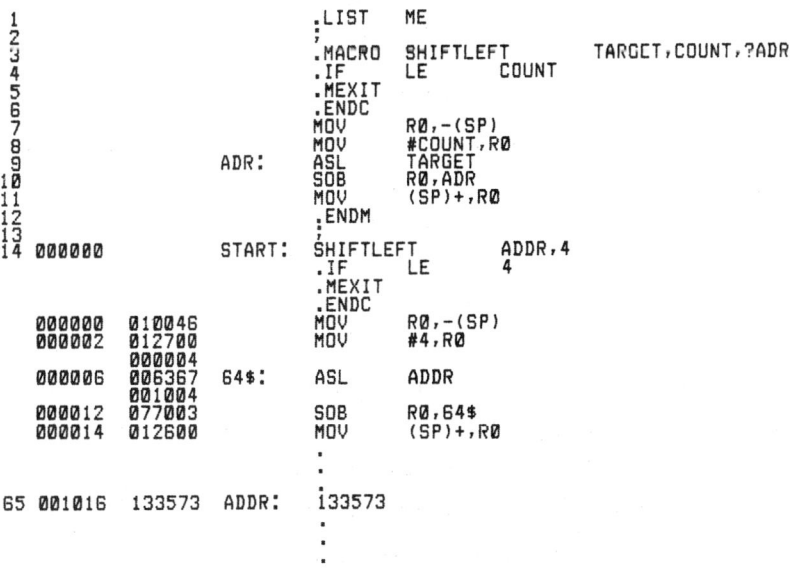

```
 1                           .LIST   ME
 2                           ;
 3                           .MACRO  SHIFTLEFT         TARGET,COUNT,?ADR
 4                           .IF     LE      COUNT
 5                           .MEXIT
 6                           .ENDC
 7                           MOV     R0,-(SP)
 8                           MOV     #COUNT,R0
 9                  ADR:     ASL     TARGET
10                           SOB     R0,ADR
11                           MOV     (SP)+,R0
12                           .ENDM
13
14 000000          START:   SHIFTLEFT         ADDR,4
                             .IF     LE      4
                             .MEXIT
                             .ENDC
   000000 010046            MOV     R0,-(SP)
   000002 012700            MOV     #4,R0
          000004
   000006 006367   64$:     ASL     ADDR
          001004
   000012 077003            SOB     R0,64$
   000014 012600            MOV     (SP)+,R0
                             .
                             .
65 001016 133573  ADDR:     133573
                             .
                             .
                             .
```

Figure 13.12.2

The macroinstruction, when invoked at line 14, was expanded as expected, since the shift count (4) was *not* less than or equal to 0 (LE). We show one more listing of this macro call, this time with a shift count that is *not* positive. As we see, no machine code was generated by the assembler (Fig. 13.12.3).

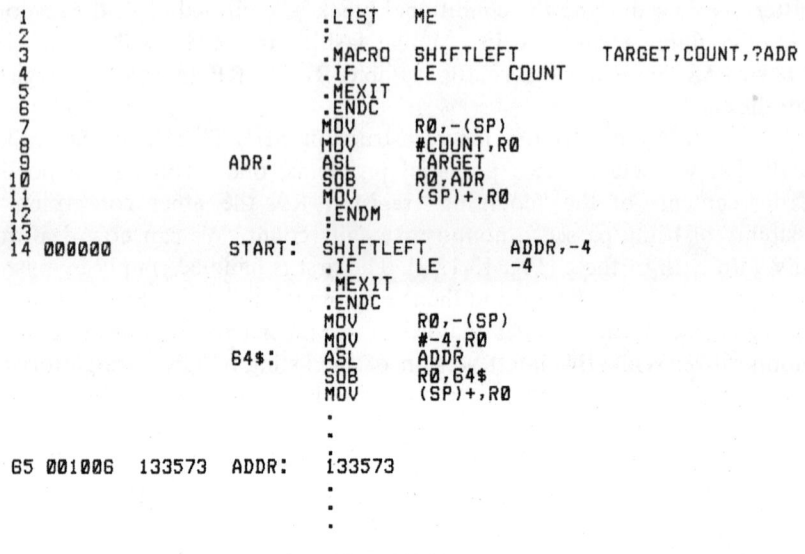

```
   1                       .LIST   ME
   2                       ;
   3                       .MACRO  SHIFTLEFT       TARGET,COUNT,?ADR
   4                       .IF     LE     COUNT
   5                       .MEXIT
   6                       .ENDC
   7                       MOV     R0,-(SP)
   8                       MOV     #COUNT,R0
   9               ADR:    ASL     TARGET
  10                       SOB     R0,ADR
  11                       MOV     (SP)+,R0
  12                       .ENDM
  13                       ;
  14 000000       START:  SHIFTLEFT       ADDR,-4
                          .IF     LE     -4
                          .MEXIT
                          .ENDC
                          MOV     R0,-(SP)
                          MOV     #-4,R0
                  64$:    ASL     ADDR
                          SOB     R0,64$
                          MOV     (SP)+,R0
                           .
                           .
  65 001006 133573 ADDR:  133573
                           .
                           .
                           .
```

Figure 13.12.3

13.13 SUBCONDITIONALS

In Sec. 13.11 we introduced the notion of conditional assemblies by selectively
assembling BGE NEXT or BLE NEXT according as the symbol FLAG was
or was not defined. While this did the job, the construction itself was somewhat awkward.

> Assemble BGE NEXT *if* FLAG is defined;
> assemble BLE NEXT *if* FLAG is not defined.

The program segment listing of Fig. 13.11.1 shows that *two* consecutive conditional blocks were required to manage this construction. What would seem
more natural, at least from an English-language standpoint, would be

> Assemble BGE NEXT *if* FLAG is defined,
> *else* assemble BLE NEXT.

In other words, if the condition tests as *true*, do one thing, but if it tests as
false, do something else. The PDP-11 assembler can generate such alternative
assemblies with the use of subconditionals.

A **subconditional** is a directive of the form .IFT (*IF T*rue), .IFF (*IF F*alse),
or .IFTF (*IF T*rue or *False*—that is, under any circumstances). These directives carry no arguments, and since the subconditional statement itself is not

assembled, it should not be labeled because the label will not be treated as a program symbol. The subconditionals divide the conditional block into subblocks, as follows: A subblock is started by any conditional or subconditional and is ended by any other subconditional or by .ENDC, the end of the conditional block. If the conditional tests as true, then the code in the conditional subblock itself, as well as the code in any .IFT or .IFTF subblock will be assembled. If the conditional tests as false, then the code in any .IFF or .IFTF subblock will be assembled. The following diagram illustrates the assembler's response to conditionals and subconditionals.

.IF   condition   (*assembled if condition is* true)
.
.
.

.IFF   (*assembled if condition is* false)
.
.
.

.IFTF   (*assembled whether condition*
.   *is* true *or* false)
.
.

.IFT   (*assembled if condition is* true)
.
.
.

.ENDC

We can now take advantage of these subconditionals quite easily to make a final repair to the macroinstruction SHIFTLEFT. To see where the problem lies, suppose we invoke SHIFTLEFT in such a way that the argument passed in place of the dummy argument TARGET is R$\emptyset$. Register $\emptyset$ is now being used as the word to be shifted *and* as the shift count, and as the listing of Fig. 13.13.1 indicates, the situation has badly come apart.

While there are a number of ways to circumvent this difficulty, the general appoach should be clear. If the word being shifted is *not* R$\emptyset$, then we can safely use R$\emptyset$ as the shift counter. On the other hand, if the word being shifted *is* R$\emptyset$, then we should use some other register—R1, for example—as the shift counter to avoid the conflict we see in the listing. This approach suggests a conditional test of the real argument replacing TARGET to determine if it is R$\emptyset$. We attack this problem by defining a *second* macroinstruction, SL (Fig. 13.13.2). Most of the action takes place in SL, and now SHIFTLEFT is used only to front-end SL. SHIFTLEFT simply decides which arguments should be passed to SL and then invokes SL itself. As we see from the listing, SHIFTLEFT tests the

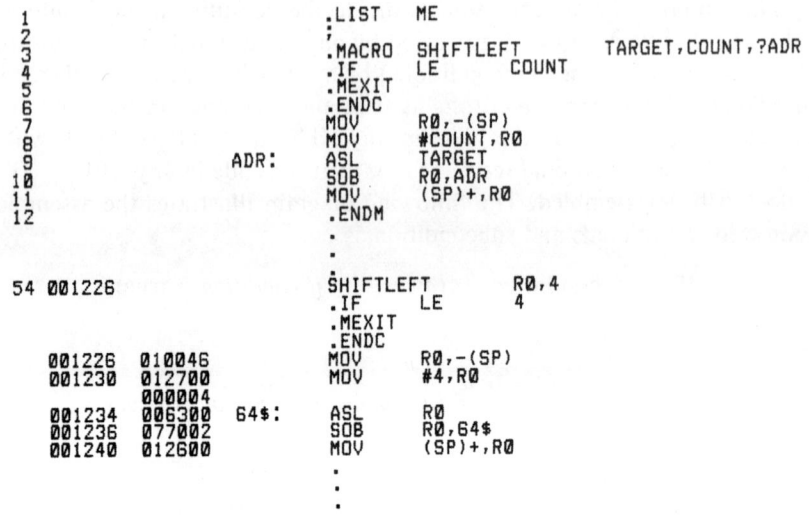

```
 1                              .LIST   ME
 2                              ;
 3                              .MACRO  SHIFTLEFT        TARGET,COUNT,?ADR
 4                              .IF     LE      COUNT
 5                              .MEXIT
 6                              .ENDC
 7                              MOV     R0,-(SP)
 8                              MOV     #COUNT,R0
 9                      ADR:    ASL     TARGET
10                              SOB     R0,ADR
11                              MOV     (SP)+,R0
12                              .ENDM
                                .
                                .

54 001226                       SHIFTLEFT        R0,4
                                .IF     LE      4
                                .MEXIT
                                .ENDC
   001226  010046               MOV     R0,-(SP)
   001230  012700               MOV     #4,R0
           000004
   001234  006300       64$:    ASL     R0
   001236  077002               SOB     R0,64$
   001240  012600               MOV     (SP)+,R0
                                .
                                .
```

Figure 13.13.1

shift count and exits if it is nonpositive. It then checks to see if the shifted word, represented by the dummy argument TARGET, is R∅. If it is, it invokes SL with the arguments TARGET, COUNT, and 1, the 1 indicating that SL is to use R1 (instead of R∅) as the counting register. If R∅ is not the word to be shifted, SHIFTLEFT can safely let SL use R∅ as the counting register, and thus it invokes it with the arguments TARGET, COUNT,0. The macroinstruction SL now does substantially what our earlier version of SHIFTLEFT did—it does the actual shifting of the target word. Again, we encourage the reader to investigate carefully the definitions of these two macroinstructions and their expansions.

We offer a final version of the macro SHIFTLEFT (Fig. 13.13.3). In this case the macroinstruction SL is defined *within the definition* of SHIFTLEFT, thereby indicating that macroinstruction definitions can be nested. This is more than a curiosity, for a look at lines 17 and 19 of the listing shows that SHIFTLEFT was able to invoke SL simply by passing the register number to SL without having to pass the arguments TARGET and COUNT. The reason for this is that whenever a macroinstruction B is defined within the definition of the macroinstruction A, any dummy arguments (and subsequently, upon a call of the macro A, any real arguments) for the macroinstruction A also become arguments for the inner macroinstruction B. This nesting of the definitions can in some cases substantially simplify the calling of one macroinstruction by another.

```
 1                        .LIST   ME
 2                        ;
 3                        .MACRO  SHIFTLEFT       TARGET,COUNT
 4                        .IF     LE      COUNT
 5                        .MEXIT
 6                        .ENDC
 7                        .IF     IDN     TARGET,R0
 8                        SL      TARGET,COUNT,1
 9                        .IFF
10                        SL      TARGET,COUNT,0
11                        .ENDC
12                        .ENDM
13                        ;
14                        .MACRO  SL      A,B,C,?D
15                        MOV     R'C,-(SP)
16                        MOV     #B,R'C
17                 D:     ASL     A
18                        SOB     R'C,D
19                        MOV     (SP)+,R'C
20                        .ENDM
                          .
                          .
45 001226                 SHIFTLEFT       R3,7
                          .IF     LE      7
                          .MEXIT
                          .ENDC
                          .IF     IDN     R3,R0
                          SL      R3,7,1
                          .IFF
   001226                 SL      R3,7,0
   001226     010046      MOV     R0,-(SP)
   001230     012700      MOV     #7,R0
              000007
   001234     006303 64$: ASL     R3
   001236     077002      SOB     R0,64$
   001240     012600      MOV     (SP)+,R0
                          .ENDC
                          .
                          .
73 002262                 SHIFTLEFT       R0,2
                          .IF     LE      2
                          .MEXIT
                          .ENDC
                          .IF     IDN     R0,R0
   002262                 SL      R0,2,1
   002262     010146      MOV     R1,-(SP)
   002264     012701      MOV     #2,R1
              000002
   002270     006300 65$: ASL     R0
   002272     077102      SOB     R1,65$
   002274     012601      MOV     (SP)+,R1
                          .IFF
                          SL      R0,2,0
                          .ENDC
                          .
                          .
                          .
```

Figure 13.13.2

```
     1                                   .LIST   ME
     2                                 ;
     3                                   .MACRO  SHIFTLEFT      TARGET,COUNT
     4                                   .IF     LE      COUNT
     5                                   .MEXIT
     6                                   .ENDC
     7                                 ;
     8                                   .MACRO  SL      C,?D
     9                                   MOV     R'C,-(SP)
    10                                   MOV     #COUNT,R'C
    11                         D:        ASL     TARGET
    12                                   SOB     R'C,D
    13                                   MOV     (SP)+,R'C
    14                                   .ENDM   SL
    15                                 ;
    16                                   .IF     IDN     TARGET,R0
    17                                   SL      1
    18                                   .IFF
    19                                   SL      0
    20                                   .ENDC
    21                                   .ENDM   SHIFTLEFT

                                         .

    63 001226                          SHIFTLEFT      R3,7
                                         .IF     LE      7
                                         .MEXIT
                                         .ENDC
                                       ;
                                         .MACRO  SL      C,?D
                                         MOV     R'C,-(SP)
                                         MOV     #7,R'C
                               D:        ASL     R3
                                         SOB     R'C,D
                                         MOV     (SP)+,R'C
                                         .ENDM   SL
                                       ;
                                         .IF     IDN     R3,R0
                                         SL      1
                                         .IFF
       001226                            SL      0
       001226   010046                   MOV     R0,-(SP)
       001230   012700                   MOV     #7,R0
                000007
       001234   006303    64$:           ASL     R3
       001236   077002                   SOB     R0,64$
       001240   012600                   MOV     (SP)+,R0
                                         .ENDC

                                         .

    89 002262                          SHIFTLEFT      R0,2
                                         .IF     LE      2
                                         .MEXIT
                                         .ENDC
                                       ;
                                         .MACRO  SL      C,?D
                                         MOV     R'C,-(SP)
                                         MOV     #2,R'C
                               D:        ASL     R0
                                         SOB     R'C,D
                                         .ENDM   SL
                                       ;
                                         .IF     IDN     R0,R0
       002262                            SL      1
       002262   010146                   MOV     R1,-(SP)
       002264   012701                   MOV     #2,R1
                000002
       002270   006300    65$:           ASL     R0
       002272   077102                   SOB     R1,65$
       002274   012601                   MOV     (SP)+,R1
                                         .IFF
                                         SL      0
                                         .ENDC
                                         .
                                         .
                                         .
```

Figure 13.13.3

13.14 SOME CONCLUDING REMARKS

The reader has doubtless noticed that the listings of the program segments of this chapter, especially those of the last few sections, were excessively long. These long listings were a consequence of the fact that if the assembler is directed to list macro expansions, it lists the definition of the macroinstruction itself each time it is invoked, and also lists any conditional blocks, whether assembled or not. Such listings can be extremely useful during the time a program module is being developed, but once one module has been debugged and tested and the next is being developed, the programmer might choose not to see the expansions in the first module listed. As the reader has already seen, macroinstruction expansions can selectively be turned on and off with the assembler directives .LIST ME and .NLIST ME, which can be included anywhere in the program. In a similar fashion, listings of **unsatisfied conditionals** can be turned on and off with the directives .LIST CND and .NLIST CND (*LIST* or do *N*ot *LIST* *C*o*N*Ditionals). Even with .NLIST CND in force, those instructions within a conditional that *are* assembled are listed.

In this chapter we examined numerous features of the PDP-11 macro-instruction and conditional assembler. The assembler has some other capabilities that we did not discuss. Our selection was based on maximum utility to the programmer, and the reader is encouraged to investigate the appropriate manuals to determine other assembler features that might be of use to him. While this chapter was devoted to the details of some of these concepts, the number of ways in which macroinstructions and conditional assemblies can be written clearly precludes the possibility of our looking at anything more than a small sampling. The conscientious programmer will develop a solid under-standing of and comfortable familiarity with these ideas by *doing*—by writing program segments with their attendant trial and error.

Finally, we saw that both macroinstructions and subroutines, while performing some task for the user numerous times, are really different concepts. The macroinstruction has the potential for a tremendous amount of flexibility in the manner in which it is invoked and thus in the code it generates. On the negative side, each call to a macro can use up a fair amount of main memory, since the expansion is coded in line. A subroutine call provides much less flexibility in the way in which it is called, but it saves space. The experienced programmer will balance the flexibility of macroinstructions with the memory conserving properties of subroutines and make appropriate decisions based on the total task to be accomplished.

13.15 EXERCISES

13.1.1. Write a subroutine to search a text string for the first occurrence of a specified target string and to return the position of the target string if it is found, otherwise to return 0. The position should be left on the stack upon return to the mainline routine. Assume both the text string and the target string end in a NUL. Thus, for example, if the text string is #SAMPLE,LP:=MT:(NUL) and the target string is LP:(NUL), the routine should return the number 9 on the stack. Let R∅ contain the address of the first byte of the target string and R1 contain the address of the first byte of the text string.

13.1.2. Show that the subroutine SAVE of Fig. 13.1.3 will execute properly if it is written as

```
SAVE:       MOV   (SP)+,RETURN+2
            MOV   R1,-(SP)
            MOV   R3,-(SP)
            MOV   R5,-(SP)
RETURN:     JMP   @#0
```

Could proper results have been achieved with

```
RETURN:     JMP   0
```

13.1.3. In the program of Fig. 13.1.2 show that the sequence of instructions

```
            CLC
            BR    DONE
EOT:        SEC
DONE:       RTS
```

could be replaced by

```
            TST   (PC)+
EOT:        SEC
            RTS
```

13.2.1. Suppose we write *two* macroinstructions, SAVE and CLEAR, defined as follows:

Definition of CLEAR
```
CLR   R1
CLR   R3
CLR   R5
```

Definition of SAVE
```
MOV   R1,-(SP)
MOV   R3,-(SP)
MOV   R5,-(SP)
CLEAR
```

How would our clerk handle a reference to SAVE? What problems, if any, would he have in expanding this macroinstruction?

13.2.2. If SAVE is the name of a macroinstruction, how would (and how should) the assembling clerk respond to the following four constructions?

(a) SAVE   (b) .WORD   SAVE
(c) MOV   R2,SAVE   (d) .ASCII /SAVE/

13.3.1. Write the two macroinstruction definitions of Exercise 13.2.1 in a format acceptable to the PDP-11 assembler. Since the macroinstruction SAVE contains in its definition a call to the macroinstruction CLEAR, could the definition of SAVE have been placed physically ahead of the definition of CLEAR? Why or why not?

13.4.1. In the program segment of Fig. 13.4.3, if the call to the subroutine SORT had been written as

```
JSR  PC,SORT
SAVE,20
```

instead of

```
JSR  PC,SORT
SAVE
20
```

what code would the assembler have generated? (We are asking the reader to make some educated guesses here. The question is resolved in Sec. 13.5.)

13.4.2. Suppose that we need frequently to increment registers or memory locations by 4, so we write a macroinstruction to do this.

```
.MACRO  INC  X
ADD   #4,X
.ENDM
```

In choosing as a name for this macroinstruction one that coincides with an assembler mnemonic, we are surely on dangerous ground. The program segment of Fig. 13.15.1 shows what happens when this macro is invoked.

```
 1                          .LIST   ME
 2                          ;
 3                          .MACRO  INC    X
 4                          ADD     #4,X
 5                          .ENDM
                            .
                            .
37 002102                   INC     R2
   002102    062702         ADD     #4,R2
             000004
                            .
                            .
```

Figure 13.15.1

The reader may be surprised to observe that apparently the assembler gave precedence to the *macroinstruction* over the *mnemonic*. And although all appears to be well, Fig. 13.15.2, in which the macro INC is defined *after*

```
 1                            .LIST   ME
 2                            ;
                              .
                              .
24 001266                     INC     R2
   001266    062702           ADD     #4,R2
             000004
                              .
                              .
P 39 001366  005005  LOOP:    CLR     R5
                              .
                              .
73                            .MACRO  INC    X
74                            ADD     #4,X
75                            .ENDM
                              .
                              .
```

Figure 13.15.2

it is invoked, shows that problems can arise. Specifically, explain in detail why the label LOOP: at line 39 was flagged with a phase error.

13.4.3. How should the assembler be expected to react to a program that contains two macroinstruction definitions with the same name? Would it make any difference if the macros specified a different number of arguments? (The reader may want to try an example of this to find the somewhat surprising answer.)

13.5.1. Using the definition of the macroinstruction SAVE given on page 297, indicate what the macro expansion will be for each of the following calls:

(a) SAVE   RØ,R1,R1   (b) SAVE   @(RØ)+,#2,#4

(c) SAVE   #'A,R1,RØ   (d) SAVE   2,4,6

(e) SAVE   1,2,3

13.5.2. Write a macro definition that will call (via a JSR) *any* subroutine using *any* transfer register, and that passes *one* argument to the subroutine in a .WORD directive immediately following the JSR instruction. Expand the macro for a few choices of macro arguments.

13.5.3. Modify the macroinstruction of Exercise 13.5.2 to pass the subroutine's argument on the stack rather than in a .WORD.

13.5.4. Consider the macroinstruction defined by

```
          .MACRO   DUMMY   A,B,C
     C:     MOV  B
            DEC  A
            BNE  C
          .ENDM
```

How would the macro be expanded for each of the following calls?

(a) DUMMY   R1,⟨R2,R3⟩,LOOP

(b) DUMMY   R1,R2,R3,LOOP

(c) DUMMY   R1,⟨R2,R3⟩

(d) DUMMY   LOOP,⟨@(R1)+,@-(R1)⟩,LOOP

(e) DUMMY   R1,,LOOP

(f) DUMMY   ,⟨R3,R4⟩,LOOP

(g) DUMMY   ,,⟨R3,R4⟩,LOOP

13.5.5. (a) In the macroinstruction of Exercise 13.5.4 we passed as a macro argument the *label* C. Thus if the third argument in a call to DUMMY were LOOP, then C: would be expanded as LOOP:. Why did this work? That is, why was C: recognized by the assembler as an occurrence of the dummy variable C, whereas (see Fig. 13.5.1) RA is *not* considered an instance of A? (The reader will have to speculate a bit here.)

(b) Could we have written this macro as

```
          .MACRO   DUMMY   A,B,C
     C      MOV  B
            DEC  A
            BNE  C
          .ENDM
```

and then called it, for example, with DUMMY   R1,⟨R2,R3⟩,LOOP:?

(c) Would the assembler recognize #X as an instance of the dummy variable X (for example, in the instruction MOV #X,RØ)?

13.5.6. Do Exercise 13.4.1 again.

13.5.7. Consider a macroinstruction similar to the macro CUSTOM of Fig. 13.5.7 that in this case invokes *another* macroinstruction, as follows:

```
.MACRO    SPECIAL  A
INSTR     A
.ENDM
```

```
.MACRO    INSTR    X
X
.ENDM
```

What would be the effect of the call
(a) SPECIAL MOV #3,R2
(b) SPECIAL ⟨MOV #3,R2⟩
(c) SPECIAL ⟨⟨MOV #3,R2⟩⟩

13.6.1. We saw in Fig. 13.6.2 that the macroinstruction SETCODE failed because the apostrophe, which we intended to be used by the assembler to generate ASCII code, was instead taken as the concatenation symbol. Our solution was to rewrite the macro definition. How could the macro, *as written,* be used to put the ASCII code for a character in RØ?

13.6.2. How will the macroinstruction

```
.MACRO  SAMPLE  X,Y
.WORD  'X''Y'
.ENDM
```

be expanded for each of the following calls?
(a) SAMPLE ADD,R   (b) SAMPLE 'ADD,R'
(c) SAMPLE ADD',R   (d) SAMPLE ADD','R

13.6.3. What will be the macro expansion TEST A,B if TEST is defined by

```
.MACRO  TEST  X,Y
.WORD  'X'''Y'
.ENDM
```

13.6.4. Consider the macroinstruction defined by

```
.MACRO  SAVE  P,Q,R
MOV  R'P,-(SP)
MOV  R'Q,-(SP)
MOV  R'R,-(SP)
.ENDM
```

How will SAVE 0,2,3 be expanded?

13.6.5. How will CODE #,H be expanded, where CODE is defined by

```
.MACRO  CODE  SYM,CHAR
MOVB  'SYM'''CHAR,RØ
.ENDM
```

13.6.6. Consider the macroinstruction

```
.MACRO  ZERO  M
CLR   RM'
.ENDM
```

How will ZERO   2 be expanded?

13.6.7. Write a macroinstruction to pop three registers from the hardware stack.

13.6.8. Write a macroinstruction to pop three registers from a stack that has as its stack pointer a fourth register.

13.8.1. Consider the macroinstruction defined by

```
.MACRO  MOVE  A,?B
MOV   A,(B)
.ENDM
```

(a) How will MOVE   R1,R2 be expanded?
(b) How will MOVE   (SP)+ be expanded?

13.8.2. Consider the following modification of the macroinstruction BIGGER of Fig. 13.8.3:

```
        .MACRO  BIGGER  A,B,C,?D
        MOV   R'A,R'C
        CMP   R'A,R'B
        BGE   L'D
        MOV   R'B,R'C
L'D:
        .ENDM
```

(a) What labels will be generated the first two times the macro is called within the same local symbol block?
(b) If the macro is invoked in *different* local symbol blocks, will the labels generated be the same? If so, will they be treated as multiply defined symbols?

13.8.3. Consider the macroinstruction defined by

```
        .MACRO  LABELS  A,?B,?C
B:      CLR   R'A
C:      MOV   #B,-(SP)
        .ENDM
```

What values will B and C be given for the first two calls to LABELS within the *same* local symbol block?

13.9.1. Would an indefinite repeat block of the form

```
.IRP  X,⟨W,X,Y,Z⟩
```

cause a conflict because of the two different uses of the symbol X?

13.9.2. Early versions of the PDP-11 assembler used %Ø, %1, ..., %7 as its register designations, rather than RØ, R1, ..., R5, SP, and PC. Write some instructions, including a repeat block, to define the appropriate register designations in terms of %Ø, ..., %7.

13.12.1. The final version of the macroinstruction SAVE (see Fig. 13.12.1) uses the argument list C,D,E,F,G,H. Why could we *not* have used A,B,C,D,E,F?

13.12.2. Write a macroinstruction to RESTORE up to six registers by popping them from the stack.

13.12.3. Write a macroinstruction RESTORE to pop up to six registers from the stack, but write this version as a companion to SAVE in such a way that the register numbers can be passed to both macros *in the same order*. For example, SAVE   1,4 should push R1 and R4, in that order, and RESTORE   1,4 should pop R1 and R4, but in the order R4 first, then R1.

13.12.4. Referring to the definition of the macro SHIFTLEFT in Fig. 13.12.2, determine how each of the following calls would be expanded:
  (a) SHIFTLEFT   R4,2
  (b) SHIFTLEFT   (R4),2

13.12.5. What would be the effect of SHIFTLEFT   (R2)+,5? (See Fig. 13.12.2 for the definition of SHIFTLEFT.)

13.13.1. Using conditional and subconditional blocks, modify the definition of the macro SHIFTLEFT so that it will shift *bytes* as well as words.

13.13.2. Our final version of SHIFTLEFT (Fig. 13.13.2) still contains a severe deficiency. If we desired to shift the word whose *address* is in R$\emptyset$, we would invoke the macro with SHIFTLEFT   (R$\emptyset$),5, for example. But then the test at line 7,

```
        .IF    IDN    TARGET,RØ
```

would be *false*, since (R$\emptyset$) is *not* identical with R$\emptyset$. Once again the macro expansion is in trouble. Correcting this will require some rewriting, and we offer some suggestions.

  (a) Do not use a register for counting the shifts. Rather, put the shift count on the stack. The shifting loop will then become

```
        D:    ASL    TARGET
              DEC    (SP)
              BNE    D
```

  (b) If the shift count is put on the stack with the instruction

```
        MOV    B,-(SP)
```

rather than

```
        MOV    #B,-(SP)
```

then SHIFTLEFT would have to be invoked with, for example, SHIFTLEFT   R2,#4 rather than SHIFTLEFT   R2,4. But this opens up a number of new possibilities, such as SHIFTLEFT   ADDR,R2 (where c(R2) = shift count) or SHIFTLEFT   ADDR,CNT (where c(CNT) = shift count).

  (c) Show that even with these modifications the situation is not completely saved because it would not be possible to shift the word that is currently on the top of the stack.

13.13.3. Modify the macroinstruction of Exercise 13.13.2 above so that it more closely emulates the instruction ASH, as follows: If the shift count is *positive*, the word is shifted *left*. If the shift count is *negative*, the word is shifted *right*. (This is perhaps not quite so straightforward as it might at first appear.)

13.13.4. We saw that macro definitions can be nested, and that macros can invoke other macros. In fact, a macro can even call *itself*, provided some care is taken to prevent infinite recursion.

   (a) Show that the following macro will generate code to calculate factorial N, provided that R1 is first set to 1.

```
.MACRO  FACT  N
.IF  LE  N-1
.MEXIT
.ENDC
MUL  #N,R1
FACT  N-1
.ENDM
```

   (b) What limitations are there on N?

   (c) Why would this macro not execute properly if we changed R1 to R2?

   (d) Modify this macro so that R2 is the register used, thereby obtaining a double-precision (32-bit) result. What limitations are now put on N?

   (e) Can this macro be rewritten (or perhaps front-ended by another macro) so that it can determine whether it is dealing with an odd- or even-numbered register?

   (f) In Sec. 8.10 we saw another example of recursion, in which a subroutine determined the address of the first instance in a block of memory of a byte containing an odd number. Why cannot this recursive procedure be written as a recursive macro?

13.13.5. The table of Fig. 13.11.3 lists six conditionals and their complements. Show that the complementary conditionals are not needed—they are implemented only for programmer convenience.

13.13.6. The reader is now in a position to understand the definitions of the I/O macros used throughout the text. In particular, look in Appendix B, Sec. B.7, and expand the macro calls $OUT.ASC #TEXT,#12 and $OUT.ASC #TEXT.

13.13.7. Conditional blocks can be nested. What is the effect of the following instructions and directives for various combinations of SYMBOL and FLAG being defined or not defined?

```
.IF  DF  SYMBOL
BGE  NEXT
.IFF
.IF  NDF  FLAG
BLE  NEXT
.ENDC
.IFTF
DEC  RØ
.ENDC
```

What might be the effect of defining SYMBOL or FLAG, or both, *after* these conditional blocks?

13.13.8. We saw that a macro can invoke another macro or even itself. In a similar fashion, consider two macros, AMAC and BMAC, each of which calls the other. How will the call to AMAC (at START:) be expanded?

```
          .MACRO  AMAC  X,Y,Z
          BMAC  Y,Z
          .ENDM
          .MACRO  BMAC  S,T
          .IF  B  S
          .MEXIT
          .IFF
          MOV  R'S,-(SP)
          .IF  NB  T
          MOV  R'T,-(SP)
          .ENDC
          AMAC  S,T
          .ENDC
          .ENDM
          ;
START:    AMAC  1,2,3
          .
          .
          .
```

13.13.9. Refer to Exercises 7.7.11, 7.7.14, and 7.7.15 and write macroinstructions to emulate XOR, MUL, and DIV, respectively.

13.13.10. While the PDP-11 has instructions to rotate 16-bit words left or right (see the descriptions of ROL and ROR in Appendix B), these are strictly 1-bit rotates. They are not *true* word rotates in that the carry bit acts as a seventeenth bit for the word, and rotations take place through the carry bit. Write a macroinstruction ROTATE that is a true 16-bit rotate, whose arguments are a *register* to be rotated and a rotate count, positive being a left rotate, negative a right rotate. (Our specifying a register as the word to be rotated is a simplifying condition which the reader may ultimately wish to remove.)

Appendix A

The PDP-11
Instruction Set

A.1 SYMBOLS AND ABBREVIATIONS

Listed below are the symbols and abbreviations used in this appendix.

Symbol	Meaning
c	condition code (binary)
c(. . .)	contents of . . .
C	condition code (octal) or PSW C-bit
d	destination (binary)
dst	destination (register or memory location)
D	destination (octal)
loc	location
n	number (binary)
N	number (octal) or PSW N-bit
PC	program counter
PSW	processor status word
r	register (binary)
reg	register
R	register (octal)
s	source (binary)
src	source (register, memory location or number)
S	source (octal)
V	PSW V-bit
x	word offset (binary)
X	word offset (octal)
Z	PSW Z-bit

Symbol	Meaning
⌊(SP)	push onto hardware stack
(SP)↑	pop from hardware stack
← . . .	is given the value . . .
∧	logical *AND*
∨	logical *OR*
⊻	logical *EXCLUSIVE OR*
∼	logical *NOT*

Processor Status Word (PSW)

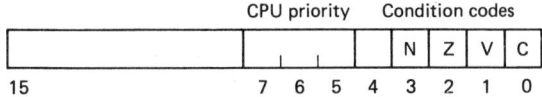

A.2 THE INSTRUCTION SET IN ALPHABETIC ORDER BY MNEMONIC

ADC   ADD CARRY TO DESTINATION   0055DD

Binary
code: 0 000 101 101 *ddd ddd*

Operation: *dst* ← c(*dst*) + c(C)

Assembler
format: ADC *dst*

Condition   N: Set if result < 0; cleared otherwise.
codes: Z: Set if result = 0; cleared otherwise.
             V: Set if c(*dst*) *was* 077777 and c(C) *was* 1; cleared
                 otherwise.
             C: Set if c(*dst*) *was* 177777 and c(C) *was* 1; cleared
                 otherwise.

Description: Adds the contents of the C-bit into the destination.

ADCB   ADD CARRY TO DESTINATION BYTE 1055DD

Binary
code: 1 000 101 101 *ddd ddd*

Operation: *dst* ← c(*dst*) + c(C)

Assembler
format: ADCB *dst*

Condition   N: Set if result < 0; cleared otherwise.
codes: Z: Set if result $= 0$; cleared otherwise.
              V: Set if c(*dst*) *was* 177 and c(C) *was* 1; cleared
                 otherwise.
              C: Set if c(*dst*) *was* 377 and c(C) *was* 1; cleared
                 otherwise.
Description: Adds the contents of the C-bit into the (byte)
              destination.

ADD   ADD SOURCE TO DESTINATION   06SSDD

Binary   0 110 *sss sss ddd ddd*
code:

Operation: *dst* ← c(*src*) + c(*dst*)

Assembler   ADD *src, dst*
format:

Condition   N: Set if result < 0; cleared otherwise.
codes: Z: Set if result $= 0$; cleared otherwise.
              V: Set if overflow occurred (both operands were
                 of the same sign, and the result is of the opposite
                 sign); cleared otherwise.
              C: Set if a carry out of bit 15 occurred; cleared
                 otherwise.

Description: Adds the contents of the source to the contents
              of the destination and places the result in the
              destination. The original contents of the des-
              tination is lost; the contents of the source is
              unaffected.

ASH   ARITHMETIC SHIFT REGISTER   072RSS

Binary   0 111 010 *rrr sss sss*
code:

Operation: *reg* ← c(*reg*) shifted *n* bits left ($n > 0$) or right
              ($n < 0$), where *n* is the signed value of the 6 low-
              order bits of *src*

Assembler   ASH *src, reg*
format:

Condition codes:

N: Set if result < 0; cleared otherwise.

Z: Set if result $= 0$; cleared otherwise.

V: Set if the high-order bit of the register changed value at any time during the shift; cleared otherwise.

C: Loaded with the last bit shifted out of the register.

Description: The 6 low-order bits of the source word are taken as a signed number n, so that $-32_{10} \leq n \leq +31_{10}$.

$n \geq 0$: The shift is a left shift by n bits. The high-order bit (bit 15) is shifted out into the PSW C-bit. The vacated low-order bit (bit 0) is given the value 0.

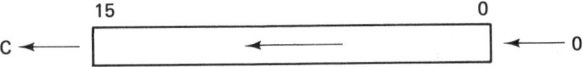

$n < 0$: The shift is a right shift by n bits. The vacated high-order bit (bit 15) is replicated. The low-order bit is shifted out into the PSW C-bit.

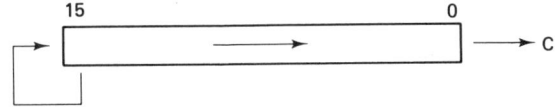

Comment: ASH is not implemented on some PDP-11 models.

ASHC   ARITHMETIC SHIFT REGISTERS COMBINED   073RSS

Binary code:

0 111 011 *rrr sss sss*

Operation: *reg, reg $\vee$ 1* $\leftarrow$ c(*reg, reg $\vee$ 1*) shifted n bits left ($n > 0$) or right ($n < 0$), where n is the signed value of the 6 low-order bits of *src*.

Assembler format:

ASHC *src, reg*

Condition codes:

N: Set if result < 0; cleared otherwise.

Z: Set if result $= 0$; cleared otherwise.

V: Set if the high-order bit of the 32-bit register

pair changed value at any time during the shift; cleared otherwise.

C: Loaded with the last bit shifted out of the register pair.

Description: The register pair *reg* and *reg* $\vee$ 1 (for example, $R2$ and $R2 \vee 1 = R3$), considered as a 32-bit double word, is shifted left or right n bits. The 6 low-order bits of the source word are taken as a signed number n, so that $-32_{10} \leq n \leq +31_{10}$.

$n \geq 0$: The shift is a left shift by n bits. The high-order bit (bit 15 of *reg*) is shifted out into the PSW C-bit. The vacated low-order bit (bit 0 of *reg* $\vee$ 1) is given the value 0.

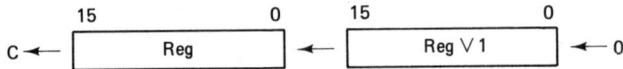

$n < 0$: The shift is a right shift by n bits. The vacated high-order bit (bit 15 of *reg*) is replicated. The low-order bit (bit 0 of *reg* $\vee$ 1) is shifted out into the PSW C-bit.

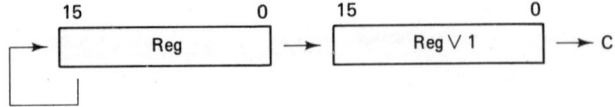

If the register number is *odd* (so that *reg* = *reg* $\vee$ 1), then a left shift is equivalent to ASH *src, reg*. A right shift is a 16-bit right rotate on *reg*:

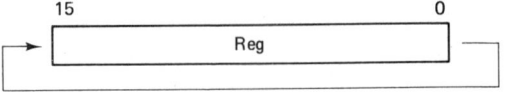

Comment: ASHC is not implemented on some PDP-11 models.

ASL   ARITHMETIC SHIFT LEFT   0063DD
         DESTINATION

Binary code: 0 000 110 011 *ddd ddd*

Operation: *dst* ← c(*dst*) shifted one bit left.

Assembler   ASL *dst*
format:

Condition   N: Set if result < 0; cleared otherwise.
codes: Z: Set if result = 0; cleared otherwise.
                V: Loaded with the *EXCLUSIVE OR* of N and C
                (as determined *after* the shift).
                C: Loaded with the bit shifted out of the high-
                order bit of the destination.

Description: Each bit of the destination word is shifted one
                position to the left. The high-order bit (bit 15) is
                shifted out into the PSW C-bit. The vacated low-
                order bit (bit 0) is given the value 0.
                ASL performs a signed multiplication by 2 of the
                destination. If, after the shift, the V-bit is set, a
                sign change in the destination has taken place.

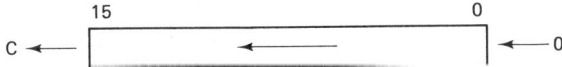

ASLB   ARITHMETIC SHIFT LEFT   1063DD
DESTINATION BYTE

Binary   1 000 110 011 *ddd ddd*
code:

Operation: *dst* ← c(*dst*) shifted one bit left.

Assembler   ASLB *dst*
format:

Condition   N: Set if result < 0; cleared otherwise.
codes: Z: Set if result = 0; cleared otherwise.
                V: Loaded with *EXCLUSIVE OR* of N and C
                (as determined *after* the shift).
                C: Loaded with the bit shifted out of the high-
                order bit of the destination.

Description: Each bit of the destination byte is shifted one
                position to the left. The high-order bit (bit 7 or 15)
                is shifted out into the PSW C-bit. The vacated low-
                order bit (bit 0 or 8) is given the value 0.

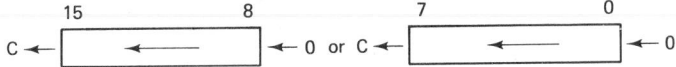

ASR   **ARITHMETIC SHIFT RIGHT**   **0062DD**
            DESTINATION

Binary code:	0 000 110 010 *ddd ddd*
Operation:	*dst* ← c(*dst*) shifted one bit right.
Assembler format:	ASR *dst*
Condition codes:	N: Set if result < 0; cleared otherwise. Z: Set if result = 0; cleared otherwise. V: Loaded with *EXCLUSIVE OR* of N and C (as determined *after* the shift). C: Loaded with the bit shifted out of the low-order bit of the destination.
Description:	Each bit of the destination is shifted one position to the right. The high-order bit (bit 15) is replicated. The low-order bit (bit 0) is shifted out into the PSW C-bit. ASR performs a signed division by 2 of the destination.

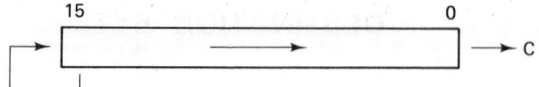

ASRB   **ARITHMETIC SHIFT RIGHT**   **1062DD**
            DESTINATION BYTE

Binary code:	1 000 110 010 *ddd ddd*
Operation:	*dst* ← c(*dst*) shifted one bit right.
Assembler format:	ASRB *dst*
Condition codes:	N: Set if result < 0; cleared otherwise. Z: Set if result = 0; cleared otherwise. V: Loaded with *EXCLUSIVE OR* of N and C (as determined *after* the shift). C: Loaded with the bit shifted out of the low-order bit of the destination.

Description: Each bit of the destination byte is shifted one position to the right. The high-order bit (bit 7 or 15) is replicated. The low-order bit (bit 0 or 8) is shifted out into the PSW C-bit.

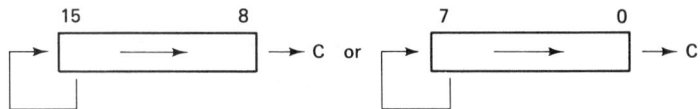

BCC   BRANCH IF CARRY CLEAR   1030XXX

Binary
code: 1 000 011 0*xx xxx xxx*

Operation: PC ← c(PC) + 2 × (offset) if C = 0.

Assembler   BCC *loc*
format:

Condition   Unaffected.
codes:

Description: The low-order byte of the instruction is the *signed word* offset from the current PC to the target address *loc*. If C = 0, twice the offset is added to c(PC). If C = 1, the instruction is ignored.

BCS   BRANCH IF CARRY SET   1034XXX

Binary   1 000 011 1*xx xxx xxx*
code:

Operation: PC ← c(PC) + 2 × (offset) if C = 1.

Assembler   BCS *loc*
format:

Condition   Unaffected.
codes:

Description: The low-order byte of the instruction is the *signed word* offset from the current PC to the target address *loc*. If C = 1, twice the offset is added to c(PC). If C = 0, the instruction is ignored.

BEQ   **BRANCH IF EQUAL ZERO**   **0014XXX**

Binary code:	0 000 001 1xx xxx xxx
Operation:	PC ← c(PC) + 2 × (offset) if Z = 1.
Assembler format:	BEQ *loc*
Condition codes:	Unaffected.
Description:	The low-order byte of the instruction is the *signed word* offset from the current PC to the target address *loc*. If Z = 1, twice the offset is added to c(PC). If Z = 0, the instruction is ignored.

BGE   **BRANCH IF GREATER THAN OR**   **0020XXX**
           EQUAL ZERO

Binary code:	0 000 010 0xx xxx xxx
Operation:	PC ← c(PC) + 2 × (offset) if N $\veebar$ V = 0.
Assembler format:	BGE *loc*
Condition codes:	Unaffected.
Description:	The low-order byte of the instruction is the *signed word* offset from the current PC to the target address *loc*. If N $\veebar$ V = 0, twice the offset is added to c(PC). If N $\veebar$ V = 1, the instruction is ignored. (Thus BGE causes a branch when it follows the addition of two positive numbers, even if the result of the addition is negative.)

BGT   **BRANCH IF GREATER THAN ZERO**   **0030XXX**

Binary code:	0 000 011 0xx xxx xxx
Operation:	PC ← c(PC) + 2 × (offset) if Z $\vee$ (N $\veebar$ V) = 0.

Assembler format:	BGT *loc*
Condition codes:	Unaffected.
Description:	The low-order byte of the instruction is the *signed word* offset from the current PC to the target address *loc*. If $Z \vee (N \veebar V) = 0$, twice the offset is added to c(PC). If $Z \vee (N \veebar V) = 1$, the instruction is ignored. (BGT behaves similarly to BGE, except that BGT does not cause a branch on a zero result.)

BHI   BRANCH IF HIGHER   1010XXX

Binary code:	1 000 001 0*xx xxx xxx*
Operation:	PC ← c(PC) + 2 × (offset) if $C \vee Z = 0$.
Assembler format:	BHI *loc*
Condition codes:	Unaffected.
Description:	The low-order byte of the instruction is the *signed word* offset from the current PC to the target address *loc*. If $C \vee Z = 0$, twice the offset is added to c(PC). If $C \vee Z = 1$, the instruction is ignored. (Thus BHI following a CMP instruction will cause a branch if the first number compared has an *unsigned* value greater than that of the second number compared.)

BHIS   BRANCH IF HIGHER OR SAME   1030XXX

Binary code:	1 000 011 0*xx xxx xxx*
Operation:	PC ← c(PC) + 2 × (offset) if $C = 0$.
Assembler format:	BHIS *loc*
Condition codes:	Unaffected.
Description:	Identical to BCC; included for programmer conve-

nience. (If BHIS follows a CMP instruction, a branch will occur if the first number compared has an *unsigned* value greater than or equal to that of the second number compared.)

BIC   BIT CLEAR DESTINATION FROM   04SSDD
SOURCE

Binary
code: 0 100 *sss sss ddd ddd*

Operation: $dst \leftarrow [\sim c(src)] \wedge c(dst)$.

Assembler   BIC *src, dst*
format:

Condition   N: Set if result < 0; cleared otherwise.
codes: Z: Set if result $= 0$; cleared otherwise.
                    V: Cleared.
                    C: Not affected.

Description: Each bit in the destination that corresponds to a *1*-bit in the source is cleared. The contents of the source is unaffected.

BICB   BIT CLEAR DESTINATION BYTE   14SSDD
FROM SOURCE

Binary
code: 1 100 *sss sss ddd ddd*

Operation: $dst \leftarrow [\sim c(src)] \wedge c(dst)$

Assembler   BICB *src, dst*
format:

Condition   N: Set if result < 0; cleared otherwise.
codes: Z: Set if result $= 0$; cleared otherwise.
                    V: Cleared.
                    C: Not affected.

Description: Each bit in the destination byte that corresponds to a *1*-bit in the source is cleared. The contents of the source byte is unaffected.

BIS   **BIT SET DESTINATION FROM**   **05SSDD**
              SOURCE

Binary   0 101 *sss sss ddd ddd*
  code:
Operation: *dst ← c(src) ∨ c(dst)*.
Assembler   BIS *src, dst*
  format:
Condition   N: Set if result < 0; cleared otherwise.
  codes: Z: Set if result = 0; cleared otherwise.
             V: Cleared.
             C: Unaffected.
Description: The destination is replaced by the contents of the
             source *OR*ed with the original contents of the
             destination. Thus each bit of the destination that
             corresponds to a *1*-bit in the source is set. All other
             destination bits are unchanged. The contents of
             the source is unaffected.

BISB   **BIT SET DESTINATION BYTE**   **15SSDD**
              FROM SOURCE

Binary   1 101 *sss sss ddd ddd*
  code:
Operation: *dst ← c(src) ∨ c(dst)*.
Assembler   BISB *src, dst*
  format:
Condition   N: Set if result < 0; cleared otherwise.
  codes: Z: Set if result = 0; cleared otherwise.
             V: Cleared.
             C: Unaffected.
Description: The destination byte is replaced by the contents of
             the source *OR*ed with the original destination. Thus
             each bit of the destination byte that corresponds to
             a *1*-bit in the source is set. All other destination
             bits are unchanged. The contents of the source
             byte is unaffected.

BIT   **BIT TEST SOURCE AND**   **03SSDD**
              DESTINATION

Binary code:	0 011 *sss sss ddd ddd*
Operation:	c(*src*) $\wedge$ c(*dst*).
Assembler format:	BIT *src, dst*
Condition codes:	N: Set if result $<$ 0; cleared otherwise.
	Z: Set if result $=$ 0; cleared otherwise.
	V: Cleared.
	C: Unaffected.
Description:	Performs a logical *AND* of the source and destination word contents and sets the condition codes N and Z accordingly. Neither source nor destination contents is affected.

BITB   **BIT TEST SOURCE AND**   **13SSDD**
              DESTINATION BYTES

Binary code:	1 011 *sss sss ddd ddd*
Operation:	c(*src*) $\wedge$ c(*dst*).
Assembler format:	BITB *src, dst*
Condition codes:	N: Set if result $<$ 0; cleared otherwise.
	Z: Set if result $=$ 0; cleared otherwise.
	V: Cleared.
	C: Unaffected.
Description:	Performs a logical *AND* of the source and destination byte contents and sets the condition codes N and Z accordingly. Neither source nor destination contents is affected.

BLE   **BRANCH IF LESS THAN**   **0034XXX**
              OR EQUAL ZERO

Binary code:	0 000 011 1*xx xxx xxx*

Operation: $PC \leftarrow c(PC) + 2 \times (\text{offset})$ if $Z \lor (N \veebar V) = 1$.

Assembler   BLE *loc*
format:

Condition   Unaffected.
codes:

Description: The low-order byte of the instruction is the *signed word* offset from the current PC to the target address *loc*. If $Z \lor (N \veebar V) = 1$, twice the offset is added to $c(PC)$. If $Z \lor (N \veebar V) = 0$, the instruction is ignored. (BLE behaves similarly to BLT, except that BLE causes a branch on a zero result.)

BLO   BRANCH IF LOWER   1034XXX

Binary   1 000 011 1*xx xxx xxx*
code:

Operation: $PC \leftarrow c(PC) + 2 \times (\text{offset})$ if $C = 1$.

Assembler   BLO *loc*
format:

Condition   Unaffected.
codes:

Description: Identical to BCS; included for programmer convenience. (If BLO follows a CMP instruction, a branch will occur if the first number compared has an *unsigned* value less than that of the second number compared.)

BLOS   BRANCH IF LOWER OR SAME   1014XXX

Binary   1 000 001 1*xx xxx xxx*
code:

Operation: $PC \leftarrow c(PC) + 2 \times (\text{offset})$ if $C \lor Z = 1$.

Assembler   BLOS *loc*
format:

Condition   Unaffected.
codes:

Description: The low-order byte of the instruction is the *signed word* offset from the current PC to the target

address *loc*. If C $\vee$ Z $= 1$, twice the offset is added
to c(PC). If C $\vee$ Z $= 0$, the instruction is ignored.
(If BLOS follows a CMP instruction, a branch will
occur if the first number compared has an *unsigned*
value less than or equal to that of the second
number compared.)

BLT   BRANCH IF LESS THAN ZERO   0024XXX

Binary   0 000 010 1*xx xxx xxx*
  code:
Operation: PC $\leftarrow$ c(PC) $+$ 2 $\times$ (offset) if N $\veebar$ V $= 1$.
Assembler   BLT *loc*
  format:
Condition   Unaffected.
  codes:
Description: The low-order byte of the instruction is the *signed*
              word offset from the current PC to the target
              address *loc*. If N $\veebar$ V $= 1$, twice the offset is added
              to c(PC). If N $\veebar$ V $= 0$, the instruction is ignored.
              (BLT following a CMP instruction will cause a
              branch if the first number compared is negative
              and the second is positive, even if an overflow
              occurred. BLT will not cause a branch if the first
              number compared is positive and the second is
              negative.)

BMI   BRANCH IF MINUS   1004XXX

Binary   1 000 000 1*xx xxx xxx*
  code:
Operation: PC $\leftarrow$ c(PC) $+$ 2 $\times$ (offset) if N $= 1$.
Assembler   BMI *loc*
  format:
Condition   Unaffected.
  codes:
Description: The low-order byte of the instruction is the *signed*
              word offset from the current PC to the target
              address *loc*. If N $= 1$, twice the offset is added to
              c(PC). If N $= 0$, the instruction is ignored.

BNE   BRANCH IF NOT EQUAL ZERO   0010XXX

Binary code:	0 000 001 0xx xxx xxx
Operation:	PC $\leftarrow$ c(PC) + 2 $\times$ (offset) if Z = 0.
Assembler format:	BNE loc
Condition codes:	Unaffected.
Description:	The low-order byte of the instruction is the *signed word* offset from the current PC to the target address *loc*. If Z = 0, twice the offset is added to c(PC). If Z = 1, the instruction is ignored.

BPL   BRANCH IF PLUS   1000XXX

Binary code:	1 000 000 0xx xxx xxx
Operation:	PC $\leftarrow$ c(PC) + 2 $\times$ (offset) if N = 0.
Assembler format:	BPL loc
Condition codes:	Unaffected.
Description:	The low-order byte of the instruction is the *signed word* offset from the current PC to the target address *loc*. If N = 0, twice the offset is added to c(PC). If N = 1, the instruction is ignored.

BPT   BREAKPOINT TRAP   000003

Binary code:	0 000 000 000 000 011
Operation:	$\downarrow$ (SP) $\leftarrow$ c(PSW) $\downarrow$ (SP) $\leftarrow$ c(PC) PC $\quad\leftarrow$ c(14) PSW $\leftarrow$ c(16)
Assembler format:	BPT

Condition   Loaded from second word of trap vector.
codes:

Description: Performs a trap through the vector at (fixed)
               memory locations 000014 — 000016.

BR   BRANCH (UNCONDITIONAL)   0004XXX

Binary   0 000 000 1xx xxx xxx
code:

Operation: PC ← c(PC) + 2 × (offset).

Assembler   BR loc
format:

Condition   Unaffected.
codes:

Description: The low-order byte of the instruction is the *signed*
               word offset from the current PC to the target address
               loc. Twice the offset is added to c(PC) (uncondi-
               tionally).

BVC   BRANCH IF OVERFLOW CLEAR   1020XXX

Binary   1 000 010 0xx xxx xxx
code:

Operation: PC ← c(PC) + 2 × (offset) if V = 0.

Assembler   BVC loc
format:

Condition   Unaffected.
codes:

Description: The low-order byte of the instruction is the *signed*
               word offset from the current PC to the target address
               loc. If V = 0, twice the offset is added to c(PC).
               If V = 1, the instruction is ignored.

BVS   BRANCH IF OVERFLOW SET   1024XXX

Binary   1 000 010 1xx xxx xxx
code:

Operation: PC ← c(PC) + 2 × (offset) if V = 1.

Assembler   BVS *loc*
format:

Condition   Unaffected.
codes:

Description: The low-order byte of the instruction is the *signed word* offset from the current PC to the target address *loc*. If V = 1, twice the offset is added to c(PC). If V = 0, the instruction is ignored.

CCC   CLEAR ALL CONDITION CODES   000257

Binary   0 000 000 010 101 111
code:

Operation: C ← 0, V ← 0, Z ← 0, N ← 0.

Assembler   CCC
format:

Condition   All cleared.
codes:

Description: Clears all condition codes.

Comment: See also the instruction CLc.

CLc   CLEAR SPECIFIED CONDITION CODE   00024CC

Binary   0 000 000 010 10c *ccc*
code:

Operation: Specified condition code(s) ← 0.

Assembler   CLc
format:

Condition   Specified code(s) cleared. All other condition codes
codes: unaffected.

Description: Bits 3, 2, 1, and 0 of the instruction correspond to the condition codes N, Z, V, and C, respectively. Any of these bits *set* in the instruction will cause the corresponding condition code to be *cleared*.

Mnemonic	Code	Action
NOP	000240	(No condition codes cleared)
CLC	000241	$C \leftarrow 0$
CLV	000242	$V \leftarrow 0$
none	000243	$C \leftarrow 0, V \leftarrow 0$
CLZ	000244	$Z \leftarrow 0$
none	000245	$C \leftarrow 0, Z \leftarrow 0$
none	000246	$V \leftarrow 0, Z \leftarrow 0$
none	000247	$C \leftarrow 0, V \leftarrow 0, Z \leftarrow 0$
CLN	000250	$N \leftarrow 0$
none	000251	$C \leftarrow 0, N \leftarrow 0$
none	000252	$V \leftarrow 0, N \leftarrow 0$
none	000253	$C \leftarrow 0, V \leftarrow 0, N \leftarrow 0$
none	000254	$Z \leftarrow 0, N \leftarrow 0$
none	000255	$C \leftarrow 0, Z \leftarrow 0, N \leftarrow 0$
none	000256	$V \leftarrow 0, Z \leftarrow 0, N \leftarrow 0$
CCC	000257	$C \leftarrow 0, V \leftarrow 0, Z \leftarrow 0, N \leftarrow 0$

Comment: Those instructions for which no PDP-11 assembler mnemonic exists can be achieved by a .WORD containing the appropriate code.

CLR   CLEAR DESTINATION   0050DD

Binary code: 0 000 101 000 *ddd ddd*

Operation: $dst \leftarrow 0$.

Assembler format: CLR *dst*

Condition codes: N: Cleared.
Z: Set.
V: Cleared.
C: Cleared.

Description: The destination word is given the value 0.

CLRB   CLEAR DESTINATION BYTE   1050DD

Binary code: 1 000 101 000 *ddd ddd*

Operation: $dst \leftarrow 0$.

Assembler   CLRB dst
format:

Condition   N: Cleared.
codes: Z: Set.
                  V: Cleared.
                  C: Cleared.

Description: The destination byte is given the value 0.

CMP   COMPARE SOURCE TO   02SSDD
         DESTINATION

Binary   0 010 sss sss ddd ddd
code:

Operation: $c(src) + [\sim c(dst) + 1]$.

Assembler   CMP src, dst
format:

Condition   N: Set if result < 0; cleared otherwise.
codes: Z: Set if result $= 0$; cleared otherwise.
                  V: Set if an overflow occurred (operands were of
                     opposite sign, and the sign of the result is the
                     same as the sign of the destination); cleared
                     otherwise.
                  C: Set if there was *not* a carry from the high-order
                     bit of the result; cleared otherwise.

Description: Subtracts the destination contents from the source
                   contents, and sets the condition codes according to
                   the result. Neither source nor destination contents
                   is affected. (CMP is normally followed by a condi-
                   tional branch instruction.)

CMPB   COMPARE SOURCE BYTE TO   12SSDD
         DESTINATION

Binary   1 010 sss sss ddd ddd
code:

Operation: $c(src) + [\sim c(dst) + 1]$.

Assembler   CMPB src, dst
format:

Condition   N: Set if result < 0; cleared otherwise.
codes: Z: Set if result = 0; cleared otherwise.
                V: Set if an overflow occurred (operands were of
                   opposite sign, and the sign of the result is the
                   same as the sign of the destination); cleared
                   otherwise.
                C: Set if there was *not* a carry from the high-order
                   bit of the result; cleared otherwise.

Description: Subtracts the destination byte contents from the
                source byte contents, and sets the condition codes
                according to the result. Neither source nor destina-
                tion byte contents is affected. (CMPB is normally
                followed by a conditional branch instruction.)

COM   COMPLEMENT DESTINATION   0051DD

Binary   0 000 101 001 *ddd ddd*
code:
Operation: $dst \leftarrow \sim c(dst)$.
Assembler   COM *dst*
format:
Condition   N: Set if result < 0; cleared otherwise.
codes: Z: Set if result = 0; cleared otherwise.
                V: Cleared.
                C: Set.

Description: The destination is replaced by its *1*'s-complement
                (each *0*-bit is set to 1 and each *1*-bit is set to 0).

COMB   COMPLEMENT DESTINATION BYTE   1051DD

Binary   1 000 101 001 *ddd ddd*
code:
Operation: $dst \leftarrow \sim c(dst)$.
Assembler   COMB *dst*
format:
Condition   N: Set if result < 0; cleared otherwise.
codes: Z: Set if result = 0; cleared otherwise.
                V: Cleared.
                C: Set.

Description: The destination byte is replaced by its *1*'s-complement (each *0*-bit is set to 1 and each *1*-bit is set to 0).

DEC   DECREMENT DESTINATION   0053DD

Binary
  code: 0 000 101 011 *ddd ddd*

Operation: $dst \leftarrow c(dst) - 1$.

Assembler   DEC *dst*
  format:

Condition   N: Set if result < 0; cleared otherwise.
  codes: Z: Set if result = 0; cleared otherwise.
             V: Set if c(*dst*) *was* 100000; cleared otherwise.
             C: Unaffected.

Description: Subtracts 1 from the contents of the destination word.

DECB   DECREMENT DESTINATION BYTE   1053DD

Binary
  code: 1 000 101 011 *ddd ddd*

Operation: $dst \leftarrow c(dst) - 1$.

Assembler   DECB *dst*
  format:

Condition   N: Set if result < 0; cleared otherwise.
  codes: Z: Set if result = 0; cleared otherwise.
             V: Set if c(*dst*) *was* 200; cleared otherwise.
             C: Unaffected.

Description: Subtracts 1 from the contents of the destination byte.

DIV   DIVIDE REGISTER BY SOURCE   071RSS

Binary
  code: 0 111 001 *rrr sss sss*

Operation: *reg, reg* $\lor$ 1 $\leftarrow$ c(*reg, reg* $\lor$ 1) $\div$ c(*src*).

Assembler   DIV *src, reg*
  format:

Condition   N: Set if quotient < 0; cleared otherwise.
codes: Z: Set if quotient = 0; cleared otherwise.
               V: Set if the register number is *odd*, or if c(*src*)
                  = 0, or if the absolute value of c(*reg*) > abso-
                  lute value of c(*src*); cleared otherwise.
               C: Set if c(*src*) = 0; cleared otherwise.
Description: The 32-bit contents of *reg*, *reg* ∨ 1 is divided by
               the contents of the source. The quotient is left in
               reg, the remainder in *reg* ∨ 1. The remainder has
               the same sign as the dividend. If the register number
               is not even, no division is performed and the V-bit
               is set.
Comment: DIV is not implemented on some PDP-11 models.

EMT   EMULATOR TRAP   104000-104377

Binary   1 000 100 0*nn nnn nnn*
code:
Operation: ↓ (SP) ← c(PSW)
               ↓ (SP) ← c(PC)
               PC   ← c(30)
               PSW   ← c(32)
Assembler   EMT *NNN*
format:
Condition   Loaded from second word of trap vector.
codes:
Description: Performs a trap through the vector at (fixed)
               memory locations 000030 − 000032.

               The low-order byte of the instruction is unused by
               the CPU's decoder. However, the PDP-11 assem-
               bler will place any number *NNN* appearing as an
               operand (0 ≤ *NNN* ≤ 377) in the low-order byte
               of the assembled instruction. This byte may then be
               accessed by the user program.
Comment: Many operating systems use EMT to invoke utility
               routines. Thus the user is advised to avoid EMT,
               using the TRAP instruction instead.

HALT   HALT THE PROCESSOR   000000

Binary
  code: 0 000 000 000 000 000

Operation: Halt the processor.

Assembler   HALT
  format:

Condition   Unaffected.
  codes:

Description: Causes all processor operations to cease.

INC   INCREMENT DESTINATION   0052DD

Binary
  code: 0 000 101 010 *ddd ddd*

Operation: $dst \leftarrow c(dst) + 1$.

Assembler   INC *dst*
  format:

Condition   N: Set if result < 0; cleared otherwise.
  codes: Z: Set if result $= 0$; cleared otherwise.
               V: Set if c(*dst*) *was* 077777; cleared otherwise.
               C: Unaffected.

Description: Adds 1 to the contents of the destination word.

INCB   INCREMENT DESTINATION BYTE   1052DD

Binary
  code: 1 000 101 010 *ddd ddd*

Operation: $dst \leftarrow c(dst) + 1$.

Assembler   INCB *dst*
  format:

Condition   N: Set if result < 0; cleared otherwise.
  codes: Z: Set if result $= 0$; cleared otherwise.
               V: Set if c(*dst*) *was* 177; cleared otherwise.
               C: Unaffected.

Description: Adds 1 to the contents of the destination byte.

IOT   INPUT/OUTPUT TRAP   000004

Binary   0 000 000 000 000 100
code:
Operation: $\downarrow$ (SP) $\leftarrow$ c(PSW)
              $\downarrow$ (SP) $\leftarrow$ c(PC)
              PC $\leftarrow$ c(20)
              PSW $\leftarrow$ c(22)
Assembler   IOT
format:
Condition   Loaded from second word of trap vector.
codes:
Description: Performs a trap through the vector at (fixed)
              memory locations 000020 $-$ 000022.

JMP   JUMP TO DESTINATION   0001DD

Binary   0 000 000 001 *ddd ddd*
code:
Operation: PC $\leftarrow$ *dst* address.
Assembler   JMP *dst*
format:
Condition   Unaffected.
codes:
Description: The PC is given the value of the address of the
              destination.

JSR   JUMP TO SUBROUTINE   004RDD

Binary   0 000 100 *rrr ddd ddd*
code:
Operation: *temp* $\leftarrow$ *dst* address
              $\downarrow$ (SP) $\leftarrow$ c(*reg*)
              reg $\leftarrow$ c(PC)
              PC $\leftarrow$ c(*temp*)
              (where *temp* is an internal processor register).

Assembler format:	JSR *reg, dst*
Condition codes:	Unaffected.
Description:	JSR calculates the destination address, saves the specified register on the hardware stack (the *subroutine transfer register*), and saves the *current* value of the PC in this register. (This saving of the PC provides the linkage from the subroutine *back* to the calling program.) Finally, the PC is given the destination address, which produces the actual jump to the subroutine. Return to the calling routine is provided by the companion instruction RTS.

MARK MARK STACK FOR CLEANUP 0064NN

Binary code:	0 000 110 100 *nnn nnn*
Operation:	SP ← c(PC) + 2 × (*NN*) PC ← c(R5) R5 ← (SP) ↑
Assembler format:	MARK *NN*
Condition codes:	Unaffected.
Description:	When arguments have been passed to a subroutine by placing them on the hardware stack, MARK may be used to clean the stack upon subroutine return, as shown in the following example:

```
MOV   R5, −(SP)
MOV   ARG1, −(SP)
    .
    .

MOV   ARGK, −(SP)
MOV   ⟨MARK  K⟩, −(SP)
MOV   SP, R5
JSR   PC, SUBR
```

(where ⟨MARK K⟩ stands for the *code* for the instruction MARK K). By the time control has been passed to SUBR, the stack will contain

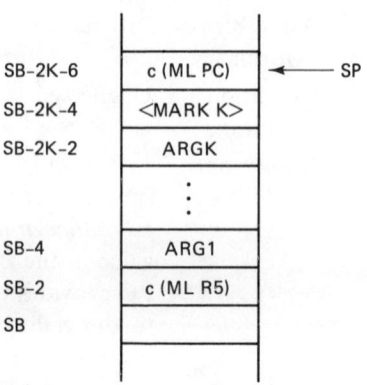

and $c(R5) = SB - 2 \times K - 4$, as a result of the MOV SP, R5 instruction. (Here, ML is an abbreviation for mainline and SB is the original stack base address.)

If the subroutine now returns with the instruction RTS R5 (and *not* with RTS PC) then the following will occur:

$$PC \longleftarrow c(R5) = SB - 2 \times K - 4$$

$$R5 \longleftarrow (SP) \uparrow \; = c(ML\ PC)$$

At this point, $c(PC) = SB - 2 \times K - 4$, so the MARK K instruction is fetched, moving $c(PC)$ up to $SB - 2K - 2$. The effect of MARK K is

$$SP \longleftarrow c(PC) + 2 \times K =$$

$$SB - 2 \times K - 2 + 2 \times K = SB - 2$$

$$PC \longleftarrow c(R5) = c(ML\ PC)$$

$$R5 \longleftarrow (SP) \uparrow$$

This last pop from the hardware stack restores R5 to its original (mainline) value and resets the stack pointer to its original value, SB.

Comment: MARK is not implemented on some PDP-11 models.

MOV MOVE SOURCE TO DESTINATION 01SSDD

Binary
code: 0 001 *sss sss ddd ddd*

Operation: *dst* ← c(*src*).

Assembler   MOV *src, dst*
format:

Condition   N: Set if c(*src*) < 0; cleared otherwise.
codes: Z: Set if c(*src*) = 0; cleared otherwise.
                V: Cleared.
                C: Unaffected.

Description: Moves a copy of the source word contents to the
                destination. The original contents of the destination
                is lost; the contents of the source word is unaffected.

MOVB   MOVE SOURCE BYTE   11SSDD
         TO DESTINATION

Binary   1 001 *sss sss ddd ddd*
code:

Operation: *dst* ← c(*src*)

Assembler   MOVB *src, dst*
format:

Condition   N: Set if c(*src*) < 0; cleared otherwise.
codes: Z: Set if c(*src*) = 0; cleared otherwise.
                V: Cleared.
                C: Unaffected.

Description: Moves a copy of the source byte contents to the
                destination byte. The original contents of the
                destination is lost; the contents of the source byte
                is unaffected.

                NOTE: If the destination is a *register*, then the
                move will be to the low-order byte of the destina-
                tion register. The *high-order* byte of the destination
                register is filled with the high-order bit of the
                source byte (which has the effect of preserving
                the arithmetic sign of the source byte contents).

MUL   MULTIPLY REGISTER BY SOURCE   070RSS

Binary   0 111 000 *rrr sss sss*
code:

Operation: *reg, reg* $\vee$ 1 ← c(*reg*) × c(*src*).

Assembler format:	MUL *src, reg*
Condition codes:	N: Set if product < 0; cleared otherwise.
	Z: Set if product = 0; cleared otherwise.
	V: Cleared.
	C: Set if product $< -2^{15}$ or $> 2^{15} - 1$; cleared otherwise.

Description: The 16-bit register contents is multiplied by the 16-bit source contents, giving a 32-bit product in *reg, reg* $\lor$ 1. If the register number is *odd* (so that *reg = reg* $\lor$ 1), the result is a 16-bit product in *reg*, the 16 high-order bits of the product having been lost. (If the product is sufficiently large that bits are lost in the odd-register case, the PSW C-bit will be set.)

Comment: MUL is not implemented on some PDP-11 models.

NEG   NEGATE DESTINATION   0054DD

Binary code:	0 000 101 100 *ddd ddd*
Operation:	$dst \leftarrow \sim c(dst) + 1.$
Assembler format:	NEG *dst*
Condition codes:	N: Set if result < 0; cleared otherwise.
	Z: Set if result = 0; cleared otherwise.
	V: Set if result = 100000; cleared otherwise.
	C: Cleared if result = 0; set otherwise.

Description: The destination word is replaced by its 2's-complement (negative).

NEGB   NEGATE DESTINATION BYTE   1054DD

Binary code:	1 000 101 100 *ddd ddd*
Operation:	$dst \leftarrow \sim c(dst) + 1.$
Assembler format:	NEGB *dst*

Condition   N: Set if result < 0; cleared otherwise.
codes: Z: Set if result = 0; cleared otherwise.
                 V: Set if result = 200; cleared otherwise.
                 C: Cleared if result = 0; set otherwise.
Description: The destination byte is replaced by its 2's-complement (negative).

NOP   NO OPERATION   000240

Binary   0 000 000 010 100 000
  code:
Operation: None
Assembler   NOP
  format:
Condition   Unaffected.
  codes:
Description: NOP is the same as "clear *no* condition codes." (See CLc.) While NOP produces no effect, it occupies one word of memory and requires a complete execution cycle upon "execution." (NOP is included for programmer convenience. For example, in a program under development containing "breakpoints," a BPT can temporarily be removed by overlaying it with a NOP.)

RESET   RESET BUS   000005

Binary   0 000 000 000 000 101
  code:
Operation: Sends INIT signal down bus.
Assembler   RESET
  format:
Condition   Unaffected.
  codes:
Description: Resets all bus devices to their power-up state.

ROL   ROTATE LEFT DESTINATION   0061DD

Binary   0 000 110 001 *ddd ddd*
  code:

Operation: C, *dst* ← c(C, *dst*) rotated one bit left.

Assembler   ROL *dst*
format:

Condition   N: Set if result < 0; cleared otherwise.
codes: Z: Set if result = 0; cleared otherwise.
                 V: Loaded with *EXCLUSIVE OR* of N and C (as
                    determined *after* the rotation).
                 C: Loaded with the bit shifted out of the high-
                    order bit of the destination.

Description: The PSW C-bit and the destination word, consid-
                 ered as a 17-bit "word," is rotated left one bit.
                 The vacated low-order bit of the destination (bit
                 0) is loaded with the contents of the C-bit. The high-
                 order bit of the destination (bit 15) is loaded into
                 the C-bit.

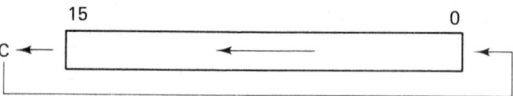

ROLB   ROTATE LEFT DESTINATION BYTE   1061DD

Binary   1 000 110 001 *ddd ddd*
code:

Operation: C, *dst* ← c(C, *dst*) rotated one bit left.

Assembler   ROLB *dst*
format:

Condition   N: Set if result < 0; cleared otherwise.
codes: Z: Set if result = 0; cleared otherwise.
                 V: Loaded with *EXCLUSIVE OR* of N and C (as
                    determined *after* the rotation).
                 C: Loaded with the bit shifted out of the high-
                    order bit of the destination.

Description: The PSW C-bit and the destination byte, consid-
                 ered as a 9-bit "byte," is rotated left one bit. The
                 vacated low-order bit of the destination (bit 0 or 8)
                 is loaded with the contents of the C-bit. The high-
                 order bit of the destination (bit 7 or 15) is loaded
                 into the C-bit.

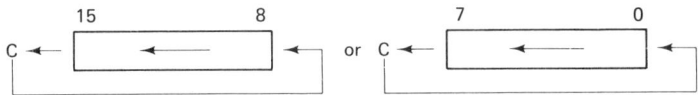

ROR ROTATE RIGHT DESTINATION 0060DD

Binary
code: 0 000 110 000 *ddd ddd*

Operation: C, *dst* ← c(C, *dst*) rotated one bit right.

Assembler
format: ROR *dst*

Condition: N: Set if result < 0; cleared otherwise.
codes: Z: Set if result = 0; cleared otherwise.
V: Loaded with *EXCLUSIVE OR* of N and C (as determined *after* the rotation).
C: Loaded with the bit shifted out of the low-order bit of the destination.

Description: The PSW C-bit and the destination word, considered as a 17-bit "word," is rotated right one bit. The vacated high-order bit (bit 15) is loaded with the contents of the C-bit. The low-order bit of the destination (bit 0) is loaded into the C-bit.

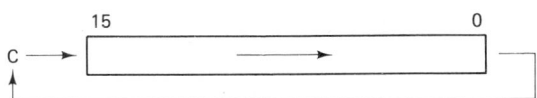

RORB ROTATE RIGHT DESTINATION BYTE 1060DD

Binary
code: 1 000 110 000 *ddd ddd*

Operation: C, *dst* ← c(C, *dst*) rotated one bit right.

Assembler
format: RORB *dst*

Condition N: Set if result < 0; cleared otherwise.
codes: Z: Set if result = 0; cleared otherwise.
V: Loaded with *EXCLUSIVE OR* of N and C (as determined *after* the rotation).

C: Loaded with the bit shifted out of the low-
order bit of the destination.

Description: The PSW C-bit and the destination byte, considered as a 9-bit "byte," is rotated right one bit. The
vacated high-order bit (bit 7 or 15) is loaded with
the contents of the C-bit. The low-order bit of the
destination byte (bit 0 or 8) is loaded into the C-bit.

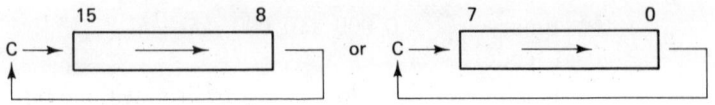

RTI   RETURN FROM INTERRUPT   000002

Binary   0 000 000 000 000 010
  code:
Operation: PC   ← (SP) ↑
                PSW ← (SP) ↑
Assembler   RTI
  format:
Condition   Loaded from hardware stack.
  codes:
Description: The PC and PSW are restored from the hardware
                stack. (Used to return from an interrupt or trap
                routine.)

RTS   RETURN FROM SUBROUTINE   00020R

Binary   0 000 000 010 000 *rrr*
  code:
Operation: PC ← c(*reg*)
                reg ← (SP) ↑
Assembler   RTS *reg*
  format:
Condition   Unaffected.
  codes:
Description: The contents of the specified register is loaded into
                the PC, and the top of the hardware stack is popped
                into the register. Used for subroutine returns.

RTT   RETURN FROM TRAP   000006

Binary code:	0 000 000 000 000 110
Operation:	PC ← (SP) ↑
	PSW ← (SP) ↑
Assembler format:	RTT
Condition codes:	Loaded from hardware stack.
Description:	The PC and PSW are restored from the hardware stack. (Used to return from an interrupt or trap routine.) RTT is identical to RTI except for a behavior which depends upon the state of bit 4 of the PSW. (See page 233.)
Comment:	RTT is not implemented on some PDP-11 models.

SBC   SUBTRACT CARRY DESTINATION   0056DD

Binary code:	0 000 101 110 *ddd ddd*
Operation:	*dst* ← c(*dst*) − c(C).
Assembler format:	SBC *dst*
Condition codes:	N: Set if result < 0; cleared otherwise.
	Z: Set if result = 0; cleared otherwise.
	V: Set if c(*dst*) *was* 100000; cleared otherwise.
	C: Cleared if c(*dst*) *was* 000000 and c(C) *was* 1; set otherwise.
Description:	Subtracts the contents of the C-bit from the destination.

SBCB   SUBTRACT CARRY DESTINATION   1056DD
BYTE

Binary code:	1 000 101 110 *ddd ddd*

Operation: $dst \leftarrow$ c(dst) $-$ c(C).

Assembler   SBCB dst
format:

Condition: N: Set if result < 0; cleared otherwise.
codes: Z: Set if result $= 0$; cleared otherwise.
               V: Set if c(dst) *was* 200; cleared otherwise.
               C: Cleared if c(dst) *was* 000 and c(C) *was* 1; set
               otherwise.

Description: Subtracts the contents of the C-bit from the byte
               destination.

SCC   SET ALL CONDITION CODES   000277

Binary   0 000 000 010 111 111
code:

Operation: $C \leftarrow 1, V \leftarrow 1, Z \leftarrow 1, N \leftarrow 1$.

Assembler   SCC
format:

Condition   All set.
codes:

Description: Set all condition codes.

Comment: See also the instruction SEc.

SEc   SET SPECIFIED CONDITION CODE   00026CC

Binary   0 000 000 010 11c ccc
code:

Operation: Specified condition code(s) $\leftarrow 1$.

Assembler   SEc
format:

Condition   Specified code(s) set. All other condition codes
codes: unaffected.

Description: Bits 3, 2, 1, and 0 of the instruction correspond to
               the condition codes N, Z, V, and C, respectively.
               Any of these bits *set* in the instruction will cause
               the corresponding condition code to be *set*.

Mnemonic	Code	Action
NOP	000260	(No condition codes set)
SEC	000261	$C \leftarrow 1$
SEV	000262	$V \leftarrow 1$
none	000263	$C \leftarrow 1, V \leftarrow 1$
SEZ	000264	$Z \leftarrow 1$
none	000265	$C \leftarrow 1, Z \leftarrow 1$
none	000266	$V \leftarrow 1, Z \leftarrow 1$
none	000267	$C \leftarrow 1, V \leftarrow 1, Z \leftarrow 1$
SEN	000270	$N \leftarrow 1$
none	000271	$C \leftarrow 1, N \leftarrow 1$
none	000272	$V \leftarrow 1, N \leftarrow 1$
none	000273	$C \leftarrow 1, V \leftarrow 1, N \leftarrow 1$
none	000274	$Z \leftarrow 1, N \leftarrow 1$
none	000275	$C \leftarrow 1, Z \leftarrow 1, N \leftarrow 1$
none	000276	$V \leftarrow 1, Z \leftarrow 1, N \leftarrow 1$
SCC	000277	$C \leftarrow 1, V \leftarrow 1, Z \leftarrow 1, N \leftarrow 1$

Comment: Those instructions for which no PDP-11 assembler mnemonic exists can be achieved by a .WORD containing the appropriate code.

SOB   SUBTRACT ONE AND BRANCH BACK   077RXX

Binary code: 0 111 111 *rrr xxx xxx*

Operation: $reg \leftarrow c(reg) - 1$;
$PC \leftarrow c(PC) - 2 \times$ (offset) if $c(reg) \neq 0$.

Assembler format: SOB *reg, loc*

Condition codes: Unaffected.

Description: The 6 low-order bits of the instruction is the *unsigned word* offset from the current PC to the target address *loc*. The contents of the specified register is decremented by 1. If the result is nonzero, twice the offset is *subtracted* from c(PC). If after decrementing, the contents of the register is 0, no branch takes place, and the next instruction is fetched.

SOB is used to control loops, with *reg* acting as a loop *counter*. Transfer of control can take place only in a *backward* fashion (to *lower* memory addresses).

Comment: SOB is not implemented on some PDP-11 models.

SPL   SET PRIORITY LEVEL   00023N

Binary code:	0 000 000 010 011 *nnn*
Operation:	PSW priority bits ← *N*.
Assembler format:	SPL *N*
Condition codes:	Unaffected.
Description:	The 3 low-order bits of the instruction are loaded into the priority bits of the PSW (bits 7, 6, and 5). Sets the CPU priority to *N*.
Comment:	SPL is not implemented on some PDP-11 models.

SUB   SUBTRACT SOURCE FROM   16SSDD
DESTINATION

Binary code:	1 110 *sss sss ddd ddd*
Operation:	$dst \leftarrow c(dst) + [\sim c(src) + 1]$.
Assembler format:	SUB *src, dst*
Condition codes:	N: Set if result < 0; cleared otherwise. Z: Set if result = 0; cleared otherwise. V: Set if overflow occurred (operands were of opposite signs and sign of the source was the same as the sign of the result); cleared otherwise. C: Cleared if there was a carry out of bit 15; set otherwise.

Description: Subtracts the contents of the source from the contents of the destination and places the result in the destination. The original contents of the destination is lost; the contents of the source is unaffected.

SWAB   SWAP BYTES OF DESTINATION   0003DD

Binary code: 0 000 000 011 *ddd ddd*

Operation: *dst high-order byte, dst low-order byte ⟵ dst low-order byte, dst high-order byte*

Assembler format: SWAB *dst*

Condition codes: N: Set if c(*dst*) *was* < 0; cleared otherwise.
Z: Set if high-order byte of *dst was* 000; cleared otherwise.
V: Cleared.
C: Cleared.

Description: Exchanges the high- and low-order bytes of the destination word.

SXT   SIGN EXTEND DESTINATION   0067DD

Binary code: 0 000 110 111 *ddd ddd*

Operation: *dst* ⟵ 0 if c(N) = 0;
dst ⟵ −1 if c(N) = 1.

Assembler format: SXT *dst*

Condition codes: N: Unaffected.
Z: Set if c(N) = 0; cleared otherwise.
V: Cleared.
C: Unaffected.

Description: Fills the destination word with the current contents of the N-bit.

Comment: SXT is not implemented on some PDP-11 models.

TRAP   TRAP   104400-104777

Binary
code: 1 000 100 1*nn nnn nnn*

Operation: ↓ (SP) ← c(PSW)
                 ↓ (SP) ← c(PC)
                 PC   ← c(34)
                 PSW   ← c(36)

Assembler   TRAP *NNN*
format:

Condition   Loaded from second word of trap vector.
codes:

Description: Performs a trap through the vector at (fixed)
                 memory locations 000034 − 000036.

                 The low-order byte of the instruction is unused by
                 the CPU's decoder. However, the PDP-11 assem-
                 bler will place any number *NNN* appearing as
                 an operand ($0 \leq NNN \leq 377$) in the low-order
                 byte of the assembled instruction. This byte may
                 then be accessed by the user program.

TST   TEST DESTINATION   0057DD

Binary
code: 0 000 101 111 *ddd ddd*

Operation: *dst* ← c(*dst*).

Assembler   TST *dst*
format:

Condition   N: Set if result < 0; cleared otherwise.
codes: Z: Set if result $= 0$; cleared otherwise.
                 V: Cleared.
                 C: Cleared.

Description: Sets the condition codes N and Z according to the
                 contents of the destination word.

TSTB   TEST DESTINATION BYTE   1057DD

Binary
code: 1 000 101 111 *ddd ddd*

Operation: $dst \leftarrow c(dst)$.

Assembler   TSTB dst
format:

Condition   N: Set if result < 0; cleared otherwise.
codes: Z: Set if result $= 0$; cleared otherwise.
              V: Cleared.
              C: Cleared.

Description: Sets the condition codes N and Z according to the
              contents of the destination byte.

WAIT   WAIT FOR INTERRUPT   000001

Binary   0 000 000 000 000 001
code:

Operation: Suspend processor operation, wait for interrupt.

Assembler   WAIT
format:

Condition   Unaffected.
codes:

Description: The processor relinquishes control of the buses
              (that is, ceases instruction fetches) until an external
              interrupt occurs. If the interrupt is honored
              (depending upon priorities), a subsequent RTI
              instruction in the interrupt routine will resume
              execution at the instruction following the WAIT.

XOR   EXCLUSIVE OR DESTINATION   074RDD
WITH REGISTER

Binary   0 111 100 rrr ddd ddd
code:

Operation: $dst \leftarrow c(reg) \veebar c(dst)$.

Assembler   XOR reg, dst
format:

Condition   N: Set if result < 0; cleared otherwise.
codes: Z: Set if result $= 0$; cleared otherwise.
              V: Cleared.
              C: Unaffected.

Description: The contents of the register is *EXCLUSIVE OR*ed with the contents of the destination, and the result is placed in the destination word. The contents of the register is unaffected.

Comment: XOR is not implemented on some PDP-11 models.

A.3 THE INSTRUCTION SET IN NUMERIC ORDER BY OP CODE

Op Code	Mnemonic	Op Code	Mnemonic	Op Code	Mnemonic
000000	HALT	0050DD	CLR	1020XXX	BVC
000001	WAIT	0051DD	COM	1024XXX	BVS
000002	RTI	0052DD	INC	1030XXX	{BCC or
000003	BPT	0053DD	DEC		BHIS
000004	IOT	0054DD	NEG	1034XXX	{BCS or
000005	RESET	0055DD	ADC		BLO
000006	RTT*	0056DD	SBC	104000	
0001DD	JMP	0057DD	TST	to	EMT
00020R	RTS	0060DD	ROR	104377	
00023N	SPL*	0061DD	ROL	104400	
000240	NOP	0062DD	ASR	to	TRAP
000241	CLC	0063DD	ASL	104777	
000242	CLV	0064NN	MARK*	1050DD	CLRB
000244	CLZ	0067DD	SXT*	1051DD	COMB
000250	CLN	01$SSDD$	MOV	1052DD	INCB
000257	CCC	02$SSDD$	CMP	1053DD	DECB
000261	SEC	03$SSDD$	BIT	1054DD	NEGB
000262	SEV	04$SSDD$	BIC	1055DD	ADCB
000264	SEZ	05$SSDD$	BIS	1056DD	SBCB
000270	SEN	06$SSDD$	ADD	1057DD	TSTB
000277	SCC	070RSS	MUL*	1060DD	RORB
0003DD	SWAB	071RSS	DIV*	1061DD	ROLB
0004XXX	BR	072RSS	ASH*	1062DD	ASRB
0010XXX	BNE	073RSS	ASHC*	1063DD	ASLB
0014XXX	BEQ	074RDD	XOR*	11$SSDD$	MOVB
0020XXX	BGE	077RXX	SOB*	12$SSDD$	CMPB
0024XXX	BLT	1000XXX	BPL	13$SSDD$	BITB
0030XXX	BGT	1004XXX	BMI	14$SSDD$	BICB
0034XXX	BLE	1010XXX	BHI	15$SSDD$	BISB
004RDD	JSR	1014XXX	BLOS	16$SSDD$	SUB

*Not implemented on some PDP-11 models

Note: Codes not included in this list are either unassigned or correspond to special-purpose instructions not used in the text.

Appendix B

The Input/Output
Macroinstructions

B.1 INTRODUCTION

Input to and output from the sample programs in the text are accomplished by macroinstructions, sequences of PDP-11 assembly language instructions packaged under a specific *name*. Upon assembly, only the name of the macroinstruction is printed on the program listing, not the sequence of instructions that make up the macroinstruction. See Chapter 13 for the details of the formation of macroinstructions.

Input and output are essential to meaningful programming. However, the actual programming involved in "driving" the devices that provide this programmer-computer intercommunication, along with the data format conversions required, is a task of sufficient complexity that we could not reasonably expect the novice assembly language programmer to manage it. Thus these macroinstructions are supplied as a means of providing keyboard input and output with a minimum of knowledge about this device and its programming.

The format of numbers *output* by the macroinstructions is *fixed* (as is the *input* format, but to a lesser extent. See Secs. B.4 and B.5). Thus the programmer does *not* have complete control over the appearance of input and output data. We claim only that the formats are reasonable and that these macroinstructions allow for the early use of input and output. The macrodefinitions are listed in Sec. B.7. Section B.8 contains the listing of $.\ldots$, the principal subroutine invoked by the macroinstructions, which also contains all of the required data format conversion routines. The experienced programmer may wish to modify these to gain added flexibility in format control, particularly in the output routines.

B.2 INVOKING THE INPUT/OUTPUT MACROINSTRUCTIONS

Each macroinstruction used for input or output is invoked by a command of the form

$$\$dir.\,fmt \qquad adr,\,cnt$$

where

dir = the *direction* of the data transfer and has the value IN (data transferred *into* the program) or OUT (data transferred *out of* the program);

fmt = the *format* of the data transfer. *fmt* can take on the value OCT (*octal*), DEC (*decimal*), BIN (*binary*, although used only for output), and ASC (*ASCII*, for reading and printing character strings);

adr = the *address* of the first word or byte of data to be transferred, the transfer taking place to or from consecutive memory locations;

cnt = the *count* of words or bytes to be transferred. (The ASCII input and output macroinstructions do not *require* this count. See Sec. B.6.)

The seven input/output macroinstructions are

$IN.OCT	*adr, cnt*	(input in octal)
$OUT.OCT	*adr, cnt*	(output in octal)
$IN.DEC	*adr, cnt*	(input in decimal)
$OUT.DEC	*adr, cnt*	(output in decimal)
$IN.ASC	*adr[,cnt]*	(input in ASCII)
$OUT.ASC	*adr[,cnt]*	(output in ASCII)
$OUT.BIN	*adr,cnt*	(output in binary)

The arguments *adr* and *cnt* passed to the macroinstructions must be used with some care. If *adr* is the *absolute address* of the first word or byte to be transferred (for example, the memory location whose symbolic address is BUFFER), then that argument must be passed as an *absolute number* (for instance, #BUFFER). Similarly, an absolute input/output count (for example, 6) must be passed as an absolute number (#6). The easiest way to determine what address and count will be used is to recognize that when the macroinstruction is invoked, the following two instructions are executed (in effect):

$$\text{MOV} \quad adr,\text{A}$$
$$\text{MOV} \quad cnt,\text{C}$$

The address used by the macroinstruction as the address of the first word or byte to be transferred to or from memory is then c(A), and the data count is c(C). Thus, for example,

$IN.DEC   #BLOCK,#6

will transfer six numbers, assumed to be in decimal format, into the six consecutive words beginning at the symbolic address BLOCK, since after MOV #BLOCK,A and MOV   #6,C we will have c(A) = BLOCK and c(C) = 6, the address and count respectively. Similarly,

MOV   #BLOCK,R4
MOV   #6,TEMP
MOV   #TEMP,R2
$OUT.OCT   R4,(R2)+

will print (in their octal format) the six consecutive numbers beginning at the address BLOCK and will autoincrement R2 by 2 in the process. Finally, note that

$OUT.DEC   BLOCK,6

is *probably* an incorrect use of the macroinstruction, since it would use c(BLOCK) as the address and c(6) as the count.

While the definitions of the macroinstructions thus allow a great deal of flexibility in specifying the address and data count, the programmer is cautioned against using R6—the stack pointer—to hold the *address*. As the listing of the macroinstructions in Sec. B.7 shows, a number of items are pushed onto the stack when a macroinstruction is invoked. By the time the address is accessed by the macroinstruction, the stack pointer has already been modified. The count, on the other hand, is the *first* item to be pushed, and thus it may successfully be transmitted through SP.

B.3 ERROR DETECTION

Potential errors are tested for by the input/output macroinstructions. The address *adr* of the first word of transfer must be *even*, that is, must be a *word* address. If it is not, the error message

?INVALID BUFFER ADDR. IN I/O MACRO INVOKED AT USER PC
= XXXXXX

is printed. This is taken to be a fatal error, and control is returned to the operating system. The macroinstructions $IN.ASC and $OUT.ASC are exceptions to this restriction, since the address is taken to be the address of a byte and thus may be odd. If the count *cnt* is nonpositive, the fatal error

?INVALID BUFFER COUNT IN I/O MACRO INVOKED AT USER PC
= XXXXXX

is printed.

The input routines $IN.OCT and $IN.DEC also test for proper input. For example, 17294 is not valid input to $IN.OCT (since 9 is not an octal character), nor is 372040 (a number that cannot be held in 16 bits). In a similar fashion, 32804 is too large a decimal number to be held in 16 bits when using $IN.DEC. In general, when $IN.OCT or $IN.DEC detect an invalid number, they print the error message

%INVALID NUMBER FOR INPUT MACRO INVOKED AT USER PC

= XXXXXX [NNNN]

where NNNN is the invalid number. This is not taken as a fatal error, however. Rather, the offending number is replaced by 0 and input continues.

B.4 INPUT FORMAT

Data input to $IN.OCT and $IN.DEC consists of numbers separated by commas. The data is in free format, in that spaces, tabs, and leading zeros are ignored. The macroinstruction $IN.DEC permits the use of a leading plus sign or minus sign. A blank field is treated as the number 0. Thus, for example, the numbers

1,,3,

used as input to $IN.OCT or $IN.DEC will be treated as if they were

1,0,3,0

and

,1,3

will be taken to be

0,1,3

B.5 OUTPUT FORMAT

Output for $OUT.OCT consists of up to nine numbers per line. If more than nine numbers are to be printed, the output is double spaced. Each octal number is six digits long, with leading zeros supplied.

Output for $OUT.DEC consists of up to nine numbers per line. If more than nine numbers are to be printed, the output is double spaced. Each decimal number is supplied with leading blanks where necessary, and negative numbers are preceded by a minus sign.

Output for $OUT.BIN consists of up to four numbers per line. If more than four numbers are to be printed, the output is double spaced. Each binary number consists of 16 binary digits.

For example, if the numbers (shown here in octal) 304, 552, 172303, 100000, 4, 0, 100001, 177777, 1232, 104401, and 2274 are printed using $OUT.OCT, the output will be

```
000304  000552  172303  100000  000004  000000  100001  177777  001232
104401  002274
```

$OUT.DEC will produce

```
  196      362   -2877  -32768       4       0  -32767      -1     666
-30463     1212
```

while $OUT.BIN will generate

```
0000000011000100  0000000101101010  1111010011000011  1000000000000000
0000000000000100  0000000000000000  1000000000000001  1111111111111111
0000001010011010  1000100100000001  0000010010111100
```

B.6 THE SPECIAL CASES $IN.ASC AND $OUT.ASC

The macroinstructions $IN.ASC and $OUT.ASC allow for input and output of ASCII character strings. Tabs, spaces, and control characters are not removed. While the character count for these routines, if specified, must be positive, the address of the first byte may be *odd*, since the ASCII codes for the characters will be at *byte* addresses.

Neither $IN.ASC nor $OUT.ASC requires a character count. If no count is specified for $IN.ASC, the transfer of bytes of ASCII code will terminate upon detection of the line terminator (carriage return). The macroinstruction $IN.ASC will then append to the block of codes that have been input one additional byte, which contains a NUL (000). Thus without a character count, $IN.ASC is compatible with the .ASCIZ directive.

If no character count is specified for $OUT.ASC, printing will begin at the byte whose address is specified and terminate upon detection of a NUL (000) byte. Thus, for example, if the response to $IN.ASC #TEXT were the string MADE IN USA, this would be entirely equivalent to

TEXT: .ASCIZ #MADE IN USA#

which could then be printed with the command $OUT.ASC #TEXT.

B.7 THE DEFINITIONS OF THE INPUT/OUTPUT MACROINSTRUCTIONS

Listed below are the definitions of the I/O macroinstructions. This file may be used as a "prologue" to source files that require the use of these macroinstructions.

```
.NLIST
.NLIST   ME
;
;************************************************************;
;                                                          ;
;                    S Y S M A C                            ;
;                    - - - - -                              ;
;                                                          ;
; DEFINITIONS OF '$EXIT' MACRO AND SYSTEM I/O MACROS        ;
; APPENDED TO THE BEGINNING OF PDP-11 MACRO-ASSEMBLER       ;
; PROGRAMS TO ALLOW FOR STANDARDIZED INPUT AND OUTPUT.      ;
;                                                          ;
;************************************************************;
;
.GLOBL  $....                    ;ROUTINE TO DO ACTUAL I/O
;
; - - - - - - - - - - - $ E X I T - - - - - - - - - - -
;
;RETURN CONTROL TO MONITOR
;
.MACRO  $EXIT
EMT     350
.ENDM
;
; - - - - - I / O   U T I L I T Y   M A C R O - - - - -
;
;INVOKED BY SYSTEM MACROS
;
.MACRO  $..     KODE,BUFFER,KOUNT
;
;(FOLLOWING TWO INSTRUCTIONS SHOULD BE:  MOV  PC,-6(SP)
;CONSTRUCTION SHOWN IS TO MAINTAIN COMPATIBILITY WITH
;ALL PDP-11 MODEL ASSEMBLERS)
;
MOV     PC,-(SP)                 ;GET USER MAINLINE PC
MOV     (SP)+,-6(SP)             ; FOR ERROR REPORTING
.IF     NB      KOUNT
MOV     KOUNT,-(SP)              ;PUT COUNT ON THE STACK
MOV     #1,-(SP)                 ;SET 'COUNT SPECIFIED' FLAG
.IFF
CLR     -(SP)                    ;PUT 'ZERO COUNT' ON STACK
CLR     -(SP)                    ;CLEAR 'COUNT SPECIFIED' FLAG
.ENDC
TST     -(SP)                    ;SKIP OVER USER PC
MOV     BUFFER,-(SP)             ;PUT BUFFER ADDRESS
MOV     #'KODE,-(SP)             ; AND CODE ON STACK
JSR     PC,$....                 ;GO TO DO THE I/O
.ENDM
;
; - - - - - S Y S T E M   I / O   M A C R O S - - - - -
;
.MACRO  $IN.OCT         BUFFER,COUNT
$..     0,BUFFER,COUNT
.ENDM
;
.MACRO  $IN.DEC         BUFFER,COUNT
$..     2,BUFFER,COUNT
.ENDM
;
.MACRO  $OUT.OCT        BUFFER,COUNT
$..     4,BUFFER,COUNT
.ENDM
;
.MACRO  $OUT.DEC        BUFFER,COUNT
$..     6,BUFFER,COUNT
.ENDM
;
.MACRO  $OUT.BIN        BUFFER,COUNT
$..     10,BUFFER,COUNT
.ENDM
;
.MACRO  $IN.ASC         BUFFER,COUNT
$..     12,BUFFER,COUNT
.ENDM
;
.MACRO  $OUT.ASC        BUFFER,COUNT
$..     14,BUFFER,COUNT
.ENDM
;
.LIST   TTM
.LIST
```

B.8 THE INPUT/OUTPUT ROUTINE "$...."

Shown on the following pages is a listing of the routine $. . . . that is called by the input/output macroinstructions. This routine performs the actual input and output and does all necessary data conversion.

```
   1                     .TITLE  MACLIB
   2                     ;
   3                     ;****************************************************;
   4                     ;                                                  ;
   5                     ;                   M A C L I B                     ;
   6                     ;                   - - - - -                       ;
   7                     ;                                                  ;
   8                     ; PDP-11 MACRO-ASSEMBLER INPUT/OUTPUT ROUTINES     ;
   9                     ; INVOKED BY MACROS DEFINED IN FILE 'SYSMAC'       ;
  10                     ;                                                  ;
  11                     ; ENTRY POINT: $....                               ;
  12                     ;                                                  ;
  13                     ; USES RT-11 STRING I/O ROUTINES INVOKED BY        ;
  14                     ; EMT 340 AND EMT 351                              ;
  15                     ;                                                  ;
  16                     ;****************************************************;
  17                     ;
  18                     ;****************************************************;
  19                     ;                                                  ;
  20                     ;            BUFFERS AND FLAGS                      ;
  21                     ;                                                  ;
  22                     ;****************************************************;
  23                     ;
  24 000000     BUFFER: .BLKB    81.            ;INTERNAL I/O BUFFER
  25 000121     BFLAG:  .BLKB    1              ;BUFFER PROTECT FLAG
  26 000122  000 CRLF:  .BYTE    0              ;CARRIAGE RETURN/LINE FEED
  27 000123     SELECT: .BLKB    1              ;ROUTINE SELECT FLAG
  28                     ;
  29     000040         BLANK=40                ;ASCII BLANK
  30     000015         CARRET=15               ;ASCII CARRIAGE RETURN
  31                     ;
  32                     ;****************************************************;
  33                     ;                                                  ;
  34                     ; VECTOR USED TO DISPATCH CONTROL TO APPRO-         ;
  35                     ; PRIATE I/O ROUTINE                               ;
  36                     ;                                                  ;
  37                     ;****************************************************;
  38                     ;
  39 000124  001614' XFER: OREAD                ;READ OCTAL NUMBERS
  40 000126  001622'       DREAD                ;READ DECIMAL NUMBERS
  41 000130  001736'       OPRINT               ;PRINT OCTAL NUMBERS
  42 000132  001744'       DPRINT               ;PRINT DECIMAL NUMBERS
  43 000134  002056'       BPRINT               ;PRINT BINARY NUMBERS
  44 000136  002154'       AREAD                ;READ ASCII TEXT
  45 000140  002230'       APRINT               ;PRINT ASCII TEXT
  46                     ;
  47                     ;****************************************************;
  48                     ;                                                  ;
  49                     ;            INTERNAL SUBROUTINES                   ;
  50                     ;                                                  ;
  51                     ;****************************************************;
  52                     ;
  53                     ; - - R T - 1 1   I N P U T   R O U T I N E - -
  54                     ;
  55                     ;BUFFER ADDRESS ASSUMED IN R1
  56                     ;
  57 000142  104340 INPSTR: EMT    340          ;GET CHARACTER
  58 000144  103776       BCS    INPSTR         ;TRY AGAIN IF ERROR
  59 000146  120027       CMPB   R0,#CARRET     ;CARRIAGE RETURN?
           000015
  60 000152  001410       BEQ    INP020         ;YES -- DONE
  61 000154  105767       TSTB   BFLAG          ;PROTECT BUFFER?
           177741
  62 000160  001403       BEQ    INP010         ;DON'T BOTHER
  63 000162  020127       CMP    R1,#BUFFER+80. ;BUFFER FULL?
           000120'
  64 000166  001765       BEQ    INPSTR         ;YES -- IGNORE THIS CHAR
  65 000170  110021 INP010: MOVB  R0,(R1)+      ;PUT IN BUFFER
  66 000172  000763       BR     INPSTR         ; AND GET ANOTHER
  67 000174  105011 INP020: CLRB  (R1)          ;INSERT A NULL
  68 000176  104340       EMT    340            ;THROW AWAY LF
  69 000200  000207       RTS    PC             ; AND RETURN
  70                     ;
  71                     ; - - R T - 1 1   O U T P U T   R O U T I N E - -
  72                     ;
  73 000202  012700 PRINTX: MOV   #BUFFER,R0    ;'BUFFER' ASSUMED ADDRESS
           000000'
```

```
74 000206 010046    PRINT:  MOV     R0,-(SP)        ;SAVE BUFFER ADDRESS
75 000210 012700            MOV     #CRLF,R0        ;SEND A
         000122'
76 000214 104351            EMT     351             ; CR/LF
77 000216 012600            MOV     (SP)+,R0        ;RESTORE BUFFER ADDRESS
78 000220 104351            EMT     351             ;CALL RT-11 ROUTINE
79 000222 000207            RTS     PC              ; AND RETURN
80                          ;
81                          ; - - - - - P A C K   B U F F E R - - - - -
82                          ;
83                          ;REMOVES BLANKS AND CONTROL CODES FROM
84                          ; INTERNAL BUFFER
85                          ;
86 000224 012703    PACK:   MOV     #BUFFER,R3      ;SET 'SCAN' AND
         000000'
87 000230 010304            MOV     R3,R4           ; 'INSERT' POINTERS
88 000232 105713    PACK20: TSTB    (R3)            ;CHECK CHARACTER
89 000234 001406            BEQ     PACK80          ;ZERO -- END-OF-BUFFER
90 000236 122327            CMPB    (R3)+,#BLANK    ;SPACE OR CONTROL?
         000040
91 000242 003773            BLE     PACK20          ;YES -- IGNORE IT
92 000244 116324            MOVB    -1(R3),(R4)+    ;PUT IN BUFFER
         177777
93 000250 000770            BR      PACK20          ; AND GO FOR NEXT CHAR
94 000252 105014    PACK80: CLRB    (R4)            ;RESET AS END-OF-BUFFER
95 000254 000207            RTS     PC              ; AND RETURN
96                          ;
97                          ; - - - - - - S C A N   B U F F E R - - - - - -
98                          ;
99                          ;SCAN BUFFER FOR DELIMITER (, OR NULL)
100                         ;R3 CONTAINS ADDRESS OF LAST DELIMITER
101                         ;
102 000256 005203   SCAN:   INC     R3              ;MOVE UP POINTER
103 000260 010300           MOV     R3,R0           ; AND SET STRING POINTER
104 000262 121327   SCAN10: CMPB    (R3),#',        ;COMMA?
         000054
105 000266 001403           BEQ     SCAN40          ;YES -- FOUND IT
106 000270 105723           TSTB    (R3)+           ;NULL?
107 000272 001373           BNE     SCAN10          ;NO -- LOOK SOME MORE
108 000274 005303           DEC     R3              ;BACK UP POINTER
109 000276 000207   SCAN40: RTS     PC              ;RETURN
110                         ;
111                         ; - - - - - - - - O 2 B I N - - - - - - - - -
112                         ;
113                         ;CONVERTS OCTAL ASCII STRING TO BINARY
114                         ;R0 POINTS AT 1ST STRING CHARACTER
115                         ;R3 POINTS AT TRAILING DELIMITER (, OR NULL)
116                         ;CONVERTED NUMBER RETURNED IN R5
117                         ;IF CARRY BIT SET, ERROR IN CONVERSION
118                         ;
119 000300 010046   O2BIN:  MOV     R0,-(SP)        ;(FOR ERROR REPORTING)
120 000302 010146           MOV     R1,-(SP)        ;SAVE USER BUFFER POINTER
121 000304 122027   O2B100: CMPB    (R0)+,#'0       ;SWEEP OFF
         000060
122 000310 001775           BEQ     O2B100          ; LEADING ZEROS
123 000312 005300           DEC     R0              ;BACK UP POINTER
124 000314 005005           CLR     R5              ;CLEAR FOR SHIFT
125 000316 020003   O2B200: CMP     R0,R3           ;AT END OF STRING?
126 000320 001420           BEQ     O2B600          ;YES -- DONE
127 000322 112001           MOVB    (R0)+,R1        ;GET CHARACTER
128 000324 162701           SUB     #'0,R1          ; AND MAKE BINARY
         000060
129 000330 020127           CMP     R1,#7           ;OCTAL?
         000007
130 000334 101010           BHI     O2B500          ;NO -- ERROR
131 000336 006305           ASL     R5              ;MULTIPLY BY 2
132 000340 103406           BCS     O2B500          ;ERROR IF CARRY
133 000342 006305           ASL     R5              ;MULTIPLY BY 2
134 000344 103404           BCS     O2B500          ;ERROR IF CARRY
135 000346 006305           ASL     R5              ;MULTIPLY BY 2
136 000350 103402           BCS     O2B500          ;ERROR IF CARRY
137 000352 050105           BIS     R1,R5           ;PUT IN LAST 3 BITS
138 000354 000760           BR      O2B200          ; AND GET NEXT NUMBER
139 000356 000261   O2B500: SEC                     ;SET ERROR FLAG
140 000360 000401           BR      O2B600+2        ; AND SKIP AROUND
141 000362 000241   O2B600: CLC                     ;CLEAR ERROR FLAG
142 000364 012601           MOV     (SP)+,R1        ;RESTORE
143 000366 012600           MOV     (SP)+,R0        ; REGISTERS
144 000370 000207           RTS     PC              ; AND RETURN
145                         ;
```

389

```
146                                 ;- - - - - - - - - D 2 B I N - - - - - - - - -
147                                 ;
148                                 ;CONVERTS DECIMAL ASCII STRING TO BINARY
149                                 ;R0 POINTS AT 1ST STRING CHARACTER
150                                 ;R3 POINTS AT TRAILING DELIMITER (, OR NULL)
151                                 ;CONVERTED NUMBER RETURNED IN R5
152                                 ;IF CARRY BIT SET, ERROR IN CONVERSION
153                                 ;
154  000372  105067    D2BIN:  CLRB    D2B800          ;MAKE 'BR' A NO-OP
             000166
155  000376  010046            MOV     R0,-(SP)        ;SAVE
156  000400  010146            MOV     R1,-(SP)        ; VOLATILE
157  000402  010346            MOV     R3,-(SP)        ; REGISTERS
158  000404  005004            CLR     R4              ;CONVERTED NUMBER
159  000406  005001            CLR     R1              ;POWERS OF 10.
160  000410  121027            CMPB    (R0),#'-        ;NEGATIVE?
             000055
161  000414  001002            BNE     D2B100          ;NO
162  000416  005200            INC     R0              ;SKIP AROUND '-'
163  000420  000406            BR      D2B200          ; AND CHECK FOR ZEROS
164  000422  105267    D2B100: INCB    D2B800          ;MAKE 1-WORD SKIP
             000136
165  000426  121027            CMPB    (R0),#'+        ;PLUS SIGN?
             000053
166  000432  001001            BNE     D2B200          ;NO -- SKIP AROUND
167  000434  005200            INC     R0              ; ELSE SKIP '+'
168  000436  122027    D2B200: CMPB    (R0)+,#'0       ;SWEEP OFF
             000060
169  000442  001775            BEQ     D2B200          ; LEADING ZEROS
170  000444  005300            DEC     R0              ;BACK UP POINTER
171  000446  020003    D2B240: CMP     R0,R3           ;DONE?
172  000450  001444            BEQ     D2B780          ;YES -- SKIP OUT
173  000452  114305            MOVB    -(R3),R5        ;GET CHARACTER
174  000454  162705            SUB     #'0,R5          ; AND MAKE BINARY
             000060
175  000460  001425            BEQ     D2B260+2        ;0 -- NO MULT REQUIRED
176  000462  002435            BLT     D2B760          ;NOT DECIMAL
177  000464  020527            CMP     R5,#9.          ;VALID DECIMAL?
             000011
178  000470  101032            BHI     D2B760          ;NO -- ERROR
179  000472  010146            MOV     R1,-(SP)        ;SAVE COUNTER
180  000474  001416            BEQ     D2B260          ;DONE IF ZERO
181  000476  006305    D2B245: ASL     R5              ;MULTIPLY BY 2
182  000500  100406            BMI     D2B250+2        ;ERROR IF OVERFLOW
183  000502  010546            MOV     R5,-(SP)        ; ELSE STACK R5
184  000504  006305            ASL     R5              ;MULTIPLY BY 2
185  000506  100402            BMI     D2B250          ;ERROR IF OVERFLOW
186  000510  006305            ASL     R5              ;MULTIPLY BY 2
187  000512  100003            BPL     D2B255          ;OK IF NO OVERFLOW
188  000514  005726    D2B250: TST     (SP)+           ;ADJUST SP BY 2
189  000516  005726            TST     (SP)+           ;ADJUST SP BY 2
190  000520  000416            BR      D2B760          ;SET UP ERROR
191  000522  062605    D2B255: ADD     (SP)+,R5        ;MULTIPLY BY 10.
192  000524  102774            BVS     D2B250+2        ;ERROR IF OVERFLOW
193  000526  005301            DEC     R1              ; ELSE DECREMENT COUNT
194  000530  001362            BNE     D2B245          ; AND MULTIPLY AGAIN
195                            ;
196  000532  012601    D2B260: MOV     (SP)+,R1        ;RESTORE R1
197  000534  005201            INC     R1              ; AND INCREMENT
198  000536  060504            ADD     R5,R4           ;ACCUMULATE
199  000540  102342            BVC     D2B240          ;NO OVERFLOW-- OK
200  000542  020427            CMP     R4,#100000      ;ONLY VALID NEGATIVE
             100000
201  000546  001003            BNE     D2B760          ;ERROR
202  000550  105767            TSTB    D2B800          ;IS NUMBER NEGATIVE?
             000010
203  000554  001734            BEQ     D2B240          ;YES -- OK
204                            ;
205  000556  000261    D2B760: SEC                     ;SET ERROR FLAG
206  000560  000404            BR      D2B820          ; AND SKIP AROUND
207  000562  010405    D2B780: MOV     R4,R5           ;SWAP RESULT TO R5
208  000564  000400    D2B800: BR      .+2             ;(1-WORD SKIP OR NO-OP)
209  000566  005405            NEG     R5              ;CHANGE SIGN IF NEGATIVE
210  000570  000241            CLC                     ;CLEAR ERROR FLAG
211  000572  012603    D2B820: MOV     (SP)+,R3        ;RESTORE
212  000574  012601            MOV     (SP)+,R1        ; THE
213  000576  012600            MOV     (SP)+,R0        ; REGISTERS
214  000600  000207            RTS     PC              ;RETURN
215                            ;
```

```
216                                   ; - - - - - - - - B I N 2 O - - - - - - - -
217                                   ;
218                                   ;CONVERT BINARY TO 6-CHARACTER OCTAL
219                                   ;NUMBER TO BE CONVERTED IN R5
220                                   ;ADDRESS OF 1ST BYTE BEYOND CONVERTED NUMBER IN R0
221                                   ;
222  000602  112710  BIN20:   MOVB   #BLANK,(R0)     ;MOVE IN A
              000040
223  000606  112760          MOVB   #BLANK,1(R0)    ; COUPLE OF SPACES
              000040
              000001
224  000614  012704          MOV    #5,R4           ;SET COUNTER
              000005
225  000620  010546          MOV    R5,-(SP)        ;SAVE THE NUMBER
226  000622  042705  BIN020:  BIC    #177770,R5      ;CLEAR ALL BUT LAST 3 BITS
              177770
227  000626  062705          ADD    #'0,R5          ; AND MAKE ASCII
              000060
228  000632  110540          MOVB   R5,-(R0)        ;PUT ASCII CODE IN BUFFER
229  000634  012605          MOV    (SP)+,R5        ;GET NUMBER BACK
230  000636  006205          ASR    R5              ;SHIFT
231  000640  006205          ASR    R5              ; DOWN
232  000642  006205          ASR    R5              ; 3 BITS
233  000644  010546          MOV    R5,-(SP)        ;STACK IT AGAIN
234  000646  005304          DEC    R4              ;BACK FOR
235  000650  001364          BNE    BIN020          ; NEXT 3 BITS
236  000652  112740          MOVB   #'0,-(R0)       ;PUT ASCII '0' IN 1ST SLOT
              000060
237  000656  005726          TST    (SP)+           ;CLEAR THE STACK
238  000660  001401          BEQ    .+4             ; AND SKIP IF ZERO
239  000662  105210          INCB   (R0)            ; ELSE SET TO 61
240  000664  000207          RTS    PC              ;RETURN
241                                   ;
242                                   ; - - - - - - - - - B I N 2 D - - - - - - - - -
243                                   ;
244                                   ;CONVERT BINARY TO 6-CHARACTER DECIMAL
245                                   ;NUMBER TO BE CONVERTED IN R5
246                                   ;ADDRESS OF 1ST BYTE BEYOND CONVERTED NUMBER IN R0
247                                   ;
248  000666  112710  BIN2D:   MOVB   #BLANK,(R0)     ;PUT IN A
              000040
249  000672  112760          MOVB   #BLANK,1(R0)    ; COUPLE BLANKS
              000040
              000001
250  000700  162700          SUB    #6,R0           ;ADJUST POINTER
              000006
251  000704  010046          MOV    R0,-(SP)        ; AND SAVE
252  000706  112720          MOVB   #'0,(R0)+       ;SET TO ASCII ZERO
              000060
253  000712  112746          MOVB   #BLANK,-(SP)    ;SAVE A BLANK
              000040
254  000716  005705          TST    R5              ;CHECK NUMBER'S SIGN
255  000720  002003          BGE    BIN100          ;SKIP IF NONNEGATIVE
256  000722  005405          NEG    R5              ; ELSE CHANGE SIGN
257  000724  112716          MOVB   #'-,(SP)        ; AND CHANGE BLANK TO '-'
              000055
258  000730  012702  BIN100:  MOV    #BIN600-2,R2    ;SET TABLE ADDRESS
              001020'
259  000734  005004  BIN120:  CLR    R4              ;SET COUNTER
260  000736  005722          TST    (R2)+           ;MOVE UP POINTER
261  000740  005712          TST    (R2)            ; AND TEST POWER OF 10.
262  000742  001410          BEQ    BIN300          ;POINTING AT 0 -- DONE
263  000744  005204  BIN200:  INC    R4              ;INCREMENT COUNTER
264  000746  161205          SUB    (R2),R5         ;SUBTRACT POWER OF 10.
265  000750  100375          BPL    BIN200          ;DO AGAIN IF NONNEG.
266  000752  061205          ADD    (R2),R5         ; ELSE ADJUST BACK
267  000754  062704          ADD    #'0-1,R4        ;MAKE COUNTER ASCII
              000057
268  000760  110420          MOVB   R4,(R0)+        ; AND PUT IN BUFFER
269  000762  000764          BR     BIN120          ;DO NEXT POWER OF 10.
270  000764  162700  BIN300:  SUB    #6,R0           ;RESET POINTER
              000006
271  000770  012702          MOV    #5,R2           ; AND SET COUNTER
              000005
272  000774  122710  BIN400:  CMPB   #'0,(R0)        ;ASCII ZERO?
              000060
273  001000  001004          BNE    BIN500          ;NO -- DONE SCANNING
274  001002  112720          MOVB   #BLANK,(R0)+    ; ELSE CHANGE '0' TO BLANK
```

```
                 000040
275 001006  005302         DEC    R2              ; AND CHECK
276 001010  001371         BNE    BIN400          ; NEXT BYTE
277 001012  112660 BIN500: MOVB   (SP)+,-1(R0)    ;PUT IN '-' OR BLANK
            177777
278 001016  012600         MOV    (SP)+,R0        ;RESTORE POINTER
279 001020  000207         RTS    PC              ; AND RETURN
280                        ;
281                        ;TABLE OF POWERS OF 10.
282                        ;
283 001022  023420 BIN600: .WORD  10000.
284 001024  001750         .WORD  1000.
285 001026  000144         .WORD  100.
286 001030  000012         .WORD  10.
287 001032  000001         .WORD  1.
288 001034  000000         .WORD  0.
289                        ;
290                        ;  - - - - E R R O R    H A N D L E R S - - - -
291                        ;
292 001036  012701 ERROR1: MOV    #ERR2,R1        ;SET ERROR ADDRESS
            001234'
293 001042  020127         CMP    R1,#ERR2+5      ;DONE?
            001241'
294 001046  001402         BEQ    ERRPC           ;YES -- SET UP PC
295 001050  112021         MOVB   (R0)+,(R1)+     ; ELSE MOVE CHARACTER
296 001052  000773         BR     ERROR1+4        ; AND CHECK AGAIN
297 001054  012700 ERRPC:  MOV    #ERR3-3,R0      ;SET UP CONVERSION
            001312'
298 001060  016605         MOV    20(SP),R5       ;GET USER PC
            000020
299 001064  005745         TST    -(R5)           ; AND DECREMENT
300 001066  004767         JSR    PC,BIN20        ;CONVERT
            177510
301 001072  012700         MOV    #ERR1,R0        ;POINT AT MESSAGE
            001214'
302 001076  004767         JSR    PC,PRINT        ; AND PRINT ERROR
            177104
303 001102  012700         MOV    #CRLF,R0        ;PRINT AN
            000122'
304 001106  104351         EMT    351             ; EXTRA LINE
305 001110  104350         EMT    350             ;RETURN TO MONITOR
306                        ;
307 001112         ERROR2:
308                        .IRP   X,<1,2,3>
309                        MOV    R'X,-(SP)       ;SAVE 3 REGISTERS
310                        .ENDM
311 001120  012701         MOV    #ERR5,R1        ;SET POINTER
            001413'
312 001124  020003 ER200:  CMP    R0,R3           ;AT DELIMITER?
313 001126  001405         BEQ    ER220           ;YES -- SKIP OUT
314 001130  020127         CMP    R1,#ERR5+7      ;END-OF-BUFFER?
            001422'
315 001134  001402         BEQ    ER220           ;YES -- NO MORE ROOM
316 001136  112021         MOVB   (R0)+,(R1)+     ;PUT IN CHARACTER
317 001140  000771         BR     ER200           ; AND DO NEXT
318 001142  112721 ER220:  MOVB   #'],(R1)+       ;PUT IN ']'
            000135
319 001146  105011         CLRB   (R1)            ; AND TERMINATOR
320 001150  012700         MOV    #ERR5-3,R0      ;SET POINTER
            001410'
321 001154  016605         MOV    30(SP),R5       ;GET USER PC
            000030
322 001160  005745         TST    -(R5)           ; AND DECREMENT
323 001162  004767         JSR    PC,BIN20        ;CONVERT
            177414
324 001166  012700         MOV    #ERR3,R0        ;SET POINTER
            001315'
325 001172  004767         JSR    PC,PRINT        ; AND PRINT ERROR
            177010
326 001176  012700         MOV    #CRLF,R0        ;PRINT AN
            000122'
327 001202  104351         EMT    351             ; EXTRA LINE
328                        .IRP   X,<3,2,1>
329                        MOV    (SP)+,R'X       ;RESTORE REGISTERS
330                        .ENDM
331 001212  000207         RTS    PC              ;RETURN
332                        ;*************************************************;
333                        ;*                                               *;
334                        ;*                                               *;
335                        ;*                  MESSAGES                     *;
336                        ;*                                               *;
337                        ;*************************************************;
```

```
338                     ;
339 001214      ERR1:   .ASCII  #?INVALID BUFFER #

340 001234      ERR2:   .ASCII  #XXXXX IN I/O MACRO INVOKED AT USER PC = #

341 001304              .ASCIZ  #XXXXXX  #

342 001315      ERR3:   .ASCII  #%INVALID NUMBER FOR INPUT #
343 001347              .ASCII  #MACRO INVOKED AT USER PC = #

344 001402      ERR4:   .ASCII  #XXXXXX [#

345 001413      ERR5:   .BLKB   9.
346                     ;
347 001424      COUNT:  .ASCII  #COUNT#

348 001431      ADDR.:  .ASCII  #ADDR.#

349                     .EVEN
350                     ;
351                     ;**********************************************;
352                     ;                                              ;
353                     ;                 ENTRY POINT                  ;
354                     ;                                              ;
355                     ; ARGUMENTS ON THE STACK AT ROUTINE ENTRY:     ;
356                     ;                                              ;
357                     ;         SP --> MAINLINE RETURN PC            ;
358                     ;               I/O MACRO CODE                 ;
359                     ;               BUFFER ADDRESS                 ;
360                     ;               <ML 'CALL' ADDRESS>+2          ;
361                     ;               'COUNT SPECIFIED' FLAG         ;
362                     ;               NUMBER OR CHAR COUNT           ;
363                     ;                                              ;
364                     ;**********************************************;
365
366 001436  012667 $....:: MOV   (SP)+,RET+2      ;SET UP RETURN ADDRESS
            000122
367                     .IRP    X,<0,1,2,3,4,5>
368                     MOV     R'X,-(SP)        ;SAVE R0 - R5
369                     .ENDM
370 001456  005766      TST     24(SP)           ;CHECK COUNT
            000024
371 001462  002410      BLT     BADCNT           ;ERROR -- NEGATIVE
372 001464  003013      BGT     $00040           ;POSITIVE -- OK
373 001466  026627      CMP     14(SP),#10       ;COMPARE CODE
            000014
            000010
374 001474  003403      BLE     BADCNT           ;ERROR -- NOT ASCII
375 001476  005766      TST     22(SP)           ;COUNT SPECIFIED?
            000022
376 001502  001431      BEQ     $00100           ;NO -- SHOULDN'T BE
377                     ;
378 001504  012700 BADCNT: MOV   #COUNT,R0       ;SET POINTER
            001424'
379 001510  000167      JMP     ERROR1           ; AND SEND MESSAGE
            177322
380                     ;
381 001514  026627 $00040: CMP  14(SP),#10       ;ASCII ROUTINE?
            000014
            000010
382 001522  003021      BGT     $00100           ;YES -- ANY ADDRESS OK
383 001524  032766      BIT     #1,16(SP)        ;ADDRESS EVEN?
            000001
            000016
384 001532  001415      BEQ     $00100           ;YES -- OK
385 001534  012700      MOV     #ADDR.,R0        ;SET POINTER
            001431'
386 001540  000763      BR      BADCNT+4         ; AND SEND MESSAGE
387                     ;
388                     ;**********************************************;
389                     ;                                              ;
390                     ;          RETURN TO CALLING ROUTINE           ;
391                     ;                                              ;
392                     ;**********************************************;
393                     ;
394 001542      RETURN:
395                     .IRP    X,<5,4,3,2,1,0>
396                     MOV     (SP)+,R'X        ;RESTORE R5 - R0
397                     .ENDM
398 001556  062706      ADD     #12,SP           ;ADJUST STACK POINTER
            000012
399 001562  000137 RET: JMP     @#0              ;RETURN TO MAINLINE
            000000
```

```
400                                                        ;(OVERLAID WITH RET ADDR)
401                                      ;
402 001566   016600   $00100: MOV    14(SP),R0        ;GET ROUTINE CODE,
             000014
403 001572   016601           MOV    16(SP),R1        ; BUFFER ADDRESS
             000016
404 001576   016602           MOV    24(SP),R2        ; AND COUNT
             000024
405 001602   116667           MOVB   22(SP),BFLAG     ;SET BUFFER PROTECT FLAG
             000022
             176311
406 001610   000170           JMP    @XFER(R0)        ;DISPATCH TO I/O ROUTINE
             000124'
407                                      ;
408                                      ;*********************************************;
409                                      ;                                             ;
410                                      ;         INPUT/OUTPUT ROUTINES               ;
411                                      ;                                             ;
412                                      ;*********************************************;
413                                      ;
414                                      ; - - - - - - - - - O R E A D - - - - - - - - -
415                                      ;
416                                      ;READ NUMBERS IN OCTAL FORMAT
417                                      ;
418 001614   105067   OREAD:  CLRB   SELECT           ;SET 'OCTAL' FLAG
             176303
419 001620   000403           BR     CREAD            ; AND SKIP AROUND
420                                      ;
421                                      ; - - - - - - - - - D R E A D - - - - - - - - -
422                                      ;
423                                      ;READ NUMBERS IN DECIMAL FORMAT
424                                      ;
425 001622   112767   DREAD:  MOVB   #1,SELECT        ;SET 'DECIMAL' FLAG
             000001
             176273
426                                      ;
427                                      ; - - C O M M O N   R E A D   R O U T I N E - -
428                                      ;
429 001630   010246   CREAD:  MOV    R2,-(SP)         ;SAVE COUNT
430 001632   010146           MOV    R1,-(SP)         ; AND BUFFER ADDRESS
431 001634   012701           MOV    #BUFFER,R1       ;SET POINTER
             000000'
432 001640   004767           JSR    PC,INPSTR        ; AND GET BUFFER-FULL
             176276
433 001644   004767           JSR    PC,PACK          ;PACK THE BUFFER
             176354
434 001650   012601           MOV    (SP)+,R1         ;RESTORE
435 001652   012602           MOV    (SP)+,R2         ; REGISTERS
436 001654   012703           MOV    #BUFFER-1,R3     ;SET DUMMY DELIMITER
             177777'
437 001660   004767   CRD100: JSR    PC,SCAN          ;GET NEXT DELIMITER
             176372
438 001664   105767           TSTB   SELECT           ;SEE WHICH ROUTINE
             176233
439 001670   001403           BEQ    CRD120           ;OCTAL -- SKIP AROUND
440 001672   004767           JSR    PC,D2BIN         ;CONVERT DECIMAL
             176474
441 001676   000402           BR     CRD140           ; AND DETOUR
442 001700   004767   CRD120: JSR    PC,O2BIN         ;CONVERT OCTAL
             176374
443 001704   103410   CRD140: BCS    CRD900           ;CONVERSION ERROR
444 001706   010521   CRD200: MOV    R5,(R1)+         ;PUT IN USER'S BUFFER
445 001710   005302           DEC    R2               ;DECREMENT USER'S COUNTER
446 001712   001002           BNE    CRD300           ;MORE TO DO
447 001714   000167           JMP    RETURN           ; ELSE RETURN
             177622
448 001720   105713   CRD300: TSTB   (R3)             ;END-OF-LINE?
449 001722   001742           BEQ    CREAD            ;YES -- READ ANOTHER LINE
450 001724   000755           BR     CRD100           ; ELSE KEEP GOING
451                                      ;
452 001726   004767   CRD900: JSR    PC,ERROR2        ;REPORT ERROR
             177160
453 001732   005005           CLR    R5               ;GET A ZERO
454 001734   000764           BR     CRD200           ; AND PUT IN BUFFER
455                                      ;
456                                      ; - - - - - - - - - O P R I N T - - - - - - - - -
457                                      ;
458                                      ;PRINT NUMBERS IN OCTAL FORMAT
459                                      ;
```

```
460  001736  105067  OPRINT:  CLRB    SELECT              ;SET FLAG AS 'OCTAL'
     176161
461  001742  000403           BR      CPRINT              ; AND GO TO COMMON ROUTINE
462                  ;
463                  ; - - - - - - - - - D P R I N T - - - - - - - - -
464                  ;
465                  ;PRINT NUMBERS IN DECIMAL FORMAT
466                  ;
467  001744  112767  DPRINT:  MOVB    #1,SELECT           ;SET FLAG AS 'DECIMAL'
     000001
     176151
468                  ;
469                  ; - - C O M M O N   P R I N T   R O U T I N E - -
470                  ;
471  001752  012704  CPRINT:  MOV     #9.,R4              ;9 NUMBERS PER LINE
     000011
472  001756  012700           MOV     #BUFFER+6,R0        ;SET POINTER
     000006'
473  001762  012105  CPR050:  MOV     (R1)+,R5            ;GET A NUMBER
474  001764  010246           MOV     R2,-(SP)            ;SAVE THESE
475  001766  010446           MOV     R4,-(SP)            ; REGISTERS
476  001770  105767           TSTB    SELECT              ;WHICH ROUTINE?
     176127
477  001774  001403           BEQ     CPR100              ;OCTAL
478  001776  004767           JSR     PC,BIN2D            ;CONVERT TO DECIMAL
     176664
479  002002  000402           BR      CPR200              ; AND SKIP AROUND
480  002004  004767  CPR100:  JSR     PC,BIN2O            ;CONVERT TO OCTAL
     176572
481  002010  012604  CPR200:  MOV     (SP)+,R4            ;RESTORE
482  002012  012602           MOV     (SP)+,R2            ; REGISTERS
483  002014  062700           ADD     #14.,R0             ;RESET POINTER
     000016
484  002020  005302           DEC     R2                  ;DECREMENT COUNTER
485  002022  001402           BEQ     CPR300              ;DONE
486  002024  005304           DEC     R4                  ; ELSE GO BACK
487  002026  001355           BNE     CPR050              ; FOR NEXT
488  002030  105060  CPR300:  CLRB    -6(R0)              ;SET END-OF-LINE
     177772
489  002034  010246           MOV     R2,-(SP)            ;SAVE IMPORTANT
490  002036  010146           MOV     R1,-(SP)            ; REGISTERS
491  002040  004767           JSR     PC,PRINTX           ;PRINT THE LINE
     176136
492  002044  012601           MOV     (SP)+,R1            ;RESTORE ADDRESS
493  002046  012602           MOV     (SP)+,R2            ; AND COUNT
494  002050  001340           BNE     CPRINT              ;YET MORE NUMBERS
495  002052  000167           JMP     RETURN              ; ELSE DONE
     177464
496                  ;
497                  ; - - - - - - - - - B P R I N T - - - - - - - - - - -
498                  ;
499                  ;PRINT NUMBERS IN BINARY FORMAT
500                  ;
501  002056  012705  BPRINT:  MOV     #4,R5               ;SET NUMBER COUNTER
     000004
502  002062  012700           MOV     #BUFFER,R0          ; AND POINTER
     000000'
503  002066  012704  BPR050:  MOV     #16.,R4             ;SET BIT COUNTER
     000020
504  002072  012103           MOV     (R1)+,R3            ;GET NUMBER
505  002074  112720  BPR100:  MOVB    #'0,(R0)+           ;MOVE IN ASCII ZERO
     000060
506  002100  006303           ASL     R3                  ;SHIFT HIGH-ORDER BIT
507  002102  103002           BCC     BPR200              ;OK -- IT'S 0
508  002104  105260           INCB    -1(R0)              ; ELSE FIX ASCII CODE
     177777
509  002110  005304  BPR200:  DEC     R4                  ;BACK FOR
510  002112  001370           BNE     BPR100              ; NEXT BIT
511  002114  012720           MOV     #20040,(R0)+        ;PUT IN DOUBLE BLANK
     020040
512  002120  005302           DEC     R2                  ;DECREMENT NUMBER COUNTER
513  002122  001402           BEQ     BPR300              ;DONE THEM ALL
514  002124  005305           DEC     R5                  ;BACK FOR
515  002126  001357           BNE     BPR050              ; NEXT NUMBER
516  002130  105010  BPR300:  CLRB    (R0)                ;PUT IN LINE TERMINATOR
517  002132  010246           MOV     R2,-(SP)            ;SAVE THE IMPORTANT
518  002134  010146           MOV     R1,-(SP)            ; REGISTERS
519  002136  004767           JSR     PC,PRINTX           ;PRINT THE LINE
     176040
```

```
520  002142  012601         MOV    (SP)+,R1        ;RESTORE ADDRESS
521  002144  012602         MOV    (SP)+,R2        ; AND COUNT
522  002146  001343         BNE    BPRINT          ;MORE TO DO
523  002150  000167         JMP    RETURN          ; ELSE RETURN
             177366
524                         ;
525                         ; - - - - - - - - A R E A D - - - - - - - - -
526                         ;
527                         ;READ ASCII STRING
528                         ;
529  002154  005766  AREAD: TST    22(SP)          ;COUNT SPECIFIED?
             000022
530  002160  003003         BGT    ARD020          ;YES
531  002162  004767         JSR    PC,INPSTR       ; ELSE GET STRING
             175754
532  002166  000426         BR     APR010          ; AND EXIT
533                         ;
534  002170  010246  ARD020: MOV   R2,-(SP)        ;SAVE VOLATILE
535  002172  010146         MOV    R1,-(SP)        ; REGISTERS
536  002174  012701         MOV    #BUFFER,R1      ;SET BUFFER POINTER
             000000'
537  002200  004767         JSR    PC,INPSTR       ; AND GET A BUFFER FULL
             175736
538  002204  012601         MOV    (SP)+,R1        ;RESTORE THE
539  002206  012602         MOV    (SP)+,R2        ; REGISTERS
540  002210  012700         MOV    #BUFFER,R0      ;SET POINTER
             000000'
541  002214  105710  ARD040: TSTB  (R0)            ;END OF BUFFER?
542  002216  001764         BEQ    ARD020          ;YES -- GET SOME MORE
543  002220  112021         MOVB   (R0)+,(R1)+     ;TRANSFER CHARACTER
544  002222  005302         DEC    R2              ;DECREMENT COUNTER
545  002224  001373         BNE    ARD040          ;MORE TO TRANSFER
546  002226  000406         BR     APR010          ; ELSE EXIT
547                         ;
548                         ; - - - - - - - - A P R I N T - - - - - - - - -
549                         ;
550                         ;PRINT ASCII STRING
551                         ;
552  002230  005766  APRINT: TST   22(SP)          ;COUNT SPECIFIED?
             000022
553  002234  003005         BGT    APR020          ;YES
554  002236  010100         MOV    R1,R0           ;SET BUFFER POINTER
555  002240  004767         JSR    PC,PRINT        ;GO PRINT USER BUFFER
             175742
556  002244  000167  APR010: JMP   RETURN          ; AND RETURN
             177272
557                         ;
558  002250  012700  APR020: MOV   #BUFFER,R0      ;SET POINTER
             000000'
559  002254  112120         MOVB   (R1)+,(R0)+     ;TRANSFER CHARACTER
560  002256  005302         DEC    R2              ; AND DECREMENT COUNTER
561  002260  001403         BEQ    APR100          ;COUNTER = 0
562  002262  020027         CMP    R0,#BUFFER+72.  ;FULL BUFFER?
             000110'
563  002266  001372         BNE    APR020+4        ;NO -- MOVE SOME MORE
564  002270  010246  APR100: MOV   R2,-(SP)        ;SAVE VOLATILE
565  002272  010146         MOV    R1,-(SP)        ; REGISTERS
566  002274  105010         CLRB   (R0)            ;INSERT A NULL
567  002276  004767         JSR    PC,PRINTX       ; AND GO PRINT
             175700
568  002302  012601         MOV    (SP)+,R1        ;GET REGISTERS
569  002304  012602         MOV    (SP)+,R2        ; BACK
570  002306  001360         BNE    APR020          ;COUNT NONZERO
571  002310  000755         BR     APR010          ; ELSE RETURN
572                         ;
573          000001         .END
```

Appendix C

Table of ASCII Codes

VALUE	CHARACTER	VALUE	CHARACTER	VALUE	CHARACTER
000	NUL	053	+	126	V
001	SOH	054	,	127	W
002	STX	055	—	130	X
003	ETX	056	.	131	Y
004	EOT	057	/	132	Z
005	ENQ	060	0	133	[
006	ACK	061	1	134	\
007	BEL	062	2	135	]
010	BACK SPACE	063	3	136	^
011	HORIZONTAL TAB	064	4	137	—
012	LINE FEED	065	5	140	`
013	VERTICAL TAB	066	6	141	a
014	FORM FEED	067	7	142	b
015	CARRIAGE RETURN	070	8	143	c
016	SO	071	9	144	d
017	SI	072	:	145	e
020	DLE	073	;	146	f
021	DC1	074	<	147	g
022	DC2	075	=	150	h
023	DC3	076	>	151	i
024	DC4	077	?	152	j
025	NAK	100	@	153	k
026	SYN	101	A	154	l
027	ETB	102	B	155	m
030	CAN	103	C	156	n
031	EM	104	D	157	o
032	SUB	105	E	160	p
033	ESC	106	F	161	q
034	FS	107	G	162	r
035	GS	110	H	163	s
036	RS	111	I	164	t
037	US	112	J	165	u
040	SPACE	113	K	166	v
041	!	114	L	167	w
042	''	115	M	170	x
043	#	116	N	171	y
044	$	117	O	172	z
045	%	120	P	173	{
046	&	121	Q	174		
047	'	122	R	175	}
050	(	123	S	176	~
051	)	124	T	177	DELETE
052	*	125	U		

Appendix D

PDP-11 Assembler Conventions

D.1 INTRODUCTION

This appendix summarizes the PDP-11 assembler conventions that pertain to the text. Assembler conventions and capabilities not referenced here will be found in the appropriate assembler manual. Throughout this appendix, references to text material are enclosed in square brackets—for example, [8.3] refers to Sec. 8.3.

D.2 THE PDP-11 CHARACTER SET

The characters recognized by the PDP-11 assembler are those listed in Appendix C. These are essentially the characters found on an ASCII-coded computer terminal. See the next section for the special assembler interpretations of some characters.

D.3 SPECIAL CHARACTERS

Those characters in the general character set that are of special significance to the PDP-11 assembler are summarized in the following table:

Symbol	Assembler Interpretation
,	(comma) separating symbol
:	(colon) symbolic label terminator [6.4]
: :	(double colon) symbolic label terminator that specifies symbol as global [9.4]
=	(equal sign) direct assignment of a value to a symbol [11.2]
#	(number sign) immediate expression symbol [6.3]
@	(commercial at) deferred addressing symbol [7.5]
;	(semicolon) start-of-comment symbol [6.7]
$\langle \ldots \rangle$	(angle brackets) grouping symbols [13.5]
+	(plus sign) addition symbol, or post-autoincrement symbol [7.5]
—	(minus sign) subtraction symbol, or pre-autodecrement symbol [7.5]
*	(asterisk) multiplication symbol
/	(slash) division symbol
'	(apostrophe) ASCII code symbol [10.7], or concatenation symbol [13.6]
↑ or ∧	(up arrow) temporary radix control symbol [D.6]

D.4 SOURCE STATEMENT FORMAT

Each line of source code input to the assembler must be in the form*

label: *operator* or   *operand$_1$, operand$_2$*   *;comment*
                 directive

All components of the source line are optional, except that if an operand is present, an operator or directive mnemonic must be included. If not, the assembler will attempt to use the default directive .WORD.

- *label.* If a label is included on a line of source code, it must be the first entry on the line, and it must be followed by a colon (or double colon). More than one label may be placed on one line, thus

    LABL1 :   LABL2 :   LABL3 :   LABL4 :

    in which case all labels are assigned the same value. See Sec. D.5 for the valid formation of symbolic label names.
- *operator.* An operator, if included, is in the form of an instruction mnemonic. The valid instruction mnemonics are given in Appendix A.
- *directive.* The valid assembler directives are given in Sec. D.8 of this appendix.

*Lines of source code that invoke macroinstructions are an exception. See Chapter 13.

- *operands.* A PDP-11 operator may take 0, 1, or 2 operands. A directive may include 0 or 1 operands (more properly, *arguments*).
- *comment.* Any part of a line (including the entire line) that is preceded by a semicolon is taken as a comment and, except for being reproduced on the program listing, is ignored by the assembler.

D.5 SYMBOLS

Symbols are of two types, *permanent symbols* and *user-defined symbols.* The permanent symbols consist of the PDP-11 assembler instruction mnemonics and directives. All other symbols are user defined.

The valid characters that may be used in a symbol are

> A–Z (the alphabetical characters)
> 0–9 (the numerical characters)
> $ (the dollar sign)
> •   (the period)

A symbol consists of one or more such characters, the first of which must *not* be numerical.* Only the first six characters are significant to the assembler, so the symbols CONTINUATION and CONTINUE would be taken as identical, namely, CONTIN.

While a symbol name *may* begin with a period, it may *not* consist *only* of a period. See Sec. D.7.

With the exception of the names of macroinstructions (Chapter 13), a user-defined symbol is assigned a value either by appearing as a *label* [6.4], in which case it is given the current value of the assembler's location assignment counter, or by appearing on the left-hand side of a direct assignment statement [11.2]. A symbol may be assigned a value by a direct assignment ($=$) more than once in a given program, its value at any time being the last value assigned to it. A symbol may *not* appear as a label more than once, nor can a symbol be assigned a value through a direct assignment *and* by appearing as a label.

D.6 NUMBERS

All numbers are assumed by the assembler to be in octal (base 8), with the following exceptions:

- Numbers followed by a period or decimal point (such as 29.) are taken to be decimal (base 10) [8.8].

---

*The exceptions are the *local symbols*, which *must* consist only of numerical characters and *must* end with a dollar sign character. See Sec. 13.7.

- The *radix* (base of the number system) may be changed by means of the .RADIX directive [D.8].
- Numbers immediately following an up-arrow construction are interpreted in the following radices:

       ↑ Bn (n is treated as a binary representation)
       ↑ On (n is treated as an octal representation)
       ↑ Dn (n is treated as a decimal representation)

D.7 THE LOCATION ASSIGNMENT COUNTER

Throughout the assembly process, the assembler maintains a **location assignment counter** with which it keeps track of the address at which each instruction is assembled. This counter may be referenced at assembly time by use of the period or dot symbol. Thus, for example, the assignment statement

BLOCK: . = . + n

is entirely equivalent to

BLOCK: .BLKB   n

The location assignment counter maintains as its value the address of the *first* word of the instruction being assembled, even for multiple word instructions. Thus, for example, during assembly of the instruction MOV   RØ,.+14, the location assignment counter will have as its value the address of the MOV operator. In this regard the location assignment counter *does not quite* reflect the value of the PC *upon execution.*

While constructions such as BNE   .+4—used to skip around one word if the PSW's Z-bit is clear—are valid, they must be used with much care; subsequent programming modifications can alter the desired displacement (.+4 might have to be changed to .+6, for instance), an alteration that might easily be overlooked and could thus result in an error that might not readily be found.

D.8 ASSEMBLER DIRECTIVES

Listed below are some of the more useful assembler directives, their arguments, and the action taken by the assembler when the directive is encountered.

Directive	Argument(s)	Operation
.ASCII	string	Generates a block of bytes consisting of the ASCII code for the characters in the string (which is assumed to be enclosed in delimiting characters) [10.5]
.ASCIZ	string	Same as .ASCII, except that a NUL character (ASCII code 000) is appended to the end of the generated string [10.5]
.BLKB	expression	Reserves a block of memory n bytes long, where n = value of the expression [10.4]
.BLKW	expression	Reserves a block of memory n words long, where n = value of the expression [6.7]
.BYTE	$exp_1, exp_2, ..$	Generates successive bytes of memory containing the values of $exp_1, exp_2, ...$ [10.4]
.END	none	Indicates physical end of the source program
	address	Indicates physical end of the source program, with the specified address saved as the transfer (execution) address [6.7]
.ENDC	none	Indicates end of a conditional block [13.11]
.ENDM	none	Indicates the end of a macroinstruction definition [13.3], indefinite repeat block [13.9], or repeat block [13.9]
.EVEN	none	Ensures that the assembler's location assignment counter contains an even number, by adding 1 to it if necessary [10.4]
.GLOBL	$sym_1, sym_2, ..$	Specifies $sym_1, sym_2, ...$ as global [9.2]
.IF	cond, arg(s)	Begins a conditional block [13.11]
.IFF	none	Begins an if-false subconditional block. Appears only within a conditional block [13.13]
.IFT	none	Begins an if-true subconditional block. Appears only within a conditional block [13.13]
.IFTF	none	Begins an unconditionally assembled block. Appears only within a conditional block. [13.13]
.IRP	sym, ⟨args⟩	Begins an indefinite repeat block, sym successively taking on as a value the arguments in the argument list [13.9]
.IRPC	sym, string	Begins an indefinite repeat block, sym successively taking on as a value the characters in the string [13.9]
.LIST	none	Causes source program, comments, object code, and symbol table to be printed (the assembler's default)
	CND	List the source code for instructions in an unsatisfied condition in a conditional block (the assembler's default)
	COM	List source program comments (the assembler's default)
	ME	List the code generated by macro expansions [13.3]

Directive	Argument(s)	Operation
	SRC	List the source program (the assembler's default)
	SYM	List the symbol table (the assembler's default)
.MACRO	sym, arg(s)	Begins a macroinstruction definition [13.3]
.MEXIT	none	Causes an exit from the current macroinstruction expansion [13.12]
.NLIST	none	Generates no listing of source program
	CND	Suppresses listing of unsatisfied conditions in a conditional block [13.14]
	COM	Suppresses the listing of source program comments
	ME	Suppresses the listing of macroinstruction expansions (the assembler's default)
	SRC	Suppresses the listing of source code
	SYM	Suppresses the listing of the symbol table
.ODD	none	Ensures that the assembler's location assignment counter contains an odd number, by adding 1 to it if necessary [10.4]
.RADIX	none	Same as .RADIX 8
	n	Changes the assembler's radix to n, where $n = 2, 4, 8,$ or 10 [D.6]
.REPT	expression	Begins a repeat block that generates n copies of the code that follows, up to the next .ENDM directive, where $n =$ the value of the expression [13.9]
.TITLE	string	Causes the string to appear at the top of each page of program listing [6.7]
.WORD	$exp_1, exp_2, ..$	Generates successive words of memory containing the values of $exp_1, exp_2, ...$ [6.7]

D.9 ASSEMBLY-TIME ERRORS

Errors detected by the assembler during the first or second assembly pass, or both, are flagged in the left-hand margin of the program listing with an error code. If more than one type of error is detected in the same line of source code, multiple error flags will be printed. The error flag, along with the offending line of source code, will be printed, even if source code listing is currently under suppression (with .NLIST or .NLIST   SRC, for example).

The error codes and their meanings are as follows:

Error	Meaning
A	Assembly error. This error code is generated as a result of a wide variety of errors, which may be broadly categorized as follows: 1. Directives. An illegal or missing argument is passed to an assembler directive. This error will also be generated by a missing terminating delimiter in a .ASCII or .ASCIZ directive. 2. Addressing. The offset in a branch instruction exceeds the range from -128_{10} to $+127_{10}$ words. A source statement contains an invalid address specification. (For example, .BLKW TWENTY, where TWENTY is a relocation-sensitive symbol.) An invalid use of the assembler's location assignment counter.
B	Bounding error. The assembler's location assignment counter contained an odd value when an instruction or word-type data was to be assembled.
D	Doubly defined symbol. Reference was made to a symbol that was given more than one value (a multiply defined symbol).
E	.END directive was not seen by the assembler.
M	Multiply defined symbol. A symbol was defined more than once, either as a label or as a label and through a direct assignment statement.
N	Number error. One or more characters in a numeric string is invalid in the current radix.
O	Op-code error. The operator or directive mnemonic is out of context.
P	Phase error. The value given to a label on assembly pass one does not agree with its value on pass two.
Q	Questionable syntax. One or more operands or arguments are missing, or the assembler completed the source line scan prior to encountering the end of the line.
R	Register error. A register was used or referenced in an invalid way.
T	Truncation error. A number is too large to be placed in a specified 16-bit word or 8-bit byte.
U	Undefined symbol. A reference was made to a symbol that is not defined within the program (by appearing as a label or in a direct assignment statement) and does not appear within a .GLOBL directive.
Z	Incompatibility warning. The instruction assembled is not compatible among all members of the PDP-11 family of processors.

Index